The
Redemption
of the
Unwanted

The Redemption of the Unwanted

From the Liberation of the Death Camps to
the Founding of Israel

ABRAM L. SACHAR

ST. MARTIN'S/MAREK
New York

Library of Congress Cataloging in Publication Data

Sachar, Abram Leon, 1899–
    The redemption of the unwanted.

    Includes bibliographical references and index.
    1. Holocaust survivors. 2. Refugees, Jewish.
3. Jews—History—1945–   I. Title.
DS126.4.S32 1983.   940.53'15'03924   83–3025
ISBN 0–312–66729–9

Design by Dennis J. Grastorf at the Angelica Design Group

FIRST EDITION

10 9 8 7 6 5 4 3 2 1

For Edward and Hindy
with love,
saluting the courage of the very much wanted.

CONTENTS

CONTENTS

LIST OF MAPS

Cartographer: G. W. Ward

ACKNOWLEDGMENTS

I have been fortunate to obtain access to files of previously unavailable material that round out the data in each chapter and, I hope, validate the accuracy of material that has accumulated since the onset of the Holocaust. One such resource is the Papers of David K. Niles whose White House career is discussed in the body of the volume. After Niles' death in 1953, his family assigned to me the custody of the papers which have been catalogued by members of my staff and are deposited in the archives of Brandeis University. They are central to an understanding of the Truman administration's effort to ameliorate the plight of the Holocaust survivors and to evaluate the role of the President in the establishment of a sovereign State of Israel.

Another resource has been the Proceedings that record hundreds of papers delivered at Institutes sponsored by Yad Vashem in Jerusalem, and published as "Studies in the European Jewish Catastrophe and Resistance." Since 1957, thirteen volumes have appeared. Yad Vashem was created by the Israeli Government primarily to evaluate the actions of compassionate Christians in European communities who risked their lives in the attempt to countermand the determination of the Nazi leadership to liquidate the Jews. But the papers delivered at the Institute by scholars from around the world have gone beyond this assignment and include narrative and interpretation that relate to the antecedents and consequences of the Nazi blight. They are usually available in the English edition in the libraries of larger universities or major cities.

But I have not relied exclusively upon the documents and

books that have appeared in great numbers in the post-Holocaust years. My wife and I undertook extensive trips to Israel, Italy, and Germany where we were cordially welcomed by many of the men and women who were active participants in the triumphant resistance.

Before we began our travels I met with Ephraim Evron, the Israeli Ambassador to the United States, and his letters to many friends and colleagues who had a role in the post-Holocaust developments, opened many doors for us. Rabbi Robert Samuels, a Brandeis alumnus and Director of the Leo Baeck Institute in Haifa and his executive assistant, Ziva Natvin, set up appointments for us and their efficient planning of our itinerary added immensely to the value and pleasure of our mission in Israel.

We were able to renew a friendship that went back to the days of Israel's founding when we met with the late General Yigal Allon, co-founder of Palmach, who had held important commands in all of Israel's wars. Our discussion turned on what he had identified as "lost opportunities" when he wrote his history of the War for Independence and of the Israeli-Arab Wars that followed. I have included in this volume a summary of Allon's reactions when, in 1948, he was overruled by Ben Gurion in his wish to continue all the way to Cairo and to mount simultaneous assaults on the Arab positions in southern and central Palestine when the Arab forces had begun to crumble. He was still firmly convinced that if his judgment had been acted upon, Israel would have achieved the frontiers that were necessary for permanent security, surrounded as it was on every side by Arab states dedicated to its destruction.

One of our most productive sessions was provided by a long morning interview with Isser Harel who was Chief of Intelligence during the incumbency of Prime Minister David Ben Gurion. The chapters that relate to the hunt for escaped Nazis after the war, and especially the scientists who found refuge in the Arab countries and South America, are strengthened by the fascinating details that Harel shared.

It was a charming experience to meet with Munya Mardor and his fifth-generation sabra wife in their lovely home in Kvar Shmaryahu, a suburb of Tel Aviv. Russian born Mardor settled in Palestine in 1933. He had an important role in the organization of Haganah and directed many of its B'richa illegal immigration projects as Chief of Rekhesch, an auxiliary of Haganah con-

cerned with the secret acquisition of arms in Europe. He is now
a senior official in the Israeli Ministry of Defence. He clarified
many of the diplomatic problems that the B'richa agents faced
in masterminding illegal immigration.

Oved Ben Ami, the perpetual Mayor of Natanya, also an old
friend, offered a veteran's insight as he discussed the experiences
of some of Israel's political leaders, especially when they sought
American aid in the disputes with the British and in the wars
against the Arabs.

Professor Yehuda Bauer, head of the Institute of Contemporary Jewry and Director of the Department of Holocaust Studies at the Hebrew University, has reviewed key chapters and has
offered detailed editorial counsel that has influenced accuracy
and perspective.

Dr. Yisroel Gutman had been one of the resistance leaders in
the Warsaw Ghetto tragedy and had survived several extermination camps. He migrated to Palestine in 1948 and participated in
the research program of Yad Vashem. When Brandeis University established an Institute for Holocaust studies in 1980, he
came as a consultant for planning its objectives and program.
We were privileged to meet with him during this trip to Israel
and again, a year later, when he was invited as a visiting professor at the University of California. We discussed one of the chief
areas of his research, the scholarly purposes of Yad Vashem. He
released to me unpublished material from the Yad Vashem files
that add detail to the chapter on Christian compassion.

Polish-born Katriel Katz, who served as Israel's Ambassador
to a number of European countries, was especially helpful in
recalling experiences as Ambassador to the Soviet Union. He
supplemented our discussion with diary material which has
helped in my interpretation of events in eastern Europe during
and following the Holocaust.

Teddy Kollek, mayor of Jerusalem, had settled in Palestine in
1934. During the war period and in the years of the struggle for
independence he was active in the United States and in European countries, organizing illegal immigration and procuring
arms. His understanding of Arab and Israeli aspirations and the
need to use reason and perspective to try to reconcile them
brought encouraging results in Jerusalem, where he continued
to win elections as Mayor with endorsements from the leaders
of both groups. We found it fascinating to hear him discuss,
soberly but with a wry sense of humor, how he has attempted

to protect the uniqueness of the Holy City by not permitting necessarily continued modernization to erase the beauty of its antiquity.

Yehiel Kadishai has been the Director of Prime Minister Begin's office. He was one of the leaders in developing the strategy of the Irgun in the battle to force the British out of Palestine. I was handicapped in our discussion of the Irgun role in the creation of a sovereign Israel, for there were several visitors in his one-room office that adjoined the Prime Minister's headquarters. But, since the subject of Irgun activities interested the other visitors as well, the interview was quite productive.

On our way to Israel we had spent a few days in Rome, mainly for discussions with the Israeli Ambassador, Moshe Alon, who steered me into a mine of material about the situation of the Jews during the collaboration of Mussolini and Hitler. On the way back from Israel we spent a week in West Germany which included a fruitful morning in Bonn with Yohanan Meroz, the Israeli Ambassador to Germany. He had been a resistance leader during the Holocaust period and in the diplomatic service of Israel after the state won its independence. His response to questions about the period and its interpretation in the German educational system was illuminating. He confirmed the dilemma of the younger generation of Germans that has grown up with little understanding of the Nazi period because its detail was virtually eliminated from the history textbooks that were used in German schools.

Dr. Hadassah (Bimko) Rosensaft had lived through several extermination camp experiences including Auschwitz and Bergen Belsen. She had been spared because, as a trained nurse, she was essential to the Nazis to contain the epidemics that struck down their guards along with their victims. When the British liberated the Belsen camp she served as an aide to Dr. Glyn Hughes when the awesome tasks of rehabilitation began. In the St. Otillien DP camp after liberation, she married Josef Rosensaft who was a leader in the many battles for Jewish self-government. Mrs. Rosensaft, now widowed and living in New York, read and filled in with significant detail the draft chapters that dealt with Auschwitz, Belsen, and the DP camps.

Arie Eliav, former Labor Party Secretary General, was one of the Mossad emissaries who was assigned leadership, during and after WW II, in guiding illegal immigration. He spent the 1980–81 academic year as a visiting professor at Harvard and the interviews that we arranged were most helpful in giving body to the chapter on the exodus from Eastern Europe.

Through the years of the DP camps from 1945 to 1950, Miss Minnie Friedman served as administrative assistant in the office of the American advisor on Jewish Affairs in Germany. When she returned to the United States she became, for a few years, one of our staff members at Brandeis. In 1980 she spent a month on our campus, and her evaluations of the successive advisors and the problems they encountered were useful when I wrote the chapters on B'richa and the DP problems of governance.

Colonel Robert Wolfe, Chief of the Military branch of the Military Archives division in Washington, read the sections that dealt with Nazi political and military policies. Since propaganda articles and books have now appeared that dispute the magnitude of the Holocaust and even that it ever occurred, Dr. Wolfe edited portions to make sure that there was unimpeachable supporting evidence to buttress narrative and judgment.

I have profited from the background which my son Howard, Professor of History at George Washington University, has brought to his research and his writings on the contemporary Middle East. He carefully reviewed the entire manuscript not with the devotion of a son but with the objectivity of a distinguished young scholar.

The generosity of several Brandeis trustees placed at my disposal a travel and research fund which was invaluable. I owe our extended travel itinerary to the generosity of the Shapiro Foundation, Joseph Linsey, Joseph Kosow, and the late Samuel Lemberg.

For many years, during my incumbency as President of Brandeis University, I had the loyal service of Mary Lou Buckley as research assistant. She has been involved in all stages of the development of this volume—the initial research, the writing, the preliminary editing. Eleanor Charter has been administrative assistant through virtually all of my thirteen years as Chancellor at Brandeis. There have been many drafts in the continuous revision of my writing. Eleanor did not limit herself to mechanical transcription, and her disciplined thoroughness has protected the text from possible lapses and omissions.

Our library staff has been most cooperative when my calls for reference data kept interrupting their routine. I am especially grateful to Miroslav Krek, who has excelled as a footnote detective.

Richard Marek's involvement in the volume has gone far beyond the concern of a publisher. He has been a warm friend, a formidable critic, and has usually had his way because of affectionate firmness. It would have been natural, in dealing with a subject that cries out in pain, to write with anger that reaches the decibels of shrillness. Mr. Marek wisely demonstrated how much more effective it is to rely on understatement, to avoid bitterness, and to let the readers judge the facts for themselves.

My copy reader in the publisher's office, Ina Shapiro, has brought her well-honed craftsmanship to the final scrutiny of a volume whose wide-ranging subjects are inevitably complicated. Her challenges on style and content were invariably put forward with disarming grace.

Erika Goldman, assistant to the publisher, employed her Argus eye to make sure that the minutest details in the preparation of the volume were always confirmed.

In my earlier volumes I expressed gratitude to my wife for sacrificial patience as the research and writing, wedged in between responsibilities at Brandeis University and regular network television broadcasts, severely crowded our family life. But this new study required considerably more travel, complicated by the exhaustion of very tight schedules. She was a superb trooper and, participating in all of the interviews, helped to place their significance in proper perspective.

I add, and not perfunctorily, that none of those who have offered assistance are to be held responsible for the use to which I have put their counsel. Dr. Bauer aptly summarized the role of a critic when he commented on the chapter on Truman, Niles and the American experience: "The material is highly original and interesting. I do not agree with some of your conclusions but you have every right to make your case." I have, and now I am at the mercy of reviewers and readers.

Distribution Of Jews
In Europe And Northwest Asia
As Hitler Came To Power, 1933

With Chief Centers of Jewish Population

OVER 10%   5-10%   LESS THAN 5%

Based on Statistics of American Jewish Year Book

```
0    100    200    300    400
              MILES
0   100   200   300    00
         KILOMETERS
```

AND
05

0.41
ONIA

ga   5.18
I A

A
7.15

WHITE
o Minsk
RUSSIA
16.1

stok

49

D

vov

MANIA
5.5
Bucharest
o

ULGARIA

ia   0.7

E
onika   9.5

Athens

RHODES

CRETE

A

Leningrad

Moscow o

S O V I E T   R U S S I A
0.36

o Kiev
Kharkov o

U K R A I N E
6.6

Odessa o
SEA OF
AZOV
0.6
CRIMEA

B L A C K   S E A

o Ankara

U   R   K   E   Y
0.5

C A S P I A N   S E A

GEORGIA
0.9 o
Tbilist
AZERBAIJAN
1.1

Baku o

Tehran o

o Mosul

P E R S I A
0.4

S Y R I A
1.6

Baghdad o

I R A Q
3.1

CYPRUS
LEBANON
Beirut o
o Damascus

KUWAIT

PALESTINE

TRANSJORDAN

Suez
Canal

A R A B I A

Cairo o
Nile R.

E G Y P T

FOREWORD

THIS IS THE STORY of the remnants of the Holocaust who, in the five or six years that followed their "liberation," transformed the image of helplessness and degradation that they had so long borne into that of a vital and self-reliant people. Some half million survivors emerged from the concentration and extermination camps, the guerilla redoubts in the forests and mountains, the convents and monasteries, and the homes where Christian compassion gave them refuge. Of these, great numbers were *in extremis,* physically and psychologically. Six million members of their families had been murdered outright or worked and starved to death, all the time manipulated by their tormentors, recorded as non-persons, denied even the dignity of identity. But because Hitler's plan for a Final Solution, the liquidation of the Jewish presence, was not entirely fulfilled, the half million who did not succumb prevailed over the fate that had been decreed for them.

What those who survived did not know when "liberation" came in 1945 was that their ordeal was by no means over. They were now to face renewed rejection, and it was to come from the governments and the peoples of the Allied world. The struggle for security and dignity had now to be fought against those whose hoped-for victory had offered the Jews their prime incentive to persevere. For where were they to go? And what was home?

Germany or *Austria?* There the Nazi doctrine had been spawned, and the hatreds of the dark years were to remain and fester until a new generation would turn its back on the past.

Czechoslovakia? Sold out by Chamberlain at Munich, it had fallen to Nazi sympathizers. Though these had now been routed, the restored democracy was threatened by the Soviet Union, and who could tell if it would survive?

The Baltic States—*Lithuania, Latvia, Estonia?* Their peoples had been caught in the attacks and counterattacks of the Germans and Russians, and those who survived were now solidly locked into the Communist empire. Many of them, hating the Russians more than the Germans, had served as Nazi auxiliary troops and as trusties, Kapos, assigned to guard fellow prisoners in the concentration and slave labor camps. Their hostility toward the Jews made them willing collaborators in liquidating the ghettos and the camps, and many regretted that Hitler had not finished the job of the Final Solution.

Poland? Even if the Poles would welcome them, and they would not, even if there were homes and jobs for them, and there were not, how could the Jews live again in a land where three million of their own had been done to death in the extermination camps? Homes, shops, schools, synagogues, even graves, had been vandalized or destroyed or taken over. Directly at war's end, when some pathetic attempts were made by a few thousand Jews to return to once-thriving cultural and religious centers, pogroms erupted. Cardinal Hlond, a prince of the Church, blamed the Jews themselves for loosing the bloodshed and destruction.

Rumania, Hungary, Greece? Though 350,000 survived in Rumania, 180,000 in Hungary, and a few thousand in Greece, life had become too insecure to reconstruct a creative community after the Nazis and their collaborators had poisoned the population with their propaganda.

The Western democracies—*Britain, France, Belgium, Italy?* Britain had demonstrated considerable compassion during the Hitler prewar days and gave asylum to several thousand refugees, mainly scholars and intellectuals and families who could be helpful to the national economy. France rejoiced over the return of its sons and daughters who had been deported to German work camps and there were Jews among them who were welcomed with honor. Léon Blum, released from the Theresienstadt concentration camp, was called once more, in 1946, to the premiership of France. Simone Veil, daughter of a Nice architect, who had endured years of deprivation in Ravensbruck, one of the subcamps of Auschwitz, resumed her

studies in law, became a judge, and was named Minister of
Health in the Cabinet of Giscard d'Estaing. In 1974 she was
elected first president of the newly established Parliament of
Europe. After the unconditional surrender of Germany, Belgium, Holland, and Italy held national celebrations as those who
had suffered through German camp imprisonment were repatriated. But while the uprooted citizens of western lands could
return, some as heroes of resistance, the disruption of their
countries' economies compelled stringent immigration safeguards that excluded outsiders. In France there were profiteers
who fought the return of homes, businesses, and other properties that had been taken over by them from deported Jewish
nationals.

Perhaps the free world beyond the seas would provide a refuge. Six million human beings had been slaughtered, more than
a million of them children; could room be found for some who
had been saved?

Canada? After 1945 it had the most restrictive immigration
laws of any western nation. Where Jews were concerned, the
remark of one official was typical: "None is too many."[1] Within
the *United States?* No, "the lamp beside the golden door" had
been dimmed for decades. Powerful labor federations, national
patriotic societies, including the Daughters of the American
Revolution, businessmen and industrialists, all were adamant
that the United States should not be "flooded by cheap labor"
nor endangered by the infiltration of Communists pretending to
be refugees.

Franklin Roosevelt spoke often in public about the obligations of Christianity, and sponsored international conferences
to explore relief measures. Yet, while Roosevelt was invested
with perhaps greater personal power than any previous American president, he found it politically impossible to accomplish
more than temporary liberalization of the immigration regulations.

The determined refusal of every Allied government to open
the doors of its lands for more than token quotas of Jews was a
traumatic shock for those who remained alive after the war
ended. An eloquent survivor, Elie Wiesel, wrote that if the people immured in the death camps had not clung to the dream of
redemption in the free world, they would have lost all will to
go on. Some of the western leaders, if we are to judge from their

statements and actions, may have hoped in their hearts that there would be just such a failure of nerve to eliminate the Jews as a tormenting problem in the postwar world.

Even if the immigration laws had been relaxed, it seems unlikely that the survivors could have qualified as viable members of an ongoing society. Hardly any emerged from their long travail who were not wracked by malnutrition, typhus, tuberculosis, anemia. Many were stunted, wizened eighty- or ninety-pound skeletons who had been deliberately dehumanized and remained tortured still by memories of those whom they had lost.

There are voluminous reports and memoirs by medical personnel who were prisoners in the concentration and slave labor camps—surgeons, internists, gynecologists, pediatricians. I have interviewed many whose needed skills had saved them from being dispatched to the gas chambers, as well as some of the medical chiefs who entered the camps with the liberating forces. All agree that at the time of the liberation, they found it difficult to distinguish between the living, the barely living, and, often, the dead. Their most dedicated efforts to salvage the human wreckage could not save tens of thousands who died in the first weeks after freedom.

At the furthest and most disheartening end of the spectrum were those who had been subjected to extremes of torture, who were without limbs, or the use of them, or deprived of eyesight, or with internal organs damaged beyond repair, or with minds now so disordered that catatonic spells were not infrequent. To be sure, new miracle drugs, developed during the stress of war, were becoming available. Sulfanilamide, in powder form, had been issued to soldiers for application to their wounds. Streptomycin and other antibiotics had been discovered and were available, when the short supplies were not stolen by black marketeers. But pulmonary tuberculosis and other ravages had in many cases progressed beyond the point of repair and carried long-term sentences of incapacity. There was other damage that even miracle drugs could not arrest. In the first months after the Nazi darkness had lifted, the occupying authorities could have filled all the sanatoria of Switzerland or Sweden, without achieving an appreciable improvement in the men and women who seemed doomed never again to be productive.

In the quest for recovery, the most haunting fear related to the effects of malnutrition. The uprooted had been deprived of all but minimum sustenance for years. Protein, fat, vitamins, minerals, almost every building block of life, had been absent from their diet, which usually consisted of liquids with only traces of food value. Their digestive systems, initially at least, could not tolerate even such simple substances as butter. A longed-for morsel, too tempting to resist after endless deprivation, could cause instant regurgitation, acute abdominal cramps, in many cases even death—as happened in the collapse of those who had overindulged during the first hours of unrestraint. The very few children who survived proved initially unable to ingest whole milk. There was, additionally, the problem of persuading them to accept food from strangers, the children having been taught to distrust outsiders, especially those wearing uniforms.

There were many women of childbearing age whose menses had been interrupted, not for months but for years, due in part to their dietary deprivations. There were girls of adolescent age who had not entered puberty, nor was there any medical guarantee that they ever would. For anemia, doctors counted upon the gradual introduction of iron-producing foods—liver, green vegetables, and supplemental iron and liver extract, which had been successfully developed in the research laboratories of Boston's City Hospital. But medical resources were hopelessly inadequate to provide the personalized care that was essential.

There was another deeply troubling concern in the case of Jewish female prisoners, namely, the alarming incidence of venereal disease caused by sexual abuse. Whether through coercion or by submission endured with the frail hope of purchasing respite, a considerable number of the younger and more attractive women in the camps had been assaulted. The doctors were confident that the physical ill effects could be remedied, but it was essential that the women be dissuaded from marriage and childbearing until the cure was complete. Offspring of the infected could be born with the most serious defects. Despite medical counsel, there were many marriages following liberation, but the joy of such fulfillment was always sobered by the fear that children might continue to pay for the years of abuse.

The physical condition of the refugees was vastly complicated by psychological problems. Long before they had reached the concentration camps there had been years of oppression and degradation. Even those who had not been crippled by truncheon, whip, or rifle butt had been stripped of human dignity.

Virtually every memoir recalls scenes in which men with highest professional standing were demeaned. It was sport for the Nazis to compel their victims to lap dirty water in a gutter or to lie prone with a jackboot on the neck. The psychiatrist Bruno Bettelheim describes a train ride with hundreds of prisoners from Vienna to Dachau where his horn-rimmed glasses marked him as an intellectual and provoked severe beatings from the SS guards. He found it safer not to wear the glasses when the tormentors were on a rampage, though he was nearly blind without them.

Bettelheim theorizes that those who had the best chance to overcome their plight were often the devoutly religious or the committed political activists. Ardent Catholics, Orthodox Jews, staunch Jehovah's Witnesses,* steadfast Communists drew strength from their singleness of purpose. Jean Améry, who suffered through several death camps, remembered the outburst of a radical German whose eyes blazed with scorn for his middle-class fellow prisoners. "Now you're sitting here," he cried, "you bourgeois bullshitters, and tremble in fear of the SS. We don't tremble, and even if we croak miserably here, we still know that after we're gone our comrades are going to line the whole pack of them up against the wall."[2]

Only a minority could look to the future with visceral conviction. And even they, when they survived, were permanently scarred. Remembering experiences that could not be erased, nightmares were a common aftermath. There was a cold sweat at the sight of a physician or a nurse in a white coat. There was panic if a child were absent for more than a few moments. There was dread when one sat or stood with back to a door or a window. There was erosion of trust even of one another. Many were psychologically unhinged by the very stratagems they had devised to save themselves, as was the captured Russian soldier who for nearly four years had pretended to be a deaf-mute lest he betray his identity as a Jew. Children of the survivors wrote of the oppressive guilt feelings carried by their parents because, by the sheerest chance, they had not died with their loved ones.

---

*"Jehovah's Witnesses were filled with a strangely contented, one might almost say radiant, exaltation, firm in the knowledge that they were about to be permitted to enter Jehovah's kingdom." From *The Autobiography of Rudolf Hoess.*

Often such children had been named for murdered members of the family and there was the unspoken expectation that they were to fashion their lives as if they were memorial candles.

These were the maimed, the unlamented, the unwanted, left in the wake of the pitiless storm that had torn the world apart. It was astonishing that a redeeming determination still flickered in bodies and minds that had been so fearfully tormented. Yet, as will be detailed, the determination was not extinguished; indeed, generated by a new breed of leadership that exorcised submissiveness and despair, it would take on a special incandescence.

As we shall see, a quarter million of the uprooted, mainly from Communist-dominated Poland and from the Soviet Union, undertook hazardous covert treks across hostile frontiers to reach the temporary shelter of Displaced Persons' Camps in the western zones.

Once there, the early months of idle, yawning routine, the shabbiness of the living quarters, and above all the long wait for relocation could easily have destroyed the will of the survivors, who found themselves again behind barbed wire. The rank and file in the occupying military, largely green draftees who had replaced the veterans, were little prepared to understand what the Jews had already endured. The top officials, like hosts who had initially extended a welcoming hand only to find that the "guests" were outstaying their welcome, felt harassed by the imposition of responsibility for those who could not be repatriated. The situation was more a product of bureaucratic unconcern than of malice, but it shocked those who had lived through the Holocaust and were now fearful that endless postponement of ameliorative action would be overtaken by abandonment. In the Allied zones, the Jews had roof and bed, food and warmth. But they were still "wandering between two worlds, one dead, the other powerless to be born."*

Yet the mood of defeatism did not remain overpowering. Under the prodding of their activist leadership, the camp inmates shook off resignation and submissiveness and began planning to make their way to remote seaports on the Mediterranean, the Adriatic, and the Black Sea, transition points on the way to Palestine. The postwar British officials, fearful of alienat-

*From Matthew Arnold, *Stanzas from the Grande Chartreuse.*

ing the Arab governments in the oil-rich regions of the Middle East, applied strenuous economic and diplomatic pressure to thwart such journeys. When the overcrowded, unseaworthy little ships occasionally eluded surveillance and managed to sail, the British hunted them down and diverted the refugees, even within sight of Palestine, interning them in detention camps or deporting them to Cyprus or distant British colonies. Refusing to be deterred, the Jews—individuals, families with little ones, and the elderly—kept coming, persuaded that every successful landing at remote Palestine shore points vindicated a dozen failures. The illegal immigrants who reached their goal melted into the earlier Jewish settlements, to join in building new settlements and strengthening the old ones.

During the war period Jewish resistance to the British was defensive, mainly action to avoid arrest or the confiscation of their meager supply of weapons. Haganah, the unofficial Jewish militia, ordered the practice of *Havlagah* (Restraint). After all, Jews and British were fighting a common Nazi foe. The campaign against the British was limited to sabotage of British installations that guarded against the infiltration of immigrants. But when the war ended, a growing activist group, armed with weapons that were stolen from the British military stores or smuggled in from abroad, ignored Haganah discipline. Violent guerilla activity was directed against the British as well as the Arabs, and terrorist disorder often erupted into open warfare.

Although they had helped to wrest unconditional surrender from the Germans, the two years from 1945 to 1947 were bitter ones for the British. The war had drained their strength and resources and had brought a victorious empire close to bankruptcy. Doubtless they could still have crushed the defiance in Palestine, especially as several years were needed for the Jews to obtain adequate manpower and equipment. But there were now challenges to continued British control in every part of the empire: Ireland, India, Egypt, and the African possessions. David alone may have been no formidable foe, but Goliath was simultaneously beset by too many slingshots. The British Foreign Secretary, Ernest Bevin, who had long resisted the humiliation of yielding to a people whom he had come to detest, bowed to the inevitable and agreed to turn the Mandate for Palestine back to the United Nations.

At this point the Jews of Palestine were no longer content with autonomy or a trusteeship where final authority for the

welfare of the state rested with outsiders. They were determined that the time had come for dependence to end, for the
Homeland promised by the Balfour Declaration of 1917, though
drastically reduced, to be given sovereign status. The battle to
gain international assurance for such an unlikely fulfillment
now shifted to diplomacy. The Arabs and the Jews lined up
their allies for the fateful decision by the United Nations, which
was scheduled for November 24, 1947. The American delegation
and the President, Harry Truman, along with some of his aides,
helped to swing just enough votes to gain international recognition for a sovereign state in a partitioned Palestine.

The Arab states had warned that they would not accept the
verdict of the United Nations if it authorized a partition of
Palestine so that both the Arabs and the Jews, now Israelis,
could have sovereign states. Even before the British relinquished the Mandate on May 14, 1948, and evacuated Palestine,
the invasion by five Arab states began, with the intent to "drive
the Jews into the sea." They were supported by a technical
British neutrality heavily tilted in their favor.

The combined assault became the climactic test of survival for
the new state. By now the Israelis were better prepared to meet
the all-frontier assault than they had been when the skirmishes
began immediately after World War II ended. Arms had been
steadily arriving for their use, the result of a carefully prepared
strategy of procurement in the United States and in European
countries. Nevertheless, no respected military critic gave the
Israelis the slightest chance of winning against such overwhelming odds. Yet in a series of several short campaigns, punctuated
by cease-fires and truces imposed by the United Nations, the
Israelis beat back all of the invading forces and compelled the
Arabs to seek an armistice that halted the war in 1949.

In five years the shorn lambs, so often led meekly to slaughter,
had grown horns. The achievement could not have been possible without the emergence of a new breed of men and women
who had cast off the supineness of the Diaspora and whose
combined talents for daring and tenacity matched the most intrepid exploits of modern times. Prewar Jewish Palestine had
already developed such leaders—David Ben Gurion, Moshe
Sharett, Golda Meir, Moshe Dayan, Munya Mardor, Yigael
Yadin, Yigal Allon, Shaul Avigur, and others whose pioneering
courage laid the foundations for a Homeland and an independent state. They were now joined by toughened and tempered

survivors of the Holocaust with a sixth sense for improvisation: Abba Kovner, Ehud Avriel, Yehuda Arazi, Menachem Begin, Mordecai Anielewicz, and scores of others. Almost all could be characterized, in Ehud Avriel's oxymoronic phrase, as "well-balanced fanatics." Working in tandem with their comrades in Palestine, they evoked courage and hope from those who were trapped in Europe and the Arab lands, directed the illegal immigration, acquired the military resources, and trained the manpower to face up to the British and the Arab states. Within a few years, repudiating Shylock's plaint, "Sufferance is the badge of all our tribe," the flotsam and jetsam of the Old World's castoffs became one of the strongest and most self-reliant of the small powers of the Middle East.

The transformed image of the Jew was perhaps best perceived by former Prime Minister Harold Macmillan in a 1968 interview with John Barkham. Barkham asked what sort of future Macmillan envisaged for Britain now that it had been compelled to relinquish most of its dominions and wondered "if the future lay along the lines of another Athens, or perhaps another Sweden." Macmillan pondered the question. "Not another Athens," he said.

> Athens was based on slave labor, ran a powerful empire, fought great wars, and eventually decayed and died. It may well be that Britain will some day follow in the footsteps of Sweden, but since, in the great war, it throve on a neutrality that impelled it to sell its products both to the Nazis and to the democracies, I'm glad I won't be here to see it. No, the future I hope for Britain is more like that of Israel. In the time of Elizabeth, we were only two million people, in the time of Marlborough, only five or six million, in the time of Napoleon only ten million. The other day [this was just after the Israelis had beaten all the Arab States in the Six-Day War], while the world debated, Israel's three million imposed their will on their enemies. They had what any great people need—resolution, courage, determination, pride. These are what really count in men and nations.[3]

Macmillan was among the first postwar statesmen to recognize the miracle in the redemption of the unwanted.

Major Concentration
And Extermination Camps Established
Before and During WW II
(Including Jewish Death Toll)

Statistics Compiled by Yehuda Bauer of Yad Vashem

GHETTO   LABOR CAMP
DEATH CAMP

* May be underestimated

G.W.WARD

The Redemption of the Unwanted

CHAPTER ONE

What the Liberators Found:
The Central European Camps*

IN THE EARLY MONTHS of 1945, after nearly six years of war in
Europe and twelve of Adolf Hitler in power, something new,
quite literally, was in the air: Allied planes could now be seen,
and their roar penetrated the concrete and cinder block installations and the electrified barbed-wire fences of the Nazi concentrations camps. The surviving prisoners cheered, even when the
Allied bombs fell among them. There was change, too, among
the prisoners' tormentors. Guards who only yesterday seemed
omnipotent had begun to shrivel. The end of their promised
Thousand-Year Reich was at hand and they knew that they
faced retribution.

Not all who raised an emaciated arm in greeting to the passing
planes would hold on long enough to savor the new day. For
many, the last ounce of stamina would seep away at the very
moment of deliverance and they would die in the arms of freedom. Other thousands would succumb in the weeks that followed. The wonder was that so many had clung to life for so
long.

The Nazis had created two types of camps for the detention
of their undesirables—Communists, dissenters, Jews, Gypsies,
and often, in violation of the Geneva Convention, prisoners of
war. One category, established first in Germany itself, later in
the overrun countries, was precisely termed the concentration

---

*The table appearing on page 45 offers a statistical summary of the Jewish
losses in the Holocaust.

camps—places where thousands of human beings were concentrated while arrangements were made for their final disposition. These, including Buchenwald, Dachau, Bergen Belsen, Mauthausen, Theresiendstadt, and scores of others, were intended as places of punishment for the recalcitrant, as well as centers, mainly in the Ruhr, for a slave labor system in Nazi factories and plants. The victims were usually transferred, when no longer productive, to the second category, the specifically created extermination camps. Most often, the transfer was unnecessary. Death spared the victims any further trip.

Many of the concentration camps were built and put into operation well before the war. In the 1930s one needed no particular ethnic or religious identification for eligibility. It was enough to be suspected of political opposition or to have assets that could be confiscated. It was enough to be known as an "intellectual" or to provide some purported evidence of "danger to the Reich." True, many of the first prisoners were Jews, since Hitler had long made their elimination in German life a prime objective. But it was part of the Nazi strategy, for a time at least, not to disclose ultimate intentions. As long as the western democracies sought appeasement and foreigners could pass in and out of Germany, the Nazis took pains to avoid overplaying Hitler's rhetoric.

There is evidence that the extermination camps were ready and waiting before the war, but they were not put into operation until after December 7, 1941, when the United States entered the conflict. Once the German Wehrmacht had extended Hitler's Reich from Calais in the west to the easternmost provinces of Poland, it became timely to create or expand such death camps, primarily in Polish-conquered territory. Each was equipped with remarkably efficient technology for wholesale torture, gassing, and cremation. In the occupied Russian areas the murders were carried out by firing squads. Some new names were now added to those that history had etched in infamy: Hitler's contribution to this vocabulary of abomination was surely the most appalling lexicography in recorded history and included Auschwitz, Treblinka, Belzec, Maidanek, Sobibor, and scores of others.

All peoples in the path of the Nazi war machine suffered during the years of appeasement and the war that it spawned. The Jews of Europe, however, lost not only millions of their families but the historic centers in which they had lived for centuries. These could not be restored. The long tradition of creative scholarship withered and died along with the learned writers who had sustained it in Poland, the Baltic States, the Balkans, Czechoslovakia, and especially in what had been enlightened Germany. It was said at the Eichmann trial that other peoples at war's end counted their losses; the Jews could count only their survivors. H. Wielneck had a point when he titled his book, *The War That Hitler Won*.

BUCHENWALD

Buchenwald, the first concentration camp to be breached by the western Allies, had been built high on the hills above Weimar, capital of the defunct democratic Republic and not far from an imperial Schloss known as Wilhelmshohe. Nearby still stood the "Goethe Oak," a noble tree to which the eighteenth-century giant of German letters had often repaired to refresh his perspective. Approximately 238,000 prisoners, many of them Jews, but also non-Jewish Poles, Russians, and dissident Germans, had been incarcerated in Buchenwald since its dedication. Even before the war exploded in Europe, it was serving the coercive purposes of the Nazis. Captured Buchenwald files recorded that already in mid-November 1938, after a Nazi Embassy official had been assassinated by a distraught young Jew, more than 10,000 people had been sent to the camp, where they were compelled to pass their arrival night in the open winter air and then were beaten and tortured. A loudspeaker kept repeating the announcement that any Jew who wished to hang himself should put a paper with his number in his mouth so that his identity could be quickly established.[1] Throughout the war years the deportation trains and convoys moved in meticulously maintained schedules out of Buchenwald to the death camps farther east. But even in this temporary detention camp, some 56,000 had died or been murdered.

When the forward platoons of Americans arrived on the morning of April 11, 1945, only about 20,000 prisoners remained. Hermann Pister, the last SS commandant,* was working frenetically to ship out as many as he could process. In the

---

*The SS were the elite in the Nazi military. The initials stood for Schutz Staffein, the protection squads.

previous week he had secretly selected forty-six of the last inmates for public execution on the home ground of Buchenwald itself. His intention was relayed to the prison underground that had been organized in the last weeks of the camp's existence. When time came for the roll call, not one of the forty-six answered. Camp personnel, aware that the Americans were already on the outskirts of Weimar, and their thoughts now mainly on escape, made a halfhearted unsuccessful search for the inmates, then drifted away.

Indeed, some panic-stricken guards who were left behind at this point begged prisoners for "good references." Others were confiscating prisoners' garb in the hope they might escape recognition in the chaos soon to come. However, few cheated retribution. Survivors with barely enough strength to walk disarmed them at the gates; only days before, even to approach a Nazi guard was to be shot down summarily. As a sign of welcome to the liberators, prisoners began to hang out scraps of cloth that had once been white. Some of the first Americans to enter the camp vomited as their eyes beheld what their minds could not absorb—bodies stacked in obscene anonymity, the barely living whimpering among the corpses, bunks full of shaven-headed, emaciated creatures who had wizened into skeletal apparitions. American soldiers put on film the scenes in rooms full of naked, unburied corpses, piled ten feet high.

Soon after the takeover, General Dwight Eisenhower, commander of the Allied Forces in Europe, arrived. "I have never felt able to describe my emotional reaction when I came face to face with indisputable evidence of Nazi brutality and ruthless disregard of every shred of human decency," he wrote. "Up to that moment I had only known about it generally, or through secondary sources. I am certain, however, that I have never at any time experienced an equal sense of shock."[2]

On that April morning the Americans brought with them news tragic for the free world. Hours before, President Franklin Roosevelt had died at Warm Springs, Georgia. The commanding American officer's first announcement at Buchenwald was for all inmates to turn out on parade for a memorial service. Of the 20,000 survivors, at least 5,000 could be described as *in extremis*. Lurching, stumbling, falling, crawling, they responded and heard a lieutenant from Norristown, Tennessee, request the immediate surrender of all arms scooped up after the Nazis fled. In peroration he urged that, as a fitting tribute to the fallen

President, all thoughts of vengeance should now be abandoned. "Let the survivors tell the world," he said, "in their names and in those of the vast numbers who had suffered and died, that their reply to barbarism was understanding, compromise and restraint."[3]

A few French prisoners began to sing the *Marseillaise;* remnants of other national groups gasped out their own anthems. The moment was most confusing for the Polish Jews. The tribute to the President called up every reserve of remaining strength, but the plea for "understanding and reconciliation," at such a point, left them bewildered. Even as they attempted to raise their voices they must have remembered the day when a train had arrived at Buchenwald from Poland with only 300 living beings of the 4,000 who had been packed into the cars. Removing the corpses had been unusually laborious since most of the bodies had been frozen together; their arms and legs snapped off in the unloading.

Some of the Hungarian prisoners must have remembered the 2,000 Hungarian girls aged between fifteen and twenty-five who had shared the miseries of camp life since the Budapest mass deportations of 1944. More than five hundred of them had been indentured as slave labor in the Krupp munitions works in nearby Essen. Their heads shaven, garbed in burlap sacks, housed in unheated barracks through the winter, set upon by dogs to prod them in their work, they had performed like robots until the intensive Allied aerial bombardment began. They were forbidden access to the air-raid shelters and huddled together in terror in open trenches. The plants destroyed, Krupp officials herded the survivors into freight cars and returned them to Buchenwald, for the girls had been merely "on loan." The German camp commandant could not accept them since he had already received thousands of other prisoners from camps also under fire. The girls were not even unloaded for bodily relief before being shipped on to dreaded Bergen Belsen. On the parade ground now, it would have been understandable if the Hungarian prisoners let their attention lapse to wonder about the fate of these exhausted girls.*

Half listening to the lieutenant was a solitary Dutchman, Max

---

*Some of the women survived Belsen to give testimony against the Krupps and the German armaments tycoons and their slave labor practices.

Nabig, the last of hundreds of his countrymen who had been deported to Buchenwald. The others in the Nabig group had perished in the Mauthausen death camp. He, a Jew from Amsterdam, had been assigned to Dr. Hans Eysele, an SS "research" physician who needed human bodies on which to test reactions to pain during operations performed without anesthesia. Nabig had undergone stomach resection under such conditions. After the operation he escaped being discarded like a laboratory animal when a compassionate nurse substituted some benign substance for the usual lethal injection. Other prisoners had kept Nabig hidden and he lived to testify at the international trials.[4] Nabig's thoughts, as he stood in tribute to Roosevelt, have not been recorded. In his testimony, however, he implied that the American officer who conducted the memorial appeared to regard the whole war effort as a sports competition in which the winners, in a show of civilized chivalry, were to shake hands with the losers.

Dr. Eysele was arrested when the camp was captured, stood trial, and was given the death penalty. But the sentence was commuted to an eight-year prison term, of which he served five. Released in 1952, the province of Bavaria loaned him, as a "homecomer," 10,000 marks "for losses due to the war." He practiced medicine for a time in Munich. He was about to be rearrested in 1955 when fresh evidence of many other inhuman experiments became available. Warned, perhaps by the police, he fled and was granted asylum in Nasser's Egypt, where he settled down to a lucrative practice in Cairo.

DACHAU

Dachau, and its network of some 150 subcamps, had been established in the Bavarian heartland, near Munich, as one of the first concentration camps. Of the hundreds of thousands who passed through its gates, more than 40,000 prisoners had died there, a substantial portion of them Jews.

The first Dachau commandant, Theodore Eicke, who had been taken by Himmler from a psychiatric ward, was well fitted for the responsibilities of his post. During Hitler's rise to power, he never questioned orders from above, including the assignment to shoot down Ernst Roehm, the Brown Shirt homosexual who had been one of Hitler's most powerful collaborators. Eicke had no compunction where discipline clashed with friendship.

The SS, he growled, was no place for the tenderhearted; weaklings belonged in monasteries. His stationery bore the motto: "Only one thing matters, the command given."[5]

The Nazis' quandary, as Allied planes began to fly low over the area, was how to eliminate, in accordance with "the command given," the 33,000 prisoners still in Dachau. Gassing? The equipment was inadequate. Shooting, or having attack dogs tear the starvelings apart? These solutions would leave an untidiness of dead bodies which, if buried hastily, would inevitably be discovered and would serve as evidence for the future. The Luftwaffe bombing the camp into annihilation? The decimated air force was needed elsewhere for last-stand defense. Deportation to other camps? Many prisoners could be thus dispatched, but there were not nearly enough trucks and trains for the rest. Nevertheless, orders from Himmler and his chief aide, Ernst Kaltenbrunner, kept coming. There must be no weakening of resolve. The personnel in charge were told to hold on, "down to the last man, to the last shot." One of the last commands was for Operation Firecloud—the demand that all prisoners, except Aryans, be poisoned.[6] The commandant was ready, but with the proximity of the American forces, the camp relapsed into bedlam.

The prisoners had hung upon shreds of hope before. In the winter of 1942, through the camp underground they had heard of the catastrophic defeat of the Germans at Stalingrad; in 1944, the stunning news circulated of Von Stauffenberg's almost successful conspiracy to assassinate Hitler; as the war wound down, every camp was agog with the ecstasy of the relief of Paris by Charles de Gaulle. But after each reassuring rumor, no German surrender had followed. Even now, though the reports had it that the German armies were in chaos, whole regions clogged with Nazis in flight, the Allies on the march everywhere, who could be sure that the rumors would not again end in frustration?*

In the last hours before the camp was captured, a convoy of

---

*Though the overwrought inmates of Dachau could not know it, New York had gone wild at dawn with the news that Germany had surrendered. President Truman, having succeeded Roosevelt less than twenty-four hours before, was obliged to announce with embarrassment that the victory celebration was still premature.

railway cars—the Grüne Minnas—windowless, airless, carrying about 7,000 prisoners who were being transferred from Buchenwald, came to a halt in the marshaling yard. There was no
need to obey Kaltenbrunner's order: no one was alive in the
doomed cargo.

By now, even the commandant realized that his men could not
carry out a successful massacre. There was barely time for the
SS to save their own skins. One ingenious officer bethought
himself of the French prisoner, Odette, who had been kept in
solitary confinement for many years. She had been spared only
because she had been a comrade and lover of Captain Peter
Churchill in the French Underground. Churchill, who had
deluded his captors into believing he was a much closer relative
of the British Prime Minister than in fact he was, had earlier
been sent to the Theresienstadt camp. The Nazi officer scooped
up the enfeebled Frenchwoman and drove her in a staff car to
the advancing Allies. The dodge did not do the Nazi much good;
he was promptly shot. But Odette survived to marry Peter
Churchill after the war.*

The SS remembered another "prize prisoner," Pastor Martin
Niemoller, who had courageously rallied Lutherans against Hitler. Niemoller was among those identified by Himmler as
"worth more to me than a whole armored division," and the
instructions were to keep him safe. There were others also
thought to be valuable hostages for exchange purposes. The
commandant was directed to march all these ransomable cap-
tives to remote areas in the Alps. But he carried Himmler's
sealed order: "If you are unable to escape from the enemy, or if
there is danger of liberation of the prisoners by Partisans, you
are to execute them all without mercy." By now the demoralized
guards no longer paid attention to orders, sealed or otherwise.
Their priority was to find ways to escape the wrath of the
advancing Allies. As each hour passed, therefore, more of Dachau's prisoners slipped away into the woods, seeking out the
Partisans for help to return to their homelands.

On the last Sunday of April 1945, the first Allied soldier, an
American scout of Polish descent, came through the gate of the
main Dachau camp. The few Nazis in the tower watched appre-

---

*There was no storybook conclusion. The marriage, in freedom, ended in
  divorce.

hensively. They were no longer there as guards; they had been ordered to stay on merely to complete the formalities of surrender. The upper ranks had already fled, to blend in among the German civilian population. The young American's first impression, later detailed in an interview, was one of "glaring chaos," thousands of ragged skeletons, in the yard, in the trees, waving little rags, climbing over one another, hysterical, completely out of control.[7] The scout went back for support and returned with a small detachment. The flags of many Allied nations had suddenly appeared. Apparently the prisoners had been secretly piecing them together over the months, from tatters and patches and strips of cloth. One prisoner, a Polish priest, exuberantly kissed an officer, learning later to his glee that she was Marguerite Higgins, of the New York *Herald Tribune*, the first American war correspondent to report on Dachau. A military chaplain came forward and asked that all who could do so join him in a prayer of thanksgiving. Then came the stunning announcements that, the night before, Mussolini had been lynched by the Italian Partisans, and that the Russians were battering away at the basement bunker in the Berlin Chancellery where Hitler had taken refuge.

Soon the advance scouts were joined by other Allied soldiers and one of the German guards came forward to surrender with what he believed would be the usual military protocol. He emerged in full regalia, wearing all his decorations. He had only recently been billeted to Dachau from the Russian front. He saluted and barked "Heil Hitler." An American officer looked down and around at mounds of rotting corpses, at thousands of prisoners shrouded in their own filth. He hesitated only a moment, then spat in the Nazi's face, snapping "Schweinehund," before ordering him taken away. Moments later a shot rang out and the American officer was informed that there was no further need for protocol.

Some of the Nazis were rounded up and summarily executed along with the guard dogs. Two of the most notorious prison guards had been stripped naked before the Americans arrived to prevent them from slipping away unnoticed. They, too, were cut down. General Eisenhower sent a laconic communiqué from headquarters: "Our forces liberated and mopped up the infamous concentration camp at Dachau. Approximately 32,000 prisoners were liberated; 300 SS camp guards were quickly neutralized."

During the next few days as the burials went forward, the sick and the dying were transferred to hospital facilities, makeshift as they had to be, and food was carefully distributed. "Prescribed" might be the better word, for the starving had to adjust their food intake with medical discipline. Only then did the American command turn to review the files that the Germans, with characteristic meticulousness, had maintained. The full record of the pseudo-medical experimentations came to light. Prisoners had been used as laboratory animals, without the humane restrictions placed on vivisection. Hannah Arendt suggested that "the camp was itself a vast laboratory in which the Nazis proved that there is no limit to human depravity." For it was remembered that these experiments were not planned or conducted by identifiable psychopaths. They were performed or supervised by professional scientists, trained in what had been once considered peerless universities and medical schools. Reverend Franklin Littell called them "technically competent barbarians." Indeed, the procedures had the full approval and cooperation of Berlin's Institute of Hygiene.

The life-and-death struggles of many of the prisoners went on long after the camp was taken over. More than three hundred expired on the first day of liberation, and for several months the daily toll was rarely less than fifty. Non-Jews who were well enough and could be repatriated were sent home quickly. Those too ill to be moved or, as in the case of most of the Jews, who had no discernible homeland to welcome them back, languished in the camp. The Americans, however compassionate and concerned, were overwhelmed by the awesome complexity of their task, its sheer numbers, and always their ministrations were slowed by the inevitable military red tape. The survivors were understandably restless and impatient, and those who could began to slip away to chance an independent search for rehabilitation. Once the danger had lessened that they were bearers of contagious disease, few attempts were made to stop them. In some weeks as many as five hundred made the break.

In the immediate postwar period, part of the camp was used to house war criminals held for trial in military courts that sat in the town itself. Within a few years the town of Dachau became a popular tourist center, situated as it is in one of the loveliest parts of Germany. German film stars and other celebrities patronized its resort facilities. From time to time, grown children of former victims, students, and research scholars came too, not for the resort, but to see the camp itself. Responses to the requests for directions were curiously vague. No one in the community seemed to know where the camp was located or much about its background. The building where the lists had been drawn that decreed life or death now displayed signs reading "Trink Coca-Cola." When visitors asked to be guided to the laboratories where the notorious Dr. Hintermeyer had conducted his medical experiments, they were told that the quarters had been converted into children's "rumpus rooms."

BERGEN BELSEN

Bergen Belsen was established near Hanover, in central Germany, in July 1943, at first to confine prisoners of war shipped there during the zenith of the Nazi conquests. By 1945 it was termed a "convalescent center," and thousands of prisoners who had become too weak to work were shipped there, to die off slowly by starvation and typhoid. In the one month of March, more than 18,000 succumbed. By the next month, with the Germans in steady retreat everywhere, it had become necessary to vacate other camps before they were engulfed by the British. Deportees from abandoned camps kept flooding into Belsen. The commandant, Josef Kramer, whose incumbency had earned him the sobriquet "the Beast of Belsen," reacted impassively to the comings and goings of the starvelings. His announced policy was simple: "The more dead Jews you bring me, the better I like it." His prescription for the uncontrollable epidemic of diarrhea was starvation. "If you don't eat, you don't shit." When railroad cars and convoys were unavailable, he dispatched the prisoners on long marches. The weakest, unable to keep going, were left to die or were shot; the roads were littered with those who had succumbed. Only rarely was an escape made when prisoners broke loose from marching columns, or leaped from trucks or trains.

Bergen Belsen was taken over by the British on April 14, 1945. In the advance tanks were three Jewish soldiers who brought the tidings of freedom, but they were not sure to whom they should be addressed. Those at the very edge of death could hardly be identified among the other thousands of unburned decomposing corpses. In garb, in appearance, in suffering it was all, in Hannah Arendt's phrase, "a monstrous equality, without fraternity and without humanity, an equality in which dogs and cats could have easily partaken." Derrick Sington, the first British officer to enter Belsen, felt that he had entered a zoo, "with its pathetic figures, once men and women of dignity and respect, now pathetic relics, the smell of ordure everywhere, like the stench in a monkey house. A sad blue smoke floated like a ground mist between the low buildings. I had tried to visualize the interior of a concentration camp, but I had not imagined it like this. Nor had I imagined the strange simian throng who crowded the barbed wire fence surrounding the compounds, with their shaven heads and their obscene prison suits, which were so dehumanizing."[8]

Dr. Hadassah Bimko (now Mrs. Josef Rosensaft), a Polish Jewess, had been brought in from Auschwitz in November 1944. She had been spared only because her tormentors believed she could help slow down an epidemic that was threatening the SS as well as the prisoners. She described for me the reactions of the head of the British Medical Corps, Brigadier Glyn Hughes, when he inspected a barracks in the camp that had been converted into a makeshift hospital. The camp now contained only 58,000 of the 1,500,000 people who had been sent there. At Belsen Dr. Bimko had continued day and night ministrations that earned her, from the despairing inmates, the title of Angel of Mercy. She led Dr. Hughes into the hospital where 1,200 inmates lay, scarcely breathing. She announced to them that she had brought help. A faint eerie cry went up from the floor, half wail, half moan, and then slowly, all over the room, arms were painfully raised, virtually no flesh on them. Hughes was overcome and could not speak. He walked in stunned silence from one such hospital to another, past the piled unburied corpses. In the next few weeks, thousands died.[9]

The inmates of Belsen had come from every part of Europe, but perhaps the most poignant tragedy was that of the Dutch. Many of the old Jewish families of Holland, especially from Amsterdam and Utrecht, had been rounded up and shipped here. In December 1944, windowless trucks brought in forty-nine Dutch children whose fathers were kept in isolation until they could teach the art of diamond polishing to "acceptable citizens." Mission accomplished, the diamond cutters were sent to their death. At Belsen died Anne Frank, the child whose diary gave the world a model of inextinguishable faith. From her attic window in Amsterdam she had seen a single chestnut tree and a patch of occasionally blue sky. "In spite of everything I still believe that people are good at heart. . . . I can feel the sufferings of millions and yet, if I look up into the heavens, I think that it will all come right, that this cruelty too will end, and that peace and tranquility will return again."[10] She did not live to mark her sixteenth birthday.

There were many other children at Belsen, brought in from Czechoslovakia and Poland and from the camps in Theresienstadt and Buchenwald. The adults, themselves worn to starvation, tried to keep the children alive by stealing food or denying themselves their own minimum rations. Most of the adult Dutch died before liberation. One historian of the Dutch tragedy describes the fate of a matron, daughter of one of Holland's most distinguished Jewish families. Beautiful and elegant upon her arrival in the camp, she had quickly wasted away, always in terrible pain, her once lovely eyes sunken in edema-swollen cheeks. She succumbed just as the liberators entered the camp. When they turned her mattress over for use by another inmate, a spotless crepe handkerchief bearing her monogram dropped out of the filthy bed.[11]

In the early hours of liberation many prisoners simply went out of control. Ravenous with hunger, desperate with thirst, they rushed to the kitchens. The guards, mostly Hungarian Nazis, not yet under complete surveillance by the British, shot down seventy-two of the prisoners. Sington noted that the liberation had brought grateful welcomes in France, Belgium, and Holland. "But the half credulous cheers of these almost lost men, of these clowns in their terrible motley, who had once been Polish officers, land workers in the Ukraine, Budapest doctors and students in France, impelled a stronger emotion, and I had to fight back my tears."[12]

The highest priority after the establishment of order and discipline was the marshaling of emergency medical help. Fourteen thousand died within the first few days of liberation. Brigadier Hughes threw the Nazis out of their comfortable barracks and converted them into hospitals. He enlisted Dr. Bimko as his chief of staff, and she organized 28 doctors and 620 nurses from among the prisoners to work with the Medical Corps. One hundred British medical students, sponsored by UNRRA, arrived, as did contingents of the British Red Cross, medical units from Sweden, and the ever ready Quaker relief units. Count Folke

Bernadotte, president of the Swedish Red Cross, urged his government to take 6,000 of the most desperate cases into its hospitals for treatment. The psychological state of the inmates as they were led or carried into the ambulances was not lost on Bernadotte's staff. The prisoners had frightening remembrances of earlier trips in cars and wagons.

Yet despite the enlistment of volunteers and the assistance of hundreds of members of the British Medical Corps,[13] Dr. Hughes still needed substantial reinforcements. He therefore drafted German doctors and nurses for the emergency, giving them to understand that their own fate was tied to complete cooperation. In the main, the Germans responded well, though their patients often cringed when attended by them. The death toll continued to climb, but many prisoners survived, and the typhus-ridden Lager was burned down on May 21, 1945, with appropriate ceremony. The main hospital was named for Glyn Hughes.

Belsen was converted into a Displaced Persons' Camp, but as the weeks of waiting for repatriation stretched into months, a further 14,000 inmates died.

MAUTHAUSEN

Situated about fourteen miles southeast of Linz, in Austria, not far from the Danube, Mauthausen was chosen by Himmler in 1938 primarily for a chain of more than fifty slave labor camps. To Mauthausen were sent about 10,000 Spanish Republicans, interned in France at the end of the Spanish Civil War and delivered to the Nazis by the French Vichy collaborators. Only 1,500 survived the first year. Of the 200,000 Frenchmen deported by the Vichy leaders, Laval and Pétain, about 8,300 ended up in Mauthausen, where most of them perished. Hundreds of Czechs were massacred there, as had been their countrymen at Lidice, in retaliation for the assassination of the Gauleiter Reinhardt Heydrich. Few of the 4,500 Italians deported there after Hitler took control of Germany lived to greet the liberators.

The Jews were among the earliest victims. Already in 1941 there had been a clash in Amsterdam between SS troops and Dutch Jews driven to frenzy by the assaults upon them. Four hundred young men were deported to Mauthausen and there quickly executed. But the majority came by way of Auschwitz, in their greatest numbers at the end of 1944 and in the spring of 1945, many of them from the doomed Budapest Jewish community.

Mauthausen contained stone and granite quarries, called the *Weinergraben*, belonging to the municipality of Vienna, and useful for paving its streets. The prisoners, weakened by dysentery, their food described as "powdered manure," were whipped up the 148 steps of the quarry in freezing weather, bearing heavy slabs of granite. If a prisoner stumbled under the weight of the load, beatings followed immediately. Sometimes a victim unwittingly, but perhaps mercifully, killed a fellow sufferer when he was unable to keep a firm hold on the stone that crashed on someone below him. Three weeks was the normal span of survival. Many of the victims, driven to desperation by their hopeless ordeal, ended their agony by jumping to their deaths from the top of the quarry. The guards referred to these as "the parachutists" and were vexed by their action since the spattered flesh and blood spoiled the neatness of the steps.

In the last months of the war forty-seven downed American pilots had been imprisoned in Mauthausen. They were among those who were compelled, barefooted, to make the climb. Men who reached the top were marched back and given heavier loads. By morning all were dead. The supervision of the quarry enterprise fell to a homosexual sadist, the notorious "Blond Fraulein"—so named by his comrades. He boasted of hacking to death a contingent of eighty-seven Dutch Jews over a period of a few days while they were digging into the sides of the quarry.[14]

By the beginning of 1945, the Nazis knew that time had run out. Panic seized them when they learned that the Allies had agreed to give the Russians the assignment to liberate eastern Austria. To fall into such hands would mean the kind of retribution that they knew only too well. There was a frantic effort to surrender to the Americans. They received unexpected cooperation from General George Patton, who had never hidden his opposition to the Russian alliance. Patton could not override Eisenhower's directive to halt the onrush of his troops, but he gladly accepted the surrender of whole German battalions and divisions. His advance reconnaissance troops burst into the Danube valley and the Mauthausen area on May 3, 1945. Lieutenant Colonel George Dyer, the senior historian of Patton's army, could barely find words to describe the condition of the scarcely living relics he encountered. In his later official history he quoted one of his officers: "Yes, it is the smell, the odor of the death camp, that makes it burn in the nostrils and memory. I will always smell Mauthausen."[15]

As at Belsen, priority was given to the plight of the deathly sick and starving. It was equally critical to establish discipline to prevent wholesale mayhem, not only against the guards who had been prevented from fleeing but against the burghers in the community. No one had expected the Austrian civilians to risk reprisal by offering help to the camp victims, but what could not be forgotten was that few parental voices had been raised when children taunted the new arrivals at Mauthausen by throwing stones and chanting: "You'll soon be up the chimney on Todesberg (Death Hill)."

The Americans were pledged to the concept of "due process." To defuse the probability of individual acts of reprisal, they set the villagers to work on cleaning up the barracks and burying the dead. A former SS football field, for example, became a cemetery. Legalities, however, were bypassed when judgment was passed on the Nazis who had participated in the killing of the American flyers and plane crews shot down during the last months of the war. Here punishment did not wait on judicial procedures.

Mauthausen's commandant, Franz Ziereis, dubbed Baby Face, had come up through the ranks and was named chief in 1939. He always appeared immaculately uniformed and bemedaled. Since Himmler had taken him from a mental asylum, Ziereis imitated his mentor by drawing the members of his personal staff from among vicious criminals. He conducted seminars to refine techniques in brutality and never denied that he shared in the satisfactions of maltreating the prisoners. He confessed to the charge that book covers and screens had been made from the skins of the camp victims, but claimed that this was the work of two of his demented fellow officers.[16] To Ziereis it was apparently entertaining to have the kitchen staff overturn pots of watery soup so that the starved creatures who shambled up for their "meal" would be forced to lick the spillage before it was absorbed into the filthy floor. He had the SS brothels secretly equipped with motion picture cameras, to monitor the possibility that messages might be passed during coitus. In his confessions he noted that he gave fifty Jews for target practice as a birthday present to his son.[17]

What was to have been Ziereis' apogee of achievement in the Final Solution turned into a humiliating loss of face. As spring approached in 1945, he was ordered by one of Himmler's lieutenants, Oswald Pohl, "if the war should go badly," to execute "all 30,000 prisoners in the Mauthausen subcamp of Ebensee." Prisoners were to be herded into the forest to "enjoy the flowers and buds." There they would be set to excavating a trench, long and wide, and into it would be moved a chain of old locomotives, carefully wired with explosives. The prisoners would be driven into the trench in advance of detonators. The prison underground learned of Ziereis' plan and prepared for resistance. When the appointed day came, the prisoners were marched into the forest and the roll call began, but no one moved. The officer in charge shouted again. Still no response. The officer hesitated for a moment, then the prisoners were returned to their blocks.

On May 3, days before the American advance forces entered Mauthausen, Ziereis fled, leaving to his underlings the gallant last stand he had pledged. On May 23, U.S. intelligence learned he was hiding in nearby Spital. Ziereis opened fire on the squad sent to arrest him and was seriously wounded in the exchange of shots. Taken to a hospital in one of the subcamps, he was put into the care of a Jewish prisoner who had been spared only because his medical skills were indispensable. The physician felt obliged by his Hippocratic oath, and his own integrity, to do his best for Ziereis. As the former commandant babbled in self-justification, hundreds of orders and records were retrieved. These, along with instruments of torture, were assembled to serve as evidence in the later trials of the war criminals. Even a cursory review of the documents indicated that between one and a half and two million prisoners had been starved or worked to death in Mauthausen and its subcamps.* Ziereis himself died in the hospital before he could be condemned and probably executed.

After the liberation, every effort was bent to speed homeward the released prisoners who were physically capable of undertaking such journeys. By the end of May, the Mauthausen camps had been emptied of all but 5,200 inmates, mostly Jews, who had no place to call home. They were temporarily lodged in one of

---

*Only one child born in the Mauthausen camp survived. She lived to study at the University of London, and later migrated to a kibbutz in Israel.

the newly established Displaced Persons' Camps in the American Zone, as a prelude to a long-delayed relocation, soon to learn that nothing is so permanent as that which is supposed to be temporary.

THERESIENSTADT

Theresienstadt (Terezin), a sleepy little Czech town, half military, half civilian, is located about forty miles from Prague. A picture-book community of about 7,000 inhabitants, it was named for the eighteenth-century empress of Austria, Maria Theresa. The Nazis chose it as the site for a special purpose prison rather than a concentration or extermination camp, an exercise, as it were, in Nazi public relations. Soon after the Nazis revealed their plans for the site, the Germans abruptly evicted the entire native population, most of whom could trace their ancestral roots to the eighteenth century. A narrow area of less than a square mile was enclosed as a detention center. In a 1941 document it was announced that "privileged people" who were to be interned for security reasons would be held in Theresienstadt—elderly men and women of distinction, decorated veterans of World War I, Jewish partners in mixed marriages and of high social standing, bureaucrats who had held high office, artists, journalists, musicians, noted church figures. Here were sent internationally respected prisoners thought by the Germans to have hostage value. It was not emphasized that 90 percent or more of those held at Theresienstadt were Jews, and the majority came from a cross section of the Czech, Dutch, German, and Danish communities.

Many Jews were deceived by the propaganda that Theresienstadt was a privileged internment center. Families about to be deported prayed to be routed there, as to a sanctuary. By the fall of 1942, 59,000 deportees had been jammed into quarters that may have been tolerable for 10,000. Then began the routine dispatch of prisoners east to Auschwitz and other death camps, at first in groups of a few hundred, ultimately in convoys of thousands. New arrivals continuously replaced the departed doomed.

The commandants, as usual, had criminal records. The last of them, Karl Rahm, a mechanic in earlier civilian life, soon disabused his charges of the idea that Theresienstadt was reserved for the privileged. To be sure, there were neither gas chambers nor crematoria there. But as the crowding increased, the facilities for daily living became ever more inadequate and degrading. Elderly people, often from comfortable backgrounds, were compelled to wait in line for hours for access to lavatories that could not be kept even moderately tidy for the traffic they had to bear. The food could hardly be digested, even by the starving.

In the spring of 1944 the Danish Red Cross, disturbed by serious charges filed on behalf of Danish prisoners, requested an opportunity to conduct a special inspection of Theresienstadt. Permission was granted, Rahm received orders to impress the Danes, and a flurry of activity ensued. The outsides of buildings were painted, streets cleaned, flowers planted, false shop fronts erected. The inmates were warned, under the gravest of threats, to say nothing about regular routines. Children were commanded to refer to Rahm as "Uncle." The dummy villages created by Prince Potemkin for Catherine II of Russia would appear artless in contrast to this Hollywood of concentration camps. The ruse succeeded in the short term; only a mildly adverse report was filed.

To back up the success, the Nazis commissioned a propaganda film entitled *Hitler Presents a Town to the Jews.* Its object was to depict a happy, serene, well-fed community, children romping in play centers, families living in middle-class comfort. The Jews who were ordered to create the film were determined to undermine its credibility by deliberately exaggerating the benevolence the community enjoyed. The stratagem worked. The film was so obviously overdone that even the Nazis understood it would only evoke derision, and it was not released. Those who had written and produced the film were packed off to Auschwitz.

Perhaps the most distinguished inmate of Theresienstadt was Rabbi Leo Baeck, prewar Germany's leader of Progressive Judaism. He was interned in 1943 and remained until the camp was liberated in 1945. There were international efforts to have him expatriated, but he refused to leave his people. His scholarly attainments won him nothing in the camp except survival. He was given such menial tasks as dragging a garbage wagon between barracks and other buildings, with the gibes of the guards in his ears.

The rabbi was not an easy man to understand, especially by those who believed in direct action even though it seemed hopeless. He was privy to reports that came to him from outside sources that his fellow Jews were marked for ultimate liquidation; he withheld the information even when there may have been the opportunity for at least token resistance or escape for a fortunate few. He followed the reasoning of some physicians when they deal with terminal cancer patients: why add to their anguish by robbing them of all hope? Rabbi Baeck's response to the evil that engulfed the camps was to turn from the wretched present to the serene wisdom of the masters of philosophy and rabbinic thought. In crowded rooms, in the limited periods when there was respite from slave labor, he calmly analyzed the concepts of Philo, Maimonides, and Spinoza. Later he would write: "I asked myself: is there another people on earth which has such a deep and true connection to the spirit as ours? . . . Although it is feeling such humiliation and danger, it asks for the word of the philosopher."[18]

Thanks, in part, to the necessity for maintaining the fiction, and in part to the concern of the Danes who requested that Red Cross representatives check on the condition of their nationals, Theresienstadt continued for some time to present a cosmetic appearance of acceptable treatment. Schools functioned for children under the age of fourteen, many of them conducted by highly talented young adults. Some teachers hid drawings, finger paintings, and poems by their pupils which, after the war, were recovered and placed in the Jewish State Museum in Prague. A selection of the work chosen from more than 4,000 items was published in the United States under the title *I Never Saw Another Butterfly*. What is extraordinary about this poignant collection is that, although the children were in no way deluded as to what lay ahead (only 100 of the 15,000 children under the age of fifteen who passed through Theresienstadt survived the war), despair and anguish are not the themes of the poems or pictures. Rather, the work is suffused with a bright-eyed melancholy.

The bizarre world of Theresienstadt was imaginatively portrayed in a novella, *The Terezin Requiem*, by Joseph Bor, himself a survivor of the camp. Bor describes the attempt of a young inmate-conductor, Raphael Schecter, to sponsor a series of classical concerts despite the difficulty of obtaining instruments, scores, and a steady supply of performers.* Schecter, who understood the direction in which he and most of his fellow musicians were headed, decided to mount a performance of Verdi's *Requiem*. He explained that he wished to expose "the mendacity of perverted ideas of pure and impure blood, of superior and inferior races, to confute them precisely in a Jewish camp, and precisely through the medium of art, a field where a man's true worth can best be recognized." He wanted to bring together the most diverse group possible, and then let all men come and hear what could be achieved by such a mixture. There would be Italian music with a Latin text, Catholic prayers, Jewish singers, and musicians from Czechoslovakia, Austria, Germany, Holland, and Denmark, many even from Poland and Hungary. . . . A Requiem studied and directed by an unbeliever, a Requiem in the ghetto."[19] Schecter conducted the concert with passionate dedication. At summer's end, the commandant kept the promise that he had made to Schecter on the night of the *Requiem*, that the company would not be separated. All the participants marched together to the wagons that would carry them to Auschwitz and the gas chambers.

By April 1945 the Americans, General Patton among them, were closing in from the west. Flying Fortresses, scattering leaflets over Theresienstadt, encouraged the inmates to hold fast. Rahm labored furiously with his staff to destroy evidence. They burned thousands of incriminating documents. Townspeople were recruited to help dispose of boxes of human ashes that had been stored in cellars. Although Theresienstadt boasted no large-scale crematoria, those who had been summarily executed or had died of disease had been cremated. The German bureaucratic mind had made sure that the containers with remains were carefully labeled as to names and dates of birth and death. The ashes of the famous or prominent had been deposited in iron boxes, the "nobodies" in cardboard. As these were hurriedly collected by the Nazi wardens to be thrown into the Ulatove River, it was considered good sport to mix the celebrities with the lesser lights. When an iron box came up the line, the guards indulged their humor: "Look out, here comes a big shot."

---

*There was, in fact, an inmate musician named Raphael Schecter. Bor kept loyally to facts in the novella except when he put thoughts in the minds of his characters.

On May 8, when the Red Cross flag suddenly replaced the swastika on the Theresienstadt tower, the inmates realized that most of their captors had fled. Rahm appeared on a bicycle. He stopped at each gate, locked it, and gathered the keys. No one moved. One of Baeck's protégés recorded the old rabbi's reaction. "Look at it," said Baeck. "This can happen only with Jews. Of all the people here, not one person lifted a stone to throw at him [Rahm]. They could have strangled him if they wanted." He added softly, "Vengeance can only be taken by God. After the Nazi brutality, the Jews still believed this to be their ultimate triumph."[20] The War Crimes Commission thought otherwise: Rahm and his chief lieutenants were sentenced to death and hanged. Nor did the younger generation of the Israelis share the sentiments of the rabbi, despite their saintly echo. They responded to them as a legacy of the Diaspora that their people's experience had compelled them to repudiate.

CHAPTER TWO

The Nazi Extermination Camps
in Poland

WHEN THE ADVANCING RUSSIAN ARMIES burst into the death camps that Hitler had established in Poland, and corroborated the monstrosities that had debauched the years of occupation, there was wonder why the Nazis had not simply killed off their prisoners. The Final Solution called for the elimination of all Jews. What purposes were served by creating the elaborate machinery of torture and slow starvation, perversions that robbed the victims of all personal dignity? Diverse interpretations have been suggested—the naked sadism of many of the executioners, the irrationality of men brutalized by unrestrained power, the contempt for humankind that the Nazis had developed.

Such explanations were in some measure validated by the behavior of the guards and the toll that it exacted. But the wellsprings of action could not have been hatred or perversion alone, even when pressed to their pathological extremes. The dehumanization that preceded death must have been a deliberate policy. By destroying the will of the prisoners, their mass extermination would be accomplished with little resistance. When they first arrived in the camps and witnessed torture and misery, they were torn apart in anguish. The suffering they witnessed and themselves endured had shaken the faith of even the most devout. Rabbi Zalman Schechter said, despairingly, "If there is a God, he doesn't exist."

But a time came when the screams of victims and their degrading deaths left fellow sufferers in an apathetic limbo. Undoubtedly also the cruelty was aimed at the enemy peoples of

Europe to create the paralysis of fear. They were being warned that loss of life was not the worst fate: an agony of drawn-out death, for themselves and for dear ones in hostage, was infinitely more to be dreaded. The strategy did not succeed completely; there were acts of defiance and resistance that no threats could stifle. But the Nazis stretched out the paralyzing intimidation long enough to fulfill most of Hitler's *Judenrein* goal.

AUSCHWITZ

If Theresienstadt was converted for visiting inspection teams into a Potemkin village, then Auschwitz, which was created in 1940 for Polish and Russian prisoners of war and became, by 1941, the main death camp for Jews, was reminiscent of the grounds of a run-down Civilian Conservation Corps camp. The plain, unadorned architecture of the gas chambers and crematoria, the row upon row of drafty barracks, the sign over the main gate with its dissembling message, *"Arbeit macht Frei"* (Work Brings Freedom), gave little clue to the diabolism of the activity within. The Russians under Marshal Ivan Konev, who stormed the camp in May 1945, discovered the truth. They learned that "work" was slave labor, and "freedom" the release of death. Among the millions tormented and murdered in Auschwitz had been thousands of captured Russians, only some 2,800 of whom survived. Marshal Konev noted in his memoirs that after liberating Auschwitz he refused to visit and inspect it because its horror was bound to affect his martial capability and his peace of mind. Rudolf Hoess, the commandant, stated at his trial that Auschwitz was "the greatest human extermination center of all time." He took credit for having done to death more than two million men, women, and children, mostly Jews.[1] The Nuremberg War Crimes Tribunal gave him an even higher rating.

The site for Auschwitz (Oswiecim), on the outskirts of a little Polish town in Galicia, thirty-seven miles west of the thriving city of Krakow, was chosen by Himmler himself. Its location, described by Hoess as "far away, in back of beyond," was ideal for its purpose. The surrounding countryside was sparsely populated and such inhabitants as there were thought it best to know as little as possible about purpose and operation. Yet, though remotely situated, Auschwitz was a railway junction where four lines converged, the better to facilitate the arrival of the trains full of the doomed who had been rounded up from the countries of conquered Europe.

Hoess had been born into a deeply religious family who nursed the hope that he would enter the priesthood. He preferred a more enterprising existence. After having served in the Imperial Army during World War I in Mesopotamia and Palestine, he enlisted, in 1919, in the roving Free Corps, made up, as he was to write, "of officers and men who had returned from the war and who found themselves misfits in civilian life." He shared the rowdyism and the vandalism with which they harassed the Weimar Republic. He joined the Nazi party in 1922 and, in the next year, was implicated in the murder of a schoolteacher. Sentenced to life imprisonment, he was released in a general amnesty in 1928, into the arms, as it were, of Adolf Hitler. He was trained in apprenticeship positions at Dachau and Sachenhausen and, in 1940, having amply demonstrated his loyalty, he was given the commandant's post at Auschwitz. He managed its murder machine until December 1943, when his record earned him appointment as chief of the Central Administration for Camps.

As the inevitability of the German defeat became clear even to the Nazi elite, the concern to escape retributive punishment that overwhelmed the Nazis in the other camps took priority at Auschwitz too. It was imperative to destroy all implicating evidence and simultaneously to kill off as many inmates as possible. The rest were to be shipped to camps that had not yet been endangered by the Allied sweep. As early as November 1944, the gas chambers that had choked out the lives of millions were closed and blown up. Incriminating documents were shredded and burned. In his autobiography, written later in prison, Hoess described how, having been promoted to an office in Berlin, he had tried to get back to Auschwitz to help supervise the transport of the Jews. Thwarted, or perhaps realizing the folly of moving toward the Russians, Hoess joined in the exodus toward the Schleswig-Holstein border of Denmark on the northwest. He wrote: "It was a gruesome journey, the men and women in flight scurrying from one clump of trees to the next, as the enemy's low flying planes continually machine-gunned the escape route."[2] The roads were clogged with dying prisoners, disoriented civilians, and deflated SS warriors and soldiers. En route, the villages were pillaged for food; but the civilian inhabitants, fully aware that they could expect no quarter from the Russians, had already turned tail, loaded down with whatever they could carry. When the news was flashed that the Führer himself had committed suicide, all discipline collapsed.

Hoess was captured in May 1945, along with several hundred thousand Germans and collaborators. He escaped early recognition and took work on a farm near Flensburg, but was rearrested by the British some months later. He had carried, as did all high-ranking Nazis, a poison phial, but claimed it had been broken, and so he was denied the honorable exit of suicide.

Hoess was a key witness in Nuremberg at the trial of one of his chiefs, Ernst Kaltenbrunner, who was to be convicted and executed in October 1946. He also testified in the trial of the tycoons of I. G. Farben, Germany's leading industrial firm, indicted for their slave labor activities during the war. In May he was delivered to the Poles, who had been waiting impatiently to deal with him.

Hoess's incarceration lasted almost a year. He used this enforced leisure to write a rambling autobiography in which, though he denied responsibility for many crimes attributed to him, he damned himself out of his own mouth. He claimed to have been a "cog in the wheel of the great extermination machine created by the Third Reich." Occasionally in the narrative there were expressions of astonishment at the mild treatment he experienced from his captors and at the fairness of his judges, "though they were nearly all Jews." There was also recognition that his acts were not benevolent, as when he described the gassing of nine hundred Russians with Zyklon B. "It made me uncomfortable: I shuddered."[3]

Hoess took pride in his exemplary family life, the devotion to his children and his pets. He recalled, wistfully, how he had been obliged to tear himself away from a Christmas gathering to attend to duties at the gas chambers. The daily death quota then was still a mere 1,500, but he was eager to make sure it was met. When one of his lieutenants was condemned to death for his part in the Auschwitz murders, Hoess and his family lamented, "Such a compassionate man, too. When his pet canary died, he tenderly put the body in a small box, covered it with a rose, and buried it under a rose bush in the garden."[4]

The evidence given at Hoess's trial repeated, in good measure, what he had written. He described, with the dispassion of a robot, how he had gradually stepped up executions, beginning with a few hundred a day and then, as methods were perfected, rising to 1,200. By mid-1942, facilities had been sufficiently enlarged to dispatch 1,500 people over a twenty-four-hour period for the smaller ovens, and up to 2,500 for the larger ones. By 1943, when the Hungarian Jews were shipped in, a new daily peak of 12,000 was achieved. Hoess described the final routines of the extermination process. These were assigned to squads of Jewish prisoners, the Sondercommandos. They marched the victims to the gas chambers, helped to undress them, removed the corpses after the gassing, extracted gold from their teeth and rings from their fingers, searched the orifices of their bodies for hidden jewelry, cut off the hair of the women, and then carted the bodies to the crematoria. Usually after several weeks of such service they were executed, first because they were Jews but also so that they would not be witnesses if ever testimony were required. One of the survivors, Dora Klein, who served as a nurse, wrote "I had a feeling that I was in a place which was half hell and half lunatic asylum"

A two-year inmate testified at the Eichmann trial that Auschwitz had become a separate planet: "The inhabitants of that planet had no names. They had no parents, and they had no children. They were not clothed as we are clothed here. They were not born there, and they did not conceive there. They breathed and lived according to different laws of Nature. They did not live according to the laws of this world of ours, and they did not die. Their name was a number."[5]

Hoess's trial in Warsaw was delayed until March 1947. He was then condemned to death and was hanged on April 7, on a site next to the house where he had lived with his wife, his children, his pets, and the recordings of classical composers.

In the last year of the war, as the horrors of Auschwitz became common knowledge, the Jewish Agency leadership made urgent appeals to the western Allies to bomb the approaches to the death camps. There had been bases captured in Italy which could be used. Although it was unlikely that the bombing could put the camps out of commission, such attacks would necessarily slow down the massive deportations. The American Air Force had bombed the synthetic oil plants of I. G. Farben and Monowitz, about five miles from the gas chambers. But none of the British officials responded affirmatively: the risks, they said, were still too great, the diversion too costly. Officials in the American State Department offered the clinching negative argument: "Such an effort," wrote John McCloy, Assistant Secretary of War, "even if practical, might provoke even more vindictive action by the Germans." By that time the Germans had already killed about five million Jews.

Most of the victims in the death camps could not cope with the overwhelming odds that destroyed them. But it is well to remember some few who, when granted a measure of survival time, were determined to challenge what seemed inevitable. One of Europe's most distinguished psychiatrists, Victor Frankl, fought back against the assault on his will by substituting fantasy for reality. In 1942 he had been deported to Theresienstadt and then, two years later, to Auschwitz. His wife and his mother died in the gas chambers. He was assigned as a slave laborer to the tasks of digging and laying tracks for railroads. The long humiliating hours were unbroken by rest periods and the diet never varied from watery soup and rancid vegetables. But Frankl would not give up. He directed his thoughts and emotions to companionship and experiences that had been precious to him, and thus shut out the world that threatened his sanity and dignity. "I understand," he wrote later, "in a position of utter desolation, when man cannot express himself in positive action . . . he can, through loving contemplation of the image he carries of his beloved, achieve fulfillment. For the first time in my life I was able to fathom the meaning of the words, 'The angels are lost in perpetual contemplation of an infinite glory.' "[6]

At another time, limping in pain in the miles-long march from camp to the work site, he forced his thoughts away from the agonies of actual experience. "Suddenly," he wrote, "I saw myself standing on the platform of a well-lit warm and pleasant lecture room. . . . I was giving a lecture on the psychology of the concentration camp! All that oppressed me at that moment became objective, seen and described from the remote viewpoint of science. By this method I succeeded somehow in rising above the situation, above the suffering of the moment, and I observed them as if they were already of the past."[7]

Frankl emerged, barely alive, from Auschwitz, and recovered sufficiently to resume teaching at the University of Vienna.

Later he headed the neurological department of the Poliklinic Hospital of Vienna and was elected president of the Austrian Medical Society of Psychotherapy. Free for research, he developed the discipline that he had applied for survival in Auschwitz into the theory of Logotherapy that became part of the curriculum of psychiatry.

Frankl resorted to fantasy as a means of survival. Others attempted more conventional forms of escape. Despite the efficiency of Hoess and the SS, 230 escape attempts were made during the years from 1941 through 1944. Most were thwarted, and a hundred-fold punishment was exacted. Some eighty attempts, however, did succeed, at least in part. The number was insignificant in the statistics of death, but the survivors fulfilled the need to bring eyewitness accounts to the outside world.

David Szmuluwski's spectacular escape may demonstrate why the SS guards could never relax their surveillance. He had left Poland as a youngster and, eluding the border guards of several countries, had made his way to Palestine. Later he fought with the International Brigade in Spain and fled to France after Franco's victory. When the Nazis took over France, Szmuluwski was shipped to Auschwitz. He was now all of thirty. Before his fate was determined, an SS guard came through the prisoners' quarters seeking roofers. Szmuluwski, who was no roofer but knew that unless he had a skill to offer he would be executed, spoke up immediately, claiming he had been trained as a tiler. His effrontery spared him.

The suddenly endowed tiler became a Jewish representative in the camp underground. He was soon recruited by another prisoner, Josef Cyrankiewicz, destined to become a postwar Prime Minister of Poland, who asked Szmuluwski to use his occupational vantage points to photograph operations inside one of the gas chambers. It was hoped that if the photographs were smuggled out, they might stir the outside world to retributive action. Szmuluwski was given a camera, stolen from one of the storerooms and passed from hand to hand in the false bottom of a soup cauldron. Special resourcefulness was needed to damage the roof of the gas chamber to justify Szmuluwski's presence there. Then, with the camera hidden beneath his jacket, he obtained three pictures of naked women on their way into the gas chambers and of bodies burning in the open pits used when there was a traffic jam in the crematoria. Cyrankiewicz smuggled the film out to resistance leaders in Krakow, where they supplied the earliest pictorial evidence of what Auschwitz was all about.*[8]

Another even more ambitious defiance was planned for the first week of October in 1944, to coincide with the expected advance of the Red Army, which was nearing the Vistula. Preparations for the attempt had begun several months earlier, for weaponry had to be manufactured by hand out of bits and pieces to be retrieved by slave workers in the neighboring Krupp munitions enterprises. The coordinating plans had to be developed by covert signals among the conspirators, since communication was forbidden.

Two leaders emerged in the long and tortuous planning stages. Yisroel Gutman had grown up in prewar Warsaw; during its liquidation, his wife and parents had perished. When the fate of those who were deported to the death camps became known to the remnants of the doomed community, Gutman, a member of the activist Zionist youth movement, joined the final ghetto uprising of 1943. He was captured and deported to Maidenek and then to Auschwitz. By now, blinded in one eye, overcome by the loss of family, he had deteriorated so much that he was counted a Musselman, the name given to prisoners who were spent physically and no longer had the will to live. He was destined for the gas chambers but was saved by a member of the Polish Underground who had infiltrated the camp to keep the spirit of resistance alive. Gutman, soon again in control of himself, was placed in charge of coordinating the acquisition of the weapons needed for the revolt.[9]

Gutman's aide was a twenty-one-year-old girl, Rosa Robota, who had been deported to Auschwitz in 1942 along with the Jews of her home town of Ciechanów. Her family had been gassed upon arrival, but Rosa had been reprieved to work in the clothing supply depot of the camp. Her assignment gave her a measure of mobility and she took advantage of it to maintain liaison with other girls from Ciechanów. The girls began filching minute particles of dynamite from the Krupp plants, hiding them

---

*In January 1960, the fifteenth anniversary of the liberation of Auschwitz, Szmuluwski returned from France, his postwar home, to receive Poland's highest honor, the Virtuti Militari, from his old comrade, now Prime Minister Cyrankiewicz.

in pockets that they had sewn into the hems of their loose burlap garments. The particles were then collected and hoarded in matchboxes. Some of the precious fragments that could pass for small buttons were smuggled to Rosa in handcarts carrying corpses to the crematoria. Others were passed from hand to hand until they reached selected Russian prisoners who were expert in bomb construction. They patiently manufactured a supply of grenades, salvaging sardine cans from garbage containers for the casings, which were then cached in an area close to the crematoria.

Suddenly the intricately planned revolt was almost aborted. The underground learned from their own intelligence sources that their leaders were marked for execution before the date set for the uprising. Preparations had to be stepped up, but too hastily to ensure complete coordination. On October 6, 1944, the revolt ignited. The chief guard of Crematorium III and four SS men were hurled into the oven, several submachine guns were seized, and the building was blown up. The electrified wire fence was cut and six hundred prisoners dashed through. Most of the escapees were rounded up or killed in flight by a massive deployment of SS reinforcements. But by now the Russians were on the outskirts of the camps and there was only enough time for the Nazis to herd 60,000 of the inmates, including Gutman, for shipment to Mauthausen, where they were liberated by the Americans.*

Rosa was not so fortunate. She and her closest collaborators were put to torture to elicit the names of the participants in the almost successful rebellion. Rosa did not talk, and she was able to get a message to the underground to remain strong and hopeful. The final Soviet drive that freed the camp came a few days later, but not in time to save Rosa. Close to death after continuous beatings, she had been hanged in the courtyard, with the remaining prisoners in compulsory attendance.[10]

The self-sacrifice of 24-year old Mala Zimetbaum in 1944

---

*Gutman, fully restored, became part of the B'richa commandos, a relief agency that was directing illegal immigration to Palestine. When the war ended, he migrated to a kibbutz in Israel and joined the faculty of the Hebrew University's Institute of Contemporary Jewry. In my interview with him in Jerusalem he would not speak of his own Auschwitz activities, but he had highest praise for his courageous fellow prisoners.

should also be remembered. She gave courage to the inmates who had been taunted by the SS on arrival with "from here one leaves only through the chimney." Polish born, a refugee in Belgium at the outbreak of WW I, Mala had been deported in 1942, and because she was proficient in languages, was made a runner (*lausferin*) by the SS command. She took advantage of the opportunity to move in relative freedom and carried news and messages from incoming transport to the camp underground. She planned an escape with a Polish prisoner, stealing the permit that would be needed to get past the guard. They were absent from the roll call on the night of the escape, and almost got through the outer gate but were recognized as they slipped by the last obstacle. Under torture, Mala refused to reveal accomplices. On the way to the gas chamber she slashed her wrists with a blade she had stolen from the kitchen. The guard, infuriated, ordered that she be burnt alive; she responded by crying out: "Murderers, the day of reckoning is near." Her mouth was taped and she was hustled, barely conscious, into the crematorium. After the war, the city of Antwerp placed a plaque on the house where she had lived that read: "Mala Zimetbaum, Symbol of Solidarity. Murdered by the Nazis in Auschwitz. 1920–1944.[11]

Auschwitz was liberated by the Russians on January 27, 1945. When the statistics of the camp were studied, they indicated that the lives of three million Jews had been destroyed. Auschwitz became a tourist attraction. The Polish government reserved some of the barracks, the gas chambers, and crematoria, and a lively souvenir trade developed on the site. Years later, when the atmosphere became too oppressive for families whose dear ones had perished there, the sale of souvenirs was dropped.*

TREBLINKA

Treblinka, sixty miles northeast of Warsaw, was set down in a dense pine forest, isolated by a nine-foot electrified barbed

---

*Walter Dejaco, of Reutte, a town in the Austrian Tyrol, who designed and constructed the Auschwitz crematoria had no trouble in continuing to fulfill building commissions. In 1963 he won warm praise from Bishop Rusk of Innsbruck for the fine Presbytery he had built for Reutte's parish priest.

wire fence. It was hard to imagine that behind the always freshly painted railway station, adorned with geraniums in neat little window boxes, a death toll of 840,000 was being exacted, using highly mechanized extermination techniques. No planes, friendly or otherwise, were permitted to fly over or near it. There were two camps. Treblinka I, created in 1941, was used to punish political prisoners who were assigned slave labor duties as part of their "regeneration." The Poles among them were usually released when their terms of punishment were completed. The Jews were either worked to death or transferred to Treblinka II, which became one of the main Nazi murder centers. At Treblinka II, 300,000 Jews, uprooted from Warsaw, were executed during the three summer months of 1942.[12] The historian of the Warsaw Ghetto uprising, Emmanuel Ringelblum, referred to it in his diary notes as "the slaughter house of European Jewry."

The term "mechanized" for Treblinka must be taken literally. The technical appointments of its gas chambers and crematoria were unsurpassed until Hoess added refinements at Auschwitz that won back for that camp the trophy for lethal ingenuity. The enterprising director of the C. N. Kori Company, when he submitted the bid for equipment at bargain prices, boasted: "We guarantee the effectiveness of the crematoria ovens as well as their durability, the use of the best materials and of course, our faultless workmanship."[13]

One of Treblinka's first commandants was Theodor von Eupen, an expert horseman who found diversion in riding about on a pedigree steed, terrifying prisoners by maiming them or even trampling them to death. When the first thirty Jewish children arrived from Warsaw, he assigned to a university-educated Ukrainian guard the task of axing the children to death. It should be added that, in the climate of the later Cold War, the murderer escaped censure and eventually returned to the teaching profession.

There was no slackening of technical efficiency when Von Eupen was succeeded by Odilo Globocnik, a veteran killer who had set up the camps in Maidanek and Sobibor and proved his mettle in the liquidation of the Bialystok ghetto. He accelerated the death process in Treblinka by channeling the gas fumes of diesel engines directly into the chambers. He saw to it that soothing music was supplied, usually by other hapless Jewish prisoners, for the march to the gas chambers, "Ascension" and

"The Way to Heaven" being among the favorite selections. Himmler found Globocnik so talented and entertaining that he promoted him to the commandant's post at Belzec.

In some camps there were opportunities, though minimal, to smuggle in arms. But not in Treblinka, unless wrested from unwary guards. Yet on August 2, 1943, an uprising occurred that involved seven hundred prisoners. Relying upon the skills of a Polish locksmith, the underground leaders obtained the impression of the key to one of the main arsenals. While the locksmith, without adequate tools, was engaged in fabricating the key, the prisoners' search for arms was intensified. Fortunately for them, most of the guards tempered the monotony of their daily rounds with generous drafts of strong Ukrainian liquor. The slowly accumulated arms were secreted in a building equipped with sprinklers for disinfecting prisoners and under corpses stacked in trucks.

When the revolt started, the gas chambers were set on fire and some of the storerooms filled with clothing were destroyed. Seven hundred prisoners made the break, after killing about twenty guards and wounding others. Hundreds of escapees were mowed down from the tower, but nearly two hundred reached the open countryside. Most of these, betrayed by the village peasants, were eventually hunted down, but a dozen got away. What mattered most in the uprising was not the survival rate; its purpose was to destroy the camp. The total goal was not achieved, but the damage was substantial and slowed down the extermination process.

When the Russians took over the Treblinka complex and the nearly dead survivors had recovered sufficiently to communicate, the tales that they poured out were not limited to the horrors they had endured. These called for no review. There was no lack of physical evidence on display, the suffocated bodies in recently arrived cattle cars, the abandoned instruments of torture and death, the files and records that the Germans had so carefully maintained. It was the repeated tales of senseless cruelty that increased the Russian fury: mothers obliged to carry their infants to their deaths (even in primitive societies a cat is led away before her kittens are destroyed); the woman on her way to the gas chamber, goaded to desperation by a taunting SS man, who threw herself upon him, and was then tortured by his comrades to emphasize the cost of remonstrance. The prisoners remembered the little boy who consoled his weeping parents on the edge of their mass grave with the assurance that the Russians would avenge them. They did so, wasting no time on due process of law.

Franz Stangl had been the last commandant at Treblinka. He had faithfully followed the procedures of his predecessor, Globocnik. One of his proudest boasts was that, in an incumbency of only ten months, he had been able to deliver twenty-five truckloads of women's hair to provide mattresses and felt slippers for U-boat crews. He managed to slip out of Treblinka before the Russians arrived, and found refuge in Brazil, where he lived for the next twenty-five years. In 1970 he was betrayed by a son-in-law who received $7,000 for his act. The spate of publicity that followed his unmasking compelled the Brazilian government to permit Stangl's extradition to Germany, but, anxious not to agitate the very large German population in the country, the condition was set that, if he were found guilty, the sentence would be comparatively light.

Stangl's trial in Dusseldorf in 1971 was one of the longest in German legal history. The defense attorney impassively offered the argument that Stangl deserved special consideration since, though under orders to carry out the executions, he had shortened the ordeal in the gas chambers by efficient procedures so that the agony of the victims was over in forty-five minutes. Stangl himself remained impenitent. "You may ask any question you like," he said. "I have done nothing to anybody that was not my duty. My conscience is clear." He was found guilty. The judges honored the German promise to the government of Brazil. The sentence was moderate, a few years; it was further shortened by a terminal cancer.

After Israel became an independent state, many bodies were exhumed from the mass graves of Treblinka and reburied in sacred ground in the Homeland, where the bereaved families gathered yearly to observe the Kaddish for their own and for the 840,000 who had perished in the camp. The Polish government devised a unique memorial at Treblinka itself. Thousands of granite slabs were gathered, each reflecting in size the number of victims from the towns and cities of Poland who were killed in the camp. Small natural rocks were scattered on the site to denote the tiniest communities, and the whole was dominated by a massive boulder that represented Warsaw's 300,000 victims.

THE LUBLIN CIRCLE

The historic city of Lublin where the Jews had for many centuries played an important role in the commerce between East and West, early caught the attention of the Nazi leadership as a possible reservation, a huge super-ghetto, in Himmler's words, where Jews "would disport themselves according to their nature." The concept, however, was abandoned when Hitler insisted that only annihilation would achieve the Final Solution. It followed from this decision that places near Lublin, such as Belzec and Maidanek, as well as Sobibor further north, would become death camps. The main camps, Auschwitz and Treblinka, were administered by men who, however perverted, had a measure of administrative ability. But the Lublin governing coterie consisted chiefly of inept *arrivistes*. There is no arrogance like servility enthroned; as camp commandants they used their posts to flaunt their fantasies of power, decked out in uniforms that must have given them mirror satisfaction. They decided life and death. A nod in one direction prescribed the gas chambers; a flip of the hand permitted a brief respite.

BELZEC

In 1939, when Germany and Russia, temporarily in a treaty of non-aggression, divided Poland, buffer areas were set up so that the two totalitarian giants could protect themselves from each other. Belzec, appropriated by Germany, was originally intended as part of this territorial shield. Thousands of conscripted Jews from the Lublin area were uprooted to construct a wall and extend ditches to cordon off the separate areas. As it happened, the wall and the ditches proved unnecessary. When the two allies went to war with each other, the wall was torn down and, together with the ditches, became the site for mass graves when Belzec, in 1942, was converted into an extermination camp.

Six hundred thousand lives were snuffed out there, nearly all of them Jewish. Not everyone went submissively to slaughter. During the process of deportation from the ghettos of Poland they put up fanatic resistance, fighting with fists and teeth against machine guns, breaking through the sides of trucks and trains that raced at speeds of forty-nine kilometers. The Ukrainian guards on top of the cars machine-gunned those who made the break. A few survived by feigning death; others, more or less seriously wounded, were able to join the Partisans in the woods. Those who were recaptured were almost invariably lined up for mass execution.

Once the deportees arrived in Belzec, there could be little further resistance. Starvation, illness, physical abuse, degradation numbed them into torpor. One survivor imagined that she had been moving through a canvas of fearsome monsters by Hieronymous Bosch.[14] It took little more than a year, from March 1942 to the spring of 1943, for the Germans to kill off their Belzec victims.

The attempt to alert the free world to this tragedy brought to prominence one of the most controversial characters of the war and of the retributive years that followed. Kurt Gerstein, born soon after the turn of the century of an old Prussian family, was early involved in Christian evangelical movements that drew to them young Germans who were repelled by the paganism of the Hitler Jugend. Gerstein believed that, since both polarized groups yearned for a strong, creative Germany, he could reconcile the passionate nationalism of the Nazis and the fervent religious sensibilities of authentic Christians. Seeking to work from within, he joined the Nazi party in 1933. From the fanatic reactions of the Hitler Jugend he realized almost at once that a formula for compromise was impossible. Outspokenly critical of Nazi blasphemies, Gerstein was expelled from the party in 1936 and, in 1938, was sentenced to a term in a concentration camp to reappraise his premises. Upon release he continued working with the Christian youth movements, but he found that, in competition with Nazi activism, they had become ineffectual.

Gerstein's prison experiences convinced him that Nazism was implacable in its determination to destroy Christianity and all other values precious to western civilization. Upon release, he came to what he called the salient decision of his life. He took it upon himself to expose the Nazi menace by gathering evidence of the extent of its depravity. Despite his "Nordic" appearance, his Prussian heritage, and impeccable family credentials (his father served as a judge in the Third Reich), he was never fully trusted, but he was put to use where it served a Nazi purpose. Gerstein had studied mining engineering and was considered an authority on the properties of gas. The Nazis were just then searching for a more economical and efficient mass method of killing, and Gerstein was assigned to Belzec to devise some method of accelerating the machinery of death. He gave a favorable report on what was called Zyklon B, a gas produced when prussic acid crystals were exposed to air, already widely used by manufacturers of particularly strong vermin sprays.

Gerstein wrote what became perhaps the most horrifying eye-witness account of death in the Belzec chambers, a process that took thirty minutes, with 600 to 700 victims crushed into an area of approximately 270 square feet: "Inside, the people were still standing erect, like pillars of basalt, since there had not been an inch of space for them to fall in or even lean. Families could still be seen holding hands, even in death. It was a tough job to separate them as the chambers were emptied to make way for the next batch. The bodies were tossed out, blue, wet with sweat and urine, the legs soiled with faeces and menstrual blood. A couple of dozen workers checked the mouths of the dead, which they tore open with iron hooks. 'Gold to the left, other objects to the right.' "[15]

The chief at Belzec was the notorious Globocnik, who prodded Gerstein to deliver ever larger quantities of gas and to step up daily quotas from the August 1942 high of 15,000. When Globocnik was disappointed in the capacity of Zyklon B to achieve faster results, the gas chambers were supplemented by firing squads. Gerstein said that he realized he was dealing with a monster when he queried Globocnik about the wisdom of creating mass graves that would be evidence for adverse interpretations by future generations. Globocnik replied: "If there should ever be, after us, a generation so cowardly and so soft that they could not understand our work which is so good and so necessary, the entire National Socialist movement will have been in vain. On the contrary, we ought to bury bronze tablets stating that it was we who had the courage to carry out this gigantic task."[16]

Gerstein later claimed that he had stalled as best he could, offering any ingenious excuse that would obstruct the orders from on high. Meanwhile, he smuggled out confidential appeals to diplomats of the free world who were posted to Germany and whom he felt he could trust. He tried the apostolic nuncio in

Berlin and several Swedish and Swiss diplomats, pleading that they make known the Nazi crimes.

On one occasion, when traveling by train from Warsaw to Berlin, Gerstein poured out his heart to Baron von Otter, a Swedish diplomat, later ambassador to Great Britain. The baron described the encounter: "From the very beginning as Gerstein described the atrocities, weeping and broken-hearted, I had no doubt as to the sincerity of his humanitarian intentions."[17] Von Otter reported Gerstein's story to his own government, which found it, as did other neutrals, too bizarre for credibility. Gerstein's appeal to the papal nuncio in Berlin, Father Orsenigo, was also ignored. Gerstein sent scores of letters to other church leaders, but if there were any replies, they must have been private, for none has come to light. Gerstein tried to explain his mission in a long letter to his father, an ardent Nazi, who was horrified by what he termed his son's "disloyalty and imprudence."

When the Nazi regime collapsed, Gerstein turned over to a French intelligence team his detailed report on atrocities in Belzec and Treblinka. His data provided the Allies in later trials with their most detailed accounts of the Nazi murder mills, and it was used at Nuremberg. Gerstein was, however, arrested by the French, who concluded that he was a war criminal now trying to weasel out of retribution. Gerstein argued that he had endangered his own life by appealing to important public figures, all of whom were ready to vouch for him. He made little headway with the French. The court noted that he was not stationed in some remote administrative office but assigned to Belzec, where the gas chamber deaths were watched by him.

In July 1945, Gerstein was found hanged in his cell. The inquest concluded that he had committed suicide. Whether or not Gerstein "worked from within" to awaken the conscience of Christians and why he committed suicide, if indeed he did, remain mysteries. The documents that Gerstein submitted and the notes that he made in his cell were lost or destroyed, deliberately or otherwise. The cemetery where he was buried, in Thais, France, was leveled, a common practice in crowded Europe, and investigation into the cause of his death could not proceed.

In 1950, a denazification court in Tübingen identified Gerstein as a willing Nazi collaborator for his role in supervising the manufacture of Zyklon B. It was not until authorities in the state of Baden Württemberg again reviewed the case, with access to considerably more documentary evidence and the testimony of reliable witnesses such as Baron von Otter, that Gerstein's good name was redeemed.[18] In the judgment of the distinguished French historian Léon Poliakov, Gerstein's testimony about the activities at Belzec remains one of the most harrowing accounts in the vast literature of the genocide.[19] The German Federal Republic Information Service distributed many thousands of copies of Gerstein's account in its campaign to disabuse the younger generation of any lingering admiration for the achievements of the Third Reich.

MAIDANEK

Maidanek was constructed in 1941 primarily as a detention center for prisoners captured by the Nazis in their initial sweep into Russia. Five thousand Soviet prisoners were shipped there within days after Hitler repudiated the non-aggression pact with Stalin. The Russians all died quickly of hunger, typhus, and brutal treatment, their fate a clear signal that the camp would honor no civilized code nor be administered with any humane concern. The message was accentuated when Maidanek was turned into a major extermination center for the Jews of conquered Poland and other centers of Jewish life in Europe. Between February 1942 and July 1944 about half a million Jews were destroyed there by gassing and by shooting. When the Soviet troops liberated the camp on July 24, 1944, they found fewer than six hundred inmates still alive, and these had been temporarily spared to obliterate the evidence of the more than two million men, women, and children who had been murdered. Much of what had happened there, the Russians already knew; in 1942 a few escapees had described the hell that Maidanek had become. But its full savagery could not even be imagined until the records and the actual physical evidence had been reviewed.

The most vivid memory was of the horror of November 3, 1943, that carried the code name *Erntefest*, Harvest Festival. Seventeen thousand Jews, rounded up after the final collapse of the Warsaw Ghetto, were machine-gunned. The victims were lined up in front of open ditches which they had dug for their own mass grave. A BBC correspondent, Alexander Werth, accompanied the Russian troops and filed the story. The BBC refused

to use it, the editor labeling it a "Russian propaganda stunt."
The sworn testimony of the camp staff, at their later trial, fully
corroborated the details of the despatch, adding other incidents
that made the Werth story appear an understatement.*

The collected belongings of the murdered Jews were sent in
truckloads to the storage rooms of one of Europe's largest department stores in Lublin, on Chopin Street. Piled up on its
shelves and in its storerooms were thousands of consumer goods
—women's dresses, knitting wool and cotton yarn, men's clothing, safety razors, penknives. There was a special room for toys,
dolls, games, puzzles, children's notebooks, and erasers. Tucked
into the neatly arranged assortments were an American-made
Mickey Mouse and the manuscript of Ernest Weil's Sonata for
Violin, Opus 15.[20]

By the fall of 1943, as the war began to go badly for the Nazis,
some of them became squeamish about the ruthlessness which
had been employed. On October 4, the increasingly apprehen-
sive guards listened to a grim exhortation from Himmler. He
had been angered because occasionally victims, using influence,
had managed to squirm out of their prescribed fate. "There
must be no exceptions," Himmler stormed. "The extermination
of the Jewish race must be total. . . . Of 80,000,000 worthy
Germans, each one has his decent Jews. Of course the others are
vermin, but this one is an A-1 Jew. Not one of those who talks
this way has witnessed it, not one of them has been through it.
Most of you must know what it means when one hundred
corpses are lying side by side or five hundred or one thousand.
To have stuck it out and at the same time . . . to have remained
decent men, that is what has made us hard. This is a page of
glory in our history which has never been written and is never
to be written."[21]

SOBIBOR

The name Sobibor was not immediately minted into the vocabulary of the West, perhaps because by the time the record of
the camp was exposed, the casualty figures of the war itself had

---

*It should be noted that until long after WW II the *Encyclopaedia Britannica*
carried no reference to Hitler's maniacal determination to destroy the whole
Jewish people.

become statistics and the capacity to respond to human suffering was blunted. Yet Sobibor was one of the six largest extermination camps and matched Auschwitz and Treblinka, not only in its death toll, but in assembly-line techniques for extermination. The floors of Sobibor's gas chambers were constructed to tilt, like the body of a dump truck, so that stacks of corpses slid out smoothly. Along with the usual barbed-wire enclosures, Sobibor was surrounded by a minefield and an adaptation of the water-filled medieval moat. Hundreds of geese were kept in special quarters, not only to appear on the tables of the SS mess but also because their raucous cackling helped drown out the screams of the doomed inmates as they were killed in the gas chambers, an unusual inversion of the classic Roman defense which depended on geese, penned at the foot of fortified hills, to warn the populace when marauders threatened the city.

It was at Sobibor that one of the most daring revolts flared, which again alerted the Nazis to the enormous danger the Jews represented once they had secured arms. Hoess of Auschwitz, in his prison autobiography, wrote that the escape and its cost to the Nazis left a trail of shame. "The Jews," he noted, "were able by force to achieve a major breakout during which almost all the guard personnel were wiped out." Himmler was so outraged by the "humiliation" that he ordered Sobibor to be destroyed and all evidence of its activity erased.[22]

The revolt was organized by a Jewish prisoner, Alexander (Sasha) Pechersky, a Red Army officer captured by the Nazis in October 1941 and shunted from Minsk to several camps until September 1943, when he finally landed in Sobibor. His ingenuity was demonstrated when an official call came for carpenters. Pechersky, who was no more a carpenter than Szmuluwski at Auschwitz was a roofer, volunteered and was plucked from the death line. It was not long before he rose to leadership in the camp underground and became the organizer of a major attempt at mass escape. He warned his comrades that there was little to be gained by waiting for the vaporous signals that might never come from the Polish Partisans in the forest. "We are not allowed to give up life," he said. "We must live in order to take our revenge. . . . No one can do our work for us."

Pechersky's realism became the credo of those who joined him in the revolt set for October 14. Each conspirator was given a station—the tailor shop or the storehouse, the cabinet makers' quarters or the armory. Each methodically disposed of an unsuspecting Nazi guard or guards by stabbing, strangling, or smashing skulls. Thirty-eight Germans and Ukrainians were killed and many more wounded. The SS lost ten of its top officers. The prisoners donned the uniforms of the slain and Pechersky gave the signal for the dash to the fence. The sudden attack and the disguise of the uniforms only temporarily delayed the counter-attack. Fleeing prisoners were strafed by machine gun fire from the watch towers. Nevertheless, about six hundred, including many women, broke out across the various barriers to the forest. The Nazis mounted a search-and-destroy mission, in the course of which all but about sixty were caught and killed. When the story broke in the international press, Himmler ordered the camp inmates to be destroyed and, as noted, leveled Sobibor to the ground. Even the geese were killed.

More than twenty years passed before a dozen of the Sobibor Nazis and their Ukrainian collaborators were brought to trial, some in the Soviet Union in 1965, the others in Germany in 1966. Pechersky, who had devoted two decades of his post-Holocaust life to hunting them down, was a chief prosecution witness. Ten of the accused were found guilty and hanged. The others, for whom no witnesses could be located to testify, received life sentences, soon commuted or suspended. A German writer, Robert Neuman, computed that the average sentence was about ten minutes of prison for each murdered victim.[23]

Perhaps it is for the psychiatrist rather than the historian to fathom the schizophrenic behavior of Nazi leaders and their menials, who could dispassionately participate in the systematic murder of men, women, and children, discharge their grisly tasks mechanically, and then return home to a devoted family, to spend the evening listening to the recordings of Bach or Beethoven without a further thought to the lives that they had just destroyed. The mystery of such behavior, endlessly repeated, has bewildered the world. If, when defeat was imminent, the officials made efforts to eliminate evidence of the brutality and the mass killing, they were not motivated by any sense of guilt or shame. Their paramount concern was to avoid the physical proof of crime. In Renaissance England, the headsman who wielded the ax on Tower Hill was always masked, unknown to victim or spectator. He customarily lived across the English Channel under an assumed name, and was sent for on occasions that demanded his professional skill. In the Nazi heyday, not only misfits but men and women who belonged to a people renowned for preeminence in science and in the arts reacted with righteous indignation when they found themselves in the prisoner's dock.

In an interview with Professor Yehuda Bauer of the Institute of Contemporary Jewry at the Hebrew University in Jerusalem, I discussed the Nazi rationale for the Final Solution. I asked for his reaction to the explanation most commonly offered, that the Nazi ideologues did not think of themselves as executioners. They were not killing human beings; rather, they looked upon Jews with the detachment of butchers who slaughtered cattle.

Bauer agreed that many of the Nazis had indeed come to equate Jews with expendable beasts of the field. But he added that many of the Nazi policy makers were obsessed by a devil theory. To them the Jews were not merely non-human: they were anti-human. Their very existence threatened the healthy growth of the human species, particularly the supreme Aryan model. Hitler's ruthless war on them was intended, once and for all, to rid the world of the sinister force that had threatened and corrupted every generation. Compassion for Jews was a fatal weakness. The grace of a twenty-year-old girl, outwardly lovely, intelligent, was really a snare to lull and divert. The infant, curled up in a mother's arms, was a cunning disguise. When a child's head was smashed against the wall of a gas chamber, it was like stepping on a cockroach. On this premise, Bauer noted, there was no evil in the teachings of the notorious anti-Semites of history. In Nazi eyes, Luther, Voltaire, Houston Chamberlain, the authors of the forged *Protocols of the Elders of Zion,* to identify only a few, were performing the highest kind of public service when they warned the world about the mortal danger of tolerating the Jews. They were exposing the lethal presence of mankind's most destructive enemy.[24]

Such views carry stunning implications for the future. They emphasize that there were fanatics loose in our nuclear world whose monomania could threaten all civilized values. Such men may never again have the opportunity to enslave and liquidate whole peoples. But in the eternity of their twelve-year Reich, the swastika came within a millimeter of blocking out the sun. In little more than a decade of Nazi domination, they created scores of Auschwitzes and Treblinkas and Maidaneks. Who could believe that Hitler, the Voice of Destruction, would have stopped after the elimination of the Jews, that he would not have continued with his attacks to extend the Final Solution to other "subhumans" whom he regarded as cattle or bacilli?

TOTAL JEWISH LOSSES IN THE HOLOCAUST

Polish-Soviet area	4,565,000
Germany	125,000
Austria	65,000
Czechoslovakia	277,000
Hungary	402,000*
France	83,000*
Belgium and Luxemburg	24,700
Holland	106,000
Italy	7,500*
Norway	760
Rumania (excluding Bessarabia, northern Bukovina and northern Transylvania)	40,000
Yugoslavia	60,000*
Greece	65,000
	5,820,960

Statistics Compiled by Yehuda Bauer of Yad Vashem
* May be underestimated.

CHAPTER THREE

Those Who Resisted:
"Be Present, Stand Up"*

For some years after World War II, the emphasis in evaluating the Holocaust was on the magnitude of its toll and the callousness with which it was achieved. The photographs that came to light at war's end, those taken clandestinely by correspondents and onlookers, and those taken by the Nazis themselves, all too frequently depicted groups of broken people shuffling along under the supervision of smartly uniformed guards. Inevitably the combination of statistics and repeated visual images induced a haunting question: How could six million Jews permit themselves to be led meekly to their slaughter? Would there not have been some dignity in their death if it came in resistance, rather than through execution or induced starvation and disease? The murdered became the defendants.

The paradox was further emphasized when several Jewish scholars of the period condemned the victims, or seemed to condemn them, for their role in their own destruction. Bruno Bettelheim, for example, seemed rather hard on the family of Anne Frank when he wrote: "But they could have sold their lives for a high price instead of walking to their deaths."[1] He did not explain how this could have been done by hostages under the most heavily armed and guarded dictatorship in modern history.

*David Knout was a Resistance leader in Nazi-occupied France. He edited an underground newspaper and gave the Resistance its rallying cry: "Partout. Présent et Faire Face." From *Soldiers in the Night* by David Schoenbrun.

Hannah Arendt equated the conduct of European Jewish leadership with the Nazi banality of evil. She berated the Judenrats, the drafted Jewish councils in the occupied communities, for collaboration with the killers. According to Arendt, the overriding resolve of the council appointees was to save their own skins: "This role of the Jewish leaders in the destruction of their own people is undoubtedly the darkest chapter of the whole dark story."[2] Raoul Hilberg, in a volume that appeared in 1961, passed censorious judgment on the centuries of the Diaspora. "The reaction pattern of the Jews," he wrote, "is characterized by almost complete lack of resistance."[3]

I asked Arie Eliav, himself a survivor, who captained a ship bearing illegal immigrants to Palestine and later became a Labor party Minister of Agriculture in Israel, to comment on the alleged lack of resistance after the murderous objectives of the Nazis were no longer in doubt. Eliav suggested that the wrong question was being asked. The wonder was, he said, not that there had been so little resistance, but that there had been so much. Eliav noted that, placed in the setting of the almost impregnable Nazi power, any resistance at all by the Jews was itself a miracle of daring. Hitler's sweep through most of Europe in less than a year demonstrated the immense force of German arms. When reprisals were ordered by the Nazis, there was no distinction between the resisters and the resigned. In the prison camps there were millions of non-Jews, nearly all of whom yielded helplessly to their fate. France surrendered in the Blitzkrieg without a major battle. The Baltic and Balkan states submitted with scarcely any defense or defiance. Their peoples were deported for slave labor, many of them never to return, and when they were herded into the trucks and trains there was little resistance from them. Some of the Jewish survivors of the death camps, placed on the defensive, asked the critics of their submission where *they* were during the Nazi dominion. Since they had not been called upon to share the ordeal of the victims, what had they done to earn the right to pontificate?[4]

Yet there *was* resistance, and the Jews were most often in the forefront. Some of the defiance in the death camps has been described earlier. There was more effective resistance outside the camps, in the urban underground, in the hit-and-run activity in mountain and forest hideouts, in the ranks of the Partisans and Maquis. The indispensable need, of course, was arms. As soon as some of the Jews, even in the camps themselves, obtained possession of a weapon, however pathetically inadequate—a rifle, a knife, an ax, a sewer cover, a homemade bomb—they used it and often took Nazis with them to death. A grudging compliment from Joseph Goebbels indicated that he understood this fully: "The joke [the reckless Jewish resistance] shows what the Jews are capable of, when they have arms." Himmler lectured his staff endlessly on "the perils of turning soft in dealing with wounded animals."

In Germany itself anti-Nazi attempts at dissent, much less resistance, were invariably crushed. Between 1933 and 1944 the courts meted out more than 32,000 death sentences for purported treason. In 1944 the young aristocrat Count von Stauffenberg, General Rommel, and other highly placed army officers plotted to eliminate Hitler, hoping thereby to negotiate better than unconditional surrender terms from the onrushing Allies. The conspiracy ended in a merciless purge. Those who were caught were denounced as "blue-blooded swine" by the Führer and were hanged from meat hooks with piano strings to intensify their agony, and retribution was visited on their families. "These are the basest creatures that ever in history wore the soldier's tunic," Hitler stormed. "We must repel and expel the scourge from a dread past who have found refuge among us." Hitler had the films of the executions shown to his aides, compelling them to sit through the ordeal. Thoroughly cowed, German resistance had no organized structure and there were no partisan groups. How then could Jews, their economic and social strength already drained, manage any significant resistance against Nazi power? In 1942, only one token defiance created a flurry of attention, the attempt by what was termed the Baum group to set fire to a Nazi public exhibition.

POLAND

Hitler's goal of *Lebensraum* for his pure Aryan race was a many-pronged affair, the two sharpest tines of which were, first, to drive fifty or more million despised Slavs into the far eastern Urals, and second to complete, once and forever, the eradication of the Jewish people. These designs accomplished, he would then colonize with Germans the richest territories of east Poland and west Russia, the granaries of the Ukraine and Crimea, the reserves of oil in the Caucausus, and the industrial resources of the Donetz basin.

Hitler's first stage began as early as 1939, when the Hitler-Stalin pact was signed. The pact lasted for two years, during which Hitler's Blitzkrieg subdued the countries of Europe and the Balkans, stalled only by the dogged defense of Britain. In June 1941, Hitler suddenly repudiated the pact, and began the invasion of the Soviet Union. He expected the victory there to be equally quick and decisive. But the Russians, drawing strength from their own soil, held the invaders at Leningrad, Moscow, and Stalingrad. They knew that defeat would mean not only destruction of their country but the end of the Slavic peoples. Hitler was astonished at the resistance. "They don't fight like men," he raged. "They fight like swamp animals."

During the course of the war Hitler pursued his second aim, the total elimination of the Jews. They had lived in Poland, however hopelessly, for many centuries. They had come to interpret the word "Poland" *(Polen)* in its Hebrew etymology, *Polin*, "Here ye shall remain." Hitler gave as high a priority to elimination of its three and a half million Jews as he gave to the conquest of the land. Wherever his armies prevailed, the Jews were among the first victims. The resistance during those bitter war years could be described as circumvention rather than defiance. The Jews tended their own sick, devised ingenious forms of ersatz foods, and shared their shabby clothing and other possessions. Though the death rate edged toward annihilation, the Jews did not die quickly enough, or in large enough numbers, to satisfy their tormentors. In April 1942 the Governor General of Poland, Hans Frank, expressed his frustration: "I wish to state that we have sentenced two hundred thousand Jews to death by starvation; the fact that the Jews are not dying from hunger will only serve to speed up enactments of further anti-Jewish decrees." To Frank, "speeding up" meant more direct action.

Soon the trucks and trains were on steadily accelerated schedules, carting off Jews to the extermination camps. There were few firearms in the ghettos and little could be obtained from the outside, even from the Polish Partisans. The anti-Jewish hostility was intense there too, though all were dedicated to fighting the common enemy. But isolated acts of sabotage and assassination were undertaken by individuals and these became more numerous as frustration mounted. The Nazis now rarely walked alone. Often they were tracked down in the most unlikely places and by the least suspected person.

There was Niuta Teitelbaum, "Little Wanda with the braids," born of a pious Lodz Hasidic family, a twenty-four-year-old who looked sixteen. Wearing traditional Polish costume, a flowered kerchief on her head, she became a valuable courier for the Jewish underground. On one occasion she charmed her way past sentinels and guards into the offices of Gestapo officials. She whispered "Private business," to the guards, who winked and let her by. Once in the presence of her target she drew her revolver, shot the SS chief, and left as calmly as she had entered. It was a simple act but its audacity electrified the ghetto.

Wanda's daring took other forms. She helped to organize women's detachments in the Warsaw Ghetto underground, acting as an instructor in many cells. She was involved in missions that blew up trains, bombed German clubs and other gathering points, and blasted artillery emplacements. One who served with her said in wonderment, "No one could lead Jews out of the ghetto, or smuggle hand grenades and weapons in, past the gaurds, as did Niuta." She survived the spring of 1943 when the Warsaw Ghetto was razed, but was captured in July. Unsuccessful in her attempt to take poison to circumvent the ordeal of torture, she managed to get a message out that nothing her captors inflicted would compel her to betray her comrades. She kept her vow. When the war was won, Niuta/Wanda was posthumously awarded the Grunwald Cross, the highest battle decoration of the new Polish government.[5]

Such acts, however dramatic, could have little effect in slowing down the deportations. Gradually the ghettos were emptied and usually razed. Only one hope to save Polish Jewry remained, a revolt by the Poles themselves. The Polish Underground in Warsaw was well organized. It was receiving substantial arms assistance through the influence of General Anders' government-in-exile in London, which was waiting for the opportune time to authorize a massive uprising, to be synchronized with an assault on Warsaw and the eastern front by the Russians. But there were endless delays. Coordination with the advancing Russians was complicated because there was no trust on either side. Only a year before, in 1938, the Russians had been the Poles' bitter enemies, participating in the conquest of Poland. Now they were storming through the land to rout out the Nazi invaders. What assurance was there that they would cooperate with the Polish Underground? If they did help to turn out the Nazis, what was there to prevent them from turning Poland into a Communist satellite? And what hope was there that even if the underground surfaced to meet the Nazis in battle, there would be any concern for the ghettos and their Jews?

By April 1943, so many Jews had been deported that there were only 65,000 left in Warsaw. The younger militants decided to wait no longer. They were the last of the three and one-half million who had once comprised the largest Jewish community in Europe.

The Warsaw Ghetto uprising of 1943 was the first mass open rebellion on the continent against the Nazis, except for the resistance of the Yugoslav guerillas under Tito. Leadership in the uprising was supplied by Mordecai Anielewicz, who emerged from the ranks of the left-wing Zionist movement. In 1942, Mordecai, all of twenty-three, helped coordinate the covert fighting units under the rubric of the Jewish Combat Organization, usually referred to by the initials of its Polish name, ZOB.

Anielewicz opposed the counsel of his elders, who wished to exercise a wary forbearance until the expected Allied intervention: "God has given life, and only God can take it away." He watched in frenzied dismay as his people were shipped out in a steady stream to the extermination camps, and told the historian Emmanuel Ringelblum that three precious years had been "wasted" in educational and cultural activities. The able-bodied in the ghetto should have been given training in the use of arms for a self-respecting defense. When Himmler himself visited the ghetto in January 1943, Anielewicz knew that the final liquidation was about to begin. He marshaled twenty-two combat units of about thirty members each, and assigned them to strategic locations in the ghetto. The planning had to be undertaken against the strenuous opposition of the Nazi-appointed Judenrat, the ghetto's governing council, whose leadership was terrified by the possible punitive consequences of defiant strategy.

What Anielewicz anticipated in January came to pass at midnight on April 19, when a strong contingent of Nazi troops backed by Ukrainian and Lithuanian collaborators, more heavily armed than usual, marched into the ghetto. Earlier, the defenders had dug a deep hole under the entry street, filling it with explosives. As a German column passed over the cache, the charge was blown, and some of the troops were killed and wounded. Further casualties resulted from a simultaneous volley of machine gun fire, hand grenades, and Molotov cocktails. A second considerably reinforced German contingent moved in. It too was routed. The Polish underground radio station, SWIT, announced that the Warsaw Ghetto had been transformed into a miniature Stalingrad. The defenders, Polish and Jewish flags flying above them, dodged from house to house, from rooms to bunkers, from cellars to sewers. They suffered heavy losses but there was exultation that Jewish casualties were exacting a toll. Anielewicz fell in mid-May in a bunker in the command headquarters. He had sent a farewell note to one of his comrades who was attempting to obtain arms in the Polish sections of the city: "We bid you farewell, you on the 'outside.' . . . The greatest wish of my life has come true. Jewish resistance and vengeance have been transformed into acts."*

The Nazi timetable called for the ghetto to be subdued in a matter of hours, at the most a day or two. But resistance went on for more than a month, against several thousand Nazis, who were reinforced with flamethrowers, tanks, and planes. As ammunition ran out among the defenders, iron bars torn from the area ways of houses and even stout pieces of furniture became weapons. The resisters made use of boiling water. They sprayed the stairs of their hideouts with gasoline and oil, setting fire to them when the enemy came seeking them. Himmler sent an angry message to Jurgen von Stroop, who had been given the assignment for the Warsaw Ghetto liquidation. "The round-ups in the Warsaw Ghetto," he wrote, "must be carried out with relentless determination and in as ruthless a manner as possible. The tougher the attack the better. Recent events show just how dangerous these Jews really are." Von Stroop was compelled to order the leveling of the ghetto, house by house if necessary. It was necessary. The ghetto defenders fought for every foot of space, even into the sewers that had to be blasted to flush out the desperate remnants. On May 16, von Stroop issued a bulletin:

---

*In Israel at Kibbutz Yad Mordechai, named for the defiant Warsaw rebellion commander, there is an impressive statue of Anielewicz by the Israeli sculptor Nathan Rapaport.

"The former Jewish quarter no longer exists . . . the *Grossaktion* is terminated." As a final vindictive measure and, by von Stroop's lights, a cautionary message to all the Jews of Poland and Europe, he ordered the Great Synagogue dynamited. Yet despite von Stroop's triumphant announcement, the resistance continued for at least another four months.

One of the most moving accounts of the ordeal is contained in a memoir by a heroine of the long siege, Zivia Lubetkin, who, by the side of her husband, Yitzchek Zuckerman, helped command the ZOB resistance. She survived and was able to reach Palestine*; her memoir, unembellished, laconic, became an epic of the resistance. She describes how at last she and a small group had reached the forests outside the leveled ghetto:

> We were remnants, clad in rags, and our bodies were caked with filth that could hardly be washed off. Everything is strange. . . . All around us is green forest, shafts of sunlight, beautifully spring. Suddenly all that was closed up for years in the midst of a choked heart blocked with a spirit of stone, trembled, shook and burst, and I started to cry. "There" I never had the desire to cry. "There" it was forbidden to cry. "There" it was a disgrace to cry, and slowly the heart turned to stone. Now, suddenly relief came in a great uncontrollable flood.[6]

Twenty thousand people died, but as Anielewicz had noted, they took a humiliating toll from the fully armed Nazis. The Polish government-in-exile in London announced, with understandable exaggeration, that 1,200 Germans had been killed and many military factories and ammunition dumps had been destroyed. But the signal for the Polish underground to join in the fighting was still withheld.

The news of the uprising received international coverage and helped to create a new image of Jewish militancy among the Allies. It had taken the Germans longer to subdue the Warsaw Ghetto than to overrun Poland itself or to bring surrender from the French. *Tribune of Freedom*, a Polish underground publication, noted, on May 15, before the ghetto had been finally re-

---

*Zivia and her husband helped found one of the Palestine kibbutzim and they continued to fight the British and the Arabs in the wars for Israel's independence.

duced: "The battle in the Ghetto has an enormous political significance for it is the greatest act of organized resistance that has been staged in the occupied countries. The Jews, who a short while ago were almost resigned, have put up a resistance which merits the applause and admiration of every country in the world." Von Stroop himself paid tribute to the fighting qualities of the virtually unarmed resistance groups: "It was combat units of eighteen- to twenty-five-years-old Jewish boys . . . that sparked off the rebellion and renewed it from time to time. These combat units received the order to resist . . . until the end and to commit suicide if necessary rather than be captured."[7]

Later, when the facts of the ghetto rebellion became more widely known, some of the Allied correspondents expressed surprise that unarmed Jews had fought with such tenacity. They concluded that the Jews had earned the right to be regarded not as supplicants, but as allies. A reporter who had analyzed the British press reaction observed: "The Jews now have a new and different kind of claim for consideration, a claim not of passive victims, but of active allies and partners who have fought the common enemy."[8]

It was not until more than a year later, in 1944, that the Polish Partisans began their own organized revolt, armed by both the Allies and the Polish government-in-exile. The war was going very badly for the Germans, whose troops were everywhere in retreat. With the Russians on the outskirts of Warsaw, the Partisans launched their rebellion, fully expecting that Stalin would coordinate his offensive with the Polish effort and the German forces would be crushed in the constricting vise. But Stalin wanted no part of a Poland under the Partisan leadership that took its guidance from the anti-Communist London government-in-exile. Hence, though Warsaw was invested by the Russian troops whose planes also had control of the air, Stalin issued orders to his marshals to arrest their advance, leaving the Partisans to the mercy of the Nazis, who were pledged to a final assault before retreat. Churchill and Roosevelt urged vehemently that the Partisans must not be abandoned, but Stalin withheld the attack. Only when the Nazis and the underground had destroyed each other did the Russians resume their attack, quickly mopping up whatever Nazi opposition remained.

The revolt in the Warsaw Ghetto was but one of the many defiant last stands that marked the end of Jewish life in Poland.

None of the others could enlist the participation that Anielewicz organized in Warsaw. But many militant men and women
shared his determination not to die submissively.

In Bialystok, an important textile manufacturing center, lived
35,000 Jews; they had priority on the early death list of the Nazis.
Here resistance was organized by Mordecai Tenenboim-
Tamarov who, in his twenties, already had an impressive record
of defiance in some of the other ghettos, notably Grodno. In
Vilna he had established friendship with a dissident German
NCO who had cooperated with him in the underground movement and had been court-martialed and shot as a traitor. Mordecai helped to organize the resistance in Warsaw and was one
of the editors of its two insurgent newspapers. Just before Warsaw fell, he was sent, although wounded, to coordinate the resistance units in Bialystok and he took command there for its
last stand.

Mordecai obtained occasional arms by paying extortionate
prices to Polish peasants, scavengers who had stripped the
weapons from the dead on the Russian-German battlefields of
1941 and 1942. Some arms were also stolen from the German
barracks. But his most effective assistance came from an anti-
Nazi German, Otto Busse, who was the director of a German
factory in the city. Busse had been smuggling food and medical
supplies into the besieged ghetto and providing homes for Jews
who took refuge in the Aryan sections of the city.*

In the Bialystock ghetto, some few crude weapons had been
manufactured—hand grenades, bottles filled with vitriol, axes,
knives, scythes. "The ghetto was a mess of blood soaked pillows,
shattered buildings, personal possessions, lying sodden in the
mud, bodies crumpled on every doorstep."⁹ With all his preparations, Mordecai's forces could do little more than offer hopeless
resistance. Nevertheless, it took the Nazis four days of bitter
fighting, supported by tanks and armored cars, to subdue
Tenenboim's little force. He was among the last to go, a suicide,
to avoid falling into Nazi hands. Before his death, he appealed
to the ghetto fighters to leave nothing of value for the enemy.
"When you leave your house, set fire to it. Set fire to the facto-

---

*After the war Busse's name was enrolled by the Yad Vashem in Jerusalem
among the Righteous Christians who took grave risks to counteract the Jewish extermination plans of the Nazis.

ries, demolish them. Do not let our assassins be our beneficiaries as well." He urged those who opted for flight to join the forest guerillas, and not leave any equipment behind, no matter how much it handicapped movement.

The combatants followed his last wishes. They exacted a toll of SS troops and damaged some valuable industrial workshop equipment. Reuben Ainsztein, one of the historians of the resistance in eastern Europe, writes: "Had only one load in ten of the arms brought by the RAF aircraft for the Polish underground reached them, the fighters of the Bialystok ghetto would have made their murderers pay a fairer price for the lives they attempted to defend."[10]

Such actions inflicted casualties and losses, but they could not of course prevail against the overwhelming German might. By the end of August 1943, all that was left of one of the great historic settlements were six girls who had escaped detection by posing as Aryans, and a few survivors whom they guided out of the doomed city to join the Partisans in the woods.

Farther east lay Minsk, the capital of Byelorussia, just outside the borders of prewar Poland. Besieged by the Nazis in the first onrush of 1941, Minsk's Jews, about 80,000 of them, were targeted for liquidation even before the completion of the death camps at Treblinka and elsewhere. The proportion of Jewish survival in Minsk was 50 percent greater than in any other section of eastern Europe and was due primarily to early organization of an underground to stand up to the enemy. During the process of liquidation, probably up to 10,000 ghetto Jews fled to the adjoining forests to join the Partisans. They found a slightly more tolerant attitude among the Byelorussians than existed in Poland, and they were reluctantly welcomed for the common effort against the invaders.

The resistance in Minsk was fortunate to have the leadership of Hersh Smoliar (Yafin Stolerovich), who exercised his command from the boiler room of the ghetto hospital. Minsk was an important industrial center and in prewar days the majority of its Jews worked in the factories. When the Germans occupied the city in 1941, at the outset of the invasion of Russia, they indentured the Jews as slave laborers for the German military machine. Smoliar's underground lieutenants infiltrated the workers' ranks and masterminded sabotage activities that tried to impede the flow of war supplies. Skilled craftsmen managed to mis-sew German uniforms so that they neither fit nor warmed. They cobbled shoes and boots that could not be worn. They spoiled leather goods irretrievably by "accidental" spills of chemicals. Those who worked in arms factories and repair shops stole weapons or spare parts for caches in the ghettos.

Smoliar was, from the outset, a marked man. In the spring of 1942 the Germans tracked him to the home of a woman courier, but he had left minutes before their arrival. An order was issued that he be immediately surrendered, else the Germans would destroy the entire Jewish community. A Smoliar lieutenant thereupon forged identification papers and dipped them in blood; the papers were delivered to the Gestapo as having been found on a ghetto dweller shot the night before. The ruse worked. The Gestapo was satisfied that the dead man was Hersh Smoliar, who by then had escaped to the Naliboki Forest to join the Partisans, where he was made deputy commander of one of the larger detachments. Soon he had developed escape routes from the ghetto and smuggled out the able-bodied, usually in groups of ten, each with a responsible leader and bearing such arms as they could procure. In six months' time Smoliar had a dozen such groups, reinforced by several hundred other fighters who were not part of the regular detachments. The Tens (as they were known) set up printing presses to manufacture forged documents and primitive radio transmitters and receivers to communicate with the ghetto and the outside world. As they became more expert, the Tens derailed German trains and ambushed convoys. Smoliar was particularly proud of his men when they made off with crates of sawn-off shotguns, invaluable in the hand-to-hand fighting of the final weeks of Partisan warfare.

Smoliar survived the war and attempted to resume a career in Polish journalism. But ever his own man and unwilling to follow the satellite Communist party line, he was expelled. In 1971 he joined his wartime comrades in Israel.[11]

No account of the resistance in Minsk would be complete without mentioning some of the children who were couriers to and from the forest hideouts. Two young boys, Banko and David, and a blond moppet, Sima, became legend. Blue-eyed Sima, her parents murdered in a pogrom, was, at twelve, already a veteran in facing death and dodging it. "Don't worry," she told the ghetto leaders, "the Fritzies will not take me alive." Armed with a pistol whose size challenged her little body, she would squirm her way under the barbed-wire fence of the ghetto to deliver small caches of arms to the Partisans in the forest. She then sneaked back into the ghetto by way of the cemetery. Sima lived to march with other decorated Partisans in the Minsk victory parade after the Nazis were driven out. She was fourteen years old.

Banko and David, both thirteen, three times a week guided Jews out of the ghetto to appointed rendezvous with Partisans in the forest. Banko still had his mother; David was an orphan. They were inseparable, although it was David who gave the commands. The children sounded for all the world like grizzled campaigners of some forgotten war. Young David would proclaim before each sortie: "I hope all will go well, and in a few hours from now you will be free people without yellow badges." For several months the children led hundreds of people, some of them doctors, out of the ghetto, David at the head of the file, Banko guarding the rear. Banko stayed with his mother each time he stole back to the ghetto. He won approval to include her on one of his sorties. "But remember," he told her, "ours is a combat detachment. You'll have to stand guard and hold a rifle. But we'll be together in a detachment in a dugout."

The Germans, in retreat from Russia in August 1943, decided to take full revenge on what was left of the Minsk ghetto and on the Partisans in the forest hideouts. Their "heroic victory" over Minsk took fifteen days and a full-scale front-line operation. Every house in the ghetto, every clump of trees, every cave they could smoke out, was systematically destroyed. Banko was taken and burned alive. David wept with his elders as the charred body of his Jonathan was buried after the Germans passed by.[12]

The name of Vilna was so closely related to the intellectual tradition of eastern European life that the city was known as the "Jerusalem of Lithuania." Here were the authoritative rabbinical academies; here the Chassidim and Mitnagdim fought their dialectic battles; here lived and taught the Vilna Gaon, the world's most erudite interpreter of Talmudic lore. The death verdict mandated by the Nazis not only destroyed the physical community; it terminated the culture of east European Jewish life. A Partisan song strove to lift spirits: "*Zog nit keynmol oz du gehst dem letzten weg* (Oh never say that you have reached the very end)." But the very end had been reached. In the first months of the war Vilna fell to the Nazis, who were welcomed with flowers by the Lithuanian population. Within two years practically all of its 60,000 Jews had been killed, with the willing collaboration of the Lithuanians either in Ponary, near the ghetto itself, or in the death camps of Poland to which they were deported.

Vilna became the prime example of the tragedy that set in when the Nazis manipulated the captive Judenrat to regulate the affairs of the community. They appointed Jacob Gens, a former Lithuanian Army officer, as liaison with the Jewish community. Gens was constantly forced into the Solomonic dilemma of either obeying the Nazis or sacrificing his entire Jewish community. As police chief, it was he who had to select the Jews to make up the quotas for deportation. Under threat, he was required to name the hiding places of resistance groups. Four rabbis, pleading with him to refuse, quoted the response given by the medieval sage Maimonides: "And should the idolators say to them: 'Deliver unto us one of you and we shall kill him, or we shall kill all of you!' let them all be killed rather than deliver a single Jewish soul." Gens's response, invariably, was "better for the few to die than to have the catastrophe swallow up the entire community." This was the *cri de coeur* of many Jewish leaders in Europe, who were compelled to perform the odious work of selection, breaking down the communal will even as the victims died. Finally the Nazis demanded the surrender of Itzik Wittenberg, head of Vilna's underground. He had been hunted unremittingly, but, with the help of loyal comrades, always managed to escape. The Nazis made the whole community hostage, declaring that, unless Gens produced Wittenberg, the ghetto would be razed and its inhabitants liquidated. Gens begged Wittenberg to give himself up to save the thousands who would otherwise die. Wittenberg emerged from his hideout and was executed immediately. "In order that certain Jews should live, I was obliged to lead others to their death," Gens claimed. "In order that some Jews should be able to leave the ghetto with clear consciences, I was obliged to wallow in filth and act without conscience."[13] Ironically, most Jews in the hostage community were killed anyway.

The few acts of defiance in Vilna did not become the pattern for the community; only a handful of survivors escaped to join the Partisan activists in the forests, led by Abba Kovner and his fiancée, Vitka Kempner. The bitterness of the young activists

impelled them to accuse men like Gens, who were labeled "traitors to their own kith and kin." His ultimate fate brought no
sorrow. Gens was killed by the Gestapo when he had served the
Nazi purpose.[14] The Nazis enjoyed no greater triumphs than
when, in this way, they set the Jews against each other. After
Israel won its independent status and brought into its midst the
surviving remnants of the Holocaust, one of the issues that split
the country was judgment on the actions of Judenrat leaders
who had been obliged to make the life-and-death decisions in the
ghettos. The wounds inflicted by the Nazis in shifting such
responsibility to appointed Jewish leaders left deep scars in the
political and social life of Israel that were never fully healed.

Kiev, on the Dnieper River, a major commercial link between
Europe and the Orient, contained a Jewish population of 175,000
on the eve of the Nazi invasion of the Soviet Union in 1941. The
Nazi forces captured the city in mid-September; within less
than a fortnight, on the 29th and 30th, nearly 34,000 Jews of the
ghetto were brought to a suburban ravine known as Babi Yar,
near the Jewish Cemetery, where men, women, and children
were systematically machine-gunned in a two-day orgy of execution. In subsequent months, most of the remaining population was exterminated.

This, the most appalling massacre of the war, is often alluded
to as a prime example of utter Jewish helplessness in the face of
disaster. But even the few desperate attempts, almost completely futile, to strike back served as a reminder that the difference between resistance and submission depended very largely
upon who was in possession of the arms that back up the will
to do or die. The Jews in their thousands, with such pathetic
belongings as they could carry, were herded into barbed-wire
areas at the top of the ravine, guarded by Ukrainian collaborators. There they were stripped of their clothes and beaten, then
led in irregular squads down the side of the ravine. The first
groups were forced to lie on the ground, face down, and were
machine-gunned by the Germans who kept up a steady volley.
The riddled bodies were covered with thin layers of earth and
the next groups were ordered to lie over them, to be similarly
despatched. To carry out the murder of 34,000 human beings in
the space of two days could not assure that all the victims had
died. Hence there were a few who survived and, though badly

wounded, managed to crawl from under the corpses and seek a hiding place.

After the main massacre, the site was converted into a more permanent camp to which thousands of victims from other parts of the Ukraine could be sent for extermination. It became known as the Syrets camp, taking its name from a nearby Kiev neighborhood. Several hundred selected prisoners were quartered there—carpenters, shoemakers, tailors, and other artisans —to serve the needs of the SS men and the Ukrainian guards. They were usually killed within a few weeks and replaced by others who continued their duties. In charge of the administration and ultimate killing was Paul von Radomski, who seemed to crave a reputation for outdoing his sadist colleagues in other camps.

By the autumn of 1943, the tide of war had turned. The great Russian counteroffensive had begun and the German forces were in bloody retreat on all the eastern fronts. A frantic effort was begun to destroy the evidence of wanton excesses and murders. For the macabre Babi Yar task, the Nazis selected about four hundred prisoners from Synets, dividing them into squads, each assigned to a special Sondercommando service. The men were called *Leichen* (corpses) and most of them must have envied those who had already become so. They were housed in bunkers close to the ravine, shackled with chains around their ankles so that they could walk but not run, and were led out at sunrise daily to work for long hours until night fell. One group dug up what remained of the corpses; another searched for rings or earrings and wrenched out the gold in the teeth; another built pyres and large ovens, each to receive hundreds of bodies. Additional groups lit the fires and kept them burning, ground up the bones that were not consumed in the flames, carried the ashes into nearby fields and scattered them for fertilizer. At night, reeking of putrefying flesh, their bodies consumed by scabies, filthy with the mud of reopened mass graves, the Sondercommandos were brought back to their bunkers. Before permitting a few hours of sleep, there was a regular wind-up routine in which a number of the half-conscious prisoners were executed for the amusement of men bored with their guard duty.

The *Leichen* never stopped concocting schemes for escape, ever hoping that at least one or two might succeed so that the world could be told of the depths of diabolism that were being probed at Babi Yar. One by one the plans, each more hare-brained than the other, usually exposed by planted spies, miscarried. The punishments that followed made death a release. Too many could not be killed, however, for there was work to be completed before the Russians arrived.

One plan did bring the desired result. It involved the use of a key to release the padlock of the grating that isolated prisoners from their guards, the laborious creation of a mechanism that would prise open the shackles on the men, and a mass rush from the bunkers to overwhelm some of the guards and wrest loose their weapons, perhaps even the capture of a machine gun. By the second anniversary of the Babi Yar massacre, late in September 1943, the task of destroying 100,000 corpses in the ravine had been completed. It was clear that the Germans were planning to eliminate what remained of the prisoners. This was the moment chosen for the suicidal assault. The padlock and the shackles were opened and the dash followed. Some of the Germans were caught off guard; they were strangled or stabbed to death with long-hidden screwdrivers and scissors. Nearly all the prisoners were caught and killed. Yet fourteen, of whom eleven were Jews, managed to escape and remain hidden until the arrival of the first Red Army units. Two were called as witnesses to tell their story at the Nuremberg Military Tribunal in 1946.

The Russians of course included the tragedy of Babi Yar in their listing of the crimes of the Nazis. But Stalin would never acknowledge that nearly all the victims were Jews; invariably they were listed in the statistics of the Russian dead. No school text carried the full story of Kiev, Babi Yar, or the final resistance there. Every request by daring Soviet intellectuals to erect a monument to the dead, to commemmorate the greatest single massacre of World War II, was refused. The Babi Yar site remained a wasteland.

One of the epic Russian novels of the war, *Babi Yar*, by A. Anatoli (Kuznetzev), who fled his homeland in 1969, was built around the narrative of Dina Muronovna Pronicheva, a survivor of the *Leichen* escape who later testified at the Darmstadt trial in West Germany when a handful of apprehended Babi Yar murderers was called to account. Kuznetzev noted in his preface that he had to write the documentary novel because "the ashes were knocking at my heart." After his defection, Kuznetzev told of the difficulties of publishing in Russia. When the manuscript was first submitted, he was ordered to omit about a fourth, "the anti-Soviet stuff." The revised draft then passed through many layers of censorship and another quarter of the text was eliminated. When it was at last published, Kuznetzev wrote, "the whole sense of the book was turned upside down." After escaping from Russia, Kuznetzev was able to smuggle out the complete text of his original manuscript and it was published in England in 1970. To demonstrate the problems of authors who are restrained by censorship in the Soviet Union, Kuznetzev's English edition was published using ordinary type for the censored version and a heavier type for the parts that the Russian censors had cut.[15]

Twenty years after Babi Yar, the Soviet policy of silence about the Jewish tragedy in Kiev elicited a bitter poetic outcry from Yevgeny Yevtushenko, Russia's most revered young poet, who mourned for the dead and expressed shame that his country's leaders, now deep in governmental anti-Semitism, had no compassionate reaction to what the Jews had endured at the hands of the common Nazi enemy:

> No gravestone stands on Babi Yar;
> Only coarse earth heaped roughly on the gash.
> Such dread comes over me; I feel so old,
> Old as the Jews. Today I am a Jew . . .
> All screams in silence, I take off my cap
> And feel that I am slowly turning grey.
> And I too have become a soundless cry
> Over the thousands that lie buried here.
> I am each old man slaughtered, each child shot,
> None of me will forget.[16]

Yevtushenko was publicly denounced by Khrushchev and the Presidium for questioning the Communist party line. Dmitri Shostakovich set the poem to music in his thirteenth Symphony, performed for the first time in December 1962, much to the chagrin of the Soviet establishment.

FRANCE

France, occupied in 1940, was divided into two administrative units, both Nazi-dominated. Policing both sections at first offered little problem to the victors. France had two coastlines, only one of which—that facing the Atlantic and the English Channel—was of even minor concern to the conquerors. The Mediterranean shores, flanked as they were by Axis Italy and "neutral" fascist Spain, presented no threat. The Germans accordingly governed the industrialized north directly and set up a vassal government in the South under the Vichy regime of Marshal Pétain, Pierre Laval, and other early collaborators.

In addition to Jewish families with ancient roots in France, there were at the time of occupation many thousands of Jews who, in flight from Hitler's long reach, had been migrating there since the early 1930s. The Nazis immediately ordered the cancellation of the French citizenship of these Jews, north or south, almost all of whom had been naturalized under French law, and Vichy complied as readily as the north. Such compliance was no problem for Pétain and Laval; they had already demonstrated their sycophancy by condemning thousands of their own non-Jewish countrymen and women to forced labor in Germany.

Detention camps for French Jews were quickly set up, the largest in Drancy, near Paris. From there 98,000 people were deported to Auschwitz, of whom only 3,000 lived to be liberated at the end of the war. These were mainly saved because of insufficient transportation facilities. The sports stadium, Vélodrome d'Hiver, was pressed into service for a week to hold 9,000 Jews, including 4,000 children, before they were sent on to the gas chambers of Auschwitz. Thirty adults, but no children, survived. Another detention camp bore the odd name of Gur, which the poet Aragon referred to as "that peculiar syllable which sounds like a sob in the throat."[17] The cruelest actions were the raiding of children's homes. The Gestapo commander at Lyon took pride in cabling his superiors in Germany in April 1944: "Early this morning the children's home at Aisier-Anne was emptied. A total number of 41 children, aged 3–13 was seized." They all died at Auschwitz.[18] All told, about 80,000 French Jews perished there.*

Resistance, even of the most token kind, was slow to develop; the French were apparently too stunned by their national disaster. But gradually it emerged, uncoordinated at first, then gath-

---

*Klaus Barbie, known as "The Butcher of Lyon," who escaped to Bolivia after the war, was extradicted to France in March 1983 to stand trial there.

ering momentum as the shock of defeat subsided. Bands of guerillas began to surface. At first they followed local and regional
leaders, some drawn from trade unions, others from demobilized former military officers, still others from the ranks of intellectuals. They were supported covertly but widely with food,
shelter, and above all, with arms. By 1943 it was unsafe for
Germans to travel unless heavily guarded.

In time a national leadership appeared, heartened by constant
broadcasts from Britain, where General de Gaulle had organized a government-in-exile whose activities were reported by
an underground of Free Frenchmen. These were mainly
younger people who resisted the draft, regarding it as forced
labor. They became part of the Résistance and appropriated the
name *Maquis* (the bush) from the Corsican tradition of vendetta
and rebellion. Churchill gave De Gaulle loyal support despite a
personal antipathy to him. He preferred to cooperate with
Pierre Mendès-France, who would one day succeed De Gaulle
as another Jewish premier. Mendès-France had avoided falling
into Nazi hands by fleeing in time to North Africa. When captured by the Vichyites there, he managed a dramatic hacksaw-
bedsheet escape and made his way to England to join De Gaulle
and to fly bombing missions into France to buoy up the hopes
of the Résistance and its governing body, the Conseil de la
Résistance.

Perhaps the most courageous defiance was offered by former
Premier Léon Blum, who stood up in a kangaroo court at Riom
to confound the Vichyites whose verdict on him had been determined in advance. Blum had organized a Popular Front in
France in 1934 to counter the gathering forces of fascism subsidized by the cosmetics king François Coty and the munitions
tycoon Eugène Schneider. The Popular Front triumph in the
election of 1936 saved French democracy temporarily from a
Fascist takeover.

The first ten weeks of Blum's incumbency rivaled the Hundred Days of Franklin Roosevelt's New Deal in the speed and
thoroughness of the legislation that was passed, including the
forty-hour work week, vacations with pay, the right to strike,
the nationalization of the Bank of France and of the armaments
industry. The legislation fundamentally altered the economic and
social structure of France. Yet it was but a temporary revolution;
within a few years, France was overwhelmed by the Nazi Blitzkrieg. The Vichy men took control under the aegis of Hitler,
and Blum and many of his political colleagues were imprisoned.

It was Pierre Laval who, in 1942, dreamed up the plan for a public trial of those who were allegedly responsible for the war against Germany and for the "fatal weakening" of France through the Popular Front. Blum was taken from his prison cell to answer for his record.

The prosecutor concentrated on what Blum described as the "venom argument," namely, that Blum had injected into French society, and especially into its economy, the toxic element of class warfare, and that this had ruined French unity. Blum's defense of the Republic and the Popular Front won international headlines. He told the court that the social welfare legislation sponsored by him was not disruptive, that it was the glory of his ministry. Indeed, the reforms had at last brought the workers into a meaningful relationship with their country. "Because we were a people's government," he concluded, "we were in its tradition, the tradition of the French Revolution. We have not destroyed the chain, we have not broken it, we have fortified and strengthened it."[19] Blum succeeded in reversing roles, placing the prosecutor on the defensive. Hitler was furious and ordered Laval to adjourn the trial. Blum was packed off to his cell and then consigned to a Nazi concentration camp. He was not executed, for he was much too valuable as a hostage. He survived the humiliations of his confinement and lived to serve again as premier in a liberated France.

Since the Jews had been singled out for special malevolence, it was hardly surprising that they were well represented in the French Resistance. They comprised less than 1 percent of the French population but many times this proportion in the ranks of the freedom fighters.

Jose Aboulker, for one, was a medical student in Algiers who, at the age of twenty-two, organized the effort to facilitate the American landings in North Africa. Albert Kohan was a Russian émigré who won his wings as a parachutist at the age of sixty-four and became a co-founder of one of the main liberation movements. There was Jacques Bingen, code name Necker, who had fled with De Gaulle in 1940 and had become one of the general's most trusted aides. Bingen, thirty-five, returned to France in 1943 to coordinate the invasion plans for the liberation of his country. Captured by the Nazi police in May 1944, he committed suicide to avoid, under torture, being forced to betray his comrades. A grateful France, later, would issue a postage stamp bearing his image.

Albert and Sonja Haasz were refugees, Albert a skilled physician reared in Hungary, Sonja, Belgian-born, a brilliant lawyer at a time when the legal profession rarely welcomed women. Their lives crossed as they sought safety in France. When the Nazis engulfed their new homeland, they became part of an ingenious intelligence network and were trained for espionage in a remote corner of Sussex in England. Assigned to Nice, they parachuted back into France in August 1943 and infiltrated the fearsome Todt organization, which had been set up by the Nazis to build and maintain the coastal fortifications. Against all probability, Albert convinced the Germans to accept him as a staff physician, while Sonja was employed at Gestapo headquarters as a translator. Once inside the establishment, she was able to identify and pass on highly classified information.

The Haaszes disclosed secret German meeting places which then were unaccountably blown up. They tracked down the site of a powerful radio transmitter in Monte Carlo that was first jammed, then destroyed. One of their major coups was to obtain a tissue-paper tracing of a map with details of German fortifications from Genoa to Marseilles. The map was indispensable as a guide to the Allies when they trained their guns on German emplacements along the Mediterranean. But this coup was also the Haasz's undoing. They were arrested in February 1944. Tortured, they did not betray their associates, even when one of Sonja's eyes was gouged out. Fortune still favored the Haaszes and they were not immediately executed; Albert was sent to Mauthausen as one of its prison doctors; Sonja landed in a small camp at Arad and, unaccountably, was placed in charge of records![20]

Some of the Jewish leaders, branded by the Nazis as special targets, petitioned the Maquis' leadership for authority to organize task force units of their own, and the request was readily granted. The guiding spirit in the Jewish Maquis was a young militant, Robert Gamzon, usually referred to by his underground name, Castor. Before the war he had founded the Jewish Boy Scouts who, in France, were much more than an organization devoted to wholesome living and communal service; the crisis of the times molded many of the older boys into highly motivated young activists, several of whom became a nucleus of Jewish resistance. They took special responsibility for placing hundreds of Jewish children in monasteries and convents and smuggling thousands of others across the borders into Spain and Switzerland.

Then there was a young Polish émigré, Abraham Lissner, who had lived in Palestine, fought against Franco's forces in Spain, and, when the Fascists triumphed there, fled to France to lead one of the Jewish Maquis units against the Nazis. His men ambushed and attacked marching German brigades in the open Paris streets, hurled hand grenades through the windows of German billets, cut off both ends of a boulevard and fired from rooftops on the trapped German troops until their columns were cut to pieces. An entry in the Lissner diary, dated January 1943, reads: "On Avenue Haveda in the heart of Paris, where police roundups occur daily, three Partisans placed two time bombs in the path of a German military detachment killing most of the soldiers. There were continuous derailments with heavy Nazi losses and with communications disrupted for considerable periods." Lissner's contingent assassinated Wehrmacht General Abt and Karl Ritter, assistant to the Gauleiter for France. They raided arsenals and cached precious stores of arms in remote places. Lissner's diary also noted that between March and November 1943, in Paris alone, nineteen hotels were set on fire, along with thirteen warehouses and twenty-three military bases. German planes were blown up and two million liters of gasoline destroyed. More than 150 collaborators and double agents were "removed."

Some Jewish resistance groups were coordinated into the Organisation Juive de Combat (OJC). It became legendary for its daring exploits, especially in smuggling hundreds of young patriots across the Pyrenees into Spain, where they planned to join the Allied forces. As many as 1,000 OJC members died in sabotage attacks on Nazi installations.

Another major triumph in 1944 was the liberation of the city of Castres, by a detachment under Charles Wittenberg, who later migrated to Toronto. Castres' 30,000 inhabitants had been dominated by Vichy and had become a strategically located Nazi garrison. Wittenberg learned that the garrison was expecting a train with fresh supplies of ammunition. He led his Jewish Maquis in the attack that intercepted and captured the train. In the aftermath, passing the surrendered Germans, each member of the victorious group exclaimed in satisfaction: "Ich bin Jude." They took the train to Castres where, with other Maquis forces, the town was liberated, and the unit went on to help drive the Nazis out of other key cities.[21]

But if the intrepid young men, and no few women, harassed

the enemy by blowing up armories and ammunition dumps, railway bridges, and other installations, there were also quieter but no less spectacular figures, such as Anny Letour, née Levy. Her family had lived for generations in Vienna. Scarcely out of a privileged girlhood at the time of the Anschluss in 1938, she had watched a distinguished Jewish doctor, head of a famous clinic, lying prone in the street, a Nazi boot on his neck, compelled to drink the gutter water while his countrymen cheered on the tormentors. Anny was fortunate enough to move to France, to continue her studies. Then, when France fell to the Nazis in June 1940 and she heard the broadcast of Pétain's submission, and the defiant response of De Gaulle vowing to restore the honor of France, Anny sought refuge for her child and joined the Resistance. She was assigned the task of forging documents and identity cards for Jews whose French nationality had been rescinded. Each of her rescue convoys included many children. She is credited with the escape of many Jews who, like Anny, had taken refuge in France before it was overrun by the Germans.

Yet in the first years of the Nazi occupation the defiance by the Résistance, their commando raids and sabotage, could be little more than diversion, hide-and-seek improvisations, or a kind of *cache-cache*, as French children called it. Strategy for a greater role had to be built on a partnership with time, until the Allies, and especially the Americans, could invade. In the interval it was essential to sustain confidence. De Gaulle's London BBC broadcasts from Studio B12, which promised that "the flame of French resistance would not die," were as vital an element in maintaining morale as the blowing up of bridges or the ambushing of Nazi columns. It was in this role, shoring up the courage of the disheartened, informing them in detail of the reinforcements of men and arms that were on the way, that two Jewish patriots made an invaluable contribution.

Jean-Pierre Levy of Lyon, little known except to the inner governing circle, developed one of the most influential Resistance newspapers. The *Franc-Tireur*, which took its name from the revolutionary paper of the Franco-Prussian War of 1870, began its clandestine appearance with a few hundred daring readers who, if caught possessing it, could pay with their lives. By the time of liberation in 1944, it had become a network with a circulation of 150,000. The most elaborate artifice was needed to obtain scarce paper supplies, mimeograph machines, and presses; to recruit the printers; and to distribute copies despite the vigilance of both Germans and Vichy collaborators. Levy's adventures—capture, imprisonment, escape—rivaled the exploits of some of the underground figures whom he featured in the headlines. De Gaulle knew his worth, and he emerged from war's end as one of its decorated heroes.

A spirited brochure appeared to supplement the newspaper network created by Levy. David Knout of Toulouse, a poet who had helped found the OJC, was not only the paper's editor but also its staff. He did not even have access to a mimeograph machine, but typed the copies by hand and distributed them, chain-letter style, to a growing circle. Its title was *Que Faire?* Knout spelled out the answer that became the rallying cry of the Resistance—*Partout Présent et Faire Face!*[22]

Paris was liberated on August 24, 1944 in a march led by De Gaulle who entered the city for the triumphant walk down the Champs Élysées from the Étoile to the Place de la Concorde. He made his way, with a long file of cars, through the cheering, weeping millions to Notre Dame for the special thanksgiving service. Then he reviewed the troops, most of them in bedraggled fatigues and, among them the haggard, emaciated but now erect Maquis, only yesterday the hunted and pursued. Many wore the yellow star of David.

ITALY

There were Jewish communities in Italy before the Christian era. The ancient settlements had, from time to time, been augmented by new arrivals, especially after the Spanish Jews had been expelled in 1492 through the influence of the Chief Inquisitor, Torquemada. A Dominican priest, some authorities believe Torquemada to have been a descendant of Spanish Jews. There had been little tension in Jewish life during the more than four hundred years that followed, except for the harassments by the Vatican. The distinguishing Jewish badge, in grotesque shapes and forms, was decreed by the Lateran Council in 1215 but was not consistently enforced, except in Rome where it was demanded by the clergy. Pope Paul IV, a post-Reformation Pope, created the Roman ghetto. Close to the disease-bearing swamps of the Tiber, it was a noisome place. But as Rome developed, the ghetto acquired a curious prestige, having attained the patina of age, custom, and gentility. Italian Jewry was well integrated into the life of the country, a Jew serving as prime minister early in the twentieth century, and another, later, as mayor of Rome.

Mussolini, when he came to power in 1929, praised the role of the Jews in Italy, never needing to be reminded that 50,000 of them already had roots in the country in the epoch of Augustus and Caesar. In November 1934 he was interviewed by Nahum Goldmann, President of the World Jewish Congress, who had come to ask for Mussolini's intercession with Hitler to end the rabid assaults of the Nuremberg laws. Mussolini reassured Goldmann. "Have no fear of Herr Hitler," he said, "for you represent a great indestructible people. I know Herr Hitler," he continued. "He is a *vaurien*, a fanatical idiot, a talker. . . . When there is no trace left of him, the Jews will still be a great people. . . . We shall all live to see his end. But you must create a Jewish state. I am a Zionist and I told Dr. Weizmann so. You must have a real country, not the ridiculous national home that the British have offered you."[23]

In 1940, however, Mussolini's earlier views evaporated. Il Duce brought Italy into the war by strafing French civilians as they took refuge in the fields along roads by which the French army was retreating. He cynically remarked that Italy needed a few hundred deaths to qualify for a place at the peace table. In Franklin Roosevelt's withering phrase, "The hand that held the dagger has plunged it into the back of its neighbor."[24]

Emboldened by his comparatively easy victory over Haile Selassie's Ethiopians, Mussolini felt that the Allies could not long hold out against the combined Nazi-Fascist might. He was sure that Hitler needed him more than he needed Hitler, a fantasy shortly to be quashed when the Greeks put up so valiant a defense against the Italian invaders that the Führer had to rush in his own legions to avoid disaster. In any event, as Mussolini became increasingly dependent upon Hitler's goodwill, he reneged on his assurances of safety to the Italian Jews and offered no objection to the enactment of anti-Jewish legislation. His mouthpiece was one of Italy's leading anti-Semites, Lieutenant Roberto Farinacci, who called himself "the Italian Streicher." In the Fascist journal that he edited he wrote, "International Jewry is anti-Fascist. Never has a Jew uttered a word of veneration or thankfulness for fascism. . . ."*

---

*Farinacci was apparently in a rage when he wrote his editorial. Many wealthy Italian Jews were members of the Fascist party.

Mussolini's scientists drew up a Manifesto of Racism that defined the sharp differences between the "pure Italian race of Aryan stock" and the Jews, who were irrevocably alien, however long their residence in the land. The legislation that Mussolini demanded prohibited intermarriage, curtailed civil and economic opportunities, and opened the way to the confiscation of Jewish possessions. Almost as soon as the new legislation was promulgated, there was a wave of emigration that left a bare 35,000 Jews, a proportion of eight-tenths of 1 percent in the total Italian population.

Mussolini now created a series of detention centers for the internment of foreign Jews. In comparison with the German camps, these were merely abominable. The Italian populace, military and civilian, had little heart for the Hitler war, and the jailers, indifferent and easygoing, were generally lenient. When there was small risk of detection, many among them offered covert help to their Jewish prisoners.

Mussolini was shortly to learn that the western Allies were not the easy victims he had presumed them to be. When the war tide turned, Italy became the entry point for the counteroffensive into Europe. In May 1943, all Italian forces in North Africa surrendered. In July, the Allies landed in Sicily, and then Rome itself was bombed to demonstrate how vulnerable the country had become. Though Pope Pius XII denounced the bombardment as endangering the holy shrines of Christendom, there was no protest from him when, in the "Great Hunt" of October 16, 1943, 1,127 Jews, 800 of them women and children, were rounded up by the Nazis and sent to die in the extermination camps.

By the end of 1943 the Fascist leaders were worrying about their personal safety. They appealed to the Italian king, who had long resented Mussolini's dominance, to repudiate Il Duce. On July 25, 1943, Mussolini was dismissed and placed under house arrest. In a bold commando coup, Hitler liberated him and brought him to northern Italy to serve as puppet head of the occupied area. But the Italian Partisans ferreted out the hiding place of Mussolini and his mistress, and shot and hanged them both by the heels in a public square in Milan. Yet despite the sympathetic reactions of the Italian people to their Jewish neighbors, the Nazi dragnet managed to destroy more than 8,000 before the Allied victory.

During the Nazi occupation, Jews were well represented among the Italian Partisans, fighting within their ranks, though not in separate ethnic groups as was the case in France. A heartening episode took place in 1943 at an internment camp set up by Mussolini at Servigliano, which held a large contingent of Jews. Word got out that the Nazi high command intended to deport the Jews to Germany. Determined to rescue their comrades, the Italian Partisans appealed successfully to the Allied leaders to coordinate their bombing with their own Partisan ground attack, and the prisoners were all freed. It was the only time during the war that the RAF joined in a special operation to free a Jewish internment camp. Inevitably there were later reflections on what the results might have been if the railroads leading to Auschwitz had been similarly bombed.

There was resistance by Italian Jews in other occupied parts of Europe. Typical was the activity of Enzo Sereni, the scion of an old Italian family whose father had been King Umberto's physician. Sereni had visited Palestine in his student days and become enamored of the land and its people. He settled there in 1927, and was given the responsibility to prepare young Jews for emigration from European countries to work in the agricultural colonies of Palestine. At the outbreak of World War II he joined the British forces and undertook radio propaganda broadcasts to the Italian people. Then came assignments in which he planned the convoyed journeys of Jews from Iraq who crossed the desert to take up residence in Palestine.

In 1943, though now past forty, Sereni volunteered as a parachutist with the British forces in the Balkans. Of the thirty men and women who volunteered for the missions, most were caught and executed. Sereni, who was to drop behind the enemy lines in North Italy, landed, because of a navigational error, on German-held territory. He was first sent to a Stalag as a British prisoner of war, but in October was transferred to Dachau, where he was shot with a captured unit of Italian prisoners. His wife, Ada, also of prestigious lineage in Italy, shared many of Enzo's adventures. After his death, she became a central figure in directing the illegal traffic to Palestine. Her access to the most influential Italian authorities won their cooperation when the British threatened to cut off Italy as a vital staging area for immigration.[25]

Many other prominent Jewish families were conspicuously represented in the resistance effort. They volunteered for sabotage missions and assisted in the escape of scores of Allied prisoners. Some of these volunteers became national heroes. Eugenio Calo of Pisa organized a Partisan unit in the Val di Piana, and Giulio Bolaffi of Turin founded and commanded the Fourth Alpine Battalion that operated in the Piedmont area. There was Eugenio Curiel, a young mathematician who joined the early anti-Fascist movements and paid for his daring with long years as a refugee in France and as a prisoner in Italian jails. In 1943, after the fall of Mussolini, he escaped to organize a major Partisan unit in North Italy, the Youth Front, to fight the Nazis. The newspaper that he published served as a liaison between the Italian Underground, the French Maquis, and the Allied liberation forces. He was betrayed by a spy and, after torture, was executed.

Twenty-three-year-old Rita Rosana was a teacher, the founder of the Partisan group Eagle, who died fighting. A grateful Verona named a street for her and a monument in her honor stands in a memorial park in Trieste.[26] Mario Vacchia, a decorated veteran of World War I, organized and commanded the Partisan unit called Freedom and Justice in the populous region of Emilia Romana. The police were alerted by an informer about a secret meeting that he attended in Parma, but he would not join the flight until all of his comrades had escaped. Because he took precious time to shred party documents, he was caught, tortured, and shot. All of these figures were in the honored group that were posthumously awarded Italy's gold medals of valor.

GREECE

Greece was an early victim of the Axis. To be sure, Mussolini's attacks in 1940 were thrown back in a resistance effort that astonished the world. Hitler was fast learning what Churchill already knew, that it was safer to have Mussolini as an enemy than as an ally. As noted earlier, the infuriated Führer was obliged to speed reinforcements to Greece, but once the Nazis entered, neither the valor nor the will of the Greeks, nor even British reinforcements, were sufficient to stand up to Panzer units and the Luftwaffe. Early in 1941 the swastika went up on the Acropolis in Athens.

At first, jurisdiction for the occupied country was shared with Bulgaria and Italy. But the alliances tottered and, by the autumn of 1943, the Nazis assumed complete control. The Greeks of course went on resisting as they had for most of their recent history, operating out of the mountains of the Peleponnesus and the north, creeping in the dark along paths that few self-respecting goats would undertake in bright daylight. As always, they paid a heart-breaking price for the realities of the rugged Greek geography. But they exacted a heavy toll. They were able to tie down more than 120,000 German troops who had been in reserve as crucially needed reinforcements on the Russian front. Hitler's anger may account for his treatment of the Greeks, which seemed far more savage than in other occupied countries. Whole villages were razed, and fifty Greeks executed for every German casualty.

For 76,000 Jews of prewar Greece, the Nazi occupation struck most lethally in Salonika and Athens, where two-thirds of Greece's Jews lived in a tradition that went back for more than 2,000 years. The New Testament, for example, refers to three successive Sabbaths when Paul preached in the synagogue of Salonika.

After the expulsion of the Jews from Spain in the late fifteenth century, Salonika became one of the centers of Sephardic influence and culture, with Ladino (a blending of Spanish and Hebrew) as its second language. In March 1943 Hitler's forces turned to the destruction of the old settlement. Transports, each carrying between 2,000 and 3,000 men, women, and children, left every few days for the death camps. There were nineteen such deportations; by the late spring all but about 5 percent of the Salonika Jewish community of 55,000 had been eliminated.

The attack on the Jews of Athens was under the command of General Jurgen von Stroop, who had directed the annihilation of the Warsaw Ghetto. Yet the majority of the Jews of Athens managed to escape, and those few hundred who were rounded up and deported did not die without exacting a price. At Auschwitz some of those who had been assigned the Sondercommando work of cremating corpses from the gas chambers participated in a suicidal resistance on October 6, 1944. They blew up two of the crematoria with help from Russian and Polish inmates. The SS had to send in a fully armed detachment to suppress the outbreak and kill off the insurgents.

In the war against the Nazis, few as the Jews now were, about 13,000 served in the armed forces and contributed far beyond their proportion to the underground resistance. Some three hundred Jewish soldiers were involved along with a thousand civilians in a number of sabotage operations. This group blew up German supply ships in the port of Piraeus and disrupted communications. A Jewish Partisan unit in Thessaly was commanded by a septuagenarian rabbi, Moshe Pesah, and it was a scene to remember as the old man roamed his mountain hideout, rifle in hand.

Perhaps the most dramatic episode in Greek resistance was the destruction of the Gorgopotamo Bridge, which was the crucial link between the Greek mainland and the Peloponnesian peninsula. Greece had become an indispensable Mediterranean base for supplying Rommel as he attempted to consolidate German control of North Africa. Any jeopardy to the efficient functioning of the bridge would undermine wide-ranging strategic plans. Leadership in the Gorgopotamo affair was assigned to Jacques Costis, an Athenian Jew who had organized a maritime sabotage squad. Costis's men successfully brought down the bridge, ruining Rommel's plans.

Even when the German Reich collapsed, the long travail was not over, for the Cold War soon turned allies into enemies. The Communists made a powerful bid to take control of the newly established Greek government, and civil war erupted. The battles were fought without mercy, the Communists supported by Russia and its Balkan satellites, the democratic Loyalists supplied with arms by the western Allies. Early in 1947 the British, deep in other problems, announced that they could no longer bear the burden of shoring up their allies in Greece, and it was then that the Truman Doctrine, enthusiastically endorsed by Congress, pledged American help "wherever the free life of a nation was threatened by aggression." The Communist drive tapered off and in 1948 the civil war came to an end.

By then the pathetic remnants of Jewish life, almost obliterated by the civil war, decided that there could be no community survival in the generations ahead, and they appealed for permission to migrate. What could they hope for, even after Gorgopotamo and their undeviating loyalty in the long struggle for Greek independence? In the animosities of the civil war, whichever side Jews joined, the other did not judge their actions as individuals but identified them with their people. Jews therefore could never be other than "the enemy." Even the tombstones in their ancient cemeteries had been uprooted to become paving material.

The new shaky government of the country placed no obstacles in the way of emigration. Indeed, it cooperated fully. Greek ports were kept open for ships headed for Palestine with refugees from other parts of Europe.*

HUNGARY

The fate of the Jewish settlement in Hungary—one of the largest in Europe—was a desolating climax to the tragic Holocaust period. Before Hitler came to power in 1933 there were about 800,000 Jews in Greater Hungary, 200,000 of them living in Budapest where, despite an endemic anti-Semitism, they were at the forefront of the cultural, scientific, and economic life of the country. Hungary was one of the first nations to fall under Hitler's sway; the obscene speed with which it joined the Nazis was appropriately termed the "Gaderine rush." Hitler rewarded Hungary's collaborating government by permitting it to take over Ruthenia from Czechoslovakia. Fifty thousand Jews in the annexed areas perished as Hungarians collaborated with the Nazi occupiers.

Hungary, as usual "valiant in velvet, light in ragged luck,"[27] chose the wrong side in teaming up with Hitler, whose early victories had turned to ashes by 1943. The Hungarian government, headed by Admiral Miklós Horthy, a Gilbertian admiral in a landlocked country, sensed the turn in fortune. As news of the Nazi rout in Russia poured in, he began to twist and turn to move away from the Axis, and he leaked his intentions to the Allies. One of his several maneuvers to demonstrate that his loyalty to the Nazis was pliable was to delay the deportation of the Jews in the annexed provinces and in Hungary itself.

Hitler, an old hand at double cross, was not taken in. On March 19, 1944, in Operation Margaret, Nazi tanks rumbled over the Danube Bridge into Budapest, paratroop units landed at airports; all strategic military and industrial points were invested, and a new puppet government under Dome Sztojay was installed. The deportations were substantially accelerated. Late in April, a month after Hitler took over Hungary, 4,000 Jews

---

*In 1947, Greece, fearful of offending its Muslim population in Mediterranean island possessions, was the sole European country that voted in the United Nations against the Partition resolution intended to set up a sovereign Jewish state.

were despatched by train to Auschwitz. Between mid-May and July 9, 437,000 more followed, until few but the Jews of Budapest were left. For their destruction, Adolf Eichmann was chosen to take charge. He too knew that the Nazi cause was lost, but he was determined that, all else failing, at least the objectives of the Final Solution would be fulfilled. He had prepared Mauthausen, Auschwitz, and other death camps in Austria and Poland to receive the one million Jews who still remained alive after the extermination campaigns in the Nazi-conquered countries.

Eichmann was proud of his Hungarian assignment and the faith in him that his Führer had exhibited. Although the Russians were already storming the outer Hungarian province on their certain way to Budapest, Eichmann exulted that he would at least fullfill his mission. Only a quarter of Hungary's nearly one million prewar Jewish population, mainly in Budapest, would live into the postwar world and new afflictions.

There had been little significant anti-Nazi resistance in Budapest, or even in Hungary, either by its Jews or by the general population. Living to some extent on the vanished glories of Hungary's importance in the old Austro-Hungarian Empire, there was probably a greater fear of the Soviets than of Germany. The more important Jewish families of Budapest, completely acculturated, counted themselves an integral part of Hungary. Still relatively strong in the economy, they could not imagine, despite the humiliating restrictions of the first years of the war period, that they would share the fate of Jews in the other occupied parts of Europe.

Most other Jews, resisting the blandishments of the host culture, nevertheless shared with the assimilated families an unwillingness to risk defiance, since they were convinced that the course of the war presaged defeat for the German invaders. They remonstrated with those who feared that there would be no exceptions as the Nazi scourge penetrated every part of Europe. They warned against spreading rumors and crying for defiance that would bring annihilation to the entire population. They counted on God's help to bring a quick and certain victory for the Allies.

With such united opposition to challenging the Nazis, it was left to a few small activist groups of Hungarian Zionists headed by an eminent engineer, Otto Komoly—tightly organized members of Hashomer Hatzair and Maccabi Hatzair, people who had already been training for a new life in Palestine—to opt for resistance.[28] Hungary had strong Zionist groups that had grown in size and influence as the situation darkened for its Jews. They had no arms; no sympathy from the general population, nor even from their own people; and no lines of communication with underground groups. One of those who refused to accept his fate supinely said, "We have to be both the fighters and the weapons." But while those who opted for resistance admitted that they did not expect any positive results from defiance, they insisted that even if there was no hope of personal survival, the message must be sent to the world, and to their own people, that death with dignity carried renewed life within it.

The stratagems to which the Zionists resorted often seemed quixotic, yet their very inconceivability caught the Nazis off guard. The president of Mizrachi, the Hungarian Orthodox Zionist group, owed his life and ultimate freedom to their audacity. He was awakened one night by the banging on his door and the shouted command, "Jew Frankel, open up!" A Nazi squad burst into his room, beat him up, and dragged him out to what he thought must be the site of his murder. Instead, hustled to a bunker in a remote part of the city, Frankel discovered that the "Nazis" in fact were disguised comrades from the young Zionists. They had learned from members who had infiltrated the Nazi inner councils that Frankel was listed for execution. They came for him in the guise of the executioners, beating him in the presence of the concierge to lend credibility to their disguise.[29]

Forty-five hundred Jews were saved through the cooperation of Raoul Wallenberg, the Swedish diplomat who, beyond offering refuge to Jews in the Swedish Embassy, rented many large houses, and, as embassy annexes, gave them the protection of the Swedish flag. Several other neutral countries—Portugal, Switzerland, San Salvador—followed the example of Sweden.* The Zionist groups, cooperating with Wallenberg, printed thousands of identity cards and passports, and every day hundreds of imperiled Jewish families were transformed into citizens of the neutral lands. One Budapest refuge center known as the House of Glass that had belonged to a mirror company was

---

*For the fuller Wallenberg story, see Chapter Four.

listed as a Swiss Embassy annex. Its ample storerooms and inner
offices were connected to dormitories, with living and dining
areas in secret cellars. Room was made for the schooling of the
children for whom, it was hoped, there would be a new life in
Palestine. The House of Glass even included a makeshift hospital, efficiently supervised by young men and women, one of
whom, Shraga Weill, survived to emigrate to Palestine where he
became a well-known artist. The extraterritorial status of the
House of Glass, to which was joined the former headquarters of
the Hungarian Football Federation, made the enclave a provi-
dential refuge until the end of 1944. Then the Nazis, though
poised for flight, bypassed the alleged neutrality of the refuge
and scooped up the Jews still hiding there.

Nothing perhaps better summarizes the role of the resistance
efforts by isolated groups of Jews in Europe than the fate of
twenty-three-year-old Hannah Senesch, the Hungarian-born
young woman who volunteered for parachute duty behind the
Nazi lines in the Balkans and was caught and shot when betrayed by collaborators in the Partisan ranks. Hannah was born
in 1921 into an affluent, highly cultured Jewish family in Budapest. At eighteen, in 1939, when girls of Hannah's background
would ordinarily be involved in university life, Hannah was
jubilant that she had obtained a certificate to emigrate to Palestine and rejoiced further when her brother decided to go with
her. Her widowed mother was aghast at their choice, for the
Senesch family's friends were thoroughly assimilated Hungarians to whom Palestine was an alien aberration.

Hannah had developed talent as a poet, but she welcomed the
laborious agricultural work of her kibbutz in Caesarea and the
military discipline that had become an essential part of it. Palestinian Jews had been volunteering to fight the Axis by the side
of the British, and Hannah hoped that she too could qualify to
join such volunteers. She listened to her comrades discuss the
usefulness of developing a parachute corps to drop behind
enemy lines in the Balkans for intelligence and rescue missions.
The Ploesti oil fields in Rumania, for example, had been repeatedly bombed, and many British and American airmen had been
shot down and were either imprisoned or were lost in the forests
of Transylvania. Parachutists could reach these downed Allied
airmen and perhaps guide them across frontiers to Adriatic
ports. Too, in 1943 there were still about a million and a quarter

Jews alive in Hungary, Slovakia, Rumania, and Bulgaria. The Palestinians could be enormously valuable in aiding these people, for many were Balkan-bred and they knew the terrain and the languages of the regions.

In her farming tasks Hannah had learned from one of her teachers the role of the calyptra, the tough cells in the sporecase that cushion the roots of plants as they penetrate the soil, then atrophy and die after they have served their mission. Hannah found poetic symbolism in the role of a human calyptra as an advance guard in resistance.

The British did not need to be persuaded that parachute infiltrators in conquered territory could be invaluable; they were already experts in this type of warfare. But they showed as little enthusiasm for a special corps of Palestinian Jews as they had when Weizmann and Ben Gurion broached the idea to them early in the war that Jewish Brigades should be assigned to the most dangerous fronts in Europe. No one doubted the courage and resourcefulness of such recruits; but would they not inevitably create problems after the war was over, exactly because they would be so well trained? It was inevitable that fighting would break out in Palestine between the Arabs and the Jews, and the British would simply be compounding their problems of mediation if they had such veterans to challenge their decisions. The Jewish militants were persistent, however, and by the end of 1943, as the war reached its climax, they finally wore down the objections of the British command. The enlistment of the special parachute corps began at once. Hannah was among the first to volunteer and she was enlisted as one of thirty-two men and women who were sent off to Cairo in January 1944 to begin their training.

After several months she was flown with two men to Slovenia and dropped among the Tito Partisans. There were many narrow escapes as they made their way more than two hundred miles through German-controlled territory across the border into Hungary, where her small party arrived in early June 1944. But her mission came to naught as one of the Partisan guides proved to be an informer. She was betrayed, as were several others who had taken different routes. Only seven of the original team survived.

Hannah was brought to a Budapest prison to be tortured into revealing the details of her mission. She had carried radio apparatus with her and her captors were eager to learn the British code signals, what communications she was receiving, and from whom. When she defied torture, the Nazis arrested her mother, who had no idea her daughter was not in Tel Aviv, and the two women had a few brief opportunities to talk. Hannah had been told by the police that unless she revealed her mission and exposed the location of its participants, her mother would be killed. Hannah gasped out why she must remain loyal to her pledge. A week later, the distraught mother, once the darling of her cultured middle-class family, set out before the permitted time to visit Hannah in prison. That same morning, Hannah had been offered commutation of her death sentence if she confessed to her crime of spying and pleaded for mercy. She had responded: "I ask no mercy from hangmen." Her mother was sitting in an office in the prison when a shot rang out from the nearby courtyard. Hannah Senesch, aged twenty-three, who had also refused to be blindfolded, had just been executed.

A few days later the Russians were in Budapest. Mme Senesch lived to escape and join her son in Israel. By then her daughter had become a legend of heroism and dedication. Her likeness in military uniform, young and radiant, was in the homes of every village and town in Palestine. And the poem that Hannah had written before her execution had become the best known and most beloved in Israel:

Blessed is the match that is consumed in kindling flame.
Blessed is the flame that burns in the secret fastnesses of the heart.
Blessed is the heart with strength to stop its beating for honor's
    sake.
Blessed is the match that is consumed in kindling flame.*

---

*"Blessed Is the Match" translated by Marie Synkin.

CHAPTER FOUR

The Carob Tree Grove:
Christian Compassion

IN AUGUST 1953, the Israeli Knesset authorized the creation of the Yad Vashem Research Institute, to be housed on Memorial Hill in Jerusalem.* It was to devote itself to an analysis of all aspects of the Holocaust, based on scrupulous scholarship. Article 9 of the resolution mandated that the research should include the identification of concerned Christians who had risked harassment, imprisonment, torture, reprisals against loved ones, even death, to save Jewish lives. The names and the nationalities of those chosen were to be inscribed at the base of individual carob trees that would become a Grove of the Righteous. The plantings, lovingly attended, flourished to remind beholders that each of the Righteous, named in gratitude, "is like a tree planted by streams of water that yields its fruit in its season and its leaf does not wither" (Psalms 1:3). The carob tree was chosen because of its endurance, resisting the hot, gusty summer and bitter winter winds of the highest hills of Jerusalem. There was felicitous symbolism too in the decision, for the fruit of the carob recalled the ministry of John the Baptist, to whom it was "The staff of life." Indeed, it is sometimes known as St. John's bread.

In the thirty years since the first plantings, about a thousand trees, in double rows, have grown up to shade the avenue leading to the Yad Vashem headquarters and museum. Each tree

---

*The designation came from the Prophet Isaiah (56:5): "I will give them an everlasting name which shall not be cut off."

commemorates an individual man or woman or a community whose acts of heroic concern have been identified and confirmed. The number seems pathetically small, given the fact that the names have been drawn from throughout Europe. Nor is the grove likely to acquire many more trees in the future. As the survivors of the Holocaust themselves grow older and die, it becomes more difficult to validate the courage, at great personal risk, that challenged the Nazis.

Nevertheless, those few daring spirits who did emerge, and whose actions can be authenticated, stand out, in Milton's phrase, "Godlike erect with native honour clad." The overwhelming majority of the Righteous seem to have arisen from among the common folk—a humble parish priest here, a minister there, a Mother Superior of a convent, a modest housewife, a shopkeeper or small businessman, the people of a feisty French village, a mini-company of laborers, a group of students. Many of the stories have been detailed in histories and biographies; others, documenting deeds as daring and sacrificial, have remained in the files of the Yad Vashem. In an overview of a period that challenges human values, it seems appropriate to include a sampling of the known and the comparatively unknown, to recall that there were valiant spirits, however rare, whose actions pierced the Stygian darkness.

Anna Simaite, a Lithuanian whose wholesome peasant face would scarcely be associated with intrigue, became a conspirator when the choice for her was to break man's law or God's. As a youthful radical when czarist Russia controlled the Baltic States, she had managed to stay clear of the police and became a teacher in a high school in Riga. Her charges were mainly waifs from the poorest families and she spent several years in Moscow to prepare for more intensive service among them. During World War II, though the Germans invested Lithuania, she managed to secure a post as a junior librarian at the University of Vilna. Many of those who frequented the library were Jewish children and she loved them dearly. But the Germans soon drove all Jews into an overcrowded ghetto area, and, as she wrote later, she knew then that her own well-being would have to be subordinated to a more compelling call.

Non-Jews were forbidden to enter the ghetto lest they be tempted to succor those whom they knew. Anna defied the order. She was admitted by the guards when she explained that her girls had been omnivorous readers and, since many of the books in the library had been taken into the ghetto, she hoped to ferret them out. Occasionally she secretly provided extra food. The coupons allocated to Aryans entitled her to obtain margarine and cheese, and she saved them for the children, who subsisted on potato peelings and cabbage. She rescued some rare books and sacred documents hidden in the synagogues and even some Torah scrolls that she stored under the floor of her lodgings and in the vaults of the university library. From the ghetto she would gather up lice-infested clothing to be disinfected, washed and ironed, and smuggled back to the owners. Occasionally when the guards' vigilance relaxed, she was able to spirit very young children out of the ghetto. Soon Anna became bold enough to bring in small arms obtained from the Partisan underground, to be hoarded for the day when the break for freedom would come. She encouraged the children to write scraps of diaries so that their experiences could be preserved; she hid the papers on her person and brought them out for deposit in the vaults of the university library.

Such subversion could not, of course, go long unnoticed. The Gestapo, using threat and coercion on weaker souls, eventually caught up with her. Anna was arrested in the summer of 1944 and tortured to reveal what she had done, and where her Jewish children were hidden. She did not break her silence and was sentenced to immediate execution; but unknown to her the university officials had interceded by bribing a Nazi guard, and she was despatched to Dachau. There, by another quirk of luck, she was at the last moment reprieved and deported to a camp in southern France. The American invasion set her free.[1]

In the postwar world Anna's ministrations, which she did not discuss, were long in coming to light. She earned a bare livelihood in Toulouse as dishwasher, seamstress, and ultimately, once again, as a librarian. During the early 1950s her Vilna experiences became known through some of the families she had rescued. The Society of Lithuanian Jews in America came to her assistance. A home was found for her in Paris. Soon she was besieged by letters from some of the children, "her children," who had settled in Israel and pleaded that she join them. Anna resisted until 1953, when she agreed to accept a little farm in Petach Tikvah, and a pension from the government.

Much of our knowledge of the last days of Jewish life in Poland comes from the diaries of a young Jewish historian, Dr. Emanuel Ringelblum, whose execution at the age of forty-six snuffed out a brilliant career. Born near the turn of the century, Ringelblum became a chronicler of Jewish life from the days when Hitler's shadow darkened occupied Poland. Early in 1938 the main Jewish relief agency, the American Joint Distribution Committee, gave him the responsibility for directing relief activities among the 17,000 Jews who were flung out of Germany and dumped across the Polish frontier. He kept a running account of those heroes who persisted in hopeless defiance in order to die with honor. Ringelblum and his collaborators hid his diaries and the documents, memoirs, reports, and writings of others in three milk pails, and buried them with the prayer that they would come to light in a better day. Two of the pails were later found and their contents published, the originals deposited in the restored Jewish Historical Institute in Warsaw, with photocopies in the Yad Vashem archives. The collection is known as the Oneg Shabbat (Enjoyment of the Sabbath) material. When the uprising was suppressed, Ringelblum was arrested, but he was smuggled back to the ghetto by the Jewish underground.

He and a few Jewish families survived because of the compassion of a simple Polish gardener, Pan Wolski, to whom his employers were precious. Wolski dug out an underground shelter, complete with kitchen and toilet, in which he hid Ringelblum and about thirty other Jews whom he secretly spirited out of the ghetto, one by one, circumventing the vigilance of police and neighbors. He topped the refuge with a greenhouse that disguised the subterranean living quarters beneath. The hideout was wretchedly crowded but it seemed to be safe, since it stood in an open field away from regular traffic. Eventually, an informer reported its operation to the Gestapo, and Ringelblum, his fellow Jews, and Pan Wolski too, were arrested and executed.[2] There was no epitaph for the courageous Polish Catholic; had there been one, it might have come from Francis Bacon, who noted that God was also a gardener, whose earliest creation for mankind was a garden.

Leodakia Yerumirska had been orphaned early and had married a poor storekeeper, one Bolek, whose hole-in-the-wall enterprise was located in a Jewish section of Warsaw. Soon after the

Germans invaded Poland, Bolek was dragged off to Auschwitz
as a political prisoner. Leodakia was drafted for slave labor in
one of the German-occupied warehouses. At daybreak one
morning, on her way to work, she heard crying and found a
newborn child, a girl, lying outside a monastery. She took the
infant home with her and named her Bugoshia, a gift of God.
Her neighbors, suspecting that the child was Jewish, were terrified that they would all be endangered by Leodakia's act of
mercy. They did not report her, but they would have nothing
to do with her that might involve them.

During the four-year occupation of Warsaw, Leodakia
managed to learn the names of the parents, faithfully promising
the mother that she would protect her confidence and assuring
her that she would care for the child as her own. She obtained
necessary extra support for the child by stealing food from the
warehouse. "After all, the Germans took it from us," she said.
She was several times visited by agents of the Gestapo but steadily insisted that the child was not Jewish. Each time her undeniable Polish appearance and her motherly devotion satisfied the
interrogators. Her most precarious moment came when she was
brought before the chief of police, who was so persistent that she
threw herself upon his mercy. "What if your own children were
abandoned in war and no one saved them?" At the end of a
two-hour grilling, Leodakia was released.

In 1944, as the Russian counterattack moved closer to Warsaw,
the main body of Germans began retreating westward, driving
thousands of Polish civilians before them. Leodakia found herself in a death-wagon convoy—trucks that preceded the main
columns to test the road for land mines. She managed to escape
and foraged her way back to desolated Warsaw, begging for
food, stealing it, hiding in barns and fields, the safety of her
adopted baby always uppermost in her concern. In Warsaw she
worked as a baker's assistant, a laundress, a farmer's handy-
woman, until at last the Russians liberated the city and its area.

Leodakia's husband, Bolek, now quite ill, and Bugoshia's father, also an Auschwitz survivor, were finally released. The
father, though deeply grateful to Leodakia for her sacrificial
devotion, wanted the return of his daughter, now more than
four years old. He pleaded with Leodakia to join him and the
child in Israel. But Leodakia could not leave her husband, now
dangerously ill; broken-hearted, she relinquished Bugoshia,
who was taken with her father to a kibbutz in Israel. The carob

tree in the Grove of the Righteous attests that Leodakia, like the child for whom she had so often risked her life, was also a gift of God.[3]

Mother Marie of Paris was another who opened her heart to those who had been marked for extermination. Born Elizabeth Pilenko in Russia, her grandmother was a direct descendant of one of Napoleon's generals who participated in the abortive invasion of Russia early in the nineteenth century. Mother Marie was the first woman to be graduated from Russia's Theological Seminary. Her early career involved her in revolutionary activity against the czar, but when communism, as interpreted by Stalin, became the state doctrine, she and a son, Yuri, by an early marriage, moved to Paris where she became a nun. Cooperating with an underground group of Greek Orthodox and Jesuit priests, she helped to organize a convent, the Little Cloister. When Hitler announced his totalitarian plans in France, her convent, which was no great distance from the Drancy concentration camp, became a center for Resistance activity and a refuge for those who had been targeted for Hitler's Final Solution. Scores of documents were forged in the convent to provide at least temporary security for Jews who had not yet been rounded up or whom Mother Marie helped to escape from Drancy.

In February 1943 the Gestapo, whose spies and agents infiltrated every underground operation, exposed Mother Marie and the secret activity of the convent. She was herself warned in enough time to avoid capture, but her son Yuri was seized. The Nazis announced that Yuri would be tortured and killed unless Mother Marie gave herself up. Indifferent to her own fate, the threat to her son brought her surrender. Yuri was murdered in Buchenwald anyway, and Mother Marie was sent to one of the women's divisions of Auschwitz, to share with 2,500 other women the starvation and the humiliations invented afresh each day.

Since her ancestry, in Nazi terms, was impeccable and she possessed a card proclaiming her an Aryan, she was not immediately doomed. It was considered a greater ordeal that she survive to live among the damned for another two years, to watch and share their affliction. However, as the Allied armies closed in on the Germans, the tempo of executions was stepped up, and Mother Marie was ordered to the gas chambers sometime before the Russians stormed Auschwitz. Too weak to walk, she had to be carried by one of the guards. Nevertheless, she summoned up enough strength to slip her Aryan card to another inmate in the hope that it might postpone a fellow sufferer's execution long enough to effect survival when the camp was liberated.[4]

For long, even the most vigilant Gestapo agents and French collaborators did not know that, shielded by the brown robe of the French Capuchin monks, Father Marie-Benoît, a tall, heavily bearded priest, had turned his modest monastery in Marseilles into one of Europe's most effective rescue points for French Jewry. Father Marie-Benoît was born in 1895 in a small French village, the son of a local miller. In his teens he entered the Capuchin Order, one of the most austere in monastic rule and practice. His novitiate was interrupted by five years of service in World War I during which he earned several medals for valor. He returned to complete his studies and was then sent to the Capuchin College in Rome, where he concentrated on philosophy and Hebraic research. He had become head of his order's monastery in Marseilles when Hitler occupied France. Marseilles was located in semi-autonomous Vichy territory and Father Marie-Benoît turned his monastery at 51 rue Croix de Rignier (The Street of the Cross) into a hiding place for hunted Jewish families.

Under his supervision, the cellar of the monastery became an affidavit factory where passports, IDs, certificates of baptism, ration cards, and other precious documents were fabricated. Applicants were carefully screened and, a few at a time, smuggled across the Pyrenees into Spain, or beyond the Alps into Switzerland, and across the Mediterranean to North Africa. Father Marie-Benoît developed remarkable skill in soliciting funds, both from international agencies and from temporarily non-threatened Jewish families in southern France.

The "underground railway" would probably have been exposed sooner or later, for 51 rue Croix de Rignier was suspiciously busy with the comings and goings of visitors. The exposure came sooner through a sudden turn in international affairs that compelled a complete revision of strategy. The Nazis, distrusting even their most compliant French collaborators when the survival of Jews was at issue, put an end to the autonomy of the Vichy government and took southern France under their own command. Nearly 50,000 Jews under cover in Marseilles, having fled from every point in Europe, were now in mortal danger. The resourceful monk opened negotiations with sympathetic Italian officials to arrange shelter in the northern border area, the Italian Tyrol, beyond Nazi control and at no great distance from neutral Switzerland. The Italians readily cooperated, for they had not only come to hate the Nazi overlords but were now worried about their own future. Again fate intervened. Just when plans for transfer were ready, the Nazis took over northern Italy as they had southern France, and hence gained control of all the escape routes in the border area.

Father Marie-Benoît had meantime moved to Italy, where he assumed a new identity as Padre Benedette. He was obliged to circumvent the vigilance of a Nazi occupying border force that operated very differently from the easygoing Italian authorities. But he had the grateful support of a descendant of an ancient distinguished Italian Jewish family, Angelo Donati, who had been living in France as director of the Franco-Italian Banque de Crédit. Through all the kaleidoscopic political and financial changes in the two countries, Donati commanded considerable influence among French and Italian bankers and he used their goodwill to ease the plight of his people.

Padre Benedette established his headquarters in the Capuchin College in Milan whose address, 159 Via Siciliani, became the new magic password for the next phase of the rescue epic. He collaborated with Delasem (Delegazione Assistenza Emigranti Profuglisi Ebrei), a committee for assistance to the Jewish refugees. One of his co-conspirators was a future prime minister of a restored democratic Italy, Alcide de Gasperi, then working anonymously in the Vatican Library. But Padre Benedette's main cooperation came from Donati, and together they brought the stranded Jews from France into northern Italy. Hundreds of men, women, and children struggled through the Alpine passes in another of the war's little-known epics. Many perished but many more were saved as they came under the protection of the new identity documents that had been prepared for them. Once again the Gestapo intervened. Three involved Jews were apprehended, and when they were unable to hold out against torture, the secret activity of the Capuchin College was exposed.

By now the betrayal did not too much matter. The Americans had landed at Anzio and were pounding away at Monte Cassino; the Nazis were in flight and the Italian resistance became bolder. The danger ended for the Jews who had been so resourcefully befriended. Donati, who had found refuge in Switzerland, could return to an Italy where the Fascist power had been repudiated. Father Marie-Benoît's heroic work was completed. Many honors came to him when his exploits became known, but his most cherished was the planting of the carob tree and its identification, "Father of the Jews."[5]

Dr. Adelaide Hautval was a well-reputed French physician who fell out with the Nazi authorities when she traveled without official permission for her mother's funeral from Vichy to the occupied zone of France. She was imprisoned in Bourges for insubordination and she learned with horror how the French collaborators rivaled the Nazis in cruelty to the Jewish prisoners. When she protested the brutality that went on all about her, she was forced to wear a yellow badge on which was written: "Friend of the Jews." Soon afterward she was sent to work as a doctor in the Auschwitz camps. Since her attempts at intercession had brought her crueler imprisonment and compounded the suffering of those whom she tried to befriend, she administered her help secretly. When a typhus epidemic wracked her block in Auschwitz, she did not report those who were stricken, knowing that they would at once be sent to the gas chambers. Instead, she hid them on the upper level of the crude bunks and ministered to them with whatever strength and skill were left to her. To her fellow prisoners she became "the angel in white." She contrived ways to avoid cooperation with several of the doctors who were conducting inhuman experiments. One of them, Dr. Christian Wirths, chided her for not perceiving the difference between the Jewish "subspecies" and her own kind. Dr. Hautval risked a sharp retort: "I have indeed perceived people different from myself, and you are one of them."

In 1963 a widely publicized trial took place in London when Leon Uris, author of *Exodus*, was sued for libel by a Polish gynecologist who claimed that he and other doctors had been portrayed as inhuman wretches in the book. Dr. Hautval testified for the defense, corroborating Uris's vignettes of those who had performed sterilization experiments on the Jewish women in the camps. The Justice, finding for the defense, went out of his way to pay tribute to Dr. Hautval, citing her as one of the most courageous women who had ever given evidence in an English court.[6]

After the 1938 Anschluss, there was a massive exodus of Jews from Austria who sought to cross into Switzerland. The Swiss authorities took prompt measures to prevent the country from being flooded with refugees and the entry points were blocked. Paul Grueninger, chief of police in St. Gallen, was the official charged with the surveillance responsibility. He had led an exemplary life, with deepest respect for the law, but he had no heart for turning away these despairing families. He disregarded the immigration restrictions and cooperated secretly with Jewish smugglers in pointing out unguarded frontier points and arranging temporary asylum for those in flight. There are no official statistics on those who were saved by his intervention, but they must have numbered several hundred. His chiefs learned of Grueninger's activity and he was tried and convicted for insubordination by the district court of St. Gallen. Upon conviction his pension was forfeited. After the European war was ended, he made no attempt to publicize his plight and the reasons for it, so the only employment he could obtain was as a low-level instructor. Those who entered Switzerland did not even know to whom they were indebted for their rescue. When the international press ultimately covered the story, the new generation of Swiss officials tried to make amends. The record of Grueninger's merciful "insubordination" was expunged, and in 1969 he was officially rehabilitated. By then he was approaching his eightieth year; he died four years later. He had never expressed bitterness over the judgment of his peers, for he had knowingly violated the Swiss law.[7] But it was difficult to understand why he had been listed for a quarter of a century as a felon who was thus denied employment suited to his talents. Switzerland was host to innumerable agencies that arbitrated international issues of justice. Apparently individual acts of compassion were better left to Heaven.

Aristides de Sousa Mendes was named by his parents for the classic Greek statesman whose countrymen, honoring his integrity, had given him the title "The Just." The young Portuguese lawyer earned both the patronym and the appellation. A devout Catholic, he insisted upon living by the tenets of his faith even though he came from a land riven with political opportunism. During the war he served as Portuguese consul in the wine center of Bordeaux, just across the boundary line that the Germans had drawn to separate occupied and Vichy France. Since

Bordeaux was a thriving Atlantic port and a way station along the coast to Spain and Portugal, the city was thronged with refugees, among them some 10,000 Jews who were trying to escape from Nazi-occupied France. Their hope was to reach Portugal by way of Spain, even though the land was swarming with Nazis.

Neutral Portugal, traditionally in alliance with Great Britain, was now menaced by Fascist states on all sides. The government determined not to risk displeasure, which could so easily harden into hostility. On the very day of the occupation of France by the Nazis, Portugal closed its frontiers and ordered its consuls to suspend the issuance of entry visas. De Sousa Mendes confronted head on the same problem that had troubled the conscience of the Swiss Grueninger. Both the streets around the consul's headquarters and around his home were overflowing with families who clamored for exit visas. De Sousa Mendes took as many into his home as could be accommodated until all rooms, staircases, floors, and the roof and basement could hold no more. Rabbi Chaim Kruger, himself a Belgian refugee, who had become his friend, joined him on the steps of his house. There De Sousa Mendes, his wife and children, and Rabbi Kruger all helped to prepare the scores of visas which De Sousa Mendes stamped hour by hour through three days until exhaustion compelled him to pause for rest. Some of his countrymen warned him that he was not only sacrificing a promising career but placing his country in jeopardy with neighboring lands that had declared war on the Jews. De Sousa Mendes sought no escape in rationalization. "I cannot let these people die," he said as he looked over the hundreds of frightened families torn by hope of reprieve and the possibility of the death camps. "Our constitution states that religion and the political views of a foreign subject shall not constitute grounds for their being refused asylum in Portugal. . . ."

The disquieted Lisbon authorities, learning of the activities of their maverick consul, despatched several officials to Bordeaux to halt his activity and to send him back to Lisbon. En route through Bayonne, De Sousa Mendes again saw crowds of refugees vainly besieging the Portuguese Consulate, which had also received instructions to issue no more exit visas. He assumed authority. "I have not yet been dismissed," he announced; "I am still your superior." De Sousa Mendes proceeded to validate visas throughout the day. Continuing his

journey technically under arrest, he reached the border town of
Hendaye, a principal rail center for travelers between France
and Spain. Passengers were obliged to change trains there and
the intransigent consul surmised correctly that at such points
the Spanish guards would exercise exceptional vigilance. He
counseled the refugees to seek out more obscure locations for
crossing, where official orders to halt passage had most likely not
yet been received. When he finally arrived in Lisbon, he went
through an unfriendly official hearing and was dismissed from
the foreign service, never to be reinstated. His property was also
confiscated. He died a decade later, officially an outcast.[8]

When Russia and Germany took over Poland in 1939 and
carved it into its fourth partition, many German businessmen
sensed opportunities for establishing profitable trade relations.
Among them was an enterprising manufacturer of kitchen uten-
sils, Oskar Schindler, who received permission to operate one of
his factories in Krakow. Schindler was completely uninterested
in ideological politics and paid little attention to the ethnic
background of his employees. He needed industrious workmen,
and he kept hiring them. Among those whom he selected were
several hundred Jews. Schindler used his business connections,
social friendships, bribery, and reciprocal favors to retain his
Jews, who in turn repaid the reprieve from the crematoria and
mass graves with fanatic devotion.

Near Schindler's factory was the notorious Plaszow camp,
and it was usually a death sentence to be sent there. Schindler
persuaded the Nazi authorities to permit him to build special
cabins for his employees, now mainly Jews, so that there would
be no interruption in manufacturing the goods that had become
so scarce in Germany. As the Russians approached in their
reconquest sweeps, almost every camp was quickly emptied by
the Nazis, and the inmates despatched to the gas chambers of
Auschwitz and other death centers. When Plaszow was liquidated, Schindler rescued three hundred women who were the
wives, sisters, mothers, and daughters of his male employees and
had them reunited with their families. This was the only time
during the Holocaust period that a large group of Jewish women
were released from Auschwitz.

After Krakow was taken over by the Russians, Schindler received permission to relocate his factory in his native Sudeten-
land, and he not only brought in the seven hundred Jews who

were his employees but five hundred others whom he now needed for the armaments manufacture that had become his new major concern. After the war about 250 of the survivors moved to Palestine, and they welcomed their benefactor in their annual reunions. At the planting of a carob tree in his honor, they were proud to be referred to as "Schindler's Juden." Schindler died in Germany in 1974; honoring his own request, he was buried in the cemetery on Mount Zion in Jerusalem.[9]

After Hitler came to power, the Protestant churches in Germany were brought under the control of Nazi-appointed officials espousing "the Aryan paragraph" of the Nazi platform. Many of the Protestant pastors resisted this assault upon their conscience and they organized a schismatic wing, the Confessional Church: by 1936 it could claim the adherence of 9,000 pastors, about 40 percent of all the Protestant canons and clerics. Martin Niemöller, who had performed brilliantly as a naval officer in World War I and then chosen a career in the ministry, was one of the founders, for he was convinced that the Nazi party was going far beyond a resurgence of nationalist fervor.

As the number of Jewish victims mounted into the millions, Niemöller could not carry his dissidence silently. His preaching, always eloquent, "spoke poignards and every word stabbed." Though he came from an important Evangelical family and had a distinguished war record, his defiance could not remain unchallenged. He was arrested and sent to one of the concentration camps, ultimately to Dachau, where he shared imprisonment with the former French Prime Minister, Léon Blum, who had been transferred from Theresienstadt.

Niemöller survived to return to his ministry, never ceasing to regret that he had not spoken out sooner before the Nazis had acquired their unlimited power. "We let God wait ten years," he declared. "These things happened in our German name and in our world. . . . I regard myself as guilty as any SS man."[10] Since for a while he had been a member of the Nazi party, no carob tree was planted for him by Yad Vashem. But the retribution for moral neutrality was never better stated than in one of his deepest felt charges to the German people: "They went after the Jews, but I was not a Jew, so I remained unconcerned. Then they went after the Catholics, but I was not a Catholic so I remained unconcerned. Then they went after the Communists, but I was not a Communist, so I remained unconcerned. Then they went after the Protestants and there was no one left to be concerned."

The examples of Christian compassion that have been discussed above relate to the actions of individuals. What they did influenced no national policy, nor did they turn the tide of events. These were men and women who rose above self to follow a vision of Christian duty. Asked why they risked so much when they had no personal stake in the result, they invariably responded that they did have a stake: they were reacting to what gave significance to their being.

Given the behavior of such spirits who chose to be their brothers' keeper, the tormenting question persists about the stance of Pope Pius XII in the nightmare years of the Holocaust. How was it that ordinary members of the domestic clergy, humble friars, priests of cloistered orders, gently bred nuns rose to the challenge while the Vatican remained silent? There were of course exceptions among the higher clergy. There was Angelo Cardinal Roncalli, the papal legate to Turkey, who later became Pope John XXIII. He was part of a large and extremely poor family in an earthquake-ridden and impoverished section of northern Italy. Retaining an unquenchable human exuberance, he had risen through the ranks of the Roman hierarchy, acquiring impressive scholarship and a command of several languages. While stationed in Ankara, he learned that transportation had been arranged for a shipload of Jewish children to safe harbor. However, the ship's destination was Lisbon, and the government of the dictator Salazar was unwilling to let the ship land and debark its cargo. Not without difficulty Roncalli, with no clear standing orders, put pressure on a Portuguese diplomat in Turkey whose child he had christened, and secured the admission of the youngsters into Portugal. After the war, when he became Pope, he greeted the Jews with the assuring words, "I am thy brother Joseph."[11]

The Pope of the Holocaust years was cast in a different mold. He was born Eugenio Pacelli of the old Roman and Vatican-connected aristocracy, a man best described, even by those who admired him most, as remote, austere, ascetic to a fault. He was chosen as Pope on the eve of war, succeeding the traditionalist but feisty Pius XI, who could berate Mussolini in language the more patrician Pacelli could not bring himself to use. There were private interventions by Pius XII on behalf of individuals

and families, witness his protection of Alcide de Gaspari, who
was to be the first prime minister of the new democratic Italy.
De Gaspari was given employment in the Vatican Library and
escaped Nazi harassment during the Mussolini period.

But the voice of Christ's vicar on earth was not heard while
the mass murders were perpetrated and the gas chambers and
crematoria operated around the clock. He had no power to inter-
vene, yet the question in the forefront was whether it was not
a sacred obligation to repudiate the inhumanity of a govern-
ment-sponsored Final Solution whose victims were destroyed
because of the blood in their veins. Pius XII's public utterances,
in response to irrefutable evidence that crimes beyond description were being perpetrated, took the form of vague and gen-
eralized references to "excesses" which he deplored. But these
could be taken to refer to Allied as well as Axis bombings of
strategic areas where there were concentrations of civilian
populations.

The Pope's silence did not of course mean that the Vatican
condoned the butchery or the inhumanity. It would have been
impossible for the hundreds of priests and nuns to carry forward their work of mercy and rescue if their Pope had forbidden it. Perhaps part of the answer lay in the statement of
Monsignor Montini, who was to become Pope Paul VI in 1976:
"The time may come when, in spite of such grievous prospect,
the Holy Father will decide to speak out." The time never came.
It never came because the duty to speak out on the barbarity of
the Holocaust was apparently always counterbalanced by the
fear of weakening Germany and thus preparing the way for the
triumph of godless communism.*[12]

Perhaps no more shining example of national courage was
offered in the teeth of Nazi occupation than that of Denmark.
Itself tiny among the peoples of Europe, it had a Jewish popula-

---

*Some Catholic observers make the point that Pope Pius XII may have been
literally "the prisoner of the Vatican," hemmed in by a bureaucracy, both
clerical and lay, that was overwhelmingly Roman, often hereditary, and in
many instances intimately related by blood to the Italian establishment outside the Vatican. They remind critics that the Pope secretly disbursed more
than $2 million of his personal or family fortune in refugee relief, much of
it specifically for Jewish victims.

tion in 1940 of about 7,300, three-fourths of whom had migrated there from Germany and other European countries in the years between the two world wars. There were also some seven hundred non-Jews who had married Jews. These people were mainly centered in Copenhagen, where they savored every opportunity for participation in Danish life. The one cloud, and it was then no larger than a man's hand, appeared in Schleswig-Holstein, the disputed province on the southern border of Germany which Bismarck had usurped in mid-nineteenth century. Schleswig-Holstein had been returned to Denmark after World War I. Fifty thousand Germans still lived in the province and occasional rumblings of anti-Semitism were heard from there, but were not taken too seriously either by the general population or by the Danish Jews.

When Hitler came to power after 1933, Nazi irredentism grew bolder. The effort to stimulate disaffection angered the Danes and their leaders. Indeed, on April 22, 1940, King Christian X attended the centennial celebration of Copenhagen's main synagogue, and spoke eloquently of Jewish contributions to Danish national life. This was a fortnight after Hitler had launched his attacks on the lands that he coveted; Denmark, along with Poland and the Baltic States, was rapidly occupied. Sweden was permitted the status of neutrality and escaped attack when it did not resist the flight of Nazi aircraft over its territory to complete the subjugation of Norway.

At first the Nazis made little attempt to bring the Danes into the Fascist fold, content to dictate economic policy and to strip the land of its rich dairy products and foodstuffs. Jew-baiting, however, began at once. The German ambassador to Denmark, Werner Best, drew up a master plan for the deportation of Danish Jews to the death camps, expecting, for this purpose, to rely upon the normal machinery of government. He requested the Danish Parliament to enact the appropriate legislation. Parliament refused.

Meanwhile, Danish writers—no mean force in so literate a society—demonstrated their defiant solidarity through an ingenious historical parallel. When the centennial of George Brandes, a Jewish intellectual and revered Danish literary critic, was observed in February 1942, the literati staged a series of celebrations. Selections from Brandes' writings were read aloud at public meetings, all chosen for their appositeness in the prevailing climate. Ernest Renan's prayer to Athena was intoned and acquired a rare popularity: "The world will only be saved by returning to you and thus shaking off the barbarism in which it finds itself." The Nazis fumed. Nevertheless, they bided their time until August 1943 when, the war going against them elsewhere, Hitler deposed the Danish king, instituted military rule, and disarmed the tiny Danish Army. He decided now to include the Jews of Denmark in the Final Solution. The dates chosen for the round-up were the High Holy Days, when most Jewish families, at worship in the synagogues, would be easily accessible. Four large ships were prepared for the mass deportation, two of which, however, were blown up by saboteurs.

What followed was high drama. The German attaché for shipping affairs was Captain Georg Ferdinand Dukwitz, a member of the German Legation in Denmark since 1939. He had close friends in the Danish Jewish community and was on good terms with the Chief Rabbi, Marcus Melchior. He risked his life and well-being when he secretly revealed the Nazi plans to the Danish leadership.[13] He was later asked what inspired his hazardous action. "It was not impetuous," he responded. "I did not think my life was more important than the lives of 7,000 Jews."*[14]

Dukwitz's warning spread quickly through Copenhagen and the few other communities where there were Jewish citizens. Overnight, as it were, a rescue organization came into being. Common folk went knocking on their Jewish neighbors' doors to offer shelter in their own homes until transport to Sweden was made ready. The motto was: "Where there's room in the heart, there's room in the house." Teams of young Danes reverently carried off about a hundred Torahs from synagogues and stored them in Protestant churches. The medical profession was especially cooperative. Copenhagen's famed Baspeberg Hospital became a staging area through which the doctors processed about 2,000 Jews for escape. There was no halt in rescue operations, even when the Gestapo brought their machine guns into an operating room when they suspected that the patient on the table was a Jew. Nurses openly kept collection boxes at their stations for small donations to aid the Jewish flight.

Meanwhile, a remarkable armada was being outfitted, not unlike the naval gallimaufry that had evacuated tens of thousands of trapped British soldiers at Dunkirk in 1940. Fishing

---

*Captain Dukwitz's name was placed on a carob tree in the Yad Vashem grove.

smacks, rowboats, skiffs, yachts, ferries, anything that could
float were placed at the disposal of the rescue committees by
their owners. No one underestimated the enormous risks of the
exodus. The Kattegat, between Elsinore in the north of Denmark and Hälsingborg in Sweden, is only two and a half miles
wide, but there are fifteen miles of choppy seas between Copenhagen and the nearest Swedish landfall, Malmö. Nor were some
of the Swedish political leaders enchanted with the prospect
that the country's precarious neutrality would be jeopardized if
they gave refuge to the Danish Jews. But these soon found that
they had to deal with a Danish Nobel Laureate, Niels Bohr,
considered one of the world's outstanding authorities in atomic
science.

Bohr's Jewish identity had, until this moment of crisis, been
quite nominal; but with 7,000 Jewish lives threatened, his latent
loyalties came to life. He and his brother were in Stockholm for
a planned stopover on the way to London, and eventually to the
United States, for collaboration in the Manhattan atomic project. When word reached Bohr that some of the Swedish political leaders hesitated to offer asylum to the Danish Jews, he
notified the Allied command that he would "sit on his duff" in
Stockholm unless there was an immediate guarantee that the
Danish Jews would be given sanctuary in Sweden. The Manhattan Project had become the most crucial secret weapon in the
victory plans of the Allies and Bohr was among the half dozen
scientists upon whom its successful completion depended.
Churchill or Roosevelt may have expressed their concern to the
Swedish embassies, for the guarantee that Bohr demanded came
quickly.

The rescue operation was a kind of mini-Dunkirk. Nazi patrol
boats were everywhere. Some small rescue crafts were sunk and
their human cargo drowned; other people were shot in flight.
But practically the entire Jewish population of Denmark, ex-
cepting those children who undoubtedly were more safely
housed in the homes of Danish clergymen, reached the Swedish
shores. A courageous Lutheran teacher, Aage Bertelson, and his
family, supervised one rescue mission that saved about seven
hundred Jews. When the Nazis moved in with their 2,000 Gestapo deportation specialists on the High Holy Days (October
1 and 2, 1943), they learned with chagrin that all but about 500
elderly and sick Jews, too weak to escape, had disappeared.[15] For
these helpless relics there was no compassion, and they were

shipped off to Theresienstadt. That most of them survived was due in largest measure to the continued concern of the Danish government. The king sent to the camp a committee of hand-picked, high-ranking Danes under the aegis of the Danish Red Cross, to observe and report on the condition of Danish prisoners there. As noted earlier, the committee was duped about the procedures in the camp, but the requirement by the Danish government for frequent reports may have had some restraining influence.

Perhaps a personal reminiscence will not be inappropriate here. The summer of 1964 marked the twentieth anniversary of the Danes' successful evacuation of their Jewish population. Brandeis University, where I then served as president, was eager to give special recognition to the compassion that illumined the darkness of the Hitler era. Through appropriate channels, we broached our wish to extend an invitation to King Frederick, son of Christian X, and to Frederick's queen, to receive a Brandeis honorary degree, even though we were aware that monarchs in general shy away from such testimonials. While King Frederick might have been willing in this case to make an exception, he responded that his younger daughter Sophie had just been betrothed to King Constantine of Greece. The wedding date had been set and it coincided with the weekend of the Brandeis Commencement.

An alternative was proposed. On every Fourth of July for many years a Danish-American association had held a festival at Rebild, in the northern province of Jutland, a festival of goodwill that had achieved the status of a Danish national holiday. The royal family frequently attended the festivities. Word came that, if it were convenient, the king and queen would be pleased to accept a Brandeis tribute on that occasion, on the hillside where the celebration was held. The tribute could not be an honorary degree since these were conferred only at commencements or special convocations on campus. Fortunately we still had a few of the gold medals struck by the United States Mint on the centennial of the birth of Justice Brandeis. One of these, along with the university's citation, went with our luggage to Denmark.

July 4, 1964, was an extraordinarily beautiful day. Tens of thousands of celebrants gathered at Rebild where the Viking king, an extremely tall man among a tall people, received and acknowledged the university's tribute to his parents and his people. Later, he directed that the medal and citation were to be displayed in the window of one of Copenhagen's most elegant downtown shops. The citation read, in part:

> Ours is a young university, named for Louis Dembitz Brandeis, distinguished American jurist, himself the son of refugees. We humbly claim kinship with a people whose tradition of sovereignty is 900 years old, whose respect for individual liberty was codified in 1814, whose cities have never known the shadow of a ghetto.*

The Swedish government found it difficult to follow a consistent course in reaction to the problems created by Nazi aggression. Its official stance was one of neutrality. This proved advantageous to its economic welfare since it could continue trading with both the Axis powers and the western Allies. Many of its steel barons cautioned against exposing the country to Nazi wrath by offering asylum to refugees. But there was so much popular sympathy for the victims of Hitler that considerable humanitarian effort, through subterfuge, was not carefully monitored. When Hitler overwhelmed Norway in 1940, there was popular pressure to appeal to the Nazis to permit the Norwegian Jews, who numbered a bare 1,700, to be permitted to migrate to Sweden. The German foreign office refused and proceeded with its plans for deportation and death. The Swedish Underground, in cooperation with some of the international Jewish organizations, began to smuggle Norwegian Jewish families over the rugged terrain shared by Norway and Sweden.

The operation was led by Od Nansen, son of the famous Norwegian Arctic explorer, who, with Peter Freuchen, a kindred spirit, was one of Norway's most dedicated freedom

---

*In summarizing the reaction of crowned heads, another example of quiet royal courage should be recalled. Elisabeth of the Belgians, then Dowager Queen Mother, is affectionately remembered for her patronage of music. During the Nazi occupation, under house arrest, she let it be known "through channels" that any child of whatever background who appeared at convents or orphanages under her personal patronage was to be admitted without question.

fighters. Both men already had a long rescue experience, guiding Austrian and Polish Jewish refugees, first to Norway and then to Sweden. The Nazi plan to deport the Jews of Norway gave these men another challenge. They supervised the escape of 930 intended victims who called up enough strength to overcome the physical hardships of the journey to the frontiers. The other 770 who were trapped in Norway were crowded into the German ship *Donau* and deported to Auschwitz. In addition to succoring the Norwegian and Danish Jews, Sweden accepted another 8,000 Jewish refugees from other countries. Many Jewish children, ill and abused, who were spirited out of the ghettos, were nursed back to health in Sweden's splendid hospitals.[16]

The defiance of the Danes and the Scandinavian peoples that saved more than 8,000 Jews is a well-known saga of exceptional Christian concern; the resistance to the Nazis of the Bulgarian common folk and their Greek Orthodox clergy that saved almost the entire Bulgarian Jewish community is less well known. Bulgaria yielded to the Nazi juggernaut early in the war. King Boris III was permitted to retain his throne as a Nazi puppet.

Some 50,000 Jews lived in the kingdom, mainly in its capital, Sofia. Boris offered no objection when, in March 1943, more than 11,000 Jews of Thrace and the Macedonian provinces that had been assigned by the Nazis to Bulgaria were deported to extermination camps in Poland. But when orders were issued to round up the Jews of Old Bulgaria, where Jews had been living peacefully with their neighbors for centuries, there was vigorous opposition from the Greek Orthodox clergy, led by the Metropolitan, Stefan. He had publicly denounced the promulgation of the Nuremberg Laws when they were forced upon Bulgaria by the Nazis in 1940. He had fought, though unsuccessfully, the deportation of the Jews from the annexed provinces. Now he warned the superstitious King that any further persecution of the Jews would put his soul in mortal danger. Joining Stefan in his protests was Angelo Roncalli, later Pope John XXIII, who had been apostolic visitor to Bulgaria from 1924 to 1934. He was promptly admonished by Rome not to concern himself with such political matters. He was constantly attacked in the Bulgarian Parliament (the Subranie) as a traitor, but he would not be silenced.

There was strong opposition too from the Fatherland Front, representing Bulgarian peasantry, headed by Nikola Petkov and

Dimitri Peshev, two of the few shining lights in modern Balkan history.[17] They took daring risks to head off the determination of the Nazis and their collaborators to deport the Jews from the annexed provinces. Peshev was censured by the Subranie even though he was its vice president.

King Boris, though prodded by Adolf Eichmann to complete the Final Solution, temporized for months, hoping that the mounting military problems of the overextended German forces would make punitive action unlikely. When the Germans were decisively defeated at Stalingrad and began their great retreat in the winter of 1943, Boris bargained more strenuously with the Nazi occupation authorities and wrung out a compromise that did not go beyond the uprooting of the Jews from Sofia and their transfer to work camps in the countryside. Since their homes and businesses would also be expropriated, it did not seem much of a compromise to Jewish families whose roots in Bulgaria went back to the Roman Empire. But they consoled themselves that their lives had been ransomed and they hoped that their dispossession would not be too long. It lasted for little more than a year, a year of disillusionment and deprivation. But on September 9, 1944, the Nazi occupation collapsed when the Red Army swept into Bulgaria. It drove out the Nazis and their puppets and installed a coalition government of the Fatherland Front Socialists and Moscow-dominated Communists. The coalition did not last. The local communists, with Soviet backing, used the next two years to undermine and liquidate their Socialist partners and, in 1947, took over the government in a spurious election. When Petkov excoriated the fraud, he was dragged from his seat in the Subranie, tried by a panel of Communist judges and, in September 1947, was hanged.[18]

Before the complete Communist take-over, however, there had been active cooperation between representatives of B'richa and the Fatherland Front leaders to facilitate Jewish immigration to Palestine. They suggested that an appearance by a leading Zionist official would offer hope and raise morale for the still badly shaken and impoverished Bulgarian Jewish community. There was jubilation in the Sofia B'richa office when Ben Gurion himself agreed to make the journey. Much of eastern Europe was still technically at war and Ben Gurion flew to neutral Turkey where, in his youth, he had been a student in Istanbul, and after some complicated maneuvering, he obtained a diplomatic visa for Bulgaria.

Ben Gurion was the first major foreign statesman to visit Bulgaria since its liberation from the Nazis, and the coalition government extended itself in paying him honor. He was installed in the specially designed parlor car previously used exclusively by royalty, and newspaper headlines hailed his arrival. He addressed a huge rally in the biggest cinema in Sofia, with thousands more crowding the narrow streets, hoping to catch a glimpse of the Messiah from the Homeland to which so many of them hoped to migrate. Ben Gurion pledged help to them if they joined the Aliya, the ingathering, to add their strength in the battle for the independent state that was then yet to come. The next day Ben Gurion was taken to an unheated medieval prison building in the townlet of Yuc Bunar where several thousand Bulgarian Jews were still housed. The men, women and children were squatting on a stone floor, numb with cold and hunger. Ben Gurion noted that none had shoes and, turning to his aide, Ehud Avriel, who had accompanied him, he said, with great effort to hold back his tears, "The first thing I will do when I return is to send out five thousand pairs of shoes for the children of Yuc Bunar." Then he paused and added, "Perhaps we should try to bring the feet to the shoes."[19] He did. But to keep this larger promise of facilitating immigration, the opposition of the Jewish Communists had to be overcome. They denounced those who wished to leave as flunkies who were being duped by "the retrograde, archaic, chauvinist nationalism of the Zionists."

The government attitude changed in 1947 after the Soviet foreign minister, Andrei Gromyko, made his speech in the UN supporting a Jewish independent state in a partitioned Palestine. It followed the Russian line and cooperated fully with the B'richa officials in encouraging Jewish migration to Palestine as an effort "to fight against British imperialism." By 1951, nearly 45,000 Bulgarian Jews had migrated to Israel. Only 7,000 remained, some hard-core communists and those too old or infirm to attempt the reconstruction of their lives elsewhere.

One of the strangest relationships during World War II brought together Hitler's chief deputy, Heinrich Himmler, and Dr. Felix Kersten, an Estonian-born physical therapist. Kersten used his influence over Himmler to become perhaps the single most effective agent of deliverance inside the Nazi empire. His relationship with Himmler was as bizarre and unlikely as that of the Austrian novelist, Louis de Wohl, who counseled British intelligence during the war years on how to treat the predictions that Hitler's astrologers were offering to the Führer.

Kersten, trained in Berlin during the 1920s by a famed Chinese physiotherapist, had made Holland his base in the prewar years. His skill gave him an international reputation, and he had built up an extensive practice in both Holland and Germany among diplomats, many of whom required physical therapy to cope with their awesome responsibilities. Henrich Himmler was one of these. He suffered from frequent abdominal spasms so violent that he often lapsed into unconsciousness: the injections and drugs prescribed by the medical establishment brought him little relief. Himmler read the report of a German tycoon about Kersten's highly successful therapy and requested his services. He fell under Kersten's spell, and told Mussolini's son-in-law, Count Ciano, that Kersten was "a magic Buddha who cures everything by massage."[20]

Kersten shortly became Himmler's chief medical adviser. As Himmler's reliance upon him deepened, he began to receive intimate confidences in the role of a kind of father confessor. These confidences included Hitler's phobias, and it soon became clear to Kersten that he was dealing with a maniac's maniac. He learned in 1941 that Himmler had been ordered to transport some three million Dutch dissidents to concentration camps in Silesia and the Ukraine. The knowledge that Hitler planned to exterminate his beloved Dutch as if they were vermin determined Kersten to go beyond his duty as a medical therapist. He planned to gain control over Himmler's political actions and his role as Hitler's surrogate. In his *Memoirs* Kersten described his efforts to persuade Himmler to ignore the order, or at least postpone it until the war was over. He also won a reprieve for the deportation to the death camps of the inmates of Theresienstadt, which held hundreds of Scandinavians and Dutch.

In these instances and in all that followed, Kersten noted that his successful intercession invariably came after he had brought Himmler out of an especially serious abdominal attack. It needed no special acumen to guide Kersten in his timing. When Himmler was well and in control, he was the authentic Nazi, dominated by command. When he was ill and had lost control, he could be manipulated. Kersten summed up the dualism of his patient: "His head contained both the plans of a Faust and the schemes of a Mephistopheles; it was the head of a Janus, for one side showed traits of loyalty, while the other revealed nothing but a skull."[21]

The domination that Kersten achieved by manipulating his patient's will did not, of course, win him any laurels from Himmler's deputies. Throughout his machinations, Kersten was never far from danger of sudden assassination. So complete was his patient's dependence on him, however, that when one of Himmler's chief aides, Kaltenbrunner, sought to discredit him, he was angrily warned by his chief, "if Kersten is bumped off, you won't survive him by twenty-four hours."[22]

By 1944 Kersten had to give thought to his personal future, if and when Himmler was toppled from power. He was already, for all practical purposes, a secret Allied agent. If he could now switch his base to Sweden, he would be out of danger in the chaotic days that must inevitably engulf the Reich. Meanwhile, as military reverses for Germany mounted, Himmler's physical condition steadily deteriorated. On one of Himmler's most despondent days Kersten asked for permission to relocate in neutral Sweden, where he would try to convince the Allied leaders that Himmler's cooperation in the waning months of the war would be worth enlisting and should entitle him to special consideration. Himmler agreed on condition that Kersten would be on call for a return to Germany whenever therapy became necessary.

The Swedish government gladly consented to an arrangement that made Kersten one of its most effective double agents. His first coup, in his new incarnation, was to persuade Himmler to release 1,000 Dutch women, 1,500 French women, 900 Polish men and women, with many Jews among them. The climax of Kersten's mission came in the last days of the war when he persuaded Himmler, first to delay, then ultimately to disregard Hitler's orders to blow up the extermination camps and all their inmates as the Allied military closed in on the last German defense strongholds. Kersten took full advantage of Himmler's anxieties as the agitated erstwhile dictator began to twist and turn, not only in physical agony, but in realization of what undoubtedly lay ahead for him with an Allied victory.

Early in 1945 Kersten arranged for Himmler to meet with Norbert Masur, who represented the World Jewish Congress, to discuss the release of Jewish prisoners to neutral countries if, in Himmler's words, "the transfers could be arranged without Hitler's knowledge." By now Himmler was describing himself as "a good friend of the Jews," insisting that he had consistently tried to thwart Hitler's mania. Himmler's belated cooperation with Masur was responsible for filtering a stream of Jewish women from the Ravensbruck camp through the lines to Stockholm for medical treatment and restoration.

Credit for this unexpected turn of events became an issue in the aftermath of the war. For many years Kersten's contributions, though they may have been exaggerated, were almost totally obscured because public attention was focused on Count Folke Bernadotte, president of the Swedish Red Cross.* Bernadotte, a strikingly handsome figure, often at the center of go-between diplomacy, can perhaps best be described by borrowing a phrase from the poet Edward Arlington Robinson: "He glittered when he walked." He was undoubtedly influential in much rescue work. What blemished his undeniable achievements was an apparent unwillingness to acknowledge the intercession of others in negotiations that were never simple. Almost immediately after the surrender of Hitler and Himmler, he rushed into print with his own story of the events, and Kersten's role was all but eliminated in the narrative. Kersten was apparently not too much concerned with his place in the rescue saga. His clientele sought him out not for a compassionate heart but for magic hands. Besides, immediately following the war and for a long time thereafter there was no distinction in a reputation for saving Jews.

When the war ended, Kersten had no desire to renew his professional life in a desolated Germany and he was eager to turn his temporary residence in Sweden into permanent citizenship. To his mortification his application was denied. According to a letter to the Dutch government from its ambassador in Helsinki, the refusal to grant citizenship was apparently instigated by Bernadotte. Those who knew of Kersten's service to Scandinavians were outraged and his Dutch champions took the initiative in protesting the shabby treatment to which he had been subjected. A special Dutch commission was appointed to investigate the facts; it examined hundreds of documents and interviewed many witnesses. Its report, issued in 1949, concluded that Kersten had indeed saved thousands of lives and

---

*Bernadotte's role as intermediary in the truce negotiations in the Arab-Israeli war is discussed in Chapter Ten.

retrieved invaluable Dutch art treasures that Nazi plunderers had appropriated. Even Walther Schellenberg, Bernadotte's ghost writer, who had also established haven in Sweden, offered testimony on behalf of Kersten's invaluable activity. The Swedish government at last acknowledged that Kersten's role had been "clear, incontestable, and important" and regretted that Bernadotte's account had "failed to do justice to Kersten's collaboration." He was granted Swedish citizenship in 1953.

Thereafter, as the history of the period unraveled, several other Allied governments offered their highest honors to Kersten. The World Jewish Congress credited him with the rescue of more than 60,000 Jews. When Kersten published his *Memoirs* in 1953, the introduction was written by Hugh Trevor-Roper, who had patiently gone through all the source material for an earlier article in the *Atlantic Monthly*. He paid tribute to Kersten's "work for humanity which he contrived to perform as a foreigner, without any power except the power of physical and intellectual manipulation at Himmler's headquarters."[23] Trevor-Roper's summary may be modified by later research revealing that Kersten had forged a crucial Himmler letter in order to discredit Bernadotte. But there is little doubt that Kersten, whatever his motives, was one of modern history's strangest instruments of deliverance.*

An as yet unsolved mystery of the postwar world concerns Raoul Wallenberg, the Swedish nobleman who undertook a mission of mercy in Hungary by means of a modern equivalent of an underground railroad and saved tens of thousands of lives. After more than thirty-five years there is still no reliable evidence as to Wallenberg's ultimate fate, despite the many investigators who have written books about him. He was last seen leaving the Swedish Legation in Budapest on the morning of January 17, 1945, in the company of a Russian officer, en route to an appointment with General Malinovski, whose troops had driven the Nazis from the Hungarian capital.

Wallenberg was of impressive lineage. One of his grandfathers, scion of an old Lutheran family, was a prominent banker and had been minister to Japan and Turkey. Wallenberg's father

---

*The reservations about Kersten were expressed by Dr. Yehuda Bauer, when he graciously read my manuscript.

had been a naval officer and, later, part of the family's banking empire. Raoul had ranged far in the course of acquiring an education, studying architecture and engineering at the University of Michigan in the United States and law in France, before returning to Stockholm to enter a leading import-export firm. His partner in the firm, Kalmen Lauer, was a Hungarian Jew. During the last months of the war, Lauer's wife and members of her family were stranded in Budapest. It was known in Stockholm that the Nazis were stepping up their extermination of Hungarian Jews, many of whom had maintained a precarious security because of shifting Hungarian political alliances. Wallenberg, who had considerable diplomatic and financial leverage, volunteered to go to Budapest to transport Lauer's relatives and whatever other Jewish families—he had a list—he could salvage. The American War Refugee Board was also eager to have a representative in Budapest to help in the release of Jews from the doomed city.

Wallenberg, then thirty-three years old, arrived in Budapest in July 1944 and quickly sized up the chaotic situation, brought on by simultaneous civil war and the collapse of the municipal administration. He decided to expand his modest family-plan mission into a full-scale rescue operation. The stakes were high. The prewar Jewish population had been slightly more than 400,000, but this figure had risen to more than 800,000 by the annexation of Polish territory and some provinces of the former Austro-Hungarian Empire. The war and deportations had taken a ghastly toll; but in 1944 there were still about 180,000 Jews left, mainly in Budapest.

Wallenberg established a special department, Section C, in the Swedish Embassy. The staff of twenty soon grew to more than six hundred, who, along with their families, were placed under the protection of the Swedish flag. Then Wallenberg began to supply Swedish identities even to those who had only the slightest family or business connection with his homeland. Section C printed "protective" passports, impressively emblazoned with Swedish stamps and signatures. Within days of his arrival, Wallenberg had taken more than a thousand families into "Swedish custody." His strategems were soon part of an effort by other neutral countries, including Switzerland, Portugal, and Spain. The papal nuncio and the Budapest director of the International Red Cross also issued protective papers and the number of those who were covered by new identities grew to the thousands. Unfortunately, while passports and other documents strengthened protection, they did not authorize a right to emigrate.

Wallenberg did not confine himself to issuing counterfeit documents. He cooperated fully with Zionist youth movement members, helping them to buy or rent thirty-two buildings that were draped, by his authorization, with Swedish flags, giving them the status of "safehouses." When Wallenberg learned that a large contingent of Jews was being taken by truck to the railroad station for deportation east, he appeared, flourishing what seemed valid credentials, demanding release for them all. His voice and tone exuded command, no doubt buttressed by the knowledge that no junior German officer could be expected to understand either Hungarian or Swedish, and that obedience to an authoritative presence was built into German military training. Wallenberg's half sister, Nina Lengergren, noted in a later interview: "Raoul was a great actor. He could imitate brilliantly. If he wanted to, he could be more German than a Prussian general."

In October 1944, barely four months after Wallenberg's arrival, the puppet chief of Hungary, Admiral Horthy, repudiated the imposed alliance with Germany and announced that he would sue for peace with the Allies. The Germans poured back, in full strength, into Budapest. Horthy was arrested, to be replaced by one of Eichmann's own men, Ferenz Szalasi. In the next weeks the Nazis seemed to give equal priority to the destruction of the remaining Jews and resistance to the Russians. No homes, whatever flags they flew, no persons, whatever documents they carried, were spared. Szalasi's underlings went on a spree of killing, burning, looting, flogging, raping. Thousands of mutilated corpses floated in the waters of the Danube.

Wallenberg continued fighting for time in the knowledge that the Russians were advancing inexorably. He was assisted by a friendship with a powerful cabinet member of the notorious Arrow Cross, the Hungarian neo-Nazi party, who had so far successfully concealed his Jewish ancestry. From him Wallenberg learned that the Arrow Cross planned a pogrom to liquidate the Jews who still remained in the desolated ghetto. Wallenberg was able to wind up his mission with another dramatic rescue. He contrived an audience with the German commander and warned him that, if the order were not canceled, he would use all his influence to have the commander tried as a war criminal. With the Russians on the outskirts of the city, their bombs already exploding nearby, the general was impressed and he canceled the order for the pogrom. Seventy thousand Jewish lives had hung on this last-minute intercession.[24]

The Nazis were driven from Budapest early in 1945, preceded by hordes of collaborators they had themselves enlisted. Wallenberg did not, as he might well have done, leave Budapest at once. He lingered on for several days hoping to obtain assurances from the Soviet general, Malinovski, that the Jews who had survived would come to no further peril. On the morning of January 17, accompanied by a Soviet motorcycle escort, he left the safety of the Swedish Legation for his fateful interview with the Russians. What happened on the way or immediately after has remained a mystery.

Over the years, the Wallenberg family and the government of Sweden have continuously appealed to Soviet authorities to explain Wallenberg's disappearance. Invariably, they received the frustrating response that he had indeed been expected at the Russian headquarters on that January morning. Period. In 1947 the Soviet Foreign Minister, Andre Vishinsky, informed the Swedish government that Wallenberg was not in the Soviet Union and was unknown to Soviet authorities. In February 1957, more than twelve years after Wallenberg's disappearance, the Soviet Foreign Minister, Andrei Gromyko, issued an official statement indicating that Wallenberg had died of a heart attack in Lubyanka Prison on July 17, 1947. The surname was misspelled. No first name was given. No explanation was offered other than that a record had come to light in the prison archives attesting to Wallenberg's death.

Despite the Russian disclaimer, hope persisted in the succeeding decades that Raoul Wallenberg had survived. One of those saved by Wallenberg, now Mrs. Thomas Lantos, who had settled in California, and several other survivors, refused to accept the Russian statement of 1957, and they kept up a persistent campaign to learn the fate of their courageous Swedish redeemer.

In May 1980, the Swedish Foreign Minister met with Andrei Gromyko, his Soviet counterpart, to urge the Russians to clear up the long-drawn-out case with its conflicting explanations and its insulting silences. What were the Russians hiding that they could not frankly reveal the events that had taken place from the time of Wallenberg's disappearance through the years that followed? Gromyko stared into space, whether listening or not, and ended the interview with the laconic statement: "We stand by our 1957 memorandum."

In the winter of 1981, an international panel headed by Ingrid Widemann, a Justice of the Swedish Supreme Court, called on the Soviet Union to reopen the case, alleging that "the original Russian statement had been based on tragic misinformation." There were nineteen sworn testimonies in Swedish hands from former cellmates of Wallenberg who had seen him in prison in Lubyanka.

Also in 1981 a bill was filed in the U.S. Congress to confer honorary citizenship on Wallenberg. The legislation was sponsored by Mrs. Lantos' husband Thomas, a concentration camp victim who was admitted to the United States after the war period on a student visa which I had obtained for him. He remained in the United States after receiving his degree, and became an American citizen. A successful political career followed, and he was the first Holocaust survivor to serve in Congress as a representative. The legislation to confer honorary citizenship on Wallenberg was unanimously adopted in September 1981. It now became possible for the American government to make official representations to the Soviet Union about Wallenberg's fate.*

Wallenberg was responsible for the direct rescue of many thousands of Hungarian Jews. Most of them are now dead or have migrated. To the younger generation, Wallenberg became a legend. There is a small building in Budapest still bearing marks of the bullets of 1945 when the Nazis were routed, and of 1956 when the freedom fighters fought the Soviet tanks to regain the liberty that had been lost under communism. A modest plaque on the house front bears the inscription in Hungarian: "To the memory of Raoul Wallenberg, Swedish diplomat whose heroic deeds saved tens of thousands of Hungarians from the final days of Nazi terror. Raoul Wallenberg disappeared during

---

*It was widely noted that honorary citizenship had been conferred only once before, on Sir Winston Churchill. This is not accurate. After the American Revolution, Congress, at the behest of George Washington, granted honorary American citizenship to the Marquis de Lafayette and his descendants in perpetuity.

the siege of Budapest." And in the heart of Budapest there is a street named for him.

In Jerusalem, the Yad Vashem several times suggested that a tree be planted in Wallenberg's memory in the Grove of the Righteous. But for Wallenberg's family to accept the appreciated honor would be tantamount to signing the death certificate. Until 1980, Raoul Wallenberg's aged mother therefore steadfastly refused permission for the memorial. After her death in that year, the rest of the family conceded that all hope was gone. A carob tree, which will not bear its fruit for another generation, has now been planted.

As one walks up the Avenue of the Righteous, each tree that lines the road tells its story of sacrificial Christian courage. The deeds that are gratefully acknowledged through the plantings saved many families, often whole communities. To be sure, in the dark world of Hitler, only a tiny minority could be counted on for redemptive service. But these kept the hope alive that rainbows would follow every storm. Sholom Asch, the dean of Jewish writers in the Holocaust generation, who was not daunted nor discouraged because there were so few Christians whose compassion outweighed their prudence, wrote:

On the flood of sin, hatred, and blood, let loose by Hitler upon the world, there was a small ark which preserved intact the common heritage of a Judaeo-Christian outlook, an outlook which is founded on the double principle of love of God and love of one's fellow man. The demonism of Hitler had sought to overturn and overwhelm it in the floods of hate. It was saved by the heroism of a handful of saints.[25]

CHAPTER FIVE

The Nuremberg Military Tribunal
and the Trials that Followed

S OON AFTER HITLER LAUNCHED his invasion of Russia in 1941,
with the rest of the continent mostly under his control, the
Allied leaders issued warnings that the Nazis would be held
strictly accountable for crimes committed against whole peoples. From their London refuge, the governments-in-exile—Belgium, Holland, Norway, Yugoslavia, Greece, Poland, Czechoslovakia, and the Free French—issued the St. James Declaration.
It was formally signed on January 13, 1942, and was endorsed as
well by Great Britain. Russia was not among the co-signers but
sent observers to the deliberations. Though the United States
remained nominally neutral during the months of drafting,
Franklin Roosevelt had already spoken out against the Nazi
treatment of civilians "that revolts the world." After the surrender of the Nazis and their allies, an International Military
Tribunal was convened in August 1945 to try some of the apprehended Nazi leaders for the crime of genocide, the name that
was given to the mass murder of whole peoples.*

In the face of irreversible defeat, twenty-nine of the major
Nazi leaders had already committed suicide, and four had disappeared. Hitler and his mistress, after a macabre wedding ceremony, died in the bunker under the Berlin Chancellery. Goebbels and his wife had their six young children injected with

---

*The word was coined by Rafael Lemkin in his *Axis Rule in Occupied Europe*,
Carnegie Endowment for International Peace, Washington, D.C., 1944,
republished in 1976.

poison, and then were shot by an SS orderly. Himmler made an unsuccessful attempt to arrange a deal with the Allied command, then bit into a phial of cyanide. Martin Bormann, another Hitler confidante, fled as the Russians closed in, but though rumors kept surfacing that he had been sighted in various foreign hideouts, there was reasonable evidence that he had not gone far beyond the bunker before he was killed. Adolf Eichmann, one of the principal administrators of the Final Solution, managed to remain at large for almost fifteen years but was tracked down in the Argentine by a team of Israelis in a sensational kidnapping.* Hundreds of lesser lights, the detritus after a catastrophe, also eluded rope and bullet by committing suicide.

Twenty-two of the master planners had been captured and were brought before the Tribunal in Nuremberg, in its Palace of Justice. The trial was to drag on for 284 days, from November 25, 1945, into October of the following year. Actually, only twenty-one sat in the dock; Dr. Robert Ley, who headed the Labor Front, hanged himself in his cell just as the legal proceedings began.

Even before the trial was underway, there were sharp misgivings about its legal validity. International courts had been functioning since early in the century at Geneva and at The Hague, but these had been empowered only to arbitrate disputes between countries, not to try individuals. Was it not a travesty, some observers asked, for a court of victors to dignify vengeance with the habiliments of due process?

At the outset, the Russians and British were inclined to oppose the idea of international trials. Stalin, brooding over twenty million Russian dead, thought it nonsense to go through with what he regarded as pantomime. He argued for quick execution of accused war criminals and almost invariably acted on the option when Nazi leaders were apprehended in the Russian jurisdiction. Churchill and Eden also felt that it would be unseemly cant to follow a barbarous war with sanctimoniousness. They knew well what their fate would have been if the roles had been reversed: their names had headed the Nazis' Black List for summary execution.

---

*The kidnapping, trial, and execution are detailed in the latter part of this chapter.

But Franklin Roosevelt and his advisers demurred. They believed that execution without trial would transform gangsters into martyrs and would provide shrines for future propaganda rallies. Besides, the primary objective of the international trial was not to validate foregone judgments but to get the story of the unprecedented evil on record, from the mouths of the criminals themselves. The purpose of Nuremberg was to identify and punish those who had ordered or committed torture and murder unrelated to the prosecution of the war. Where the evidence was not sufficient to prove complicity, the defendants would not be convicted. The only imperative was for the trial to be conducted with every legal safeguard for the accused so that judgment would be rendered on the basis of confirmed evidence.

One embarrassment could not be avoided: the Russian presence in the court. Before the war, the Russians had been in a devil's compact with the Nazis. They had devoured the Baltic and Balkan states. Stalin had ordered the massacre of more than 10,000 Polish officers in the Katyn Forest. How, reasonably, could Russian judges, always in military uniform, sit among the gowned representatives of the courts of England, the United States, and France, to try aggressors for "crimes against humanity"? Airey Neave, a young British officer attached to the Tribunal staff, suspected that, of the two Russian judges, one was a secret agent set to watch the other![1] The Russians, while they made no secret of their contempt for the democracies' naivete and obsession with "fairness," would not, however, submit to exclusion. So the trial was undertaken with eight judges to represent the eighteen nations that had fought the Nazis.

In the bombed-out city of Nuremberg, which had so often been the site of flamboyant Nazi rallies, the accused sat in the prisoners' rows in the Palace of Justice. It was difficult now to identify them as the powerful men whose words had sealed the fate of millions, and whose actions had kept the world in terror. One American correspondent sized up the "fallen eagles" as just a "seedy assortments of soldiers, rowdies, bureaucrats . . . who had broken every law, human and divine, and now sought refuge in legalism."[2] Rebecca West, covering the trial, limned memorable descriptions of the deflated power-mongers, who "defined themselves by oddity rather than character." Hermann Goering, long the Deputy Führer, was likened to "the fat women with their sleek cats seen in the late morning in doorways along the steep streets of Munich." Rudolf Hess, another

Hitler deputy, who had spent most of the war years as a prisoner in England, "sat in a lunatic daze." Hjalmar Schacht, who manipulated the Nazi voodoo economics, his demeanor questioning the right of the victors to try him, was "stiff as an iron stag in the garden of an old house." Julius Streicher, whose publication, *Der Stürmer*, reeked of anti-Semitism, seemed "a dirty old man of the sort that gives trouble in parks." And Seyss-Inquart, who had been Gauleiter in The Netherlands, looked like a "thin-lipped monster, the murderer with a whip."[3] One of the American reporters noted how frightened Ribbentrop was throughout: "Even his cough contained a shudder."

Through the trials, what emerged with hyaline clarity was that the abuses and massacres were not acts of irrationality, bursts of hatred from offscourings of the gutter raised to authority. They were deliberately planned by a major government to terrorize dissidents and to eliminate any who threatened the racially pure Nazi society. It was this incontrovertible conclusion that impelled Hans Frank, who had been Gauleiter of Poland, to break down before he was led to the scaffold after judgment. He sobbed, "a thousand years will pass and still Germany's guilt will not be erased.*

Attorneys for the defense appropriated the arguments advanced by concerned jurists in the Allied countries, that the Tribunal, representing "military victors," was a fraud. Further, they argued, their clients had been bound by "sacred vows" of obedience. Riveted to their oaths, it was not for them to question the Führer's authority, or the orders that came from his appointed deputies. There was no alternative to complete compliance unless one were prepared to court certain personal disaster. Significantly, "the higher authorities"—Hitler, Goering, Goebbels, Himmler—who were invariably cited were those who, with the exception of Goering, were now dead and could be reviled with impunity. As his honor-bound comrades testified, Goering kept glowering in the dock, muttering "Schweinehund." A British journalist covering the trial noted that Goering, to the end, was "an unashamedly, unrepentant gangster."[4]

---

*The diary of Frau Frank described impassively the administration of her husband and the gruesome activities that elicited his belated *mea culpa*. The original diary is in the archival collection of Nazi documents at Brandeis University.

The main summation of evidence was presented by Robert Jackson of the U.S. Supreme Court. Some of Justice Jackson's associates had argued that it was inappropriate for a member of the U.S. Supreme Court to participate in the Tribunal proceedings. Similar objections were to be offered later, when Justice Owen Roberts was drafted for the trials of the Japanese warlords, and when a reluctant Chief Justice Earl Warren was commanded by President Johnson to head the commission to investigate the assassination of President Kennedy. But Justice Jackson had been eager to serve at Nuremberg, and he worked with his aides to reconcile the diverse national legal traditions that had to be respected.

Jackson ridiculed the claim that the Tribunal was a kangaroo court whose *ex post facto* proceedings were applied to defendants for actions that had never before been identified as crimes. There was no comparison, Jackson said, between the military procedures of the Germans who had fought World War I and the inhuman behavior of the Nazis who had laid Europe waste. Furthermore, because there had been misgivings about *ex post facto* judgment, scrupulous regard had been given to due process. Every avenue of defense had remained open to the accused. Jackson asked for verdicts based primarily on evidence offered by the defendants themselves. His characterizations of the culprits emphasized barbarity rather than illegality: Walther Funk, "who banked the gold that was extracted from the teeth of gas chamber victims in probably the most ghoulish collateral in banking history," and Fritz Sauckel, "the greatest and cruelest slaver since the Pharaohs of Egypt." Referring to rules of evidence that had protected the defendants' rights, Jackson said that the Allies "had provided them the kind of trial which in the days of their pomp and power, they never gave to any man."

> We are not trying them [the accused] for possession of obnoxious ideas. The intellectual bankruptcy and moral perversion of the Nazi regime might have been no concern of international law had it not been *used* to goosestep the *Herrenvolk* across international frontiers. It is not their thoughts, it is their overt acts, which we charge to be the crimes.[5]

Jackson called upon Rudolf Hoess, commandant at Auschwitz, to testify about the statistics of extermination that had not been believed when revealed by escaped survivors: 34,000 human beings gassed and burned daily in two shifts, with an ultimate toll of three and a half million victims in the Auschwitz camps alone. Hoess's orders had been signed by Wilhelm von Keitel, now in the prisoners' dock, who hung his head while Hoess droned out the statistics. The Tribunal had to be adjourned many times when survivors, reciting their experiences, were excused to recover their composure.

The verdicts were reached quickly, on October 1, 1946. The prosecution had avoided, where it could, allegations of aggression, recognizing that such charges could be leveled by victors against vanquished in any war. There was almost exclusive concentration on evidence of mass inhumanity. On the basis of these charges alone, all of the defendants except the banker Schacht, the "diplomat" Franz von Papen, and Goebbels' public relations aide, Hans Fritzsche, were found guilty. Eleven were sentenced to death by hanging; the others received terms of imprisonment ranging from a few years to life.

Von Papen was acquitted not because he had early fallen out of Hitler's favor, but because it was judged that there was insufficient evidence to link him with "inhuman" behavior. But outraged anti-Nazi elements in Germany could not forgive him for his role in bringing Hitler to power. After his acquittal by the Tribunal, a lynching was threatened, and Von Papen had to remain in American custody until he could be whisked away to safety. He was rearrested, tried by German courts, and sentenced to eight years imprisonment in a labor camp where he was beaten up by fellow prisoners who had been incarcerated for civil felonies. He was released in January 1949 and, shunning public appearances, was permitted to live out shabby and inglorious years.

Fritzsche had been an assistant to Goebbels, a cog in the Nazi propaganda apparatus, and he hardly belonged among the major defendants. The judges concluded that what the media concocted in the heat of wartime passions could not be legally classed as criminal behavior. Here, too, the first German denazification courts took a sterner view. When tried by them, in 1949, Fritzsche was sentenced to nine years at hard labor, but was pardoned after three years and succumbed to the agonies of cancer.

The two admirals, Erich Raeder and Karl Doenitz, did not ask for leniency. Raeder, at seventy, pleaded in vain to be shot. He was sentenced to life imprisonment. After a few years even the

Russians relented to let the old man, hobbling on two canes, move into a new democratic Germany that he neither recognized nor understood. Doenitz had been named by Hitler as his successor, a hollow honor, since the appointment was announced while the Führer was trapped in his bunker and the Third Reich was everywhere in ruins. He had been included in the criminal company because he was accused of violating the international military code when he made no attempt to rescue British survivors in U-boat engagements. To the end Doenitz maintained his adoration of Der Führer as beyond criticism: "Compared with him we others are worms." He was sentenced to ten years.

The failure of the Tribunal to impose any punishment on Schacht created widespread indignation, most of all among the officials of the successor government that was striving for international rehabilitation. Schacht was immediately rearrested and tried in a German court, but was again freed. The travesty was not lost on the survivors of the Holocaust that the "money man" retired to a secure old age, serving as adviser in financial affairs in the governments of Syria, Egypt, Iran, and Indonesia.

Fritz Sauckel had worked under Albert Speer, Hitler's Minister of Armaments, and had carried out his chief's orders to round up masses of foreign workers as slave labor for the German war machine. His directive had been blunt and direct, to exploit this labor "to the highest possible extent and the lowest conceivable degree of expenditure."[6] Speer was given a twenty-year sentence but Sauckel was condemned to death by hanging. Bewildered by the verdict, Sauckel said, "I have never been cruel myself." He had good reason to wonder at Speer's escape from the noose though the Russians had argued strenuously for execution. The evidence had been clear that Speer had planned and supervised the war economy and had approved the acquisition of building materials for barracks for 132,000 Auschwitz inmates.

Hugh Trevor-Roper believed, from this evidence, that Speer was the real criminal of Nazi Germany, who sat at every center of political power: "He had a cold precise mind but no regard for human suffering."[7] Bargaining for his life he sold out his fellow prisoners, identifying their complicity in war crimes, and he revealed to the prosecutors his conversations with Hitler that expedited the Final Solution. The prosecution treated his craven conduct with contempt, but his revelatory evidence was valuable and the twenty-year sentence was a tradeoff. When released, Speer wrote a book, *Inside the Third Reich*, with heavy advance royalties, in which he expressed regret that he had "not given attention to what was happening to the Jews." A new generation, removed by twenty years from the barbarities of the Holocaust, treated him as a celebrity—"Just imagine, he actually knew Hitler personally!" Speer garnered a fortune from interviews, lectures, TV appearances, articles, and book royalties, and a Harvard professor, Eugene Davidson, wrote an introduction for the Speer memoirs, extolling the decency of the repentant sinner.[8] In a novel by Günter Grass, *Dog Years*, one of the characters develops an intriguing invention, a pair of magical spectacles which, when worn by the young, enables them to look back into the past and to note what their parents were doing then.

Rudolph Hess, Hitler's Deputy Führer, had fled to Britain at the outset of World War II and the mystery of his flight was never solved. Had he hoped to persuade Chamberlain to accept a compromise peace so that Germany could apply its full strength to the destruction of Russia? Had he become disenchanted with the Führer and sought asylum in Britain? Not even highly expert British psychiatrists could agree on his likely motive. Imprisoned in Britain through the war years, he was returned for trial in Nuremberg. He was given a life sentence in Spandau, the prison in West Berlin administered by all four of the wartime Allies. He outlived all of his confederates and became the prison's sole ward. After twenty-five years the western Allies found him no longer dangerous and were ready to release him, but the Russians remained adamant whenever appeals for release were presented. At this writing (1983) Hess still haunts the virtually empty prison.*

Walther Funk, a former senior editor of Germany's leading financial newspaper, the *Berliner Boersenseitung*, had succeeded Schacht as Minister of the Economy. Schacht described him as a harmless homosexual and a drunkard, who brought a "Ja, mein Führer" approach to his task. He had drawn up the 1938 laws

---

*Recently another theory has attained wide currency. It suggests that Hess was in the employ of the Russians and explains their determination to keep him incommunicado at Spandau lest, in freedom, some of his disclosures might prove highly embarrassing.

that expelled the Jews from German economic life; during the concentration camp years he loaded the vaults of the Reichsbank, where he was president, with gold teeth torn from the mouths of those who had been shot or gassed. "When they are dead," he told his Nuremberg guard, "it is easier." In the dock, often weeping, he acted the contrite penitent, babbling endlessly his regret that he had not restrained the behavior of the "fanatics." "I placed the will of the State before my own conscience and my inner sense of duty," he sobbed. His fellow prisoners hung their heads as he spoke. He was given life imprisonment but was released in 1956 when the prison physicians testified that he was suffering from a terminal cancer.

The twelve who were condemned to die went to their execution on October 12 and 13, trying for a show of stoic courage, but many of them caved in at the last moment.* Streicher had to be dragged to the gallows in his underwear, screaming: "Purim Feast, 1946!"† There were flurries of criticism from those who opposed capital punishment even for the Nazi defendants, and indignation because the hangings were marred by technical inefficiencies that broke the noses and bloodied some of the condemned as they hurtled through the trap door. After the executions, the ovens of Dachau were relit, the bodies of the condemned were cremated, and the ashes strewn over the River Iser, though the identity of the river was not made public until many years later.

The proceedings of the historic trial, published in English, French, and German, required forty-two volumes. It was expected that the monumental record would become a research archive for all the future. There had been fear that a legend, feeding on ersatz glory, might surface to provide a rallying point for neo-Nazism. The memory of Hitler did survive, but it was, with some exceptions, a memory of barbarity, a warning of what Germany henceforth must avoid. For more than a generation the Nazis had fostered the canard that the Jews had been

---

*Goering swallowed cyanide that had been smuggled to him just before his intended execution.

†A reference to the Jewish holiday that commemorated the hanging of Haman, a notorious anti-Semite of the fifth century B.C. who had plotted the extermination of the Jews in Persia but was hanged on the gallows he had prepared for Mordecai, his Jewish court rival.

responsible for Germany's disastrous defeat in World War I and that they were a bacillus that had to be exterminated. In a moment of rare candor, Chancellor Adenauer, who eventually inherited the wreckage to which Hitler had reduced the country, referred to the generation that had capitulated to the Führer as "carnivorous sheep." He knew the dangers of a fickle public opinion, and the long-range effects of hate and envy. His primary historic obligation was not to resurrect a blasted economy, though that was also a priority, nor to restore national respect in the councils of the nations, though that called for singular imagination. His most challenging task was to make sure that the lust for world power, the corrupting myth of Aryan supremacy, would be diffused with the ashes of the criminals of Nuremberg and those who had listened to their call.

After the Military Tribunal judgments of 1946, there were totally dissimilar responses from the Soviet government and its satellites and the western Allies to their pledges that there would be other trials to reach beyond the major war criminals for accountability. The Russians never relented in pursuit of the commandants and of their retainers, who had willingly followed the directives of their chiefs. As the Red Armies made their way back to the home areas that had fallen to German occupation, every region turned up mass graves. Their shoes kicked up the ashes of the dead in the crematoria where millions had perished. One of the poets of Leningrad, who had survived a thousand days of starvation blockade, wrote: "Let no one forget; let nothing be forgiven."

Hence, in the early months of the reconquest, the Russians rarely took prisoners and devoted little attention to the prosecution of cases in courts of law. Only after the first spate of wholesale military executions did they turn to arrests; the prisoners were usually given just enough time before sentence to offer confessions. The persistent hunt continued right up to the present, by which time only a few old fugitives, protected in exile, remained on a most-wanted list.

The satellite countries followed the Soviet model. Once the native Communists had established their control of Poland, they made short shrift of the Nazi functionaries who fell into their hands. After all, it was on Polish soil that Auschwitz, Treblinka, Belsen, Belzec, Maidanek, and scores of other death camps had exacted their fearsome toll. When the Polish courts turned to

deal with the accused ringleaders, there were nearly 2,500 con-
victions that brought 630 sentences of death, with long prison
terms for most of the others. Ludwig Fisher and Rudolph Hoess
of Auschwitz were executed in 1947. SS General Jurgen von
Stroop, who had suppressed the Warsaw Ghetto rebellion, was
hanged in 1951. Overall the Polish tribunals called to account
about 40,000 Nazis and their collaborators. Where there were
delays of several years in meting out punishment, they occurred
because some of the murderers were so skillfully hidden and
protected that it took undeviating persistence to flush them out.

In the western zones, after the Military Tribunal at Nuremberg was over, the determination of most of the occupying authorities to track down war criminals soon cooled. Even during
the trial, after the early weeks of dramatic evidence, the crowds
of spectators dwindled. Horror loses its impact as sensitivity is
blunted by repetition. Rebecca West noted that the proceedings
turned into "a water torture, boredom falling drop by drop on
the same spot on the soul."[9] The American officials had no wish
to be saddled with the continuing responsibility and expense of
trying thousands of lesser functionaries. They preferred to let
the West German and Austrian courts deal with them.

In the first denazification years after 1945, these German
courts, reorganized to eliminate, as far as possible, any Nazi
taint, brought in verdicts that reflected their desire to satisfy the
occupying powers. More than 5,000 of the accused were convicted and death sentences were carried out for about 500. There
were twelve trials in Nuremberg itself, from 1946 to 1949. Some
of them made international headlines for they involved many of
the commandants of the extermination camps and their chief
aides. In the trials in Dachau, more than 1,500 people were
judged guilty of inhuman behavior and 278 were executed.

But after 1947, when the Cold War shifted alliances and West
Germany was welcomed into an anti-Russian bloc, further trials
were no longer pressed, and there were only perfunctory efforts
to capture criminals who had fled and were living under new
identities in Spain, the Argentine, Egypt, and other countries
that offered asylum, tacitly or otherwise. The most influential
elements in Germany began to insist that the time had come to
bury or play down the past. What purpose, they asked, was to
be served in perpetuating "resentments"? For that matter, many
of the government officials and the judges, too, had records that

might not read too well if the scrutiny were thorough. They joined in the move toward *Totschweigen,* hushing up the tragedy of death.

There were also technical problems. Witnesses were now scattered throughout the world and it was difficult to persuade many of them to return, especially those who never again wanted to set foot in the land that evoked such sorrowful memories. Many who would have gone through the ordeal of the trials, if only to help bring the murderers of their families to justice, were old and ill. Some of the few who still lived in Germany and Austria feared that, if they served as witnesses, they might lay themselves open to the reprisals of only superficially denazified neighbors. Hence, only when an occasional notorious culprit was tracked down and identified did the provincial governments, or Bonn itself, feel compelled by the pressure of world opinion to bring the accused to trial.

Nor were the French or the British government officials—busy wrestling with somersault international diplomacy in which former enemies and friends became allies and adversaries—eager to complicate their foreign affairs by keeping the war resentments alive. The French largely limited their quest for punishment to collaborators who had acquiesced in or, indeed, promoted the enslavement of their own people by yielding to Hitler's threats. Since there was no reliable test to determine who had acted under compulsion and who had gladly embraced a vassal status in the Fascist order, there were only scattered trials. A few of the most notorious killers were executed, but most of the convicted were let off with cosmetic prison terms, soon commuted.

Two major cases, however, demonstrated how deeply the infamy of Vichy had corroded the national spirit. They brought to the dock the former prime ministers Marshal Henri Pétain and Pierre Laval. These were the men who had quickly capitulated to Hitler. It could be argued, as they did, that they had no choice if they were to save their country from the destruction suffered by Holland and other lands where even token resistance was avenged with utter desolation. But they could not be forgiven for agreeing to send large numbers of their own people into foreign lands for slave labor. They had gone far beyond the pressure of compulsion in enforcing anti-Jewish legislation and deportations, filling the Drancy concentration camp with uprooted Jewish families, very few of whom survived. Pétain was dealt with leniently, for it was remembered that he had been a heroic figure in World War I. He was sentenced to death, but he was already in his late eighties and there was little indignation when General de Gaulle commuted the sentence to exile and nominal imprisonment. Pétain did not long survive.

All the pent-up hatreds, however, exploded in the trial of Pierre Laval. He had set up many courts to destroy his political enemies; now he faced one himself. The scenes recalled a lynching. The jurors took turns shouting at him, vilifying him as a renegade, a swine, a scoundrel. Laval was condemned to death and, after a thwarted attempt at suicide, was carried half-conscious to the execution post and shot as a traitor.

In the British Occupied Zone, the main trials were conducted in Lüneberg, Hamburg, and Wuppertal, and the accused numbered about 1,000 men and women whose ruthlessness could not be hidden behind pleas of coercion; 290 were condemned to death. Retribution finally overtook Josef Kramer, "the Beast of Belsen," who had topped his reputation for acts of barbarism by shipping the corpses of one hundred Jewish prisoners to the German scientists at the Reich Anatomical Institute to add to their anthropological and racial skeleton collections. But once the most notorious criminals had been punished, even Winston Churchill, who had vowed that there could never be amnesty for wanton murder, modified his sense of outrage and called for a fresh start. "Draw a sponge across the crimes and horrors of the past," he said, "and look for the sake of all our salvation towards the future. There can be no revival of Europe without the active and loyal aid of all the German tribes."*

Only the Dutch, among the western Allies, refused to allow time to grass over the crimes of the war criminals. Their hunt was persistent. The evidence presented in the Doctor's Trial in The Hague shocked even those who had been sated by the endless tales of horror. There was national satisfaction when Hans Rauter, the police chief in Holland, was flushed out in 1948, tried in The Hague court, and hanged.

---

*The use of the term "the German tribes" would seem to indicate that the sponge did not completely erase his contempt.

Initially the Americans, or rather, a small circle of associates close to President Truman, were determined not to let the wartime pledges lapse. They were deeply concerned, not so much with legally ordained punishment as with guarantees that the German lords of finance and industry would never again be able to exert the influence that had brought Hitler and his minions to power and enslaved the western world. Since the British and the French were reluctant to treat civilian cartelists as war criminals, Truman, as soon as he became President, authorized General Telford Taylor, a chief counsel at the Nuremberg International Tribunal, to organize a task force to gather evidence of financial and industrial complicity.

Taylor and his chief aides, James Martin and Josiah DuBois, Jr., soon found themselves in a quagmire of dilatory maneuvers. When General Lucius Clay's office distributed a questionnaire to four hundred sections of the American military government, requesting relevant information and evidence, there were only two replies. Clay's chief of staff explained that the almost complete disregard of the directive was not the result of apathy or ineptitude. He wrote: "They [the occupation military government] are responsible for the apprehension and extradition of actual war criminals and have no direct responsibility in connection with German business leaders and industrialists."[10] Indictments were filed but were pressed only when there was widely publicized evidence that the financiers and "the smoke stack barons" were guilty of slave labor practices and other abuses that just stopped short of actually pushing the victims into the gas chambers. Taylor wrote later that there was damning evidence that would easily have convicted thousands of civilian collaborators whose brutality matched their greed.[11] But though he and a zealous staff followed every clue, only twelve trials were authorized. They resulted in the conviction of the directors of six corporate entities who were given nominal sentences, soon thereafter commuted by General John McCloy, High Commissioner for American Occupied Germany.

The rationale most frequently offered for the retributive pledge turnabout was that, after 1946, the Soviet Union had become the more dangerous enemy, and the resources of a reconstructed Germany were indispensable in the effort to halt Communist aggression. Indeed, even before the war had ended, there was intense competition between the western Allies and the Russians to obtain the services of German scientists who could be helpful in strengthening postwar military establishments. An elaborate operation that went far beyond "forgive and forget" was launched by American military officials, and scores of German experts were courted and "signed up" to apply their skills to expand the American arsenal. A correspondent noted that in the last period of the war, the United States and Russia began playing "a sinister game of hide and seek . . . and behaved far more like enemies than allies."[12] Werner von Braun, the German rocket expert, and his Peenemünde team, whose V-2 rockets had nearly pounded Britain into submission, were welcomed to the United States and given citizenship and high honors as they set to work on guided missiles. Rabbi Stephen Wise, head of the American Jewish Congress, said with deep concern: "As long as we reward former servants of Hitler while leaving his victims in Displaced Persons' Camps, we cannot even pretend that we are making any real effort to achieve the aims we fought for."

Investigators appointed by the Truman administration to gather evidence for use in the trials that were to follow the Nuremberg Military Tribunal hearings, in summarizing their experiences, made it clear that the emergence of the Cold War was not the only factor in creating the climate that favored general amnesty or nominal punishment.[13] In their reports and in later memoirs they emphasized that the compelling influence was the intercession of Allied industrialists and heads of banking syndicates who sought the speedy reestablishment of working relationships with those who had been their cartel affiliates. Even during the war period, legal maneuvers were employed to prevent the disruption of "business as usual." To some highly placed American industrialists, and law firms who resorted to pettifogging even when their country was in mortal peril, enmities were apparently transient political digressions that could not be permitted to block the resumption of routine sale-and-profit cooperation. Many who had the closest professional connections with German conglomerates and their legal counsel came to Washington as "dollar a year men" to assume policy positions in the stepped-up war production program. When the hostilities were ended, some of them moved up to policy posts at the Navy, War, and Defense departments, even into State. There was clear evidence that they consciously or unconsciously circumvented attempts to punish their prewar associates or used their influence to restore their German industrial

empires. Just before America entered the war, the German cartelists had employed skillful legal talent to incorporate the
American affiliates, usually in the state of Delaware, to gain
protection for their holdings from seizure as alien enemy property. Now, the hostilities over, they instituted proceedings to
retrieve legal title and to reincorporate crucial resources under
German control. This policy of switching ownerships was referred to by the Justice Department investigators as the "New
German Christmas Tree economy."[14]

In his memoir, James Martin named names and cases, describing in detail the strategems employed. There had been a trial,
in the summer of 1942, of eight Nazi saboteurs who had landed
in America with the mission to blow up some of the key factories of the United States. The strictest security was maintained
in bringing the prisoners daily to their trial. But, as Martin
notes, the intended sabotage of the accused was in reality quite
peripheral. There were legal agreements between German and
American producers of magnesium, indispensable to aircraft,
that severely limited production in the United States. Germany
in 1939 produced 13,500 tons of magnesium and during the war
nearly tripled its tonnage; the United States had been limited to
5,000 tons and it took the toughest legal battles, during the war
period, to effect an increase in production. There were no facilities ready to effect any major increase. Martin writes: "Plants
which have never been built are more dead than plants which
have been bombed, for there are no blueprints and no trained
labor force to move into action. . . . Here was a case, where
American 'business is business' men had, knowingly or un-
knowingly, helped a German firm to close some valves over
here, with far more effect than the eight saboteurs could ever
have achieved even if they had been allowed to do their utmost."* It took the combined pressure of the War Department,
the Navy Department, and the War Production Board to suspend the restrictions that affected industries considered important in the war effort.[15]

Martin offered an equally shocking example that described

---

*There is no intention to cast aspersions on any of the current executive
officers of those corporations, which during the war period and the years that
immediately followed, sponsored activity on the borderline of technical legality.

how the Department of Justice in 1942 had to resort to court battle to restrain Standard Oil of New Jersey from sharing technological information and joining in patent pooling arrangements with the American affiliate of I. G. Farben, one of Hitler's strongest industrial assets. Immediately after the war Standard Oil sued the Alien Property Custodian to recover ownership of 2,000 patents that it claimed were bought from the German firm just before the outbreak of war and, as "American" property, ought never to have been seized. But the investigators, after a long search, discovered cabinets with secret files that had been hidden in an underground air-raid shelter in the Harz mountain area. The records revealed that the "sale" to Standard Oil had been a subterfuge. The documents contained an agreement, signed by Frank Howard on behalf of Standard Oil, in a secret meeting at The Hague, that I. G. Farben could redeem the property "when it was safe and convenient." During the trial another document was flushed out that was marked *"Nach Kriegs Kamouflage"* (Postwar Camouflage). The Circuit Court of Appeals dismissed the claims of Standard Oil in unusually sharp language: "The Court found that these were sham transactions designed to create an appearance of Jersey ownership of property interests which nevertheless continued to be regarded by the parties as I. G. owned. The parties intended that after completion of the war and the resulting disappearance of the danger of United States Government controls, the property would be formally returned to I. G. and the prewar relationship resumed." The court added a vigorous reprimand of Standard Oil's president, Frank Howard, as "not a credible witness."[16] The Standard Oil attorney was not prosecuted for perjury.

A more spectacular three-way arrangement was exposed that involved aircraft equipment manufactured by Bendix of the United States, Siemens of Germany, and Zenith of England. The American firm had an agreement with the Siemens firm, still binding as late as 1941, that forbade Zenith to grant licenses so that the Allies could expand their production of aircraft carburetors.[17] The consequence of limiting production even as the war clouds gathered was substantial and costly. After the United States became a belligerent, the attempts to modify agreements that interfered with the war operations required drawn-out litigation. As soon as hostilities ended, action was instituted to reinstate the prewar arrangements; in most instances, it was successful. Legal and banking talent that had served prewar Germany, now in United States government posts, emerged as leading opponents of appropriate punishment for the crimes and excesses of the war. It was John McCloy, an American lawyer turned banker who had been named High Commissioner for Occupied Germany, who, in 1951, commuted the death and prison sentences of all the convicted bankers and industrialists and signed the documents that returned their empires to I. G. Farben, Siemens, and Krupp.

Another example pointed up practices that moved very close to treason. When the United States entered World War II, security measures were intensified for American ships that carried men and supplies to the war fronts. Millions of dollars were spent on all forms of surveillance. Yet American ships were sunk, often before they had proceeded far beyond the loading ports. It seemed that German intelligence had penetrated the secrecy and obtained precise information about the movement of the ships and the location and operation of the expanded war plants. But we now know that such highly classified information was not gained through astute German spy work. The ships, the plants, the war materiel, had all been heavily insured. Following the usual practice where major risk is involved, the underwriting was shared by insurance affiliates in European countries who took fractional shares. There were firms in neutral Luxembourg and Switzerland that were branch offices of major German companies, centered mainly in Munich. The location of the American war plants, blueprints of their structure, the ship cargoes, their value, the dates of their sailing plans, were all carefully documented and sent on to the European firms for reinsurance. The Luxembourg and Zurich branches of the German firms received much of this business, and had no trouble in keeping the German high command informed. Attempts to stop the flow of such information were ensnarled in red tape. Martin described how, in the summer of 1945, he came upon the files of the Munich Reinsurance Company, "bundles of photographs, blueprints, and detailed descriptions of whole industrial developments in the U.S., many of them obtained through insurance channels."[18]

Even before cases of this sort kept surfacing, President Roosevelt, in the fall of 1944, wrote an urgent letter to the Secretary of State, Cordell Hull, exclaiming that "The history of the I. G. Farben trust by the Nazis reads like a detective story. Defeat of the Nazi armies will have to be followed by the eradication of these weapons of economic warfare." But when the war ended, the high-priced American lawyers who had long represented the German cartels, went into action to influence the decision that businessmen were not to be listed as war criminals. The Roosevelt warning was consigned to a filing cabinet and the cartels were back in business.

If such covert practice could be lost in the maze of bureaucratic idiocy, it is easier to understand the vexation of the investigators when their most damning evidence—in the cases of Siemens, Holske, Stinnes Industries, Mannesmann, Rohrenwerke A. B., and scores of other involved cartels that siphoned profits from the bodies of their slave laborers—were cavalierly dismissed "because there was not enough concrete indictable evidence." Martin summed up his frustrating experiences in a weary statement: "After two and a half years [attempting to advance the prosecution for war crimes of the cartelists] I came back from Germany quite well aware that I had been wrestling with a buzz saw. We had not been stopped in Germany by German business. We had been stopped in Germany by American business."[19]

The trials of Friedrich Flick of the Stahlverein, of I. G. Farben, and of the Krupp dynasty, and the token verdicts that resulted, may be considered as prime examples of the international power of the great cartels before, during, and after the war.

Friedrich Flick, who enjoyed being called Friedrich der Grosse, had built his Stahlverein, the monumental steel union, by ruthless competitive practices in Germany and by plundering European competitors in conquered countries. He added industrial companies to his empire as sedulously as any coin collector. His conglomerate, one of the world's largest, included everything from iron and coal products to dynamite, plastics, and automobiles. To achieve its ever-mounting quotas, Stahlverein indentured thousands of Poles, Russians, and Jews as slave laborers. One of the few 350-calorie-a-day survivors noted how much worse than slaves they were treated in the chain gangs. Slaves, he commented, were at least property who, however little regarded, were protected as production assets. "We, on the other hand, were like a bit of sandpaper which, rubbed a few times, becomes useless and is thrown away to be burned with the garbage." Flick blandly offered the conventional defense: "My actions were forced. Failure to meet quotas risked severe punishment. I had no animus to Jews. I had to howl with the wolves." The investigators countered his disclaimers with piles of documents that verified how he regularly initiated the demands for the slave laborers.[20]

The verdict after a six-month trial came down in June 1947 and it stunned the prosecution, for whom the case was a test for the others to follow. The judges accepted the pleas of the defendants that any lack of cooperation would have subjected them to severe penalties; that though their profits from compliance were enormous, they were hostages chained to the Führer's will. No sentence was severe. Flick was given seven years, some directors a few more, some a few less. The imprisonment at Landsberg was country-club style. There were regular visits for staff consultations with Flick's attorneys and bankers. Hermann Abs, Flick's chief aide, holding one of the highest positions in the Deutsche Bank, had been condemned to death in absentia in a Yugoslavian court for fueling the Nazi outrages in the Balkans. But, tried also in a German court, he had escaped punishment when it was ruled that he could not be held responsible for the use to which the bank loans had been put. After his acquittal in Germany, Abs retained his key position in the bank and continued to counsel the Flick directorate on plans after an expected commutation of Flick's sentence.

The release by General McCloy came in 1951, when less than half of Flick's sentence had been served. His directors too were freed and the far-flung holdings of the empire were returned. McCloy's rationale fitted the new international climate. During the trial the Flick defense team had insisted that Communists were the chief threat to private enterprise and that the German effort had been concentrated on stopping them. Who better than the efficient German industrialists could manage the effort in the renewed bitter competition with the Russians? Within a few years, Flick was in control of over 150 companies. McCloy had hoped that Flick, now seventy-six, would exhibit a modicum of compassion by offering some token compensation to survivors, those against whom he had avowed "no personal animus," most of them ill and poverty-stricken. Modest claims were made on their behalf; but Flick grimly refused to pay out a single mark to any of them or their families. He died in 1963, at eighty-nine, one of Europe's most influential billionaires.[21]

The pressure for leniency was equally persistent in the case of the I. G. Farben cartel. Martin and his staff built a solid case of I. G. Farben plunder and abuse, perpetrated primarily in Austria, Poland, and France, as it appropriated the facilities for every variety of chemical product. When the empire invested 900 million Reichsmark in a plant for the manufacture of gas (for the extermination chambers) and the production of synthetic rubber, slave labor was so urgently needed that it was deemed most practical to establish I. G. Auschwitz, a special adjacent subcamp, to house the workers. I. G. Farben paid the SS Corps 3 Reichsmarks daily for unskilled labor, 4 marks for skilled, and 1.5 marks for children. The overall coordinator of the project confessed at the trial that Kapos were selected from among professional criminals in Auschwitz and other concentration camps. The laborers were treated with such pitilessness that the average rate of survival was three months.

The I. G. Farben directors were unabashed. Gathering data before the trial, Martin confronted one of the vice presidents, Baron von Schnitzler. Martin's investigative visit was greeted with aplomb. The record of brutality that Martin read to Schnitzler was interpreted as no more than the expected conventional give and take of war. Schnitzler expressed relief that "all this unpleasantness is over" and looked forward to the "renewal of friendship" with his old cartel colleagues. As the trial proceeded, one of the judges, drawn from a local court in North Dakota, remarked: "We have to worry about the Russians now. It wouldn't surprise me if they overran the courtroom before we are through."[22]

The verdict on I. G. Farben, announced in July 1948, followed the pattern in the Flick case. All but one of the judges accepted the plea of the defendants that they could not oppose the practices in the work camps without risking life or status. Carl Krauch, inventor of the Bosch magnets, and head of the I. G. Farben empire, claimed ignorance of the abuses of the I. G. Auschwitz workers. He received a sentence of six years, also only partially served. DuBois, another of Taylor's aides, commented that the sentence was light enough to please a chicken thief or a driver who had irresponsibly run down a pedestrian, and concluded that Krauch, whom he described as "a general in a grey suit," must have held only an honorific title and was really just the office boy emeritus.*

Léon Blum, returning to the premiership of France after his imprisonment in a Nazi concentration camp, observed wryly that the only real internationalists were the bankers and the industrialists, whose cartels inevitably placed profit above patriotism. He could not have offered more convincing proof than in the disposition of the charges against the House of Krupp. For nearly a century the Krupps had been the armament kings of Germany, their influence in international affairs only briefly interrupted by the German defeat in World War I. There was quick reemergence in the early thirties when Germany violated its treaty obligations and began surreptitiously to rearm.

Gustav Krupp directed the empire during Hitler's rise to power; but since he suffered a stroke in 1942, his son Alfried, well trained for succession, took over the management of the empire and became the Third Reich armorer during the Nazi conquests on the continent. When the list of war criminals to be tried at Nuremberg was drawn up, Justice Jackson, not too well briefed, mistakenly included Gustav's name instead of Alfried's. After the error was discovered, Jackson attempted to substitute Alfried's name, but the British jurists insisted on adhering to procedures and ruled that a substitution would be illegal. It was therefore agreed that, when the promised separate trials for the industrialists were set, Alfried Krupp and his directors would be placed high on the list to face prosecution.

Taylor's staff, here too headed by James Martin, still smarting from the Flick verdict, hunted out every shred of evidence to offset any possible legal chicanery. The bill of particulars pointed up the ruthlessness of Krupp's drive for power and fortune. More than 250 witnesses were called and more than

---

*A campaign mounted by supporters of the defendants claimed that DuBois was an activist left-winger, a fellow traveller motivated by his desire to discredit the capitalist system. But DuBois had written: "Today a great struggle is being waged for the political allegiance of men. The United States of America has been steadily losing in that struggle since the end of World War II. In seven years, the free world has lost to Communism half of Europe and large areas of Asia. This amounts to the loss of over eight hundred million people who once regarded themselves as our friends and allies."[23]

3,000 documents detailed the avarice of the Cannon King. To feed his plants and reach his production quotas, he, like I. G. Farben, demanded large contingents of prisoners and inmates of the concentration camps, and thousands were shipped to Essen in cattle cars and cargo vans. Later, following the Farben Auschwitz precedent, to salvage the time used to transport the victims, Alfried had special camps established adjacent to the Krupp munitions plants and factories. Food, medical care, and shelter were no better for the Krupp labor battalions than for those who were doomed in Auschwitz. Even hope was denied. As the Allies kept up their bombing and their forces neared the plants, the inmates were warned by the SS guards to attempt no insubordination: "The last five minutes will be saved for us."

Krupp was sentenced to twelve years at Landsberg, his chief directors from two to twelve years. Reporters noted that he was unmoved when the sentence was pronounced, for he was sure the imprisonment would be substantially modified. But he turned white when he heard that his empire was to be confiscated. He was right about the sentence. As in the cases of the other cartelists, it was imprisonment in name only. The sentences were served in special comfortable quarters. Ample office space was assigned where conferences with aides and lawyers could be conducted. Gourmet food and exotic wines were brought in regularly to enable the prisoners to maintain their luxurious lifestyle.

In the 1951 general amnesty, McCloy released Alfried and his directors. McCloy explained that Alfried had already paid his debt to society by the months of humiliating incarceration. "He felt that he had expiated whatever he'd done by the time he had already served in jail." The directors were welcomed back to their Essen offices with an elaborate champagne breakfast. Alfried moved into his castle with its two hundred rooms overlooking the valley of the Ruhr.

A few months after the release, again through action by General McCloy, all the family holdings were returned. One important restriction, the Mehlen Accord, was imposed by McCloy in the amnesty directive: to break their monopoly, the Krupps were to divest themselves of their coal mine and steel manufacturing divisions. Alfried simply ignored the mandate and there was no pressure to compel compliance. Indeed, he undertook more extensive diversification, and the Krupp plants began turning out locomotives, trucks, planes, and ships for eager purchasers in India, Greece, Pakistan, Brazil, Canada, even Soviet Russia. NATO, too, turned to the Krupp empire as a major supplier. By 1957, the sales of the sixty-nine factories in the consortium had reached beyond three quarters of a billion dollars.[24]

After Alfried's death in 1960, his heir, who preferred the life of a playboy to the rigors of managing a vast industrial empire, sold out his holdings and relocated in Florida. He was granted American citizenship and became a prime catch for the Palm Beach high society life.

After the trials of the bankers and the industrialists, interest waned considerably in tracking down even the most notorious fugitive Nazis, many of whom had settled into comfortable quarters and affluent careers. As relations with the Soviet and its satellites locked the West Germans ever more closely to the western Allies, the story of the Nazi period virtually disappeared from the curricula of the German school system. It was given a few sanitized paragraphs in the textbooks, where it was treated as an unfortunate aberration that the older generation was glad to forget and the younger generation had no incentive to learn.

In 1958 there was a brief upturn in concern in the western world about the large number of Nazi leaders who were still at large. Some of the renewed interest in exposing them was due to the patient accumulation of data about the Holocaust by Yad Vashem, the research institute that had been set up in Israel. Some was due to the persistence of a small group of Nazi hunters whose families had been destroyed and who had dedicated what was left of their lives to flushing out the predators of the extermination camps. But most of the reawakened concern was stimulated by facts that came to light in the much-postponed Einsetz-Kommando-Tilsit trial of 1958, which was held in Ulm. The evidence offered there of the atrocities in Nazi-occupied Lithuania was shocking to the younger generation, who had long been shielded from learning the truth. How could what was described have happened, and why were so many of the proven criminals still at large?

An initial result of the renewed world publicity was the creation, in cooperation with Yad Vashem, of a special agency in Ludwigsburg, near Stuttgart, to intensify the search efforts. A central catalogue was set up, which identified many of the fugitives about whom evidence had been gathered. After the elimination of the names of those who were now dead or presumed dead, and those who had already been tried and sentenced or freed, a master list of many thousands was compiled. Efforts to track down and arrest those people were now given new impetus by the embarrassed West German government.

At intervals the news would be flashed that an extermination camp commandant or a chief aide or a cold-blooded doctor had been discovered. If he was living in Germany, he would be put on trial, though usually after many delaying maneuvers. If his presence was brought to light in Egypt or Spain or the Argentine, where nests of now wealthy Nazis had bribed their way to security, extradition was perfunctorily requested but rarely honored.

The hunters of the fugitives persisted, and each new capture kept the Nazi period in at least a hazy focus. There were trials involving the officers of Treblinka, Sobibor, the ghettos of Lwów, Stanislawów, Czestochowa, and scores of more obscure death points. In 1964, after years of tenacious hide-and-seek, some of the long-sought Auschwitz ringleaders were hauled to court in Frankfurt for one of the longest trials in the postwar world. Two hundred fifty witnesses who came from fifteen countries offered testimony and the proceedings were recorded in eight volumes. The indictments alone required about 2,000 pages. All the accused seemed to suffer from mass amnesia. They could remember very little about unnatural practices at the camps where they had carried pivotal responsibilities. One of the adjutants, Robert Muller, who had become a prosperous Hamburg importer after the war, was indignant that he had been arrested, insisting: "I did not know that Auschwitz was an extermination camp." Karl Hoecker, the last commandant at Auschwitz, confessed that he suspected something must have been going on "because of the reek of burning bodies," but he was surprised to learn that there were murders under way. "No one told me that 25,000 victims were gassed and disposed of daily."

After the first weeks of the new trials, during which some of the most lurid episodes still created a stir, interest again lagged. Nearly thirty years had passed since the days of the Final Solution, and what had happened, even when recorded in books, now belonged to past history. The most harrowing details had become rhetoric. The gap between action and narrative had muted the thunder, and, as the Polish folklore has it, when the thunder is not heard, the peasant forgets to cross himself.

It was the trial of Adolf Eichmann in 1961, conducted in Israel, that most effectively recreated for the short-memoried world all the bestiality of the Nazi period. Eichmann had disappeared after Germany's defeat. Rumors persisted that he was living under constantly changing aliases in Spain, in Egypt, in the fastnesses of the German Alps, in the Argentine, even in Israel. As noted, a team of Israelis, themselves survivors of death camps, had dedicated their lives to the hunt for escaped Nazi criminals, and Eichmann headed their list. Isser Harel, the head of Israeli intelligence and a trusted associate of Ben Gurion, was assigned responsibility for the search. The Prime Minister gave him carte blanche to bring in alive the man who had boasted that he would "go laughing to his grave, having killed millions of Jews."

For years Harel and his staff explored every possible clue to Eichmann's whereabouts. They developed their strategy as if preparing for a major military encounter. It took months to make certain that a man known as Klement, living quietly in a secluded suburb of Buenos Aires, was Eichmann. Every precaution had to be taken not to alert Klement that he was under surveillance. There was no point in seeking legal extradition, for it would most likely be denied by a government that welcomed Nazi escapees. Too, Eichmann might be whisked away again, aided by a secret international ring of highly placed Nazis, the notorious Odessa File terrorists.

After the identification had been established, further months of patient planning were necessary to effect the capture at a propitious time, to hide Eichmann until he could be secretly moved, to transfer him to an Israeli-bound plane past specially trained immigration officials, and to minimize the inevitable international repercussions of a kidnapping from a sovereign state. There had to be endless rehearsals to ensure that there would be no slip-up. Eichmann's family ties were closely studied, his habitual movements, his hours of arrival and departure at work, the transportation that he used, the exact moment when he reached his street and home. Several apartments in Buenos Aires were rented where Eichmann could be held or moved about if necessary.

When I interviewed Harel in his home in Israel many years later, he had already recorded the story of the Eichmann capture.[25] I had read it and was fascinated by the thoroughness of the kidnapping preparations. Yet even its dramatic narrative could not fully convey the extraordinary precautions that had been patiently rehearsed, down to the remotest detail. Harel himself was a shy and soft-spoken man, and gave not the slightest impression of being one of the world's shrewdest intelligence agents. But as his low-keyed discussion continued, supplementing his book with details of forged documents, arrival and departure times of the diplomatic plane, subterfuges to lull the ever suspicious Eichmann family, bribes not too inadequate but also not too generous, I could understand better why the much later complicated Entebbe rescue had succeeded so well, how the Nazi scientists in their refuge in Egypt had been thwarted in their work on atomic weaponry, and how the blasting of the Iraqi nuclear reactor had been brought off.*

Eichmann was seized on the evening of May 11, 1960. In less than an hour, handcuffed, he lay trussed on the floor of one of the houses that had been secretly rented. An Israeli plane, having synchronized its flight to Buenos Aires with a diplomatic mission sent to join in the observance of an Argentine patriotic anniversary, waited on the apron of the Buenos Aires airport. Eichmann, drugged and disguised as a pilot who had overcelebrated his revels in the capital, was carried on a stretcher past the airport officials. It was agonizing for the captors, all survivors, to sit disciplined on the plane so close to the man who had been responsible for the deaths of millions of their people. Even when the plane was well beyond the Argentine airspace, no word had leaked out. Only when it was on Israeli soil did Prime Minister Ben Gurion make the electrifying announcement to the Knesset that the arch criminal was in Israeli hands and would stand trial.

As expected, the Argentine government immediately protested the violation of its sovereignty. Ben Gurion sent a personal message to the president expressing regret that Israel had no recourse but to act as it did. "Only a very few persons in the world," he wrote, "would fail to understand the profound motivation and supreme moral justification for this act." The Argen-

---

*On a wall in Harel's home in a Tel Aviv suburb is an autographed photograph of Ben Gurion with the salute that Harel had been Israel's "eternal sentinel".

tine government felt obliged to defend its national honor and temporarily recalled its ambassador, lodging a formal complaint in the United Nations. There were further Israeli apologies, both in the United Nations and in Buenos Aires; after four months, diplomatic relations between the two countries were reestablished.

The repercussions of the unprecedented act, of course, did not end with the diplomatic maneuvers. For more than a year the legality of the kidnapping was vigorously debated throughout the western world. The various protests against Israel's action were later incorporated in the defense counsel's testimony at Eichmann's trial. Israel, it was argued, had disqualified itself to try Eichmann because it had committed the felony of kidnapping him. Israel had no right to speak in the name of the total world Jewish community. How could Israel pass judgment on the crime of genocide if such a crime did not exist when Eichmann carried out his mission? He could be tried legally only in an international tribunal, or perhaps in a German court.

The Israeli government was not diverted by the avalanche of argument. It proceeded with the trial, careful however that every legal protection was afforded Eichmann. The prosecutor contended that Israel's jurisdiction was precisely what is claimed by other nations when they try cases of piracy or slave trading. The method of bringing an alleged criminal to trial has no bearing on a country's right to try him. Israel, the argument proceeded, had as much right to speak for the world Jewish community as it had to receive reparations from the West German government in symbolic contribution for Nazi crimes. Besides, what other body would try Eichmann? Germany wanted no part of him. It was impossible to reconvene a Nuremberg Tribunal—and, even were that possible, could there be a meaningful trial in the climate of the Cold War? Above all, why all these legalisms in the attempt to deal with a crime that had destroyed millions of human beings?

Justice Gideon Hausner, the chief prosecutor, reviewing the trial in a book he wrote later, reiterated that the main purpose of the trial was not simply to gain a conviction. How could Eichmann's wretched life atone for the misery he had brought upon the world? The trial had been planned and held to set down the record, unimpeachably validated—a record to challenge the Christian conscience, to remind the civilized world that what had begun as an assault on one people had quickly engulfed all civilized values.

Eichmann's trial lasted four months, from April until August 1961. It was conducted in Jerusalem, presided over by three judges, all of them German-born, who had fled Nazi Germany before the war. Five hundred journalists from all parts of the world attended. Every word, every action, was fully reported, from the testimony of the long parade of witnesses to the behavior of the defendant in the glass-enclosed, bullet-proof prisoner's dock. Eichmann was given efficient and resourceful counsel, headed by a Cologne attorney, whose fee was partially covered by the Israeli government. The basis of Eichmann's defense was not a denial of the mass murders, but rather insistence that he had been a petty functionary in the rigidly organized Nazi apparatus. He had loyally fulfilled the orders that he had received from above.

The prosecution refuted this claim, reminding the court that a similar defense by the top Nazi leadership had been rejected in the Nuremberg Military Trial of 1945–46. Eichmann was identified as a new type of mass killer, the man who exercises his bloody craft as a faceless bureaucrat. A new word was coined to describe the role of all the Eichmanns of the soulless hierarchies, *Schreibtischmorder*—the murderer at the desk.

The chief prosecutor elicited from the witnesses evidence of Eichmann's personal involvement. One instance served for all that Hausner grimly detailed, the episode of the starving boy in a Hungarian camp who had been accused of stealing a few cherries. With so little strength left in his body that he could hardly find voice to defend his action, the child was seized personally by Eichmann and dragged into a toolshed. When Eichmann emerged alone, he was heard to mutter, *"Ubriges mistvolk* (superfluous dung people)."

There was no doubt about the court's ruling: it was quickly reached. But the panel of judges annotated the verdict of guilty to refute the core of the defense argument that Eichmann, like thousands of Nazis everywhere, was merely executing orders in a society where obedience to authority was the highest national imperative. "In fulfilling [his mission]," the judges averred, "the accused acted in accordance with general directives from his superiors, but there still remained in him wide powers of discretion, which extended also to the planning of operations on his own initiative. He was not a puppet in the hands of others. His place was amongst those who pulled the strings."[26]

Eichmann was hanged on May 21, 1962, and his ashes were scattered over the Mediterranean waters.

The oscillation of interest by the general public in the Holocaust tragedy was quite natural. Ordinary people usually remain viscerally concerned only with matters that affect them
personally. Abstractions are rarely moving. Hitler's sneering
comment was significant when he was warned that planning for
the Final Solution would undoubtedly earn him a reputation for
pitilessness. He dismissed the caution with the reminder that a
million and a half Armenians had been butchered by the Turks
in 1915, "and who ever speaks about the Armenians today?"

Nevertheless it was crucial for the Jews at least to remember
the Hitler nightmare. Their sages had stressed the injunction
when the story of the escape from Egypt was annually repeated
at the Seder table: "Tell the story, though thousands of years
have passed, as if it had happened to you." Ever vulnerable as
historic scapegoats, it was incumbent upon the Jews to keep the
Holocaust experience fresh and to prevent the outside world
from forgetting. For Auschwitz and Treblinka and Mauthausen
were not isolated phenomena. Their horror could be repeated
unless the earliest signs of criminal demagoguery were not
quickly dammed before they engulfed whole peoples.

It was this concern that kept the Nazi hunters from slackening their effort, or becoming discouraged by failure. The punishment of a Nazi murderer was a minor incentive for them. It
could not bring back lives that had been snuffed out, nor could
it erase haunting memories. But the capture of a notorious Nazi
killer, a trial that dramatized his actions, that recorded the influ-
ences that impelled his pathology or his calculated malevolence,
the social forces that gave him his opportunities, the noncha-
lance of the righteous bystander who would not be involved—
these were the factors that gave meaning to the persistent hunt
and that recognized no Statute of Limitations.

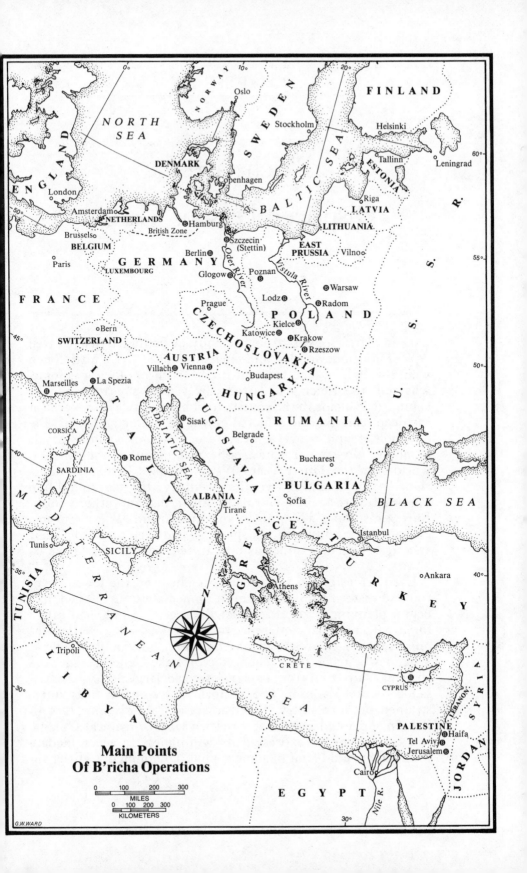

**Main Points
Of B'richa Operations**

G.W.WARD

CHAPTER SIX

B'richa and the
Displaced Persons' Camps

W HEN HITLER CAME TO POWER in 1933 he predicted that, cleared of its undesirables and unassimilables, his Third Reich would stretch beyond ten centuries. His chronology was somewhat off: the Reich had lasted barely twelve years when he committed suicide in the courtyard of his hideaway bunker. But the deep scars that he inflicted on the economic and social life of whole peoples gave a measure of ominous validity to his bombast. No similar catastrophe had engulfed the western world since the Thirty Years' War of the post-Reformation period. In the civilized twentieth century, the eleven million uprooted were mainly Germans, Austrians, and other central Europeans, Poles, Ukrainians, and Russians in eastern Europe, and the Baltic and Balkan peoples. All had been torn from their ancestral moorings either as military conscripts or as slave laborers.

Even before Hitler had precipitated his war, the Jews of central and eastern Europe, the most immediately threatened, had begun planning flight. President Roosevelt, in 1938, had called for an international conference to explore possible resettlement opportunities. Representatives from thirty-one countries met at Évian-les-Bains on the French shore of Lake Geneva, under the chairmanship of Myron Taylor, later special American ambassador to the Vatican. The rhetoric of sympathy was unrestrained, but no country offered any practical assistance, though Britain suggested a tract of unsettled land in tropical Guiana, and San Domingo expressed its willingness to accommodate Jews who could bring in some capital. Undoubtedly Hitler interpreted the lesson of the conference to mean that the world was very little concerned with the fate of the Jews.

Their bleak isolation was dramatized in the fate of the *St. Louis*, a vessel that sailed for Cuba from Hamburg in mid-May 1939 carrying 930 Jews. Cuba, under pressure from Britain, and caught in a battle between rival political factions, had canceled the visas that had been issued and the ship, upon arrival, was refused landing. Many of the passengers, convinced that the dreaded concentration camps awaited them if they were returned to Germany, threatened suicide. The Cuban authorities were unable to modify their prohibition and the ship was ordered to leave port at once. Shadowed by an American Coast Guard cutter, it drifted aimlessly in Florida waters. Representations to the American government on behalf of the refugees were of no avail. Only when the American Joint Distribution Committee, the major international Jewish relief agency, guaranteed that those who were given emergency asylum would not become public charges did France, Britain, Belgium, and Holland each agree to admit, temporarily, limited numbers of the distraught passengers. The *St. Louis* was the forerunner of hundreds of barred vessels and their myriads of boat people, who were to test the world's compassion in the next decades.

As the war drew to a close, thought had to be given to the disposition of the stranded remnants, once they were technically "liberated." Roosevelt had dutifully convened another of his international conferences, and forty-four nations sent delegates to the White House to lay the groundwork for the later United Nations Relief and Rehabilitation Agency (UNRRA). When Germany surrendered in 1945, UNRRA was in place, and it organized the homeward journey of the great majority of the nationals who had lands to which to return. Within little more than a year, nearly all had been repatriated and resettled.

But many thousands remained, a long-range problem for the occupying Allies. Most of these were collaborators who, during the war, had more or less eagerly volunteered to serve the Nazis and, knowing that their countrymen would punish them as Quislings, dared not return. Rabbi Judah Nadich, the first Adviser on Jewish Affairs to General Eisenhower, termed them "Nazis to the very core of their beings." At the outset, thrown together with them as non-comrades in limbo, were about 50,000 Jews who had survived the death camps, emerged from the forests and mountains, monasteries and convents, or had been hidden in Christian homes. Their scars, physical and psychological, were indelible. Now there were others to be inflicted, almost as hard to bear because they were unexpected.

Fifty thousand Jews could be sheltered in the Displaced Persons' Camps with a measure of comfort and hope, even in the midst of the postwar chaos. The American officials had won high marks for their organizing skills. But when Jews from Poland and then from Rumania and Hungary poured in, bringing the number of refugees to nearly half a million, the camps lapsed into an agony of confusion and frustration. The DP ordeal and its dateless limits were poignantly sensed by the German poet, Nelly Sachs, 1966 Nobelist in Literature:

> Someone comes
> from afar
> who moves like a dog
> or
> perhaps a rat
> and it is winter
> so clothe him warmly,
> or he may have
> fire beneath his feet . . .
> a stranger always has
> his homeland in his arms
> like an orphan
> for which he may be seeking
> nothing but a grave.[1]

When the Germans invaded Poland in 1939, great numbers of Jews had fled eastward deep into Russia, where they were given asylum, mainly in remote areas. They shared the hardships inflicted by the war on all Russians, but they survived in reasonably good health and often with their families intact. Now that the Germans had been driven back, the Soviets offered to grant those who preferred to leave, for whatever reason, a special strip of expropriated German territory in Upper Silesia, which was to become part of the new Poland. No one familiar with the etchings and lithographs of Käthe Kollwitz, who lived for decades in Silesia and drew from her experiences there some of the grimmest scenes of twentieth-century art, would have thought of the assigned territory as being precisely a land of milk and honey. Nevertheless it beckoned as a possible sanctuary. Demobilized Jewish soldiers who had fought in the Russian armies were joined by thousands of other adrift Polish Jewish families, in the expectation that they could perhaps now settle into a less precarious routine. One of the historians of this period noted that, by 1946, some 80,000 Jews who had been scattered far into the Russian outposts, even into Siberia, had registered for such Polish relocation.* He wrote: "It appeared that Lower Silesia might become the Land of Promise to Polish Jewry."[2] It was not to be.

At first, attempts were made by the Communist-dominated Polish government to check the exodus of the Jewish survivors. Many of them had usable talents, particularly in professions. Government officials urged faithful party members to encourage the survivors to cast their destiny with the new Poland, promising long-denied rights and opportunities. The Jewish Communists painted pictures of a resplendent era in Poland free of exploitation, and ridiculed the naivete of families who "kept sitting on their shabby suitcases" waiting for a bourgeois Utopia in Palestine. But the propagandists made few converts. Even families that had opted for an experimental interlude in Lower Silesia kept hoping that ways would be opened for them to reach the American Zone in occupied Germany and Austria and thence to seaports for the onward trip to Palestine. Though B'richa, the illegal Jewish rescue organization masterminded from Palestine, whose agents were already in Poland, had been outlawed by the government, it cooperated surreptitiously with such families and helped them plan their flight.

The least guarded routes out of Poland in 1945 were through uncharted areas, "the green fields," though the movement across them was constantly impeded by woods, rivers, and pathless hills. The days and nights had their recurring crises, and their casualties too, but every rumor of possible escape trails encouraged expectant families to try to reach them. One of the B'richa leaders told of an emergency birth in an open field; a sympathetic Christian farming family provided temporary care despite all risks. When the mother was asked how, in a far advanced pregnancy, she had slipped by the vigilant B'richa

---

*The historian was Joseph Tennenbaum, president at the time of the World Federation of Lithuanian Jews.

screening committee, she replied impassively that her sister had taken her place in the application line and then, just before boarding the trucks, places were again changed. "She could wait for the next group. Obviously I couldn't." Such incidents were not uncommon.

The attempt was now made, in the teeth of Polish government opposition, to bring order and discipline into the inchoate plans for flight and rescue. Rovno, once a thriving commercial center, became a staging area for thousands of Polish and east European Jews in preparation for their attempts to reach Palestine, seemingly the only hope for secure settlement. Since the sixteenth century Rovno had been a focus of Jewish communal and scholarly activity, and it was one of the first objectives of the Nazi invasion of 1941. Almost the entire community of 30,000 Jews had been immediately destroyed. In the single day of November 6, 18,000 men, women, and children had been machine-gunned in a suburban pine grove, as much the victims of their neighbors as of the invading Nazis. Now Rovno was to return to Jewish history.

The initiative for the ingathering at Rovno was taken by a small group of Zionists who, though scarcely in their twenties, were already veterans in the artifices of resistance. In December 1944 the handful of promoters, including girls, met to launch their plan to reach into the remotest areas of Poland and eastern Europe to gather up those who had survived. Their leader, Abba Kovner, seemed an unlikely strategist for missions of such complex logistics. He had been reared in Vilna, the ancient Lithuanian city renowned for its Talmudic scholarship. Its Jewish leadership had become resigned to what Kovner had stigmatized as a demeaning docility. He worked with the Zionist militant organization, Hashomer Hatzair; with him they resisted the views of the elders that if Jews were to die it was in compliance with God's will. To Kovner there was no nobility in martyrdom; he was an heir of Chaim Nachman Bialik, the literary conscience of the early twentieth century whose "City of Slaughter" had castigated the people of Kishinev for meekly submitting to pogrom.

At the end of the war Kovner found his way to Lublin in Poland, where he was enlisted by B'richa for its mission of shepherding Jewish families out of Poland. He was thoroughly seasoned to give leadership to the migration program initially centered in Rovno. Kovner began dispatching scouting expeditions to the farthest parts of Poland, the Baltic States, Rumania, Hungary, and Czechoslovakia to prepare routes over which the abandoned refugees could make their way to the Displaced Persons' Camps and selected seaports. Rescue teams then fanned out, and during the next months, convoys crisscrossed eastern Europe. Permission was obtained from Rumanian and Yugoslavian officials to use their countries as transit points, but no transports could proceed without encountering officials and guards whose consent to their journeys had to be won by extraordinary resourcefulness. Often the migrants in the overloaded trucks must have repeated Job's plaint: "I was not in safety, neither had I rest, neither was I quiet. Yet trouble came."

At one point it appeared that the entire leadership would be liquidated. In March 1945, Kovner and his chief lieutenants were arrested by some Red Army officers stationed in Poland, and they were put through severe questioning. During the ordeal an old colonel approached the interrogation desk and whispered some words to the officers in charge. The young conspirators were led into a cellar and then, expecting to be shot, were pushed through a door onto the street. The colonel met them there and said in Yiddish: "Go, and bless you."[3]

The adventure of the so-called Rumanian Rescue Train was typical of the hairbreadth line that often separated escape and annihilation. In the spring of 1945 two resourceful emissaries, Moshe Agami and Jacob Schmitterer, who had been positioned in Bucharest, successfully negotiated with the Rumanian Red Cross for a train to be sent from Oradea Mare, near the Hungarian border, to move slowly through Hungary, Czechoslovakia, and Poland repatriating Rumanian survivors. The train, with from ten to fifteen freight cars attached, in each of five long circuitous trips chugged back and forth from Rumania, stopping at towns along the way where reports indicated that there were stranded families to be evacuated. Those selected were supposed to be of Rumanian origin, but Jews of other lands were often able to bribe guards to let them board. When identities were challenged, documents to validate eligibility usually appeared. There was one heart-stopping experience when hundreds of documents in good order, in the keeping of the B'richa leader, mysteriously disappeared. Forgers worked throughout the night to create new ones; they beat the inspection by minutes.[4]

On one of its trips, the train made a stop at Auschwitz to

transfer the few remaining inmates who had been too ill to be moved earlier and had given up hope that the outside world remembered where they were. There were galling delays when officials suspected that the train carried spies or disguised Nazis. The suspicion was not too fanciful, for many war criminals sought to escape retribution by infiltrating as Jews into the rescue convoys. It was usually not the guards who penetrated the disguise but rather the Jews themselves. In one instance three Nazis in flight, having mastered a core Yiddish vocabulary, tried to act out a refugee role. They were asked offhandedly about Jewish leaders in the community from which they had purported to come. One questioner asked if they knew *Modeh Ani* or *Lecho Dodi*, these being the opening words of traditional Jewish prayers. The Nazis responded with fond recollection of such fine characters. It did not take long to turn them over to the Poles, who dealt with them as Nazi collaborators.[5]

There were other, more serious problems. As the train wound through hostile countryside, outlawed Fascist collaborators sniped at it from woods or hidden roads along the way and had to be fought off, often at severe cost in casualties. It was estimated that by summer's end in 1945, about 15,000 Jews, mainly from Poland, had been brought into Rumania. But their ordeal was still not over. Communists and anti-Communists were fighting for control of the government and stability was under constant threat. New routes therefore had to be devised for still other journeys through Hungary, Yugoslavia, and Italy, on into the American Zone of Germany and Austria. It was counted a near miracle when 433 orphans, gathered from every part of eastern Europe, were brought at last, bewildered and exhausted but alive and restorable, to the shelter of the Displaced Persons' Camps in the American Zone.

All through this first period of liberation, B'richa was obliged to limit itself to the relocation of families or small communities through such operations as the Rescue Train. Larger-scale transportation was an almost insoluble problem. These were desperately difficult months for the refugees, especially the elderly and the infirm, the women and children, who endured day and night rides in crowded trucks and carts. When transportation was unavailable, they traveled on foot through hostile territory, giving up meager possessions as bribes to accelerate their passage to the frontiers.

In June 1946 a breakthrough occurred that made possible a

major expansion in B'richa operations. Poland annexed a large section of Prussia, and millions of Germans living in the appropriated areas were expelled and forced further west into Germany. The Polish government created a special agency, PUR, to direct the deportation of the Germans, and the recolonization of the evacuated territory by Poles brought in from other parts of the reconstituted state. The B'richa leaders quickly grasped the opportunity to slip first hundreds, then thousands, of Jews into the expulsion convoys, arming them with documents that validated their identity as "returning German prisoners" or as dispossessed German Jews who had fled the Hitler terror. By the beginning of July about 20,000 Jews had been dispatched by the B'richa emissaries in Poland to Stettin, a Baltic port that was incorporated into the new Poland. Its location close to Berlin made it an ideal transfer point. The Jews were housed and fed by the American Joint Distribution Committee and sympathetic officials of UNRRA. Several large houses and some partially repaired bombed-out buildings were made available to take care of the transients who were to be moved on into Germany. Some went by train, a thousand at a time, to the Baltic port of Lübeck, others to Berlin by truck or on the Oder River by ferry.

Many of the PUR officials were Jews who tried to be helpful to those who wished to leave Poland. Every effort was made to assign separate compartments on the trains for the Jews. At one time the B'richa men were able to load 1,200 Jews from east European countries into a train that was registered to transport 1,500 "returning Germans." Since the PUR convoys had to pass through British Zone territory, the journey was especially precarious. A crisis developed when a British team was dispatched to investigate the heavy overload of "German" Jews. B'richa sponsored a festive party for the British and, through a long bibulous evening, the investigators became uproariously drunk. They overslept and arrived late. The convoys had already left. The embarrassed British thanked the B'richa officials profusely for having covered their tardy arrival by attending effectively to all the details of despatching the convoys.[6]

Soon there was no need for subterfuge in planning and attempting flight from Poland or eastern Europe. While many of the Polish government officials had kept promising the Jews that opportunities would not be denied to them, the general population remained hostile to any Jewish settlement even by former neighbors. They expressed their hostility with increasing insult and violence. A common note was sounded: "If only Hitler had finished the job of the Final Solution!" On July 4, 1946, a pogrom erupted in Kielce, a city of 200,000 inhabitants, during which Polish townsfolk lynched scores of Jews who had returned to learn the fate of loved ones or to reclaim their homes and property. As so often before, the pogrom was ignited by the ritual murder canard that had plagued Jews throughout the centuries. When an appeal was made to the bishop of Lublin to calm the frenzied Catholic population, he replied as if he had just been reading the *Protocols of the Elders of Zion:* "At the Beilis trial, many ancient and modern books were presented in evidence, but the question as to whether or not Jews use [Christian] blood in their rituals has not yet been clarified."* Nor did the primate, Cardinal Hlond, agree to condemn the massacre. "The fact that their condition is deteriorating is to a great degree due to the Jews themselves, who today occupy leading positions in Poland's [Communist-sponsored] government and endeavor to introduce a governmental structure that a majority of the people do not desire."[7]

The hastily reorganized and none too secure Jewish communities in Poland immediately felt repercussions of the pogrom and its aftermath. It had probably been too much to expect that appropriated Jewish property and assets would be willingly relinquished, and religious bigotry was obviously a convenient rationale for the retention of the property. Now even the Jewish Communists who had denounced as unpatriotic those who wished to leave Poland scrambled to find ways for their own flight. Their promises had never been valued as more than cant. Yehuda Bauer referred to the rhetoric of the officials as "mere shadow play on the gray edge of nothingness."[8]

An exodus began that soon became a stampede. In one night early in August 1946, 3,800 Jews crossed the frontier into neighboring Czechoslovakia on their pell-mell way to the American Zone. During the next three months another 75,000 joined in the flight. The Polish government had acquiesced in July and entered into an informal agreement with B'richa to permit an orderly migration. Since the British were vigorously opposed to extralegal migration of Jews to Palestine, the condition was

---

*Beilis, a Russian Jew, had been accused in 1911 in Kiev of using the blood of a Christian child for the Passover ritual.

set that the exodus must be managed without public fanfare.

B'richa was now assigned by the shadow government of Jewish Palestine the primary responsibility for converting the individual and group exploits, courageous as they were, into a disciplined, carefully planned migration that would bring another 150,000 Jews into the Displaced Persons' Camps. It undertook to screen those who were likely to withstand the inevitable hardships, arrange for the way stations en route, acquire the resources for supplies of essential food, clothing, and medical reserves, and, above all, prepare whatever diplomatic or economic influence had to be utilized to circumvent the mounting vigilance of the British.* Assigned to direct this complicated international flight and rescue network was Shaul Avigur who, like Kovner, had emerged during the Holocaust period and after to help shape a self-reliant future.

Avigur, born in Dvinsk, Russia, in 1899, had migrated on his own to Palestine as a boy of thirteen. There he joined one of the earliest kvutzoth in Galilee. He became a leading force in the creation of Haganah, the unofficial militia, and of Sherut Ye'diot, the agency that directed the intelligence network. After 1938, and throughout the war, he commanded widely dispersed rescue operations in Europe and the Middle East. One of Avigur's underground missions brought him to Istanbul at a time when the Turks, nominally pro-Axis, watched the struggle from the sidelines, waiting to leap to the assistance of the winning side. When the thousand-year-old Jewish settlement of Baghdad came under threat from Iraq's Nazi-dominated government in 1941, Avigur managed a clandestine emigration to Palestine that salvaged remnants of the ancient Jewish community. After the war, operating out of Paris in offices on the same street as the Allied military headquarters, he consolidated the stepped-up rescue efforts. He assigned to the Displaced Persons' Camps scores of veterans of the demobilized Jewish Brigades who had fought under the British flag, to provide leadership to survivors who had been funneled there as a prelude to their hoped-for migration to Palestine.

Reviewing Avigur's career, one understands better the reverence of his associates for their often dour and taciturn chief, who

---

*In Hebrew, the illegal immigrant was known as the *ma apil*—a phrase that carried the connotation of one who ascends a steep mountain.

had little of the personality of the cloak-and-dagger operator. I interviewed some of them a good thirty years after Israel's independence had been won; to a man, they included Avigur with the giants who had transformed the Jewish spirit and created the sovereign state. They admitted their impatience with the limits he had set on their "calculated irresponsibility," but recognized his sure instinct as a dependable statesman, who knew when to hold with anchor and when to venture with sail.

No one better exemplified calculated irresponsibility than Yehuda Arazi, a modern Scarlet Pimpernel, who lived by the philosophy of *toujours l'audace*. Even Avigur, rarely given to fervor, held Arazi in open admiration. He was born in 1907, in Lodz, Poland, and migrated to Palestine in 1923 with his parents. He grew up in the kibbutz tradition and early became a member of Haganah. Recognizing his innovative talents, his Haganah superiors directed him to join the British domestic police with the assignment to penetrate its intelligence system. For many years Arazi operated as a member of the constabulary while he passed information to Haganah, helped the escape of Jews imprisoned by the British, and smuggled arms for the expected showdown with the Arabs. During the Holocaust years and until after the war, Arazi lived the precarious life of a double agent in Poland, in the Balkans, in North Africa; in 1945, his identity was discovered and he narrowly escaped arrest by the British, who put a price on his head. He turned up in Italy in a British Army uniform and fitted into the B'richa operations for the promotion of illegal immigration.

Arazi had neither funds nor transport, camps nor provisions. But he took advantage of the dislocated economy and functioned almost entirely through the black market. Military conditions in Europe were weighted down by bureaucratic confusion, "slack and unbuttoned," as he said. No Yankee trader was more adept at the art of swapping questionable goods for necessary services and questionable services for necessary goods.

Arazi's first move was to get in touch with the 462nd Transport Company in Milan, a senior Jewish Unit of the British Eighth Army that had fought in both Africa and Italy.* The

---

*The Jewish leaders of Palestine had urged that special units made up of Jewish volunteers be permitted to serve in the British military in the common

company's base in Milan was an ideal front for refugee-running from the northern frontiers of Italy. His plan of action was bold. Each Jewish Brigade within the British forces in Italy was ordered to allot a number of vehicles for the transport of refugees. Isolated feudal villas and farms were requisitioned "on behalf of the military" and set up as refugee camps, supervised and provisioned by the Brigade units under the direction of B'richa. The soldiers were asked to give up their weekly ration of a bottle of whiskey or gin for the "liquor bank" from which Arazi drew to barter for spare parts, food, and other supplies. On one occasion Arazi persuaded the Italian Admiralty office at Taranto to accept a case of whiskey in trade for a detailed map of the minefields along the coastlines of Italy. It was a godsend for Arazi's anticipated problems in "shipping."

By the beginning of 1946, however, what remained of the Jewish Brigade units in Milan were summarily ordered to North Africa for demobilization, and Arazi lost the military presence that had ensured getting his forty truckloads past British and Italian police checkpoints. He reacted with his customary audacity. If a military unit was essential to his operations, why not invent one? Why not create a phantom force, fully equipped and supplied with all appropriate trappings to lend it legitimacy? The stratagem was so incredible that at first Arazi's Haganah chiefs dismissed it as mad. He persuaded them that, in the circumstances, rashness was a more acceptable fault than faintheartedness. The doubters swallowed their hesitation and authorized Arazi to create the phantom army unit.

Using forged requisition papers, Arazi took over a large courtyard and garage in the center of Milan. Here he set in place every detail of an authentic army unit, complete with workshop, regimental police, MP signboards, guards, and all the documents necessary to validate them. Soldiers and staff from the demobilized Jewish Brigade were sent back to Milan on Haganah's orders to bring the unit "up to strength." Under the cover of the phantom unit, a fleet of vehicles went up and down Italy, transporting the refugees to their assembly points while teams of Arazi's men brought in fuel and provisions for the sailings. The relocation of the refugees and the dispatching of the ships

---

war against the Nazis. Churchill at first demurred but then, by 1942, yielded, on condition that the volunteers serve outside Palestine.

to Palestine were made possible by the very men who were being hunted by British intelligence. "The sheep were hiding in wolf's clothing," noted two historians of the period, themselves part of the B'richa contingent.[9]

With B'richa agents operating in every part of eastern Europe to direct one of the great migration movements of the postwar period, the occupation authorities were soon overwhelmed by the magnitude of their responsibility. The refugees were exhausted by their ordeal and inevitably impatient. The DP officials were pressured by the unexpected demands upon them, and a crisis climate soon enveloped all relationships. At first the American command found ways to evade its enlarged responsibilities, especially when it was also overburdened with the complexities of governing a fragmented, defeated country in which essential services were everywhere almost totally inoperative. An American general, irritated beyond patience, expressed his reaction to Dr. William Haber, one of the advisors of Jewish Affairs: "The people [DPs] have been here a long time and we are tired of them."[10] Further, though the plight of the stateless Jews was pitiable in the extreme, they were not the only disjointed wanderers in chaotic Europe. Czechoslovakia, struggling to survive as a democratic nation, had expelled millions of Sudeten Germans who had created irredentist disruption before the war. The Germans in Schleswig-Holstein, who had served Hitler well as a fifth column, had been ousted by Denmark, and they too had somehow to be absorbed. The population of Germany, despite the casualties of war, was thus swollen almost out of control; food, clothing, medicines, and above all shelter, were in shortest supply.

The American military chiefs, pointing to these complications, sought to prevent further inundation of the Displaced Persons' Camps. President Truman recognized their dilemma; but he insisted in a firm order that, come what may, the American zone was to remain open to the new floods of Jewish refugees. Depots and stations for transients were set up in Germany and Austria. From there the hastily organized family groups, thousands of whom had been traveling on foot for weeks, struggled to reach the camps. By the time the borders were closed, in April 1947, there were approximately 150,000 Jews in the Displaced Persons' Camps in the American Zone in Germany and another 27,000 in Austria. In addition there were about 15,000 in the

British Zone, a few thousand more in the French Zone, and the rest scattered in southern Europe. The Jews, two years after the war ended, comprised about one-fourth of the population in the camps.

The American officials, and certainly the rank and file, harassed and resentful, rarely went farther in their imposed duties than they had to. They followed the conventional military routine: do only what the regulations call for. They were tendered little appreciation. For the refugees, the years of war and terror, of debasement, and of families destroyed, had drained out such graces. And receiving scant acknowledgment for offering asylum, most of the army administrators applied rigid regulations, with few concessions, as a cover for their mounting hostility. Even General Eisenhower, easygoing and imperturbable, could not understand why the Jews were so sullen and ill disposed. He knew little about them, and what they had endured was as much a blur to him as an unremembered footnote. Colonel Abraham Hyman, who directed the Office of Adviser on Jewish Affairs, related that in 1955, on the tenth anniversary of deliverance from the extermination camps, Eisenhower, now President of the United States, was invited by survivors to receive a plaque that expressed appreciation to the "Liberator of Auschwitz." "By the way," Eisenhower asked at the ceremony, in genial innocence, "where *is* Auschwitz?"[11]

It was probably sheer obtuseness rather than hostility that was responsible for the directive to assign the Displaced Persons to camps according to their country of origin. In practice, this billeted together those who had suffered from the Nazi blight and the collaborators who would have rejoiced in a Nazi victory. It yoked Jews in too many instances with their recent, none too repentant tormentors among the Poles and Ukrainians. The military stood on high principle. Would not segregation of their charges according to ethnic identification be tantamount to an endorsement of the Nazi racial policies? The Jews, among whom were men and women who had been effective community leaders before the war, explained with ill-concealed impatience that the tragic facts of life could not be governed by the abstractions of bloodless categories. The highly emotional billeting controversy dominated the concerns of the first months in the camps.

Equally oppressive were the living conditions. Here, too, this was less the product of malice or indifference than of unpreparedness for the magnitude of the task. The refugees were assigned primarily to makeshift quarters, abandoned German and Austrian military barracks, airplane hangars, garages, all overcrowded and short of toilets and washing facilities. The monotonous rations of black bread, cheese, and soup were served cafeteria-style to men and women, regarded as mendicants, waiting sullenly in long queues.

Perhaps even the harshest physical living conditions might have been endured; when resentment ebbed, the complainants conceded that the problems of refugees dumped on the occupation forces was indeed a thorny one. But what perverse judgment confined survivors of death camps behind barbed-wire fences, under the surveillance of armed guards? Just outside their makeshift quarters there were German and Austrian burghers who still lived in comfortable homes, tended their gardens, moved about freely, and continued to hate the victims whose destruction had not been fulfilled.

Perhaps the situation that existed in the Rothschild Hospital in Vienna best pointed up the mood of the refugees who had been pouring into the city in the B'richa convoys until the frontiers were closed. When the hospital was built by the famous international family, it was one of the best equipped in Europe, serving both as a healing facility and as a center for advanced medical research. Austria fell to the Nazis and the hospital was renovated to provide elegant living and administrative quarters for the commanding elite. After the war it was requisitioned to house refugees and, within months, overcrowding and perfunctory maintenance had converted it into a quasi-prison camp. When it was inspected by one of the many United Nations teams, the report of the chief of the Guatemala delegation, Jorge Garcia-Granados, was devastating.

"At the beginning of our tour of the Rothschild Hospital," Garcia-Granados wrote,

> we were shocked by the words of a German Jewish physician, Dr. Otto Wolken, a harassed little man who had been the prison camp doctor at Auschwitz. 'I have X-rayed 2000 people at random here,' he told us. 'Of them 1400 have tuberculosis now, or are arrested cases. The sanitary conditions are incredible. We have 15 toilets for 4000 people. Half of these people are suffering from malnutrition. You can imagine their mental state. . . . Little by little, as we began slowly to explore this incredible building, it dawned

upon me that I was in the presence of one of the great shames of modern times. . . . I am a healthy, normal man and I have never known dizziness. But now my head began to spin and I knew that I was about to faint. By a tremendous effort I pushed my way through the people . . . to a window opening on the courtyard. I put my head out and began to gulp the blessed air. The court was crowded but above it was the blue sky of Vienna. I remained there for two or three full minutes, breathing deeply, and sick at heart for all mankind.[12]

In the first months of the Displaced Persons' Camps most of the inmates were too ill or exhausted to challenge the authorities. Gradually, however, a less compliant leadership began to emerge and protests mounted against the slow pace of the military bureaucracy. By April 1945 a protest committee was organized and Dr. Zalman Grunberg, a native of Lithuania, one of the few fortunate Jews who had received a sound medical training in Switzerland, was chosen to head it up. His professional eminence had earned him no respect from the savage mobs of Kovno who stormed the ghetto and collaborated with the Nazis in cutting down its Jewish inhabitants. Grunberg's wife had been packed off on a death train. His son, Imanuel, smuggled out of the ghetto in a potato sack by a compassionate neighbor, had disappeared. Grunberg himself had spent the next years in Dachau, saved from a mass grave only because his medical skills had been useful in the camp. In his gaunt and wrinkled face, a man of thirty-nine could scarcely be discerned. On the backs of prescription blanks, serving, he said, as a "stenographer of destiny," he had kept a running account of what his people had endured. The record was preserved not to deplore the lacerations of fate but to keep memory fresh for the obligations that it imposed upon survivors. Arriving in the Displaced Persons' Camp at St. Ottilian in the American Zone, he wasted no time on grief. Appearing before the authorities, he insisted on and received authorization to turn a substandard barracks into a hospital and staffed it with medical men and women among the DPs. He scrimped for equipment and supplies, and set an accelerated tempo for service to the desperately ill.[13]

Teams of representatives from the Jewish relief agencies, especially the Joint Distribution Committee, sent reports that were quickly relayed to American political leaders. The first Adviser on Jewish Affairs, Judge Simon Rifkind of New York, appealed to the officers in command of the camp for emergency measures to head off possible scandal. The uproar was heard in the White House and impelled Truman, within a few weeks of his swearing in as President, to move with dispatch for remedial action. He commissioned a special representative, Earl Harrison, dean of the University of Pennsylvania Law School and a member of the Intergovernmental Committee on Refugees, to conduct an on-the-spot investigation.[14]

Harrison, far from finding that published accounts had exaggerated the plight of the uprooted, concluded that their living conditions had been understated. "Beyond knowing that they are no longer in danger of the gas chambers, torture and other forms of violent death," he wrote, "they see—and there is—little change. . . . As matters now stand, we appear to be treating the Jews as the Nazis treated them except that we do not exterminate them. They are in concentration camps in large numbers under our own military guards instead of the SS troops. One is led to wonder whether the German people, seeing this, are not supposing that we are following or at least condoning Nazi policy." An immediate action, Harrison urged, should be to offer the Jews refuge in camps of their own. He also called for an appeal to the British government to release 100,000 certificates for those who were eager to emigrate to Palestine. Finally, he strongly recommended legislation to modify American immigration laws so that survivors who had relatives in the United States could be reunited with them.

Responding promptly, Truman was sharp in his message to Eisenhower. He directed him to give priority to those who had suffered most. "We must make clear to the German people," he cabled, "that we thoroughly abhor the Nazi policies of hatred and persecution. We have no better opportunity to demonstrate this than by the manner in which we ourselves actually treat the survivors remaining in Germany." Privately, Eisenhower resented the President's scolding for what he believed were exaggerations in the Harrison Report. In his official reply, however, he muted his anger and offered rebuttal to the implication of unconcern, noting that the problems of a prostrate Germany were overwhelming. How could newly arrived, inexperienced young officers be expected to work miracles when trained social workers and doctors were baffled by the magnitude of the chaos that had to be resolved? He reminded the President that reforms were already under way even as Harrison had been drafting his report, and promised that others would follow.

On September 17, Yom Kippur day, Eisenhower visited one of the German camps at Feldafing, briefly attending services. He then inspected the camp and was visibly appalled by its squalor and degradation. On his way back to headquarters, he stopped in Stuttgart and was again upset by the contrast between the facilities assigned to the Jews and the homes in which the civilian Germans lived. The inspection tour disabused him of the idea that the Harrison Report had exaggerated the treatment of the Jews. His shocked reaction received worldwide coverage.[15]

In truth Eisenhower was not being well served by many members of his top staff. The case of General George Patton, while extreme, was not entirely unique. Patton was a brilliant field commander and had become a legend for the daring that brought victories in North Africa and, in the final actions of the war, in Germany and Czechoslovakia. Eisenhower regarded him as his "champion end runner," but the professional respect had not been reciprocated.

With all his Hotspur courage, Patton was unstable and harbored deep prejudices. Commanding the Third Army in Europe, he caused embarrassment when he publicly questioned the military usefulness of black soldiers. He had little understanding of the evil core of Nazism. In a press conference that centered on denazification, he referred to "this Nazi thing" as "just like a Democratic and Republican election." Patton had the professional soldier's attitude that neither winners nor losers should "carry a grudge." Moreover, he never bothered to disguise the anti-Semitism he had imbibed in his southern California childhood. On August 31, he wrote to his wife: "Actually the Germans are the only decent people left in Europe. It's a choice between them and the Russians. I prefer the Germans. So do our cousins." He resorted to a double pejorative when he described the wife of a man prominent in the American government as "a very Jewy Jewess."

Patton reluctantly accompanied Eisenhower on the Yom Kippur visit to Feldafing, and reacted violently. In his diary there was a stinging reference to the Harrison Report:

One of the chief complaints of [Earl Harrison] is that the DPs are kept in camp under guard. Of course, Harrison is ignorant of the fact that if they were not kept under guard they would not stay in the camps, would spread over the country like locusts, and would eventually have to be rounded up after quite a few of them had been shot and quite a few Germans murdered and pillaged. . . . Harrison and his ilk believe that the DP is a human being, which he is not, and this applies particularly to the Jews who are lower than animals.[16]

After Eisenhower returned from his inspection tour, he ordered drastic reforms in the operation of the camps. The barbed wire was removed and the guards were supplanted by unarmed Jews who did not interfere with the mobility of camp inmates. Daily rations were increased to 2,500 calories and more varied food was made available. Overcrowding was ameliorated by measures that included the requisition of some German homes. But reforms came more slowly at lower levels, despite explicit directives from General Eisenhower's headquarters.

The bickering between the guardians and the guarded seemed to be interminable. A common criticism, entirely unrelated to living conditions but apparently an influence on the attitude of some officials, was that "too many of the Jews were wheeler-dealers." The cigarette black market was the most frequently cited example of sharp practice. In the economic and social chaos of Europe in 1945, American cigarettes provided one of the few stable forms of currency, from Danzig-Gdansk to Calais. The price of a package of American cigarettes in the immediate postwar period was about 20 cents. At the Post Exchanges and Ships' Stores, the cost was considerably less. A PX pack of cigarettes exchanged for other goods could support a small family for a full day. American soldiers, sailors, and merchant mariners, not merely officers, regularly traded their cigarettes for cameras, prewar binoculars, souvenirs, or even sexual favors. The Jewish camp inmates had no access to the PXs, but they too followed the accepted practice of bartering their few cigarettes, often given to them by sympathetic soldiers, receiving in return fresh vegetables, milk for their children, or extra blankets to improve comfort and privacy in the barracks.

The officers who brought fixed prejudices to their tasks or were irritated by Jews who seemed to be ever-complaining and overdemanding simply filed and ignored directives that called for ameliorative action. Typical was the reaction of Colonel Epes, one of the officers in the 26th Division stationed in the American Zone in Austria. He could not be persuaded that Jews who refused to be repatriated to their "home" countries should be given sympathetic consideration. On October 3, 1945, he ordered clearance of the camps at Hart and Haag, and their Jewish inmates transferred to Camp 55. The director of the Joint Distribution Committee, James P. Rice, pleaded in vain with Epes not to insist upon the order. He had visited Camp 55 and found it deplorable—"barbed wire, pill boxes, leaky roofs, broken windows." The UNRRA representative had no greater success with Epes, who insisted that the Jews would have to go to 55, and "his men would be armed with live ammunition to enforce the order." A sit-down strike, followed by more vociferous demonstrations, drew sufficient public attention to compel Epes to retreat. General Mark Clark, in charge of the Austrian area, publicly reprimanded him and added a warning: "I think I know why you have not obeyed my orders. It is because you are not in sympathy with them. . . . I don't give a goddamn whether or not you are interested in or in sympathy with my orders on Jews. You will obey them." Following the reproof, the hotels in the resort town of Bad Gasten were requisitioned for DP needs.

By the end of 1945, even the most uncooperative officials realized that Eisenhower and his commanding generals were in earnest about sympathetic treatment of the Jews. Before returning to Washington for new assignments, Eisenhower had written:

> My recent visists in several Jewish centers made a poignant impression. I saw thousands of men and women who had suffered in the German concentration camps and had looked so hopeless on their liberation. But now, many of them have improved in health and are imbued with new faith. . . . I do not know when the stateless Jews will be given a permanent home. It is my aim, until that time, to make it possible for them to lead a normal and useful life.[17]

The letter was accepted as a charge by his successors, General Lucius Clay, the new Military Governor of Germany, and General Joseph McNarney, his associate. General Clay demonstrated his cooperation when he attended memorial services in the American Berlin Sector in Schlestensee, and General McNarney attended a Hanukkah party for two hundred orphans in Lendenfels, joining with the children in the *bora*.

Self-governing units had now been authorized in all the camps, with elected committees and a full democratic apparatus. An overall coordinating Central Committee was officially acknowledged as representative of the Jewish population. A news-broadcaster over the Armed Forces Network recognized the significance of the recognition. "This act of General McNar-ney's," he said, "writes a new page in our history. He has recog-nized the existence of a little democracy of 160,000 people liber-ated in the heart of Germany. The Central Committee of Liberated Jews is now a government without a flag." Another of the Jewish leaders hailed the flagless government "as repre-sentative of the dead as well as the living." Soon the UNRRA director at Landsberg, Leo Srole, was able to write: "Total camp administration was turned over to the DPs with overall supervi-sion by the IRO teams. All services indispensable to the mainte-nance of life, health, order and welfare of any normal town were performed exclusively by camp residents, out of a sense of per-sonal, social responsibility, a moral regard to work, and the normal drive to develop one's skills and talents for the future."[18]

Once encouragement had been offered by the senior officers and self-government had been inaugurated, a more tolerable way of life developed. Its most encouraging aspect was the to-tally unpredicted soaring birth rate. In the concentration and death camps the Nazis hardly needed to prohibit and punish pregnancy. Children deported to the camps had usually been the first victims of the gas chambers and the crematoria. Even outside the camps, who in the ultimately doomed ghettos would want to father or mother a child in an era dominated by Hitler and his executioners? When the Allies set up the first Displaced Persons' Camps in 1945, they housed few if any children under the age of six. Now there appeared an unarticulated determina-tion to replace the lives snuffed out or prevented. Dr. Samuel Gringauz, president of the Council of Liberated Jews in the American Zone, charged the young people: "You may not, and dare not, live with the memory of the dead and with lamenta-tions. You must live and build. . . . Remember the words of one of our great writers, 'not even the devil has prepared a revenge fitting for the spilled blood of a little child.' Your children, the carriers of our revenge, must find revenge in existence."

By the end of 1946, due in large part to the influx of refugees from the regions that had been under Russian control, children under six accounted for 8.5 percent of the camps' Jewish popula-tion, and for 12 percent of the inmates between the ages of six and seventeen. By that time, also, nearly 1,000 babies were being born each month. There were now more than 26,000 children in the camps, 5,700 of them orphans.

Through the leadership of Dr. Josef Rosensaft, who had married Dr. Bimko, the children were enrolled in more than a hundred schools. The facilities were still primitive, with few teaching tools, an extreme shortage of books, blackboards, or chalk. But the teachers, themselves often untrained, made do. Marie Syrkin, an American educator who had been commissioned by the Hillel Foundation in 1946 to identify students who could be recommended for college scholarships in American universities, was impressed by the imaginative use to which the limited facilities were utilized and by the maturity of the young people. She referred to the response of several of the seven- or eight-year-olds as typical:

A Bible class, studying the life of Moses, came to the episode where the infant Moses was left by his mother among the bulrushes. The teacher asked if the mother was justified in abandoning her child to an unknown woman, the Egyptian princess. Was that how a real mother would act? This was no problem for the children. There was no effort of the mind and imagination beyond their years to produce replies. Of course, they responded, that is how the real mother would act. One little girl mentioned mothers whom she had seen tossing children out of trains in the hope of saving them from certain extermination. Perhaps a compassionate passer-by would pick up the child. Another youngster had been present when a baby had been thrown over a fence during an "action." And, finally, a boy got up and said, "Some of us in this class were given by our mothers to Poles. That is how we escaped."[19]

Adults too refused to succumb to idleness during the interminable wait for employment or migration. They organized schools, which were labeled rather grandiloquently as "People's Universities." There were special sessions in the makeshift synagogues where Bible, Talmud, and their commentaries could be studied and discussed. Surviving teachers and students in two of the famous Yeshiboth (seminaries) of Poland, the Lubovitcher and the Lubliner, were transplanted en masse to the camps. For those who wished to sharpen their vocational skills, there were training workshops. And for those who looked ahead to a transformed life in Palestine, there were agricultural training centers for communal life modeled on the kibbutzim and kvutsoth of the hoped-for Homeland. Through the indefatigable efforts of Dr. Bimko, a newspaper, *Unser Styme* (Our

Voice), came into being. There were no typewriters, no printing equipment, very little paper; but the "newspaper" appeared. It was widely circulated in the camps and abroad. And there was a Yiddish theater whose activity elicited the tribute of an amazed visiting actor: "I never played to such a grateful audience. They clapped and laughed and cried. When we gave, as our last item, the famous song, 'Think Not You Travel to Despair Again,' the thousand people in the hall rose to their feet and sang with us."

In the fall of 1946 a series of revolutionary developments transformed the political alignments of the postwar world. The coalition of Russia and the West, precariously held together during the defense against a common enemy, collapsed, and all the suspicions harbored by the Communists and the free world against each other reemerged. Stalin locked the "liberated" Baltic States and the Balkans firmly into the Soviet empire. Using infiltration, coup, and conquest, he bludgeoned the states contiguous to Russia into a ring of satellites, to make certain that the Russian heartland would never again be in jeopardy. The Big Three of the Allies—Britain, France, and the United States —fearful that Communist penetration would not only be extended in eastern and middle Europe but would threaten the security of the West, reacted sharply. Through an apocryphal story, Churchill, in his *Memoirs,* illustrated how yesterday's allies had become today's enemies. He told of an Englishman, a Royal Marine, who was being shown the sights of Moscow by one of the Intourist guides. "This," said the Russian, "is the Eden Hotel, formerly the Ribbentrop Hotel. Here is Churchill Street, formerly Hitler Street. And here is Beaverbrook Station, formerly Goering Station. By the way, comrade, will you have a cigarette?" The Marine took the cigarette and then replied, "Thank you, comrade, formerly bastard."[20] By 1946, other names could again be substituted as the Grand Alliance disintegrated.

Nowhere did the divergent interests of the former Allies more clearly express themselves than in their revised objectives for defeated Germany. The western bloc had planned to dismember it, to postpone sovereignty, to prevent any possibility of rearmament. Instead, as the Cold War tightened its grip, East and West began to vie with one another to add the potential German strength to their own side. Two new Germanies arose.

Russia coerced its Eastern German Zone into becoming a full-fledged satellite. The West combined its three zones to create the Federal Republic of Germany and planned a major program of assistance for its reconstruction. A visiting Michigan senator, Arthur Vandenberg, remarked: "We will soon have little control over the fate of Germany; it will be Germany that, in the long run, will decide the fate of the former allies." The realistic wisdom of the nineteenth-century British Prime Minister Palmerston was validated: "There are no permanent friendships, there are no permanent enmities, there are only permanent interests."

How far the pendulum had swung was pointed up in a memorable speech by James Byrnes, the new American Secretary of State, when he addressed an assembly of 1,500 American military and government personnel in Stuttgart on September 6, 1946. One hundred fifty Germans working in the American occupation administration were in the audience. Byrnes said: "The German people throughout Germany, under proper safeguards, should now be given the primary responsibility for running their own affairs. . . . The American people want to help the German people to win their way back to an honorable place among the free and peace-loving peoples of the world. All that the Allied governments can and should do is to lay down the rules under which German democracy can govern itself. I look forward to welcoming a rehabilitated Germany into the western bloc."[21]

This was a far cry from the October 1945 Truman statement, which had defined the principal objective of the western Allies as being "to prevent Germany from becoming a threat to the world," and had warned the Germans that "they cannot escape responsibility for what they have brought upon the world and upon themselves." Little wonder that the Germans in the audience wept in relief. Here was an outstretched hand, a magnanimity that could not have been imagined less than a year before.

The Russians, remembering their twenty million dead, their ruined cities, their uprooted populations, the extermination camps, were outraged by this ominous courtship. They suspected that the Allies would soon begin rebuilding Germany, strengthening it, perhaps even rearming it. The western Allies responded that the Kremlin had only itself to blame for the changed diplomatic climate after its brazen subversions in east-

ern Europe and its incessant calls for Communist revolutions in
Europe and Asia.

By the summer of 1947, acting upon the re-ordered strategy of
rapprochement, the Allies announced that most of the restrictions that had been in force in German economic and political
life would be abolished. In the following March, representatives
of the United States, Britain, and France met in London to
consider plans for the establishment of a sovereign West German state. When the Four Power Council convened in Berlin
ten days later, the Soviet general demanded to know the Allied
intentions for German unification. General Lucius Clay, the
American representative, refused to divulge details. The Soviet
general walked out and the quadripartite administration of Germany disintegrated amid angry charges and countercharges.

The developing Cold War, with its dramatic shift in alliances,
inevitably affected the relationship of the Germans to the DPs
in their midst. All the hidden hostilities surfaced as the Germans savored their new favored status. Anti-Semitism did not
take dangerous forms, but Jews, now permitted to leave the
camps, heard ugly remarks, ever more overt. "It is perfectly
clear," Rabbi Philip Bernstein, the current Adviser on Jewish
Affairs, wrote on May 12, 1947, "that only the presence of the
American military safeguards the Jewish people." Since Truman's directive to Eisenhower, many of the DPs had been permitted to take up residence outside the camps. But after stones
were thrown at the homes where they lived, many moved back
to the camps to ensure protection. Even more troubling to them
was the lack of understanding among the replacements for the
seasoned veterans in the American occupying forces who, by
1946, had almost all been demobilized. Many of the newcomers
were raw recruits who, when drafted, had been hauled un-
ceremoniously out of college and entry-level jobs. They knew
little about the war and its objectives and they cared less. Some
of them no doubt enjoyed the favors of attractive German
women eager to fraternize with purveyors of nylon stockings,
chocolates, cigarettes, and other luxuries obtainable only from
the camp PX. They were given distorted versions of what had
to be unfairly endured by the defeated German people. Those
who came from German-American backgrounds understandably identified with the general population rather than with
gaunt, scrawny Jews who were only just recovering from their
dehumanizing concentration camp experiences. A poll taken in

1946 on the reactions of the American soldiers produced ill-omened findings: 51 percent replied that Hitler "had done many good things for the Germans"; 22 percent said that "the Germans had good reason to distrust the Jews"; 10 percent thought that "the Germans were justified in launching the war." Of course these were the reactions of eighteen-year-old GIs. But they could not be ignored, especially when the earlier policy of barring entry of refugees into the American Zone again went into effect on April 27, 1947. The pressure on behalf of the Jews to migrate to Israel or to western countries that would accept them became overwhelming.

A good proportion of the DPs had dreamed of ultimate settlement in the United States. In Earl Harrison's report of 1945 he had strongly recommended that his country share some of the responsibility for easing the plight of the Jewish survivors by modifying its restrictive immigration laws. These had been enacted in 1924, and they established a quota of 2 percent of each nationality resident in the United States in 1890, before the immigration tides from eastern and southern Europe had become a significant social force. The historian Samuel Eliot Morison, himself a New England Brahmin, believed that the underlying purpose of the legislation had been to exclude Jews who were applying from countries that had turned to communism, and Italians, among whom there well might be Mafiosi elements.[22]

There was little likelihood that the restrictive quotas would be lifted after World War II. Millions of demobilized GIs were returning to claim jobs and housing. For all of Truman's goodwill, he knew that Congress would resist any effort to provide a haven for more than an inconsequential fraction even of those who had relatives in the United States.

Jewish officials examined every possibility for other immigration outlets. Rabbi Bernstein undertook an extensive placement mission and interviewed many heads of state, including the Pope. His report of May 12, 1947, was utterly disheartening. Countries willing to accept very small numbers sought skills in mining, forestry, farming, and shipping, useful for their own economies; but few among the Jewish Displaced Persons could qualify by experience.

More than two years had now dragged by since the war had ended and there were still tens of thousands of survivors marooned in Europe, most of them in the Displaced Persons' Camps, their desperation further deepened by the conviction that they had been abandoned. By now they had become an international nuisance, castoffs, unwanted, the Christian conscience blunted by the intractability of the problem, compassion giving way to irritation and even to hostility. Palestine, more than ever, even for those who had originally dreamed of a new life in the western lands, had become the only hope for a solution to their status of dependency on authorities who, inevitably, were guided by their own national interests. Since Hitler's day this wretched flotsam had lost even the dignity of identity. In the concentration camps they had been numbers: the tattoos on their arms reminded them and all who observed them that they were non-persons. In the temporary shelters of the western military zones, offered as a humanitarian gesture, they were anonymous DPs.

In October 1945, on his return to Palestine from Jewish Agency meetings in Paris, David Ben Gurion, the emerging leader of the Yishub, had made a special stopover in the DP Camps of the Munich area. The ride to Landsberg from Munich was on the road of the Tyrol March, during which thousands of doomed Jewish prisoners had died in the few days preceding liberation. Ben Gurion passed the prison in which Hitler had written *Mein Kampf.* He addressed more than 2,000 cheering DPs who crowded the Landsberg sports arena. "Palestine," he exclaimed, "is no longer only a vision, a dream, a hope. It will become a reality in the near future. . . . I speak in the name of six hundred thousand Jews who have suffered countless trials in establishing our Homeland. They believe that, despite British politics, they will determine their own fate. If England attempts to keep the doors of Palestine shut, our youth will open them: and even if our hopes are stifled, we will meet the situation like a nation confident in its cause and in its strength."[23]

The delirious audience was fired by Ben Gurion's unquenchable faith. The international commissions of the next few years that inspected the camps and took testimony reported near unanimity in the yearning of the DPs to make Palestine the home for their renewal. It was clear that for them the era of deference and resignation had ended. They were determined never again "to carry their Homeland in their arms."

President Truman had several times urged Britain to issue 100,000 certificates for a mass immigration to Palestine, at least to empty the Displaced Persons' Camps. But Ernest Bevin and his Labor government had tenaciously resisted, determined not to alienate the Arabs of the Middle East. No argument made the slightest impression, even the unanimous recommendation of a special commission that Bevin had himself appointed and had pledged to honor. The DPs faced the stark prospect that, if their hearts' desire was to be fulfilled, it would have to be in the teeth of British opposition, even armed opposition. Ironically, by his very intransigence, Bevin thus became the less than legitimate father of Aliyah Bet, the clandestine operation for illegal immigration that was to dominate international headlines until Israel emerged independent in 1948.

CHAPTER SEVEN

Af Al Pi (Despite All):
Illegal Immigration to Palestine

THE TENACIOUS ATTEMPTS to get the Jews out of eastern and central Europe and shepherd them to the Displaced Persons' Camps or to the seaports of the Mediterranean, the Black Sea, and the Adriatic, was the assignment of B'richa under the direction of Haganah. But this migration represented only part of the overall objective. The actual sea journeys to reach Palestine called for even greater resourcefulness and risk, for here the opposition of the British was direct, through their own Royal Navy, and it often led to confrontation and violence. The responsibility for the sea journeys of the refugee ships fell to Mossad, another arm of Haganah.* The closest cooperation had to be maintained with B'richa agents, and the evacuation from European lands and the onward voyages by sea often became an extended operation.

The Holocaust brought out the worst in many people. There were others in whom it brought out the best; the agents of Mossad were such. In daring and improvisation, they matched the leadership qualities provided by B'richa. They were a cadre

---

*References to the Mossad are sometimes confusing because it had different roles during the war and after. During WW II it was an arm of Haganah and cooperated with B'richa in bringing displaced Jews to seaports for onward journeys to Palestine. After the war and the establishment of Israel, it was reorganized to become an intelligence system to protect the security of Israel, including the search for Nazi criminals and the penetration of intelligence activity of the Arab states.

of near-buccaneers—Ehud Avriel, Yehuda Arazi, Ruth Aliav, Eliahu Golomb, Moshe Agami, Yulik Braginski, Munya Mardor, and scores of others—who did not flinch when they had to cope, in refugee vessels, with the might and omnipresence of the Royal Navy. Some of their names were linked to specific exploits, but in most instances what they accomplished was the result of teamwork.

When Hitler came to power in 1933, the effort had already begun to circumvent the Chamberlain White Paper–imposed monthly limit of 1,500 immigrants to Palestine. The first ships began to make the precarious voyage to Palestine, usually by way of Greece. One of the early experimental ventures was undertaken in 1934. A tiny craft, the *Velos*, was chartered in Greece by Irgun Zionists, headed by Yulik Braginski, and loaded with 340 immigrants who had made their way with B'richa guidance from Poland. The *Velos* landed on a remote beach in Palestine and the passengers were quickly absorbed into the kibbutzim in the area. The ship then returned at once to Greece hoping to repeat its success; but the British had been alerted and on the second journey, the intercepted *Velos* did not reach port.

In the next two years British vigilance continued to thwart nearly every effort. But the probability of failure was no deterrent. Mossad kept multiplying the number of small boats and every completed landing was hailed as justifying frequent failures. Braginski, chided for efforts that seemed so picayune in relation to the magnitude of the problem, exclaimed: "What the hell, Columbus discovered America in a 49-foot barge."[1] He and his colleagues managed in 1938, after many near failures, to load a much larger ship, the *Attratto*, and arrange for its sailing from the Yugoslavian port of Lousak to Palestine. He was euphoric when the code message announced that the nearly 1,400 "books" that had been shipped had finally arrived.

But much more ambitious undertakings were soon forced upon the Jewish world as Hitler's conquests expanded. It was necessary now to plan well-coordinated efforts, with representatives in the main cities of Europe—depots to receive the refugees, trucks to transport them to seaports, and negotiations for the lease or purchase of ships. It was also necessary to arrange for the debarcations, the distribution of the immigrants if and when they landed, and care for their welfare if they were apprehended and committed for internment, imprisonment, or, worst of all, for deportation to their points of origin. Experienced agents were recruited; within a year, scores of them were operating in every part of Europe and the Near East.

A few months before the Chamberlain White Paper was issued in 1939, three barely seaworthy ships, carrying more than 1,000 refugees who had fled from Germany and Rumania, reached the shores of Palestine. They were promptly turned away by the British coastal police. The Colonial Secretary, Malcolm MacDonald, was sharply questioned in Parliament how such action could have been taken when it inevitably resulted in sending the refugees to German imprisonment. MacDonald replied that "the responsibility rests with those who had organized the illegal immigration." He reinforced his decision by ordering port authorities "to shoot at or into" any ship bringing illegals to Palestine.[2]

The illegal immigration was accelerated as the war drew close. One ship, the *Tiger Hill,* whose 1,400 Polish refugees were brought together at a port in Rumania, was halted under British pressure for several days. It was released by the intervention of King Carol after a personal appeal by Ruth Aliav, one of the legendary heroines of the Mossad who operated out of Rumania. When the *Tiger Hill* reached the coast of Tel Aviv, it was greeted with a British fusillade, the first shots fired by the British after the declaration of war on Germany. Three women and one man were among the earliest casualties of the war between the Allies and the Nazis.

By the fall of 1940 the German concentration camps were in full operation. The desperation that now motivated the refugees was dramatized in a succession of tragic episodes that brought the full light of world publicity on British policy. On November 11 two broken-down ships, the *Pacific* and the *Milos,* arrived in Haifa, from Black Sea ports, with 1,800 fugitives. The majority of the passengers were Zionists who had been training in secret European camps for life in Palestine. The British authorities arrested them. To discourage other attempts to enter Palestine, the deportation announcement declared that the passengers would be interned in Mauritius, the tropical island in the Indian Ocean. "Their ultimate disposal," the announcement added, "will be a matter of consideration at the end of the war; but it is not proposed that they shall remain in the colony to which they are sent, or that they should go to Palestine. Similar action will be taken in the case of any further parties who may succeed in reaching Palestine with a view to illegal entry."[3] The intercepted refugees were then transferred to the 12,000-ton *Patria*, a ship that the British had seized from conquered France to prevent its being taken over by the Nazis. The departure for Mauritius was scheduled for November 25.

The Haganah leadership was determined to prevent the ship from sailing. A plan developed to cripple it, expecting that in the confusion of planned sabotage, perhaps several hundred of the refugees would have a chance to escape and blend into the Palestine villages. The effort depended on perfect timing and the success of every detail. It was necessary to float a large barrel with dynamite past the vigilant British guards, to attach it to an exact point on the side of the ship, and to set off an explosion with enough force to disable the vessel but not so much as to cause loss of life. Young volunteers carried out their assigned responsibilities skillfully and the sappers who swam out to the ship were able to attach the barrel of dynamite to its side.

But the plotters could not know how decrepit the vessel had become, and the charge for the explosion proved too powerful. It shattered the *Patria*, killing 240 of the passengers and 50 members of the crew. For the next few days frantic attempts were made, mainly by the Haifa Jews, to rescue those who were trapped in the hulk of the ship or trying to stay alive in the Mediterranean waters. Those who were rescued were imprisoned in Athlit, one of the British detention camps in Palestine. Although appeals came from all over the world for the British to exercise compassion after what the survivors had already endured, the deportation decision remained unchanged.

During the *Patria* crisis, another ship, the *Atlantic*, had arrived in Haifa with 1,875 more fugitives. They too were sent to Athlit. There was an angry confrontation when Moshe Sharett of the Jewish Agency upbraided the High Commissioner for callousness in imprisoning the refugees in Athlit and then ordering them deported to another end of the world. He deeply resented the argument that Communists might infiltrate any contingent that would be admitted to Palestine. "Not a single such case has ever happened," said Sharett. The High Commissioner replied blandly, "Well, Governors sometimes have to handle unpleasant situations."[4] A fortnight later, though every military resource was needed by the Allies in this decisive period of the war, 1,650 of the *Patria* and *Atlantic* internees were marshaled for deportation. Police dragged them out of their cages in Athlit, one by one, many of them on stretchers, to be dispatched to Mauritius for internment during the five years that the war lasted. In the first period of the confinement the men were lodged in cells in an old French prison, the women and children in primitive huts, twenty-four to each hut. Visits of two hours were limited to three times weekly. During the internment 130 people died of tropical diseases.*

Meanwhile another ship, the *Salvador*, carrying more than 350 passengers, most of them refugees from central Europe, set sail from the Bulgarian port of Varna, by way of Turkish waters. The British ambassador to Turkey warned that the ship would not be permitted to land in Haifa. Upon arrival there, it was turned away and ordered back to its point of sailing. When it reached the Sea of Marmara in mid-December 1940, the overload caused the vessel to capsize. Two hundred passengers drowned, including children. T. M. Snow, who headed the British Foreign Office Refugee Section, found a salutory caution in the catastrophe. "There could have been no more opportune disaster from the point of view of stopping this traffic," he said.[5]

The *Salvador* tragedy did not divert Mossad from its illegal traffic. After the Japanese sneak attacks on Pearl Harbor in December 1941, which brought the United States into the war, the Germans no longer had any lingering concern about American reactions to their policies. As Hitler escalated the process of Jewish extermination, the desperation of the Jews in the conquered lands encouraged cooperative planning by Mossad emissaries and the generally obstreperous Irgunists, who had regarded Haganah as too cautious.

How desperate the risks taken by Mossad had become was pointed up by the tragedy of the *Struma*, a small converted cattle boat that was leased by the Irgunists to attempt the transport to Palestine of 769 refugees from the Axis-dominated Balkans. It left the Rumanian port of Constanta in December 1941 under a Panamanian flag to make its way to Palestine via Turkey. When it arrived in Istanbul, it could not proceed, for major repairs were needed that could not be accomplished for many weeks. The Turkish authorities, wary of being saddled with the un-

---

*Of those who had escaped internment and deportation, 150 joined the British forces in the Near East, and the first to die fighting the Germans at Tobruk in North Africa was a Greek Jew who had survived the *Patria* tragedy.

wanted passenger load, would not permit disembarcation unless the British agreed that the refugees would be admitted to Palestine. The British refused.

For two months the wretched families, including more than four hundred women and children, remained holed up on a ship that had one lavatory, no fresh water, and a limited reserve of food and medical supplies. They survived only because the Jewish community of Istanbul managed to provide bare subsistence. Even the official British naval reports described conditions on the boat as "appalling." The Turkish authorities kept threatening to tow the boat out to the international waters of the Black Sea unless the British gave the required assurances. After nine weeks, they lost patience and ordered the *Struma* to leave.

A few shocked voices were heard in the British Parliament and in the press. Eden's secretary, Oliver Harvey, was one of the government aides who pleaded for more compassionate consideration. "Must His Majesty's Government," he asked, "take such an inhumane decision? If they [the refugees] go back, they will all be killed." He suggested that perhaps they could be interned in Cyprus camps and sent on to Palestine later as their quota number came up. But Harvey was not speaking for Eden, nor for Churchill, who, Harvey wrote, though deeply touched was unable to give more than fragments of time to such problems when the war was going so badly in the Pacific.[6] Indeed, on the day that Harvey made his appeal, Singapore fell to Japan. The British ambassador to Turkey, overcome by his eyewitness appraisal of the tragedy, suggested to the Turkish authorities that they need have no fear of being saddled with the refugees if they let them disembark, "for if the refugees reached Palestine they might, despite their illegality, receive humane treatment." The statement infuriated Lord Moyne, then Colonial Secretary, who again admonished all officials to remember that concession, however compassionately motivated, would simply encourage hordes of other refugees to imitate the effort. He advised the Turkish government to divest itself of all responsibility since the refugees should not have made the attempt in the first place. "Send the boat back to where it originated, in Rumania," he said.

On February 23, 1942, all avenues of diplomacy having been exhausted, eighty Turkish police stormed the *Struma* during the night and, without providing fuel, food, or water, prepared to have it towed into the Black Sea. A few hundred despairing passengers tried to resist, but they were quickly overcome. In the midst of the mêlée the ship's boilers exploded and it sank. Of the 769 refugees, only one who was able to swim the few miles to the shores of Istanbul survived. No rescue effort to the drowning victims was offered by any government agency.

During the drawn-out negotiations it had been urged that, of the seventy children on board, those aged from eleven to sixteen should be released and sent overland to Palestine. But the Turkish government refused to accept responsibility for their fate in the difficult journey on Turkish land, and the British could find no shipping to transport them. All the children were drowned when the ship sank. A pregnant woman had been taken off earlier and brought to a city hospital; the baby died in birth. Her husband was drowned when the *Struma* sank. Both she and the one survivor of the sinking were denied British visas to go on to Palestine.

The horror over the fate of the *Struma* and other floating coffins was swallowed up by additional tragedies of the war in the two years that followed. But the bitterness of the Jews of Palestine could not be softened, for even when the war ended, the British maintained their policy of intercepting "illegal" ships. The Irgunists listed the British with the Nazis as common enemies. They mounted posters all over Palestine in Hebrew and English with photographs of Lord Moyne and the British Commissioner in Palestine, Harold MacMichael. The posters proclaimed them "wanted" as murderers for their pitiless role in the tragedies of illegal immigrations.

Some youngsters in the extremist wing of the Irgun party who had witnessed the tragic *Patria* deportation planned retribution. The attempt to track down MacMichael failed; but Moyne, when he later became High Commissioner in Egypt, was assassinated in Cairo as he was leaving his office on November 6, 1944. The two boys who were responsible were captured and hanged for murder by an Egyptian court.* It should be

---

*In 1979, in an interview with Gershon Avner, president of the University of Haifa, he related an experience that indicated the young terrorists might have shot down Moyne when he was apparently fast changing his mind about the White Paper and Partition. Avner was British born and attended Oxford where, in 1942, he became president of the Oxford Union. He migrated to

added that there was considerable sympathy for them among Egyptian young people, who hated the British exploitation of their country as much as the assassins hated Moyne.

The end of the war in April 1945 did not yield modification of the British immigration restrictions; the rigid quotas were still enforced. The Jews of Palestine had been loyal allies throughout the war, while the Arabs were either in sullen boycott or outright opposition. Acknowledgment however was not a diplomatic virtue. The new Labor government under Clement Attlee, despite its earlier promises, refused to repudiate Chamberlain's White Paper; the Arabs, undeviatingly opposed to a Jewish presence in the Near East, were not to be further estranged. But Ben Gurion and the leaders of Haganah were no longer inhibited about jeopardizing the war effort by resisting British immigration policies. All parties in Israel, though with differing intensity, now united in their effort to outmaneuver and resist the British surveillance.

In August 1945, the first postwar boat slipped out of a lonely port on the South Italian coast, a 25-ton fishing smack named *Dalin.* It successfully made the 2,500-mile journey with thirty-five passengers drawn from many parts of Europe. After *Dalin,* other small boats were dispatched, all of which reached their destination and returned to their Italian bases. The *Petro* made several such runs, each with about 170 illegals, before Mossad decided that the tiny craft had become too well known to the British to be of further use.

Mossad continued to take advantage of British global colonial troubles. A loyal Athenian, Spiro Gaganis, affectionately called

---

Israel and served in the Foreign Office and filled a number of ambassadorial posts before becoming president of the University of Haifa. There was a tradition at both Oxford and Cambridge that brought national figures weekly to the university union for debates on controversial public issues. Each of the two guests teamed up with outstanding students. Avner was in the debate when Lord Moyne came as one of the guest speakers in 1942. After the debate he drew Avner aside and told him that, as events unfolded in Europe and the Middle East, he was reanalyzing the British position on Palestine and was moving much closer to the Jewish position. Avner hurried the information to Dr. Chaim Weizmann, but by that time Britain was ensnared in the most desperate phase of the war and could not venture a revision of its policy that would critically alienate the Arab world.

by his Jewish friends "the Goose," became a valuable liaison for procuring shipping for the onward journeys from Greek ports to Palestine. Typical was his resourcefulness in acquiring a 200-ton boat that had been built for forty passengers. He undertook the complete reconstruction of the vessel and his carpenters stretched their efforts, a further incentive being their dislike for the British. When the boat was ready to sail, more than two hundred passengers were crammed into it. It was renamed the *Berl Katzenelson* for a recently deceased Zionist Labor theoretician.

Lights out and radio silent, the vessel stole past the British patrols and reached its goal. Palyam men were ready with rowboats to bring the passengers to shore, some of them carried on the backs of the rescuers. By the time the British arrived at the debarcation point, all but eleven had landed and had been distributed among neighboring kibbutzim. The eleven, some elderly and the others children, together with the Greek crew and captain, were taken for internment to Athlit. The crew were soon released to return to Greece, where they began at once to plan with the Goose for another rendezvous in Palestine. In October 1945, Haganah units penetrated the Athlit detention center in a daring exploit and most of the internees were freed.[7]

Then came a day in April 1946 when a spectacular effort to thwart the blockade, and give it worldwide publicity, was made. The responsibility devolved on the veteran Yehuda Arazi, who was reassigned from planning B'richa migrations to isolated embarcation points, to operate out of major ports. He chartered the *Fede*, a large vessel capable of carrying more than 1,000 passengers, and acquired the license to carry a shipment of salt to Sardinia, from La Spezia on the Italian Riviera. The port authorities were bribed or cajoled into cooperation, and the sailing from La Spezia was set for April 4. But the destination was not to be Sardinia, but Palestine. And the cargo was not salt, but refugees.

For a moment the enterprise backfired. The arrival at the port of so many army trucks, packed almost beyond capacity with people, however shielded with impressive documents, roused the suspicion of the regular Italian police. They presumed that Arazi, despite his British uniform, was smuggling Polish Fascists into Franco's Spain. Arazi, at bay, decided to risk a candid confession about the real purpose of the venture. He summoned some of the refugees who had suffered most in the camps to appear before the head of the police and had them expose their arms with the tattoo numbers on them. They told the story of their ordeal and what Palestine meant now.

Arazi's intuition was vindicated. The carabinieri were most sympathetic and began helping the refugees to board the vessel. But the inevitable delay was long enough for the British to get wind of the affair. Their gunboats arrived quickly and prevented the *Fede* from sailing, though the trucks got away. When the British commander ordered instant disembarcation of all passengers, on penalty of being taken off by force, Arazi coolly responded that his passengers had found Europe "inhospitable" and they had no intention of turning back. If the British laid a hand on any of them, Arazi threatened to have the ship blown up with all on board, including such British as participated in the attempt to remove the passengers. The commander and his men withdrew to determine their next move, but one of their warships moved alongside the *Fede* and the port was sealed off by British tanks.

Arazi now went public. Radio messages went out to Attlee, Truman, and Stalin, noting that 1,000 survivors of Hitler's death camps were crowded into a small ship in an Allied port and were besieged by the tanks and warships of the world's greatest navy. Reporters and correspondents arrived to cover one of the most dramatic stories of the postwar period. Hundreds of Italians from the town and the area crowded the quay daily to encourage the beleaguered refugees. Arazi made daily speeches from the port gates, emphasizing that all the survivors wanted now was the opportunity to begin new lives in Palestine. And the crowds cheered.

The British were compelled to move their troops to a distance from the quay, for the demonstrations were becoming ever more difficult to contain. The windows of the British commander's house were smashed, army reinforcements had to be brought in, and the tension mounted. Arazi then employed bolder actions. With the consent of the municipality he put up a sign at the port entry reading, "The Gate of Zion," and he hoisted the Italian and Zionist flags there. In daily press conferences he displayed immigration certificates that he had designed, imprinted with quotations from the Bible, the Balfour Declaration of 1917, and the San Remo affirmation of 1920 in which all the Allied nations had validated the right of the Jews to their Homeland.

In Palestine itself the Jewish shadow government faced a grave dilemma in determining how to react publicly. For if there was evidence that the *Fede* defiance had the cooperation of the Jewish authorities, the British had the power to impose sanctions. Moshe Sharett, later Israeli Foreign Minister, indicated that Arazi was a loner and was not following official directives. Actually, Arazi was adapting a stratagem used when the nineteenth-century Italian Red Shirt hero, Garibaldi, challenged Austrian authority in Italian provinces that he was determined to liberate. The Prime Minister, Camillo Cavour, condemned him in public as a provocateur and then, in his private quarters, embraced him as a patriot.

Arazi moved rapidly to broaden his challenge. He declared a hunger strike. Next to the "Gate of Zion" sign he placed a large billboard on which two numbers were posted daily: the number of hours of the hunger strike and the number of refugees on board who had lost consciousness. The figures mounted steadily and were flashed to the world, with the implicit message that the besieged were all survivors of death camps and Hitler's work of extermination was being completed by British implacability. The crowds of demonstrators grew, and in nearby Genoa the port workers went on strike. By the third day the deck of the *Fede* was covered with inert bodies that had been carried outdoors for full public view. Not a sound came from the ship, no moans, no cries, just an eerie silence. Arazi made public the messages of sympathy that came from the Italian Prime Minister, Alcide de Gasperi, and from other notables throughout the world, including the admiral of the Italian fleet. He then held another press conference in which he told reporters that he was not playing a political game, that his desperate charges had come through the agonies of the ghettos and the extermination camps, and that they would rather die now than be obliged to go back to the Europe that had destroyed all their loved ones and offered no hope for them. He warned the Attlee government that it would have to bear the responsibility for the developing tragedy.

On the fourth day, two British cars drew up to the port carrying embassy officials, including Harold Laski, a high-ranking member of the British Labor Party and scion of an influential Jewish family. He had been implored by one of the outstanding Italian Jewish leaders, Rafaele Cantoni, to intercede. Arazi agreed to a conference and Laski urged him to return the refugees to their European camps while he would counsel the government to issue certificates for Palestine. Arazi insisted that unless the refugees were permitted to sail at once, ten would commit suicide each day on the deck until only a coffin ship would be left. The first ten had already volunteered; their suicides would begin the next morning.

Laski was convinced that a lunatic was leading a shipload of survivors who were distraught enough to carry through their threat. He pledged to Arazi that if the hunger strike and the suicide threat were canceled, he would discuss the situation with Attlee and Bevin and recommend that negotiations for a compromise be opened. Arazi accepted the offer on the assurance that no police would be brought in while the British government's reply was awaited, and an early time limit was set. The strike and the suicide threat were then lifted and a truce was declared just before the Passover holidays were to begin.

The Seder on board the *Fede* was exultantly celebrated. Leading local authorities were invited and they brought abundant food with them. Arazi announced that if the *Fede* was released and sailed to Palestine, it would bring back Italian prisoners whose repatriation had been long delayed by the British ostensibly because there was a severe shipping shortage. The announcement made Arazi the toast of Italy.

Soon the response of the British government arrived, offering 679 entry certificates to be deducted from the 1,500 that were the regular monthly quota for Palestine. The rest, it was promised, would be issued in the following month. Arazi refused to modify his conditions. On May 8, the British gave in and agreed to the immediate admission of all the passengers, without reference to any effect on future quotas.[8]

Arazi turned the *Fede* back to its regular commander, and went down the ladder to a waiting motorboat that took him to the mainland. Since there was no further need for harrying the refugees on the overcrowded *Fede*, about half were transferred to another ship. The two vessels sailed to Palestine, where their passengers and crew were received as heroes. The six-week battle had been won. The victory involved much more than the 1,000 refugees who had challenged an empire to gain their objective. The rationale for illegal immigration had been explained in its most dramatic form.*

The British were determined that the *Fede* incident would not stand as a precedent. They decided that they would make an overwhelming effort that would once and for all end the defiance of the Jews. The test came in July 1947 with the voyage of the *Exodus*. More than 4,000 inmates of DP Camps in Germany holding forged visas for South American countries boarded the ship at Sete in France. They reached Palestine and, unsuccessful in the attempt to break the British blockade, were herded into the deportation cages of three British transports to be returned to Sete. But the French refused to accept any who would not disembark of their own free will. Only 130 people, sick, old, or pregnant, yielded. The British then sent the vessels on to Germany, intending to intern the passengers in several of the former Nazi concentration camps. Arriving at Hamburg the passengers of two ships disembarked, but no threat could compel any of those on the third ship to come down voluntarily. As the British began forcing the passengers off the ship, those who still resisted were beaten with clubs and hoses in the presence of German civilians who crowded the quay and watched the incredible scene only two years after Hitler's suicide.†

Winston Churchill heartily condemned the "callous hostility"

---

*The *Fede* episode is included with other daring exploits in illegal immigration in the autobiographical volume by Ehud Avriel, one of the chief Mossad leaders. For many years after independence, he was in charge of Prime Minister Ben Gurion's office and served in several European capitals as Israeli ambassador.

After the sovereignty of Israel had been declared, Yehuda Arazi returned to Palestine, where Ben Gurion offered him the choice of a government post. He declined and turned to civilian life. Envisaging an enormous tourist interest in an independent Israel, he pioneered a hotel training school, but such tranquil activity could not satisfy his restless spirit. He died in an airplane crash in 1959.

†A month later the internees were transferred to Displaced Persons' Camps at Pöppendorf and Amstau, in the British Zone. In November most of them were smuggled into the American Zone. They were given priority in the illegal immigration of the next few months and the last of them reached Palestine in September 1948.

of the Bevin policy as "the Labour Government's war with the Jews," but Bevin cabled his "expression of personal appreciation" to the troops. The revulsion aroused by this ugly episode caused many of the Jewish moderates in Palestine to side with the Irgun and Lehi extremists, who were now making a supreme effort to compel the British to relinquish their Mandate for Palestine. It needed little more to convince the British people that Palestine was becoming another Ireland, where the guerilla resistance of the Sinn Feiners had long since obliged Britain to reappraise its imperial role.

Apparently Bevin needed further persuasion. He calculated that his firm, unrelenting handling of the *Exodus* had demonstrated the futility of illegal immigration, and that the democratic world's opprobrium would fade. He was soon disabused. The ships continued to come. The *Haim Arlosoroff*, sponsored by the Irgun, broke through the blockade with highly sophisticated seamanship and crashed on the shore of Palestine, at Cape Carmel. One of its plates, taken from a ship that had earlier vainly attempted to run the blockade, bore the phrase "*Af al pi*" (Despite all), which became the rallying declaration in the defiance of the British. The passengers, triumphantly fulfilling the motto, melted into the kibbutzim of the area.

Bevin at last realized the enormity of his problem when naval intelligence reported to him that emissaries from Palestine had purchased two 4,500-ton ships, the *Pan York* and the *Pan Crescent*, both much larger than any carriers of the past. The plan was to load them with 15,000 refugees whose defiance would strain to an intolerable point the British capacity to enforce their Mandate.

Early in September 1947 the *York* arrived in Marseilles with a mixed crew of Palestinians, Americans, and Spaniards. The *Crescent* docked in Venice; there were delays for repairs when the vessel was severely damaged by British saboteurs. Then both ships sailed for the Rumanian port of Constanta, trailed by British destroyers. They were guided into port by a Soviet gunboat. In the continuing propaganda war, the British circulated the story that a fresh wave of Jewish immigrants, mainly Communists from Rumania, were planning to flood Palestine. The British pledged that they would not allow the position of the Arabs to be prejudiced by such immigration. There was intense diplomatic pressure by the British to persuade Anna Pauker, the Rumanian Foreign Minister, to delay the sailing of the ships.

Pauker was caught in a conflict between her anti-Zionism and her hostility to the British, though outwardly she remained neutral.*

The British had appealed to the United States to persuade the Jewish leaders, and specifically Moshe Sharett, the Foreign Minister, to order the ships not to sail. At the United Nations the debate on Partition was approaching its climax.† Sharett and even Ben Gurion realized that Partition itself might be voted down if massive illegal immigration were interpreted as an untimely provocation. They urged postponement of the sailing. But the captain in charge of the operation respectfully asked that the order be rescinded. He pledged full loyalty to his chiefs in Palestine while insisting that this was one order he could not obey.

The two ships were loaded with their 15,169 passengers and set sail. A turning point in the long confrontation came when they were not blocked by Turkish authorities, who permitted them to sail through Turkish waters into the Mediterranean. Once on the open seas there was no alternative but for the vessels to continue their voyage and the British were forced to a painful decision, whether or not to attempt to turn them back when they reached Palestine. A compromise was wearily arranged. It was agreed by the British Colonial Secretary and Haganah that the ships would sail directly to Cyprus, but with the public understanding that the Jews were "yielding to duress." The more than 15,000 refugees were landed at Famagusta in Cyprus, joining the thousands who were already there to await the time for entry into Palestine.

Britain now realized that it could not spare limited resources to what had become a full-fledged attack upon its immigration policy. Harassed by colonial uprisings in many parts of the world, how long would it be able to absorb the cost of holding back the tireless efforts of the Jews to reach Palestine? And how long could it preserve its good name as the details of the deporta-

---

*Anna Pauker was a Jewess whose father and mother and many close relatives were among the first settlers from Rumania in the State of Israel.

†The compromise solution for Palestine, dividing the country into independent Jewish and Arab states, is discussed in detail in Chapters Nine through Eleven.

tions were widely reported in the world press? To save face, the British continued their technical opposition to immigration, and issued proclamations that they would not betray Arab hopes. But when, in November 1947, the Partition resolution was adopted by the United Nations, Britain announced that it would relinquish its Mandate in May 1948.

In the immediate postwar years, from 1945 to 1948, Haganah and its agents in the Mossad had directed the sailing of sixty-five ships. Most were intercepted; but though the passengers were interned for long periods, 115,000 immigrants had been brought into Palestine. About eight hundred who served in the War of Independence gave their lives on the free soil of Israel. Many of the boats that had been impounded by the British, subsequently released, were adapted to become the first warships of the Israeli navy.

CHAPTER EIGHT

Truman, Niles, and the American Effort

HISTORY, AT LEAST WHILE IN THE MAKING, rarely follows an orderly course. Constantly influenced by the unexpected, it may be said, and not altogether frivolously, to have a whim of iron. Certainly there could be few less likely shapers of the destiny of the Holocaust survivors and the establishment of the State of Israel than Harry Truman, President-by-accident, and his administrative assistant, David K. Niles. The one was a blunt no-nonsense Missouri politician who, to the astonishment of party, country, and himself, had been chosen by Franklin Roosevelt as his compromise fourth-term running mate. When he was nominated, even the best informed European statesmen did not know who he was. The American jest was "Harry who?" The other, Niles, was a round-faced, inscrutable promoter of adult education from Boston who had come to Washington as a protégé of Harry Hopkins, Roosevelt's closest intimate.

But for failing health, Hopkins would probably have been Roosevelt's choice for the vice presidency or even the presidency. Truman, though he had them, needed no charismatic qualities for his pronouncements to carry weight. He was chief executive of the one victorious western Allied nation that had emerged from the costliest war in history with augmented military and economic strength. He had the power to offer a shattered world such major reconstruction projects as the Marshall Plan, the Truman Doctrine, Point Four, the Berlin Airlift, and others that had global impact.

It was Truman, among the leaders of the free world, who ordered that the borders of the American zones in Germany and Austria be opened to the survivors trapped in eastern Europe and the Balkans. It was he who insisted that the Displaced Persons' Camps be administered as shelters rather than as quasi-prisons. He persisted in applying unremitting pressure on the British government to modify the White Paper that severely restricted Jewish immigration to Palestine. In all this he accepted the counsel of Niles, as he did in the long battle—where their opponents included senior members of his own State Department—to win UN consent for the establishment of an independent Jewish state. He obtained congressional approval for massive grants and loans to Israel in the crucial years when the newly born state struggled to become a viable entity in the family of nations. He was realistic enough to be aware of the political advantages of his actions. But some of his turning-point diplomacy was undoubtedly firmed up by his genuine Christian compassion for people who had endured such sustained torment.

By his side, providing the briefing that challenged the views and pressures of those who insisted that it was not in America's best interest to endorse a sovereign state of Israel, was his passionately loyal aide, David K. Niles, who had earned Truman's complete confidence and, with it, an influence that often proved decisive at critical junctures. When, on Friday evening May 14, 1948, Truman announced de facto American recognition of Israel, he telephoned Niles a few minutes later, even before he had notified the American ambassador at the UN, and said to him: "Dave, I want you to know that I've just announced recognition. You're the first person I called, because I knew how much this would mean to you."[1] The President of Israel, Dr. Chaim Weizmann, wrote to Niles after the Israeli Declaration of Independence, expressing gratitude to him as a basic architect in this fullfillment:

> We are living in great days: it is perhaps too soon to evaluate their meaning for history. For many years now you have played no insignificant part in the making of this history, and I feel certain that when you look back upon these years, you will have good reason to be proud and satisfied that it had been given to you to help bring about a proper understanding of the ideals of our cause in high places in Washington. . . .*[2]

---

*There are frequent references to the David K. Niles Papers. These documents have been extracted from memoranda and letters exchanged between

Yet Niles, then as now, was an enigmatic figure, hardly known to the general public, and a source of mystery even to Washington political columnists. Few first-hand accounts, let alone later histories, refer to Niles in more than a perfunctory aside. It was very much Niles' own choice to avoid the limelight. Throughout his Washington experience of more than a decade, he returned to Boston almost every weekend, living at the modest home of a sister and attending the Saturday evening performance of the Boston Symphony. He usually held court for young protégés on Saturday and Sunday mornings, carefully steering discussion away from any of his own political involvements. Niles may have been one of the last of his breed in American presidential politics. In part because his career preceded the proliferation of television sets in American homes, and of on-the-spot television news coverage, Niles was able to protect the personal privacy which he considered essential to his function as a presidential adviser.

Niles was born in 1890 in the village, Baltrementz, a Polish part of Russia. He was brought as a child to the United States in 1891. The family name was originally Neyhus, legally changed before David was out of his teens. The family lived at first in Boston's North End, and he received his introduction to ethnic politics in the feisty Irish and Jewish neighborhood (now homogeneously Italian) so well described in Joseph Dineen's novel, *Ward Eight*. His father earned a precarious livelihood as a tailor; but the usual hard work and rigid discipline of Jewish immigrants gradually improved the family living standard and permitted a move to the more attractive Grove Hill section of Roxbury.

Young Niles entered Boston Latin School and took great pride, which all alumni of perhaps the best public preparatory school in the country felt, in sharing his alumni association with Benjamin Franklin, Ralph Waldo Emerson, and Bernard Berenson, among others. He must have had special satisfaction, as did "Honey Fitz" Fitzgerald, mayor of Boston and grandfather of John Kennedy, in reminding friends that Boston Latin was a year older than Harvard.

Niles and the president or other public officials. Those papers relevent to this chapter are noted in the references; those that have major bearing are included in full in the appendix section. The complete set of documents is indexed and filed in the Brandeis University library archives.

Niles did not continue his education in college; few sons of immigrant families in the early years of the century could afford that luxury. His first "grown-up" job was a minor one in Filene's department store, headed by Edward A. Filene, the merchant prince who was then in the heyday of a career that combined aggressive business acumen with concern for social betterment. Niles was soon drawn to the Ford Hall Forum, established in 1908 by George Coleman, a pioneering enterprise that offered free lectures on controversial subjects by nationally known speakers—editors, educators, senators, congressmen, judges. It still does. As Boston was the cradle of the American public school (only Boston, perhaps, would commemorate public education's first important champion, Horace Mann, by erecting a statue of him, toga-clad, on the State House lawn), so it was also the nursery of what we now call adult education. Ford Hall was to become the most constant element in Niles' career. He came to it not only as an avid listener but as a paid assistant to George Coleman, who was impressed by his quiet, well-spoken, eager-to-be-of-use protégé.

When, in World War I, Coleman accepted an assignment in Washington as Director of Information in the Labor Department, he took the bright twenty-three-year-old Niles with him. After the war, Niles was involved with short, ineffectual ventures in the infant motion picture business, then centered in Long Island. He was relieved to return to Boston in 1924 upon being offered the post of administrative director of Ford Hall. Postwar Boston rocked with controversy over all the major national issues of the time, and no few of Boston's own, from the police strike that helped to make Calvin Coolidge president to the later Sacco-Vanzetti case, the reverberations of which were felt as far away as Moscow. There could have been no better "university" for learning the art of politics, or for meeting the men and women who were on the inside of its practice.

Niles was very much a part of the national political battles of the next two decades. In 1924 he undertook the direction of the campaign Speakers' Bureau for the Presidency of a maverick senator, Robert LaFollette, "the little giant from Wisconsin," and in 1928 he marshaled the support of independent voters when Alfred E. Smith, the Catholic governor of New York, challenged Herbert Hoover for the White House. The 1928 campaign was bitter and scurrilous and Niles learned a great deal about religious bigotry as a weapon in politics. His skill in working with minority groups won the admiration of Harry Hopkins, who had by then become one of Franklin Roosevelt's most influential confidantes. Niles was given the task of enlisting independent voters, primarily those who had their roots in minority groups, to help elect Roosevelt as President in 1932.

With Roosevelt's overwhelming victory, Niles became a more important part of the White House inner staff, and in 1942, during Roosevelt's third term, he was named one of the President's administrative assistants. He had used his long apprenticeship with Hopkins to hone the skills that were to serve two presidents in the New Deal revolution at home and in the problems of World War II and its aftermath. Roosevelt entrusted to Niles many of the problems that had become pressing, among them civil rights, immigration, and relief of the dispossessed through the agencies of the WPA. One of Niles' first assignments was to steer a major reform through the shoals of military prejudice that made possible the enlistment of American blacks, Filipinos, and Hispanics.

But Niles' most compelling responsibility was to offer counsel on ways to deal with the plight of the European Jews. During the two final years of Roosevelt's administration, while the war was in progress, there was little that could be done for the victims of the Holocaust; the Nazis, though now in retreat, were still in solid control of the extermination camps. The conferences of the Allied powers that were sponsored in Roosevelt's name usually ended with pious resolutions but with no western government willing to offer practical amelioration.

In April 1945 Roosevelt died suddenly, scarcely having begun his fourth term, and Truman in succeeding him asked Niles to remain as his administrative assistant with responsibility for the problems that, with the war winding down, could now be placed on the front burner. Truman wrote that Niles' service was more critical than ever: "You have had a hand in many of the important events of the last decade. It will be of great service to have the benefit of your ability and conscientious service and the experience and information you have acquired during these years will be most valuable."[3]

Niles was ready, and the President called upon him repeatedly. He drafted most of the policy directives that dealt with the opening of the American Occupied Zone for the east European refugees, the key negotiations with Britain to modify its restrictions on Jewish emigration to Palestine, and the complicated diplomacy that, eventually, brought about the Partition vote in the United Nations and the de facto American recognition of the sovereign State of Israel. With few exceptions the drafts were accepted and released by the president.

One wonders how a man with such impact on White House policy could have remained so obscure. Niles wanted it so. It was not mere modesty; Niles found larger opportunity to perform by shielding his anonymity. He believed that if the influence he wielded became known, those who opposed it would try harder to undermine it. In the many cartons of letters and records left by Niles, only a small percentage are copies of anything that he himself wrote; the vast bulk of the material comprises messages *to* him. Niles invariably preferred to conduct his negotiations, or to express his reactions or sentiments, in person or by telephone, and in the case of the latter, with utmost care that the instrument was not tapped. He was irritated if the media carried news of his political, even his social, activities. He shunned parties and, as noted, fled to Boston on weekends. His confidential secretary, Jeanette Hurley, who served him for most of his public career, admitted that she never even knew what his middle initial stood for.

The background of Niles is given here in detail to help explain how he was able to win such surprising support for highly contested issues that crowded the Truman years. He cultivated the powerful, including the president's intimate friend and legal counsel, Clark Clifford, enlightened financiers, liberal Democratic party leaders, diplomats in the United Nations, opinion molders in the bewilderingly fragmented world of Jewish affairs. He was a formidable power broker in large measure because he never asked for or sought anything for himself.

The war in Europe was already winding down on that April afternoon in 1945 when Franklin Roosevelt suffered the fatal cerebral hemmorrhage at Warm Springs, and a stunned Harry Truman was called to the presidency. "Pray for me, boys," he said to the reporters, "the sun, the moon, and the stars, have all fallen on me." His daughter Margaret wrote, years later, how she had answered the telephone in the vice-presidential home and had chattered on to her father about a party she expected to attend that evening, while the new president pleaded quietly, over and over, "Please let me speak to your mother."[4]

Truman, an early riser, worked assiduously to assimilate the briefing he needed on the global problems that he inherited—whether or not to use the atom bomb to hasten the Japanese surrender; the overwhelming public demand to "bring home our boys," millions of whom were being demobilized; how to convert a war economy into a peace economy without precipitating an economic depression; the confrontation at the Potsdam summit to decide the fate of Europe and the world. With remarkable aplomb, Truman took all the problems in stride. It was a hopeful symbol to have the President of the United States play Paderewski's "Minuet in G Major" for Stalin and Churchill after a state dinner in Potsdam.

Truman had to wrestle, too, with conflicting plans for the disposition of the uprooted peoples of a devastated Europe. The millions of war prisoners and demobilized soldiers who had countries to receive them were effectively repatriated, often within a few months. But the Jews who had survived the death camps or their hunted underground resistance, or who had emerged from hidden refuge points, found themselves in a limbo of the unwanted.

It could no longer be argued by the Allied strategists that the fate of the Jews had to be subordinated to the drive for victory. The Final Solution had exacted its fearful cost. Six million Jews had perished. The overwhelming wish of the survivors was to get to Palestine, away from the helpless dependence that had been largely responsible for the magnitude of their disaster. Since Britain held the Mandate for Palestine, and the United States contained the largest Jewish community in the world, it was the clear responsibility of the two main war Allies to deal with the fate of the Jews in Europe as a high priority.

Britain, with slight deviations, maintained a consistent policy throughout. Despite the promises of the Balfour Declaration, the government was determined that the Arabs in Palestine and the Arab states surrounding the country, whose oil reserves fueled the economic life of the world's industrial countries, were not to be alienated. Hence, immigration of Jews must be held to a minimum and remain strictly controlled. Complicating Truman's own policy in the face of the British refusal to modify the White Paper was the almost unanimous support of the British position by the senior members of his own administration. General George Marshall, Chief of Staff, James Forrestal, Secretary of Defense, James Byrnes, Secretary of State, and most of the career officials were concerned about the effect on the Arabs if restrictions on Jewish immigration to Palestine were eased. They argued that to preserve a strong American presence in the Middle East, Arab goodwill was essential, even though the Arab leaders had cooperated with the Germans all through the war. The State Department warned that the Arab governments, in control of precious oil reserves, could strike at the jugular if, as they had threatened, they were to cut off the oil supplies upon which the United States depended so completely.

Rabbi Stephen Wise, president of the American Jewish Congress and a dominating force in the American Jewish community, alarmed that key officials in the cabinet held views about the disposition of the Palestine problem that would severely limit the aspirations of the Jewish Agency, sought and received an appointment with Truman for April 20, 1945. Edward Stettinius, a former Secretary of State, cautioned the President to go slowly with Wise. "There is continued tension in the situation in the Near East," he wrote in a memo, "largely as a result of the Palestine question, and we have interests in that area which are vital to the United States. We feel that this whole subject is one that should be handled with the greatest care and with a view to the long range interests of the country."[5]

Joseph Grew, an Undersecretary of State, sent Truman two memoranda, warning him not to give any assurances to the Jewish advocates. He reminded Truman that, "although President Roosevelt gave expression to views sympathetic to certain Zionist aims, he also gave certain assurances to the Arabs which they [the Arabs] regard as definite commitments on our part."[6] Grew was referring to the statement by Roosevelt to King Ibn Saud and other Arab leaders after the Yalta Conference of 1945 that "in the view of this Government there should be no decision altering the basic situation in Palestine without full consultation with both Arabs and Jews." This was typically skillful Roosevelt yes-no-perhaps vocabulary, a model of diplomatic equivocation. He used the word "consultation," which did not commit, nor did it confer any Arab veto power.

Truman, briefed by Niles and by his legal counsel, Clark Clifford, an advocate of Jewish claims in Palestine, disregarded the warnings of his cabinet members. He saw Dr. Wise and assured him that he was not impressed with the arguments of "the striped pants boys" because "they didn't care enough about what happened to the thousands of displaced persons who were involved." Nor did he believe that his great concern for those who had suffered so much and so long was prejudicial to American interests.[7]

The impression that Truman was a novice in diplomacy, and brought insufficient background to the complex problems that had to be faced, quickly dissipated as he met both his advisers and his critics head on. In one of the last interviews that Dean Acheson gave, a few days before his death, when I was preparing for a televised evaluation of the Truman years, his long-time Secretary of State spoke glowingly of the President's decisiveness. I asked Acheson for his reaction to the general impression that his chief had come to his tasks with little preparation and that he often followed the frontier habit of shooting from the hip.

"Nonsense," Acheson snorted. "Truman did not need formal schooling for his great decisions. He needed fact and judgment, and these he had in uncommon degree. He had read widely, going through virtually every volume on history and politics in the library of Independence, Missouri. He had been toughened by experience in his political tasks at home and in the Senate. He demonstrated again and again, at global strategy meetings, that he had fully briefed himself to come to informed judgments. By temperament he avoided shilly-shallying. He had no need of the reminder on his desk, 'The buck stops here.' "[8]

As the stalemate continued over the problems of modifying immigration restrictions for Palestine, Truman accepted the suggestion of Clifford and Niles to authorize an investigation of living conditions in the DP Camps. Disquieting reports had been pouring into the United States from correspondents abroad and observers from the international agencies. They emphasized that the makeshift camps in the American Zone were being insensitively administered by the military authorities. All through the spring of 1945 Truman kept Niles busy preparing briefing papers on the refugee problems. He called for carefully documented counsel on the role that the United States should undertake in coping with the issues that made the Middle East so diplomatically volatile. In June, a commission was appointed to visit the DP Camps in the American zone in Germany and Austria to explore the views of the military commanders and the condition of the inmates. The commission was instructed also to confer with the heads of the successor governments in Europe and the Middle East. Niles meantime promoted overwhelming affirmative resolutions in both Houses of Congress for quick relief in the camps. He obtained strong endorsements for such action from the governors of all forty-eight states. The call upon the British government to open the doors of Palestine to the survivors in the DP Camps was written into the mid-term Republican and Democratic platforms.

Niles recommended that the commission be headed by Earl Harrison, former dean of the University of Pennsylvania Law School, who had amassed considerable experience in studying the disruptions in Europe when he served on the Intergovernmental Committee on Refugees. Niles also suggested that Dr. Joseph Schwartz, of the Joint Distribution Committee, who had supervised the major relief programs for Jewish refugees for many years, ought to be at Harrison's side to make sure that his itinerary was not limited to areas chosen by the American military officials. Truman agreed. The choice of Harrison and his team of advisers ensured thoroughness in the investigations and the preparation of the report for the President.[9]

While Harrison's commission set about taking evidence, Truman wrote, once again, to Churchill, on July 24, 1945: "Knowing your deep and sympathetic interest in Jewish settlement in Palestine, I venture to express to you the hope that the British government may find it possible, without delay, to lift the restrictions of the White Paper on Jewish immigration in Palestine."[10] Three days later, Churchill was defeated in the British general election and Labor took over the conduct of state. To the dismay of the Jewish Agency and its constituency, the new British cabinet, despite Labor's pre-election pledges, was to make no substantive changes in the White Paper immigration restrictions.

Harrison's committee completed its investigative work with dispatch; its report was in Truman's hands at the end of August. The description of the misery of the Jewish camp inmates and their sense of hopelessness elicited a stern command from Truman. General Eisenhower was ordered to improve living conditions in the camps to maintain at least the standard that had been established for the German civilian population.*

The Harrison Report's second and longer-range recommendation was for the President to urge the British government to

---

*Eisenhower's aggrieved reaction has been detailed in Chapter seven.

modify Chamberlain's White Paper and to open Palestine to the 100,000 refugees already in the DP Camps (the number was to grow to 250,000). On the very day, August 31, that the report was submitted, Niles drafted the letter for Truman to the new British Prime Minister, Clement Attlee. It stated that the only human solution to the problem of the refugees was to grant their plea for transfer to Palestine. "No other single matter," Truman's message read, "is so important for those who have known the horrors of concentration camps for over a decade as is the future of immigration possibilities into Palestine. . . . If it is to be effective, such action should not be long delayed."[11] The response was more than prompt. Before the Harrison recommendation had been made public, Labor's Colonial Office had already notified Dr. Weizmann that the White Paper would be strictly enforced. Its message to President Truman, while couched less abrasively, was substantively the same.

Ben Gurion, head of the Jewish Agency, and a master of realism, was one of the few who had taken Labor's election promises with a measure of skepticism. He had warned his colleagues that the British parties, in or out of office, followed a common imperial line, and he urged the continuation and expansion of illegal immigration.* He was not at all surprised when the Foreign Secretary, Ernest Bevin, repudiated his party's earlier pledges. But he did find it difficult to understand the lack of discipline in the American cabinet, the virtual defiance of the President of the United States by his own appointees.

Early in September 1945, substantially increased illegal immigration was the immediate Jewish reply to the rejection of the Harrison Report by the British. The American Secretary of State, James Byrnes, alarmed by renewed warnings, often thinly veiled threats, that came from the Arab capitals, sent another strong message to Truman, cautioning him against condoning illegal immigration. Truman had expected the British reaction to the Harrison Report and was already exploring ways to combat it. But he was angered by the internal resistance to his efforts

---

*"The great majority of the members of the Colonial Civil Service are anti-Zionist as they have been since the time of the Balfour Declaration. . . . Let us not underestimate their influence on the Labor Government." David Ben Gurion. *Israel, A Personal History.* New York, Funk & Wagnalls, 1971, p. 56.

from his own senior officials, and the encouragement that this evidence of divided counsels was offering to the British negative resolve. When Byrnes reminded the President of Roosevelt's promises to Ibn Saud, Truman reached the limits of patience with being told what "the President," meaning Roosevelt, had said or done. He sharply reminded Byrnes that he, Harry Truman, was now the President. He wrote later that "the State Department continued to be more concerned about the Arab reaction than about the suffering of the Jews."[12]

Yet the pressure on Bevin and his cabinet was beginning to have an effect. The British government was in the midst of negotiations for a multi-billion-dollar loan from the United States to bolster its seriously sagging economy. Bevin's resistance on the immigration issue was endangering favorable action in Congress, which had taken a stronger stand than even Truman had in urging the modification of the restrictive White Paper. Already earlier in the summer both Houses of Congress, by large majorities, had petitioned the President to urge Britain to establish Palestine as "a free and democratic Jewish Commonwealth at the earliest possible moment," and all forty-eight state governors had endorsed the resolution. At the time, Truman had preferred to move less precipitously on the issue of a Jewish Commonwealth, but the congressional charge was in his armory. These political realities in the United States made it clear to Bevin that the threat to the loan was not limited to what he had earlier sarcastically dismissed as "the Zionist lobby."

On October 19, Bevin suggested to Truman the appointment of an Anglo-American Commission to investigate the problem of the refugees and its relation to Palestine. There was grave concern among some of the American Jewish leaders that Bevin's offer to consider the recommendations of still another investigation commission was a delaying tactic. Rabbi Stephen Wise and Rabbi Abba Hillel Silver wrote the President on October 30: "We beg of you not to countenance further commissions and inquiries at a continued cost in human life and human misery, which can only ascertain facts already well known."[13]

The Arab leaders were hopelessly divided by national rivalries but they cooperated warily in their opposition to Jewish immigration into the Arab world. They too were exercised by the naming of another commission, fearful that it might be influenced by the Harrison Report and recommend a modification of the White Paper. Once again officials in the State Department took it upon themselves, in a secret memorandum, to reassure the Arab states that the appointment of the commission did not presage any change in the current situation. Truman felt that it was important to test Bevin's willingness to break the impasse, and he promised Wise and Silver that he would not permit the United States "to become a party to any dilatory tactics."

The personnel of the commission was strong in diversified representation and experience. The British co-chairman was Sir John Singleton, a judge on the king's bench; the American co-chairman was Joseph C. Hutcheson, a circuit court judge from Texas. Their colleagues were men who were concerned with the national interest, but were apparently determined to be as fair as realism permitted. When the commission had been named, the President expressed full confidence in its "spirit of cooperation" and his hope that its deliberations would be productive. Bevin later promised, when he met the commission in London, that, "if [it] achieved a unanimous report, he would personally do everything in his power to put it into effect."[14] Bevin's condition of a "unanimous report" caused considerable uneasiness among those who hoped that the refugee tragedy in Europe could be quickly resolved; but the high caliber of the commission's membership, and the recognition of the gravity of its responsibilities, gave pause to obstructive protest. The proceedings began harmoniously.

During the week of February 5, 1946, teams of commissioners visited some of the largest DP Camps in the American and British zones. Everything that had appalled Earl Harrison brought similar reactions from the more widely diversified binational investigators. Living facilities were bleak and overcrowded, and the inmates were swallowed up in the aimlessness and indignity of prison camps. Armed guards were posted to prevent the "liberated" from leaving the premises without permission. Polls were taken to determine where the uprooted wished to reconstruct their lives if ever the day should come that they were repatriated. The results of a typical questionnaire in a Bavarian DP Camp produced astonishment even among those who were determined not to be beguiled by propaganda. The polled group numbered 22,000: 13 opted to stay on in some European land; 596 hoped that they could find a haven in the United States, in one of the British dominions, or in a Latin American country; more than 21,000 people chose Palestine. An analysis of all the polls indicated clearly that those who had survived preferred almost unanimously to resettle in a land where they would no longer live on the caprice of countrymen to whom they would always remain strangers.

When the commissioners reached Vienna, Bartley Crum, a San Francisco attorney, urged the publication of an interim report that would reflect the mood and will of the camp inmates. He believed it would immeasurably raise their morale if they knew how seriously their plight was being considered by the prestigious bi-national commission. While sobered by the evidence that their investigations had produced, Crum's colleagues strongly demurred. They believed that any such action at this stage would seriously compromise the impression of impartiality that had to be maintained. Truman supported this judgment and so informed Hutcheson, who asked Crum to modify his persistence. "Word has come from the White House," Hutcheson said, "asking that no interim report be made; instead, that short-term recommendations be made when we file our final report."[15] Crum was upset by the intervention of the White House, interpreting it as part of the anti-Zionist machinations of some of the State Department officials. He threatened to resign.

Truman in turn was dismayed by the thought of losing Crum and thereby playing into Bevin's hands. He called in Niles and asked him to intercede with Crum and to persuade him to exercise more patience. Niles turned to Loy Henderson, the leading opponent of Truman's policy on Palestine, "to help him" in editing the message "in any way you see fit."[16] Niles then called Crum: "There are rumors that you are getting madder every day and that you are threatening to resign with a blast. I can understand the provocation, but you must be patient and calm down if these rumors have any foundation. The President talked to me this morning and he wants to assure you that he has every confidence in you and that he hopes you will do nothing rash. . . . I know you are a good sport and will see it through [the commission's mandate] as intelligently as you have always operated." Crum did not resign. Had he done so, he would have doomed any possibility of gaining a unanimous commission report.

Niles had other problems, among them the continuous pressure of irascible American Zionists. He used to banter that one of the difficulties in Jewish life was the pontification on Jewish issues, indeed on all issues, undertaken by men and women who were not inhibited in speaking out by the absence of a representative mandate. Truman expressed envy to Ben Gurion after the Israeli State was established because the Prime Minister had to contend with only a few million people whereas he, Truman, had to cope with nearly two hundred million. Ben Gurion insisted that his own problems were more nerve-wracking, for he had several million prime ministers-in-embryo in his constituency. Truman felt that he had at least that many during the refugee crisis. Letters, wires, and telephone calls poured in, and Truman's patience wore thin. Many berated him for the "disgracefully" slow rate of progress in relieving the misery of families who had risen from the grave. Many more vilified him for trying to placate "Arab dictators in a desert" at the expense of the only democratic society in the Near East. Rabbi Silver threatened to try to stop the loan to Britain by an appeal to political figures who supported the cancelation of the White Paper. Truman asked Niles to take over the care and feeding of the hawks. The Niles files bulge with recorded telephone messages that explained, placated, scolded, reasoned—all intended to persuade irate critics to trust the good intentions of the President.

Niles was eyes, ears, and even, to some extent, whipping boy for the President as the American delegation groped their way to reconcile the State Department's concerns and the determination of President Truman to ameliorate the plight of the refugees. Judge Hutcheson exercised surprising agility in treading a fine line between the alarmed rhetoric of Forrestal, Lovett, and other State Department officials who leaned to the British view, and the impatience of Bartley Crum and his colleague on the commission, James McDonald, later the first American ambassador to sovereign Israel, who were exasperated by British obduracy. Hutcheson often wearied of his role as mediator, and Niles urged Truman to offer him the encouragement of personal commendation. He drafted a letter for the President that acknowledged Hutcheson's difficulties and expressed the hope that he would persevere in holding his colleagues firmly "to a program that is in accord with the highest American tradition of generosity and justice."[17] Hutcheson, with second wind, obtained unanimous consent from his delegation, emphasizing the urgent need to provide 100,000 certificates "for admission into Palestine of the Jews who had been victims of the Nazi and Fascist persecution." He counseled the postponement of proposals that required long-range solutions.

The commission's report was completed and signed on April

19, 1946. It was obviously the product of considerable compromise. There was no recommendation to create an independent or autonomous Jewish Homeland, and there were vague assumptions that the Mandate for Palestine would be retained by the British until it could be converted into a UN Trusteeship. Yet the report did address itself to the plight of the inmates in the DP Camps and recommended priority for the quick admission of 100,000 to Palestine.

Though Bevin had pledged that he would honor the recommendations of the commission if its report were unanimous, a conflict erupted at once over the intent of his pledge. Truman expected that, since the commission had urged speedy admission of 100,000 refugees into Palestine and he was in agreement that the other long-term recommendations could be delayed for further study, there would be early action to end the deepening tragedy of the DP Camps. Bevin was chagrined that even his British representatives had joined in the recommendation for the immediate release of the immigrants. He now insisted that the report could not be acted upon piecemeal. He cautioned the President to defer any statements about the commission's report, fearing that the focus of international attention would be on the positive recommendation to free the Displaced Persons for migration to Palestine.

The President decided to press ahead as the only way to compel Bevin to abide by his pledged word. He planned to make the report public at once, and he asked Niles to prepare an accompanying statement that would emphasize the commission's strong recommendation for the admission of 100,000 refugees into Palestine. Niles tried to persuade the President to include his views on the issues that were temporarily postponed. Here Truman preferred not to widen the battle too quickly. In a private note to Niles, he wrote: "Dave: The late President [FDR] made a commitment to the King of Arabia in a famous letter, which I later confirmed. We have to consult both sides. I doubt if the 1,000,000 [sic] necessarily means any change of policy, but the whole report does. HST."[18]

Nevertheless, when the report was made public on April 30, Truman's accompanying statement went quite far: "I am very happy," it read,

> that the request which I made for the immediate admission of 100,000 Jews into Palestine has been unanimously endorsed by the Anglo-American Committee of Inquiry. The transference of these

unfortunate people should now be accomplished with the greatest dispatch. . . . I am also pleased that the Committee recommends in effect the abrogation of the White Paper of 1939 including existing restrictions on immigration and land acquisition to permit the further development of the Jewish National home. . . .[19]

On May 8 Truman followed his statement with a message to Clement Attlee urging early consultations to try for a meeting of minds. The British leaders wre furious with Truman for placing them on the defensive. Attlee and Bevin insisted that conferences on refugee policies be postponed for at least a month.

Truman had expected these dilatory tactics. Crum had kept Niles informed with ever-growing pessimism about British intentions. Within a week after the report had been signed, Crum wrote a long personal letter to Niles in which he said: "It is now quite apparent that the British do not intend to move at all to implement our report."[20] But what concerned Truman most of all was that his own men were encouraging the British in their reluctance to fulfill their promises. The head of the Joint Chiefs of Staff again warned the President that it would require force against the Arabs to go forward with any mass immigration, that there was grave danger of bringing the Soviet into the Middle East, and that oil supplies for the United States might be seriously endangered. Barely a week later, on May 15, a letter came from Myron Taylor, the President's personal envoy to the Vatican, listing all the disasters that were likely to ensue from the President's position. Taylor wrote:

> Having the best interests of the Jews at heart, and without offend-
> ing the Moslem world, I believe the solution is a broad dispersion
> of the Jews, not a concentration anywhere. To create a purely
> racial state is contrary to American traditions and ideals. In my
> opinion time, patience, and resonable control of the number of
> Jewish people in Europe, with the acceptance of a reasonable
> number of emergency cases now by Palestine, and a large number
> by all other countries, is the best solution.

And of course, Taylor cautioned, there was Russia on the threshold of "the dark skinned Eastern world," all ready to take advantage of the complications that would be created by Arab hostility against the United States.

It was difficult for Truman to contain his temper at the naive-

te of sentiments that pontificated glibly about European countries accepting a "reasonable" number of Jews when pogroms
often occurred if even a small number attempted to return to
their former homes. Truman asked Niles to draft a reply to
Taylor, recognizing that he was unable to restrain his language
when he dealt with men whose understanding of European
immigration realities was so superficial.

In a draft memorandum Niles patiently refuted each of Taylor's arguments, including the impracticality of expecting refugees "to be absorbed by other countries." He noted that "there
would be terrific resistance if we attempted at this time to bring
even a small portion of the refugees into our own country beyond the quota limitation. I don't see how we could ask other
countries to do what we ourselves are unable to do." Taylor was
also reminded that, "in the war period, the Jews of Palestine
fought at the side of the Allies and offered considerable help.
The Allies got no help from the Arabs at all." As for Russia,
"members of the Anglo-American Commission were told privately that the Russians would not look with disfavor on the
transference of 100,000 Jews to Palestine."[21] Truman accepted
the memorandum in toto and sent it to Taylor. He noted that
"having in mind the difficulties of reconciling the aspirations of
Jewish and Arab nationalism," he had set aside the long-range
proposals of the commission for further study even though he
was convinced that the Homeland promised in the Balfour Declaration and validated in 1921 by the League of Nations should
be honored and encouraged.

Temperate discussion and negotiation were seriously jeopardized when Bevin, who had been brooding over Truman's release
of the commission's report, suddenly exploded with remarks
that applied flame to highly combustible fuels. Addressing the
Labor Party Conference in Bournemouth on June 12, he jibed
that the Americans were so enthusiastic about opening Palestine to the refugees because "they did not want to have many
of them in New York." Simultaneously the combative Zionist
leader, Rabbi Silver, threatened to bring all possible influence
to bear to defeat the American loan to Britain whose authorization was just then slowly making its way in Congress.

Niles had all he could do to cool Truman's formidable temper.
A press conference had been scheduled, and Niles suggested
that it would be an opportune occasion for a low-keyed but firm
response to the inevitable questions that would be asked about
the statements of Bevin and Silver. At the press conference

Truman performed admirably, carefully muting his expected resentment. He affirmed his determination to press for admission of the refugees to Palestine and that no impolitic remarks elsewhere "would alter his determination to serve the humanitarian needs of the world, whether it be to help Jews or other needy peoples." He turned aside Silver's threat by suggesting "because Mr. Bevin may be taking an unmoral attitude, that is no justification for our people here to do the same thing."

After the press conference, Niles solicited letters from moderate Zionist leaders to reassure the President of their opposition to Silver's views. Rabbi Stephen Wise, in a letter Niles passed on to Truman, wrote: "We should proceed to counteract the Silver mischief. I am not prepared to hurt the interests of the American and British people, alike involved in this loan, to spite a man [Bevin] however hasty his speech and however lamentable his conduct against Zionism."[22]

Meantime, in Palestine there was little patience with the exchange of notes couched in diplomatic niceties. With all his good intentions, Truman was apparently unable to gain immigration concessions for the frustrated families who were still chafing in the DP Camps. The more extreme elements in Palestine had already escalated the violence. They had been convinced, even before Bevin made his gesture of accepting a joint Anglo-American Commission to seek a peaceful solution, that only the argument of force could prevail over the force of argument. Now Haganah—hitherto bound by the discipline of *Havlagah*, or Restraint, to use force only for self-defense—joined Irgun and other right-wing Partisans in attacks against British installations and shore patrols.

On June 18, while Truman and Bevin were exchanging notes, Haganah units blew up nine bridges and gutted a number of Haifa workshops. They were signaling the British that the inflicted damage was the lesser part of their objective, that the Jews of Palestine would no longer wait passively for the camps to be emptied. The British command moved quickly to meet the challenge before it became serious. Reprisals were drastic. Three thousand Palestinian Jews, including leaders of the Zionist governing council, were rounded up and placed under arrest. A curfew was imposed in Jerusalem and Jewish Agency headquarters were sealed.

The actions of the British High Commissioner boomeranged. The Jewish population in Palestine united in the determination to turn from negotiation to outright revolt. In Britain, Richard Crossman, a highly placed Labor party member who had pleaded with his colleagues on the Anglo-American Commission not to goad the Jews into desperate acts, solemnly warned the House of Commons that Britain was losing the cooperation of the moderates. "No Jew anywhere," he said, "least of all Dr. Weizmann or the Haganah, can be won over to the Government by the arrests of thousands of their brothers." Bevin's reprisal rages were converting a law-abiding people into a resistance movement.

On July 7, only three days after the Kielce pogrom in Poland, Niles asked Ben Cohen, a counselor in the State Department, if he could arrange an appointment for Ben Gurion with Secretary of State James Byrnes, to explore fresh ways to resolve the refugee dilemma. Cohen telephoned Ben Gurion that Byrnes had not only refused an appointment but had expressed his deep resentment over the importunate tactics of the Zionists. Nahum Goldmann reported the incident to Niles, who relayed it to Truman. The harassed President was just then deep in complicated international problems. A handwritten note went back to Niles, who was still shaken by the news from Kielce, and the Polish exodus. "Dave," wrote the President, "I don't blame him [Byrnes] much. Imagine, Goldman [sic; president of the World Jewish Congress], Wise & Co. coming in after a round with a bandit like Molotov on Trieste and the Tyrol!—reparations, displaced persons, and hell all round. Think probably, I'd tell him [Goldmann] to jump in the Jordan."[23]

Truman's mood of exasperation passed quickly. The President was already exploring a final effort for a possible breakthrough in a situation that was deteriorating dangerously. The violence in Palestine was now being condoned by the moderate elements. There was unrest in the DP Camps, illegal immigration was engaging British naval units in running battles with crowded refugee ships. There were ugly recriminations among the highest officials of two committed Allies. Truman suggested that teams of experts on the Near East from Britain and the United States should meet in London to lay the groundwork for a negotiated settlement. Dr. Henry Grady of the State Department and his colleagues flew in the President's official plane to meet Herbert Morrison, who headed the British team. He carried a promise from Truman that if the certificates for admission were issued, the United States would pay all the costs of transportation. But the sessions were wasted effort, for Bevin set the terms of discussion as soon as the two teams convened. Any solution, Bevin declared, had to start with the premise that most of the Jews would remain in Europe, and that Palestine was not to be considered as a possible Jewish Homeland.*

After several weeks of meetings the committee came up with a jigsaw puzzle Partition plan, a cantonized Palestine, dotted with Arab and Jewish areas, self-governing only in purely domestic concerns, Jerusalem and the whole Negev remaining as part of the British Mandate, all other areas also under firm British jurisdiction. The United States would provide $50 million to help the Arabs develop their territory. One hundred thousand refugees would at last be permitted to enter Palestine over a year's time, but further immigration would depend upon "absorptive capacity"—and this would be determined by the British.

It was an arrangement with little viability except for the British, and especially disappointing because it had been developed after the unanimous Anglo-American Commission's report. One of the British officials described it with brazen candor: "It is a beautiful scheme. It treats the Arabs and the Jews on a footing of complete equality in that it gives nothing to either party, while it leaves us a free run over the whole of Palestine." The plan died without any further discussion since, among other objections, it was promptly rejected by both the Arab and the Jewish leaders.

Even if the Grady-Morrison proposals had been judged negotiable, a point had now been reached where dialogue seemed no longer to be useful. For on July 22, the most violent terrorist act in the tragic history of the Mandate period occurred. The King David Hotel in the heart of Jerusalem, which had served as headquarters for many of the highest ranking British officers and their staffs, was blown up by Irgunist agents. Ninety-one people—British, Arabs, and Jews—were killed and more than

---

*During the Grady-Morrison discussions, a confidential letter was hurried to Eliahu Elath, Israeli Ambassador to the United States, from Oscar Gass, a consultant to the Israeli embassy, warning that Grady was "acting as a British stooge," and pleading that the President be warned that his program was being completely abandoned by his own representatives (Niles Papers).[24]

forty injured, many seriously. The Irgunist command insisted that a thirty-minute warning had been given to avoid loss of life, but that the warning had apparently either been treated as a hoax or had not been efficiently transmitted by the hotel staff.

Warning or no, there was almost universal condemnation of the action as criminal lunacy. But how to cope with a situation now clearly out of control was differently decided by each of the chief parties involved. Though Haganah had approved the plan, Ben Gurion, alarmed by the extremism that had been employed, repudiated identification with the terrorism. His cooperation with Irgun, he claimed, had not envisaged wanton bloodshed. He called upon the Jewish community to turn in the Irgunists, who, he declared, had gone far beyond the plan to harass the establishment.

The British dismissed Ben Gurion's statement as contrived buck-passing and issued orders for a massive display of force. The commanding officer in Palestine, Sir Evelyn Barker, extended the punishments and reprisals to the whole civilian population. He imposed a curfew in Jerusalem and Tel Aviv with orders to shoot on sight any who violated it, and he placed all Jewish businesses out of bounds for his men and their families. In his uncontrolled anger he added a stinging comment that was to haunt the British case: "We will punish the Jews in a way the race dislikes as much as any, by striking at their pockets and showing our contempt for them." Later he deeply regretted the outburst. "It was a rotten letter, written on the spur of the moment. I ought to have restrained myself for an hour or two before putting pen to paper."[25] The insult was linked in the international press with Bevin's earlier sneer that the Americans were so eager to have the Jews sent to Palestine because they did not want them in New York. Barker's tirade had the effect of turning attention from the King David outrage to the implied anti-Semitism of the British government leaders, and Bevin and Barker had a large part in losing the propaganda war.

The most important declaration—ultimately the one that dramatically broke the long stalemate—came from President Truman. While condemning the Irgunist action, he expressed his conviction that peace was no longer possible unless some form of partition was authorized by international action. His statement of October 4, issued on the eve of Yom Kippur, was based on a draft prepared by the Jewish Agency in cooperation with Niles. There is no record to explain whether the timing was a coincidence or the result of planning. "The Jewish Agency," the President declared, "proposed a solution of the Palestine problem by means of the creation of a viable Jewish state in control of its own immigration and economic policies in an adequate area of Palestine instead of in the whole of Palestine. It proposed furthermore the immediate issuance of certificates for 100,000 Jewish immigrants. . . . From the discussion which has ensued (in press and forum), it is my belief that a solution along these lines would command the support of public opinion in the United States. . . . To such a solution our Government should give its support . . ." and he was sure that it ". . . could be worked out by men of reason and good will."

Protests and warnings poured in from opponents of the proposal, including threats from the Arab states that Truman was leading the world to war; but he refused to be diverted. The issue had become too explosive for half measures that satisfied none of the contending parties. His message to the king of Saudi Arabia, transmitted as well to the other Arab capitals, contained his determined response to all the critics, foreign and domestic: "I do not consider that my urging of the admittance of a considerable number of displaced Jews into Palestine, or my statements with regard to the solution of the problem of Palestine, in any sense represents [sic] an action hostile to the Arab people."[26]

The militants in Palestine, sensing that their opportunity had arrived, did not let up in their attacks on the Mandatory government. They were aware that a good portion of the British civilian population at home was weary of the burden of maintaining an outpost of dubious value in Palestine. In the midst of other pressing imperial problems in every part of the globe, it was not worth further bloodshed and expense, to say nothing of the strain in the collaboration with their American allies. The Irgunists, now undoubtedly enjoying the support of many moderates in Palestine, engineered almost daily bombing, rioting, and the damage of war materiel. Their hit-and-run sabotage became so serious that in January 1947, the wives and children of British servicemen were ordered evacuated. In the month before, as if to underscore the turn from moderation, the international Conference of the Zionists at Basel in Switzerland did not reelect the revered Dr. Chaim Weizmann as president—the office he had held since the Balfour Declaration had been obtained by his effort almost a quarter century previously. But in deference to the old statesman's historic contributions, the office was left vacant.

The instinct of the militants was sound. Faint signals now emanated from the British cabinet. Harassed by unrest and revolt in many parts of the Commonwealth and the deteriorating relationships with the United States, the cabinet appeared ready to retreat from its inflexible position on Partition. Already in November 1946, Lord Inverchapel, British ambassador to the United States, in conference with Secretary of State Dean Acheson, and later with Nahum Goldmann, had indicated that Bevin was considering the possibility of having the United Nations review the changed situation in Palestine. There was no hint that an independent Jewish Homeland was under consideration; but the informal conversations seemed to suggest that Bevin might compromise and accept the formula of a trust territory, to be overseen by the multinational body. Reports of these conversations were immediately relayed to Niles and helped to strengthen Truman in his resolve to achieve the breakthrough.

Behind the scenes, diplomacy began to cut through obstacles that had long impeded progress. Ben Gurion was invited to meet with Bevin. The conference brought no commitment, but during the discussion Bevin expressed willingness to consider some revision of Britain's Mandate. Ben Gurion, for his part, promised that if the Jews established a state in a partitioned Palestine, the British could count on air bases in initially agreed-upon sites. Such air bases would protect the British positions in the Middle East and the route to India and the Far East if the long-held dream of the Egyptian nationalists to eliminate the British colonial grip in Egypt was fulfilled. Ben Gurion added that concessions would also be arranged for oil drilling in the Negev, and access to Haifa Harbor, the terminus for the pipeline from the Gulf states' oil fields.[27] The confidential dialogue was hedged in with reservations. Later the Colonial Secretary, Arthur Creech-Jones, warned that Britain had made no commitment to consider relinquishing its Mandate. Yet on February 17, 1947, Bevin announced to the House of Commons that he planned to refer the Palestine problem to the United Nations for review and possible new lines of action.

Ben Gurion and his colleagues remained wary. What was the wily cantankerous Foreign Minister up to? Preparing a trap, convinced that the necessary two-thirds majority in the UN

could not be corraled for a Partition resolution? Was he hoping
that if Partition failed, Britain would retain control of Palestine
on its own terms? Indeed, Harold Beeley, Bevin's personal adviser on Palestinian affairs, admitted to one of the Jewish
Agency diplomats that Bevin expected the East-West conflict to
prevent a favorable vote on Partition in the United Nations.
Apparently he also counted on allies in the American State
Department, where high officials were almost solidly aligned
against their President's Partition proposal.

It was suspicion of Bevin's good faith and the animosities in
the American State Department that impelled the Irgunists to
pursue their sabotage in Palestine. As diplomacy moved slowly
to reach agreement upon procedures for the UN debate, their
violence kept mounting. Terror again brought swift reprisals
from the British. Several Irgunists, captured during a raid on
the Acre prison, were court-martialed and executed. Their comrades responded by kidnapping two British sergeants, completely innocent of any complicity, and hanging them, "a life for
a life." The world looked on aghast as two peoples, historically
oriented to respect the law and the dignity of human life, lost
themselves in the passionate intensity of the struggle.

The British imposed martial law on nearly half the settlements of Palestine, bringing trade and commerce to a virtual
standstill. But even martial law did not halt the tempo of the
violence. Each episode provoked the opposing forces into more
extreme retaliation. Whole communities were subjected to mass
searches by British forces to uncover weapons or to round up
the conspirators. The continuous curfew blacked out normal
living. At last on April 2, 1947, the Secretary-General of the UN
received the request from the British government that a special
session of the General Assembly be called to pass upon recommendations that could then be considered for a final judgment
at the regular UN Assembly in November. On April 28, the
special session was convened at Lake Success.

After a protracted debate it was agreed that the United Nation's Special Committee on Palestine (UNSCOP) should include only representatives from comparatively uninvolved
countries. On May 13 the composition of the committee was
announced: two members from the British Commonwealth
(Australia and Canada), two from the east European bloc (Czechoslovakia and Yugoslavia), three from Latin America
(Guatemala, Peru, and Uruguay), two from western Europe

(Sweden and The Netherlands), and two from Asia (India and Iran). It was also agreed that there should be no specific directives for the committee that, in the words of the chief American delegate, Herschel Johnson, "would hamper them in reaching an entirely objective recommendation or set of recommendations for the General Assembly."

But the latitude in the terms of reference could not guarantee such objectivity. Wherever members of the committee traveled seeking information or evidence, they were overwhelmed by the intensity of the passions that the simplest questions loosed. For example, UNSCOP members visited Displaced Persons' Camps on the very day that the British military court sentenced three young Jews to death for their attack on the Acre prison. The committee was in Palestine when the two British sergeants were hanged in reprisal by Irgun comrades. There were four UNSCOP members in Palestine when 5,000 illegal immigrants on the *Exodus 1947* were herded back on prison ships and forcibly returned to Germany. Commenting on the reaction to the *Exodus* tragedy, Abba Eban, later Israeli ambassador to the United Nations, wrote in his autobiography: "I could see that they [the UNSCOP delegates] were preoccupied with one point alone. If this were the only way that the British Mandate could continue, it would be better not to continue it at all."

By August the news began to circulate that the UNSCOP members would very likely recommend the establishment of independent Jewish and Arab states in a partitioned Palestine and the termination of the British Mandate. As his plans evaporated, Bevin lost command of judgment. In the early days of August when Eban was in London for conferences with editors and members of Parliament, Richard Crossman summarized for him an interview with an enraged Bevin. The essence of the discussion was related by Goldmann to Eban, who in turn relayed the information to Niles for President Truman's information and guidance. It read:

The present trend of Mr. Bevin's thinking was luridly revealed to me in my conversation with Mr. Crossman, who had seen him on August 4th. Crossman described Bevin's outlook as corresponding roughly with the Protocols of the Elders of Zion. The main points of Mr. Bevin's discourse were: (a) the Jews had organized a world-wide conspiracy against Britain and Mr. Bevin. When Crossman suggested that Mr. Bevin's Palestine policy was isolating Britain from world public opinion, Mr. Bevin replied: "That proves my point exactly. They have successfully organized world opinion against me." (b) "The whole Jewish pressure was a gigantic racket run from America." When Crossman pointed out that the Irish Republic had also been a racket run from America, but that Britain had been forced to concede a State, Bevin replied, "Yes, but they did not steal half the place first." (c) In a reference presumably to the latest Irgun outrage, Mr. Bevin said that he would not be surprised if the Germans had learned their worst atrocities from Jews. . . . From this tirade, Mr. Crossman drew the moderate deduction that Mr. Bevin was insane on this issue. . . .[28]

The rumors that had circulated for many weeks about the probable recommendations of UNSCOP were validated at the end of August when the official report was transmitted to the UN General Secretary. Seven members favored the division of Palestine into independent Jewish and Arab states; three, representing India, Iran, and Yugoslavia, opposed Partition but recommended some loose form of federal union; Australia, because the report was not unanimous, abstained.

No one realized more clearly than Niles that the majority recommendations from UNSCOP for a partitioned independent Palestine by no means assured their fulfillment. There would still be many difficult battles ahead. Could a resolution for any kind of Partition, which required a two-thirds vote, pass the General Assembly where the Arab bloc was solid and where it had many allies in the Third World, and, for that matter, in the western world as well? Would the partitioned states be related to a Mandatory power, or to a UN Trusteeship Committee, or would they be completely independent? What land would be assigned to the Jews and the Arabs in the partitioned states; and since "assignment" would assuredly not be peacefully yielded, how could a major war be avoided? The American and British oil interests, much worried about the danger to their investments, had enormous resources with which to wield influence in the media and the many voting states. Niles knew also that there were many powerful opponents of a partitioned Palestine within the advisory groups of the U.S. delegation itself, in the departments of State and Defense, and in the Joint Chiefs of Staff. Above all, since the Arab states threatened all-out war if Partition were attempted, would President Truman be able to hold to his support, or would he wish to? How far could even the President of the United States go in commitment to enforce Partition?

Niles marshaled his allies in Congress, in both political parties, and in the media, and then moved into the final battles whose outcome was to transform the political and military future of the Near East. First, it was necessary to make sure that the advisers to the American representatives in the United Nations would faithfully support the wishes of the President. The advisers were the specialists who often deeply influenced policy; they did more than the staff work for the official representatives, who were usually political appointees. Yet in the period when the immigration and Partition issues took on major significance, the main advisers were not all supportive of Truman's views. They sided with Robert Lovett, a senior State Department official, with James Forrestal, Secretary of Defense, and with other cabinet-rank officials who did all they could to scuttle the Partition proposals. Niles already had many examples of the outright opposition views of Loy Henderson and George Wadsworth, Undersecretaries of State.

On July 29, Niles had sent a long memorandum to the President, pointing out how crucial it was, in the protracted debates and decisions that lay ahead, to have loyal personnel in the advisers' role: ". . . on the basis of their [Henderson and Wadsworth's] past behaviour and attitudes, I frankly doubt that they will vigorously carry out your policy. But your administration, not they, will be held responsible." Niles did not go so far as to suggest their removal, unreliable though their record proved them to be. He recommended instead that "at least one of the advisers be a vigorous and well-informed individual in whom you, the members of the United States Delegation, and American Jewry have complete confidence." His nominee was Major General John H. Hilldring, who had been part of the military government in Germany and had demonstrated unique understanding and compassion in the administration of the DP Camps.*[29]

Truman was much impressed with Niles' counsel and he

---

*This memorandum is included in full in Appendix, Letter J. It is a good example of the influence that can be exerted on his chief by a trusted presidential administrative assistant.

acted upon it promptly, appointing General Hilldring as a chief adviser. It was a timely action, for as late as a fortnight before the General Assembly opened its sessions, Lovett kept exhorting cabinet colleagues and their aides to remember the strategic interests of the United States in the Near East, the American dependence on oil, and the crucial importance of sustained Arab and British friendship. Even after the Assembly had begun its deliberations, Lovett was still speaking and conferring in opposition to the UNSCOP recommendations on Partition.

The chief American representative to the United Nations, Herschel Johnson, welcomed the appointment of Hilldring, who was solidly behind Truman's policies. David Horowitz, later the first director-general of Israel's Ministry of Defense and governor of the Bank of Israel, wrote that Hilldring was a pillar of strength in the Partition negotiations from the outset and "the moving spirit in the American delegation for a firmer and more active line."[30] The two worked together admirably, and their cooperation was indispensable, especially after an announcement by Sir Alexander Cadogan, head of the British delegation to the UN, that if Partition should be adopted, and there should be resistance from the Arabs, his government felt no obligation to "carry the baby." Furthermore, the British government would take no action during the transition months of Mandate authority to prepare for the new order. Cadogan's statement was an ominous warning that, if conflict broke out, the British would not even exercise police authority to restrain violence, nor would it allow any UN mission to enter the land to deal with emergencies. Herschel Johnson remarked sarcastically that "the British were not entirely helpful."

Forrestal, Lovett, and some of the other State Department dissentients, having clearly lost the battle to sidetrack Partition, now concentrated on the attempt to placate the Arab representatives by obtaining extensive territorial concessions for the projected Palestine Arab state. UNSCOP had already made such concessions and had again reduced the original Balfour Declaration allocation; but it retained Safed, the fertile areas in Lower Galilee, the vale of Beisan, and the Valley of Esdraelon for the Jewish State. These were not only indispensable for the future of the Israeli economy but were integrally linked with the most precious biblical associations. Johnson and Hilldring kept their troops in line and succeeded in preventing the emasculation of the UNSCOP recommendation. Deborah, Barak,

Gideon, and other biblical heroes, were not to be deported.

A climactic battle, almost as important as the Partition vote itself, was to be fought over the disposition of the southern Negev Desert and its port of Aqaba. At this point in history it seemed to have almost no value except geographical size: a large sail-shaped wasteland that abutted the Sinai, neglected through the centuries, left to the nomadic Bedouin tribes. A few widely separated Jewish settlements had been established there since World War I that were beginning to send out fragile tendrils of green into the almost lunar landscape. The UNSCOP report had assigned the entire Negev to the proposed Jewish State. The American delegation was urged by the State Department to separate the Aqaba port area and to reassign it to the Arabs.

But to Weizmann and Ben Gurion the barrenness of the land was the result of neglect and did not lessen its significance for the future. They had watched for nearly thirty years, in successive British attempts to achieve peace, the steady diminution of territory that had been promised to the Jews in the Balfour Declaration. The whole of the Kingdom of Transjordan had been carved out of the original Balfour Declaration assignment. There could be no more retreat now. The Jews counted upon their specialists in desert ecology, and on the achievements of modern technology, to bring the Negev Desert back to fruitful irrigation. Even more, they counted on Aqaba as assurance of access to the Red Sea and trade routes to Africa and the Orient.

The crucial importance of the Negev in assuring a viable Israel loomed large enough to warrant a direct personal appeal to President Truman by Dr. Weizmann. Niles called the ailing old statesman and pleaded with him to make the trip from Israel to the United States for a hoped-for interview. Weizmann complied, but President Truman was by now so tired of the acerbic skirmishes over Partition that he had determined to see no more advocates. Indeed, only a few weeks before, he had received a violent letter from a Chicago Zionist leader that said "a fascist Arab military organization in Palestine was wearing U.S. Army surplus uniforms," and Truman had flared in an angry note to Niles, "It is such drivel as this that makes anti-Semites. I thought maybe you had better answer it because I might tell him what's good for him!"[31]

Niles knew that he had to proceed softly. He called in Truman's old friend, Ed Jacobson, who had been Truman's partner in a haberdashery store in Kansas City in their early days. Tru-

man had never forgotten their relationship and he had promised
Jacobson that the door of the White House would never be
closed to him. Given the choleric mood of the President, even
Jacobson found his "courtesy" call difficult. But he managed to
bring the conversation around to a request for the President to
see Weizmann. At first Truman remained obdurate. As Jacobson tells what followed, he indicated that Weizmann was to the
Jews what the outstanding heroes in American history were to
Americans, and particularly what Andrew Jackson was to Truman. He hoped that the President would give one of the world's
elder statesmen the courtesy of a brief interview. "You bald-
headed old SOB," the President then retorted, "I'll give you
your way and see Dr. Weizmann."*

On the morning of November 19, only a few days before the
opening sessions of the General Assembly, Weizmann came
through a side door of the White House for the historic interview. He fascinated Truman not only by his awesome personal
presence but by the graphic logic with which he presented the
case for the southern Negev in the redemption of the Jewish
State. The President's daughter wrote later: "Weizmann's vivid
description of what Israel could do with the Negev ignited the
enthusiasm of the former Senator who had toiled for years to
create regional development and flood control for Missouri."[32]
Truman was entirely persuaded, and promised to instruct the
American delegation to insist upon the retention of the whole
of the Negev for a Jewish Palestine, as recommended by
UNSCOP.

Truman's change of view was almost bypassed because of a
failure of communication. The American delegation, not having
received Truman's directive, was preparing to follow instructions from the State Department to inform Moshe Sharett, the
Jewish Agency secretary, that the southern Negev would not be

---

*Truman describes the visit with Jacobson in his *Memoirs*, Vol. Two, pp.
160–161. Later a legend was built upon the incident, which made it appear that
Jacobson could wrest any concession about Israel from his former partner.
The legend angered Margaret Truman, who insisted that her father had been
most circumspect in resisting the influence of purely sentimental friendships.
Jacobson himself, a quite modest character, was proud of his relationship
with Truman, but never tried to capitalize on it; his role had been blown out
of proportion by the enthusiasm of friends.

part of the Jewish State. The news of the meeting with Sharett and its purpose reached Truman just before the conference was to begin. "I assured Dr. Weizmann that the American delegation would support the retention of the Negev for Israel," he exclaimed. "He will think I am a liar!" He placed a telephone call. Johnson and Hilldring then excused themselves from the Sharett conference and learned of the President's wishes. They returned to the highly mystified Sharett to tell him nonchalantly that they had nothing important to convey. The American delegation went into the UN session pledged to support the land allocation that would include the whole of the Negev for the Jewish State.[33]

Saturday, November 29, had been set for the UN Assembly vote on the Partition issue. In the weeks preceding, the most feverish activity had been mounted as the adherents maneuvered to line up their votes. Niles was in charge of the campaign to bring in the required two-thirds majority for Partition. Every influence was exerted by both sides—political considerations, quid pro quo favors, tradeoffs, business incentives, government loans, appeals to personal friendship. The most unholy means were considered fair to settle the fate of the Holy Land. The memoirists of the period relate dramatic stories of the extraordinary scramble, and the often capricious circumstances that decided switches and abstentions, ayes and nays.

There was very little doubt about the affirmative votes that had been committed by countries such as Norway and Canada, none of which could be swayed. Nor was there any doubt about the votes of Soviet Russia and its satellites, for the determination to get Britain out of the Near East would have tempted the Russians to resurrect Ivan the Terrible. There were about half a dozen swing states, however, whose decision vacillated until almost the last moment. France was one of these. The delegation was of divided counsel, but the chief French delegate, Alexandre Paroli, worried about the North African colonies and their Muslim population. Niles appealed to Bernard Baruch, who had important friendships in the French delegation. Though a non-Zionist, Baruch was persuaded to think of Palestine as the only refuge left for the unwanted survivors of the death camps. Dr. Weizmann appealed to former Premier Léon Blum, who was still a revered figure in French politics. Two hours before the vote had to be cast, French approval for Partition came through.

Greece, too, had serious problems because of its large Greek minority settlement in Egypt. Niles appealed to an old Boston friend, Tom Pappas, a heavy investor in his native Greece, and to Pappas' countryman, Spyros Skouras, the cinema magnate. They were crestfallen that they could not deliver the Greek vote because Niles had broached his need too late for them to wield enough influence. Greece voted no.

Liberia was a tiny African state with little concern for Near East affairs, but its vote counted as much as one from India or Russia. Its chief delegate had intended to oppose Partition. Niles persuaded his friend Robert Nathan, a Washington economist, to approach Edward Stettinius, a former Secretary of State, no enthusiast for Partition but now president of the American Liberian Development Company and a Nathan client. Stettinius agreed to talk to Firestone Tire and Rubber Company officials, the corporation having vast interests in Liberia. Liberia ultimately voted yes.

The dictator of Nicaragua, Somoza, had been suffering from severe stomach problems that required delicate surgery. Two friends, Dewey Stone and his brother, Judge Harry Stone, of Brockton, Massachusetts, prevailed upon a leading Boston surgeon to take the case and to perform the delicate operation. Somoza did not forget the intercession of the Stones and he brought his own and several of the Latin American countries into the affirmative line.*

Christian Ethiopia had been betrayed in the old League of Nations by the European world when Mussolini trampled out its independence, and after its sovereignty had been restored, it had cast its lot with its Muslim neighbors. David Horowitz and Moshe Sharett must have given Ethiopia's delegates a lesson in sentimental history and reminded them of the happy romance between the Queen of Sheba and King Solomon that linked Ethiopia with the land of Israel. At least, the purported history lesson made a good story. The Zionist leaders refuted Jeremiah's plaint,† and an intended negative vote was turned into an abstention.

---

*Confirmed by Lewis Weinstein of Boston, who had served as chief of the liaison section in General Eisenhower's European command and was a close personal friend of Niles.[34]

†Jeremiah 13:23: "Can the Ethiopian change his skin or the leopard his spots?"

Chance had often conspired against Jewish destiny. But here, during the critical UN debates, it was kinder. There was a revolution in Siam (Thailand) in late November, and the prince, who planned to oppose Partition, had his authority nullified; his vote in the ding-dong battle became an abstention. Carlos Romulo, the Philippine ambassador to the United Nations, was opposed to Partition but, just before the vote, he was called away from New York. Niles prevailed upon Justice Felix Frankfurther and Justice Frank Murphy of the Supreme Court to intercede with the Philippine ambassador to the United States. The ambassador issued a directive to his country's UN delegation to vote in the affirmative.

Late on the Sabbath afternoon of November 29, the decision was made. With only three votes to spare, the United Nations authorized the establishment of independent Arab and Jewish states in a partitioned Palestine.*

The world response, both Christian and Jewish, was overwhelming. Five thousand Jews gathered to express gratitude for the miracle of redemption at the base of the Arch of Titus in Rome, erected two thousand years before. Some of the more learned Jews of Egypt, though intimidated into silence, must have thought of the famous parchment of Mnepthah kept in the Cairo Museum. One of the earliest of the Pharaohs, Mnepthah, had written thirty centuries before: "Israel is no more," using the name for the first time in recorded history to introduce Israel with the salutation of an epitaph. Yet in 1947 there were still Jews in Egypt, even in the Holocaust countries, to hail the United Nations' decision.†

The rejoicing and the anxiety about the future were elo-

---

*Truman, commenting in his *Memoirs* on his immediate de facto recognition of Israel, noted, "I was told that to some of the career men of the State Department that announcement came as a surprise. It should not have been if these men had faithfully supported my policy." (Vol. Two, p. 164)

Niles continued to serve Truman into the second presidency. His additional year in the White House is briefly summarized in the Appendix, Letter K.[35]

†Bevin was never reconciled to the failure of his Palestine policy. A recorded trans-Atlantic conversation between President Truman's legal counsel, Clark Clifford, and James McDonald, the newly appointed first American ambassador to Israel, reflects the attitude of the frustrated foreign minister.

quently recorded by a young sabra, Moshe Dayan, who was to become one of Israel's most brilliant military guardians. In his memoirs, he recalled the historic November night: "We were happy that night, and we danced, and our hearts went out to every nation whose UN representative had voted in favor of the resolution. We had heard them utter the magic word 'yes' as we followed their voices over the airwaves from thousands of miles away. We danced—but we knew that ahead of us lay the battlefield."[36]

CHAPTER NINE

Forcing the British
to Relinquish the Mandate

THE CONSENSUS AMONG THE Jews of Palestine to break all ties with the Mandatory power and to fight for the establishment of a sovereign state was reached slowly, after agonizing disputes. Different factions held varying views on the practicality and the risks in seeking such a drastic solution to end the dependence of Jewish security upon the self-interest of other nations and peoples.

The Jewish militants, spearheaded by the Irgunists led by a Polish immigrant, Menachem Begin, needed no prodding to conclude that there was no alternative to the bid for independent status. Even before Chamberlain's White Paper of 1939 had all but repudiated the Balfour Declaration, they derided the expectation that Britain would be influenced by sentiment or compassion or would honor the pledges of its earlier leaders if these seemed no longer to serve specific British interests. They were not in the least surprised when Lord Halifax, the British Foreign Minister in the Chamberlain government at the threshold of World War II, said bluntly, in issuing the White Paper: "There are times when considerations of abstract justice must give way to those of administrative expediency."

Following a more conciliatory policy than that of the Irgun, Dr. Chaim Weizmann, who was the decisive influence in 1917 in securing the Balfour Declaration, persisted in his faith in Britain's pledged word to fulfill the establishment of a Jewish Homeland in Palestine. He clung to the hope that when the war against Hitler ended, Britain would honor the promises of Lloyd George, Balfour, and Churchill, validated in the most uncompromising language by the leaders of the Labor party. Herbert Morrison, the Home Secretary in the wartime Coalition government and one of the most respected leaders in the party, had gone so far as to advocate an exchange of populations that would send such Arabs in Palestine as consented to other Arab lands, and would open Palestine to Jews who wished to leave the Arab lands where they now lived as virtual hostages.

During most of the war period the great majority of the Palestine Jewish community shared Weizmann's views. Their resistance was not to the British administration under the Mandate; they treasured the advantages of British Commonwealth status. During the war, they offered more than their proportion of volunteers to the fighting forces, while the Grand Mufti, head of the Arab League, was Hitler's guest and Axis collaborator in Berlin. They were determined, however, to oppose the White Paper quotas on immigration and on the expansion of Jewish settlements in Palestine. Ben Gurion aptly summarized their attitude when he said: "We shall fight in the war as if there were no White Paper, and we shall fight the White Paper as if there were no war."

Hence through the years that remained of the Chamberlain government and those after 1940, the leaders of the Jewish Agency encouraged the staking out of settlements, founding and expanding nearly fifty of them, defying British arrest and detention. Many fell under Arab bomb and bullet, but no settlement was abandoned, in the north, at the Jordan, on the hills, in the valleys. The White Paper, indeed, accelerated the pace of settlement. Volunteers from adjacent areas would arrive on a chosen site in the dark of night. By morning, the foundations of a kibbutz were laid—stockade, watch towers, barracks, and fences in place, each another link in the Jewish defense system. The British, fighting for survival against the Germans and faced with colonial turmoil in many parts of the Commonwealth, could not move in to destroy the settlements.*

By 1942, accounts of the Nazi death camps began to circulate in the Allied world. At first, little credence was given to them. Statesmen and publicists in the West remembered the atrocity stories of World War I, many of which were apparently deliber-

---

*Some episodes contained in previous chapters are briefly summarized here to provide continuity to the story of developments in Palestine.

ately manufactured for propaganda purposes. But by the end of 1942 the genocidal objectives of the Nazis could not be denied. Eyewitness reports by escaped prisoners of the camps validated the macabre fact that the Final Solution (made official at Wannsee, a Berlin suburb, on January 20, 1942) was not hysterical rhetoric.* The Allied governments issued a formal condemnation of "this bestial policy of cold-blooded extermination."

But the Jewish leaders in the United States—Stephen Wise, Abba Hillel Silver, Henry Morgenthau—and David Ben Gurion, Yitzchak Ben-Zvi, Moshe Sharett, and Golda Meir in Israel —among others, knew that pious protests by the Allied leaders would not stop the massacres. They convened an international meeting at the Biltmore Hotel in New York early in May 1942, and every shade of opinion was represented among the six hundred delegates. Dr. Weizmann participated, though he was brokenhearted over the loss, three weeks earlier, of his younger son, Michael, an officer in the Royal Air Force who had been killed in action off the coast of France. He still counseled the continuation of diplomatic pressure for accelerated immigration to Palestine, but urged that there must be no action that would sacrifice the quarter century of earlier British concern.

Although the convention was in no mood for patience, there was hesitation to risk the gamble of a complete break with Britain. Hence, the resolutions adopted at the Biltmore Hotel were couched in general terms that did not go beyond the demand for lifting the restrictions of the White Paper and the encouragement of actions to impel British concessions. Nevertheless, Ben Gurion, not Weizmann, emerged as the recognized leader, supported by the majority of Palestinian Jews and by the most concerned elements in American Jewry.

Encouraged by such a mandate, Ben Gurion gave full support to the B'richa network directing the underground flight from occupied Europe. But his reluctance to take more vigorous measures, such as attacking British installations, brought him into direct conflict with Menachem Begin. The contrast in experience and personality between the two men was antipodal.

David Ben Gurion had been born in Poland in 1886 when it

---

*The Wannsee discussion and text, entered in evidence at the Nuremberg Military Tribunal, is included in Raul Hilberg (editor), *Documents of Destruction: Germany and Jewry, 1933–43*. London, 1972, pp. 89–99.

was still part of czarist Russia and where, periodically, government-encouraged pogroms made every Jewish family potential victims. He was early caught up in the dream of Zion and made the journey to Palestine as a young man of twenty. He was a man of sober logic but lyrical when he spoke of Palestine as a homeland. Galilee, where first he settled, was a wilderness in the early years of the century, promising little more than privation and bare survival. Yet he wrote, "We had left behind our books and our theorizing, the hairsplitting and the arguments, and came to the Land to redeem it by our labor. We were all still fresh; the dew of dreams was still moist in our hearts. . . ."[1] With his fellow pioneers, he labored to drain marshes, plant trees, and to prepare the foundations for self-supporting communities, many of whose pioneers perished in the reclamation struggle. His effort to organize the first immigrants for their own protection was interpreted by the Turkish authorities, then in control of Palestine, as political agitation, and he was arrested and deported; his papers were stamped, "Never to return." He was in the United States at the outbreak of World War I and slipped away to join the Jewish Legion, which fought with distinction in the Near East under British auspices.

After World War I, Turkey having been driven out of the Middle East, Ben Gurion returned to Palestine. Though still only in his middle thirties, he quickly rose to leadership in Histadrut, the all-encompassing labor federation that was later to dominate the economic and political life of Israel and was part of the Jewish Agency.

He was a stocky little man, this "lion's cub" from Plonsk—blunt, tough, truculent, whose corona of white hair rose in disarray around a face deceptively cherubic. Prophet and pragmatist, visionary and dogged negotiator, Ben Gurion could walk like Agag through the labyrinths of diplomatic councils, yet, when necessary, remain as contumacious as the head of any local in a longshoreman's union. He was broadly self-educated, immersed in the Bible, the Greek classics, and the Buddhist wisdom of the East.*

---

*Some years ago in Dublin for a television interview, I discussed Ben Gurion with Eamon de Valera, the founding Irish president. He envied Ben Gurion for the tenacity with which he fulfilled Ben Yehuda's pioneer dream of making Hebrew the common language of Israel, a land that had absorbed

Ben Gurion's view of Jewish history was unabashedly simple. His people had been defeated by Roman legions in A.D. 79 and had been driven from the land of Israel. In an audacious act of faith he leaped a hundred generations to link the present struggle for regeneration with the courageous though unavailing resistance that occurred when the Second Temple fell. For him, the intervening centuries represented nothing more than sterile chronology. His contemporaries were the spirits who had created the Bible—the Maccabeans who had defied the Syrians, and the zealots who defended Masada to the last breath against the might of Rome. Ben Gurion made this leap across the flux of time with no resort to fantasy. Every mile he walked, every hill he climbed, every corner he turned, validated the reality of his vision. Here was the Jordan, the river of the Bible. Here Gideon confounded the Midianites. Here Deborah inspired Barak in his victory over the Canaanites and the chariots of Sisera. Here Joshua brought down the walls of Jericho. Here another diminutive David challenged Goliath. For Ben Gurion and his comrades there was an ongoing role in the drama where the People of the Book had only temporarily stood offstage.

Determined to lead his people in their struggle to regain security through statehood, Ben Gurion was faced with a rival who shared his objectives but believed that even terrorist tactics were not too extreme to achieve them. Menachem Begin had been born in 1913 (into a family of timber merchants) in Brest Litovsk, a fortress city on the Polish border. He earned a degree in law in 1935 at the University of Warsaw, but his earliest remembrances were of the intense anti-Semitism that all his people endured. "As students we were forced to sit on the left side of the room during lectures. Anti-Semitic students often used to beat us up. But we were not frightened Jews who succumbed to persecution. We used to retaliate. I remember pitched battles with these students. . . . But when we finished university, we had no future. We couldn't get jobs as lawyers, we couldn't do anything." Begin was deeply influenced by

---

Jews from the ends of the earth. "With all of our Sinn Fein success in beating the British," de Valera said, "our hope to establish our ancestral Gaelic as the common language of the new Ireland did not go beyond a limited literary circle. We must conduct our daily lives in the language of our historic oppressor."

Vladimir Jabotinsky, the Russian poet-orator who organized an extreme right-wing unit of Zionism that endorsed the maximalist demand of a Jewish independent state, to be obtained by forcing the British out of Palestine. There had to be an end to this role of "timid supplicants for protection."[2]

Begin joined one of the militant Zionist societies, Betar, and, at twenty-five, became its leader in Poland. During the riots in Palestine in 1936 to 1938, he organized demonstrations near the British Embassy in Warsaw and was imprisoned by the Polish police. When the Nazi forces occupied Warsaw in 1949, he and his wife, Aliza, sought refuge in the Soviet-occupied parts of Poland and Lithuania. In September 1940 he was again arrested, this time by the Soviet police, and convicted as "a dangerous element in society." He spent many months in a Russian prison and in a labor camp in Siberia. During his exile and imprisonment, his parents, his family, and his comrades were all murdered by the Nazis. In 1942 a deal was worked out by Russia with the western Allies and the London Polish government-in-exile that permitted several thousand Polish prisoners in the labor camps to enlist in a Polish division under General Anders. The unit, which Begin joined, was sent to Palestine for training under the British. Once in the land of his dreams, in May 1942, he promptly deserted the Polish force and joined the paramilitary Irgun underground. His reputation for defiance in Poland and his militant advocacy of Jabotinsky's objectives for Palestine brought him to leadership of Irgun.

Begin had little in common with the more moderate pioneers who had ridden the desert and slept under canvas with the Bedouins. While they shared his dream of an ultimate Jewish state, he had been tested in a different crucible, that of Middle Europe in the late 1930s and 1940s. His biblical first name was Menachem (Comfort), but he was no comfort even to fellow partisans. Though one of his biographers, Eitan Haber, claimed that he had acquired the patina of Polish aristocratic etiquette, it was difficult to discern it, for he had little of the urbane graces. His style was often abrasive, and he had no memories of Christian compassion to temper his distrust of the non-Jewish world.

Begin was convinced from the outset that the Mandatory power had no intention of modifying the White Paper, and he pressed his view for the strategy of harassing the British by attacks on their installations. He declared that it was encouragement to the Nazis to set no limits on their plans for the Final

Solution. What did the Nazis have to fear when their most ruthless barbarities were treated with unconcern? "First they [the Nazis] imprisoned the Jews, and noted the world's indifference," he said. "Then they starved them and still the world did not move. They dug their claws in, bared their teeth. The world did not even raise an eyebrow." He was among the first therefore, to repudiate Fabian tactics. "A Jewish state alone can save us. Our people are living on a volcano. . . . Ancient Judaea collapsed in fire and blood. The new Judaea will rise in fire and blood. What use was there in writing memoranda? What value in speeches? If you are attacked by a wolf in the forest, do you try to persuade him that it is not fair to tear you to pieces, or that he is not a wolf at all but an innocent lamb? Do you send him a "memorandum"? No, there was no other way. If we did not fight we should be destroyed. To fight was the only way to salvation." Through the 1940s he was public enemy number one to the British, who put a $30,000 price on his head.

Begin seemed to be vindicated in his cynicism about British long-range intentions when there was no modification of the White Paper even during Churchill's incumbency as Prime Minister after 1940. His activists stepped up their efforts to circumvent British vigilance and to get shiploads of immigrants into Palestine. The Colonial Office clamped down hard; so strict was the surveillance that even the limited immigration authorized by the White Paper was not achieved.

The effort of the British to prevent the landing of the Jews was often charged with a hostility that verged on outright anti-Semitism. As the number of murders in the death camps began climbing into the millions, British cabinet officials were deluged with protest. Sir John Shuckburgh, an undersecretary in the Colonial Office, referred to such protests as "unscrupulous Zionist sobstuff." When the Allied war losses mounted, Shuckburgh justified strong measures in fighting illegal immigration, even firing on refugee ships. "There are days," he said, "in which we are brought up against realities and we cannot be deterred by the kind of perverse pre-war humanitarianism that prevailed in 1939." During the war period, as the wrath of the militants in Palestine turned into acts of violence, he burst out: "This sort of thing makes one regret that the Jews are not on the other side of this war."

Not all the British political figures were in agreement with the hard line taken by the Colonial Office. There were many sharp exchanges in the House of Commons when the government policy was questioned. On December 14, 1943, during one of these debates, a member of the Opposition, Eleanor Rathbone, declared that "if it had not been for the restrictions placed on immigration to Palestine in the prewar years, even before the Palestinian White Paper, imposed partly for economic reasons and partly to please the Arabs, tens of thousands of men, women, and children who now lie in bloody graves, would long ago have been among their kindred in Palestine. That is something I shall never forget, and I hope the House will never forget it either."[4]

In mid-February 1944 open war on the British flared as Begin's men dynamited the immigration and tax offices in Jerusalem, Haifa, and Tel-Aviv. At first every care was taken to avoid casualties. But by March 23 these precautions became secondary. When the Irgun bombed a number of police offices, a few British lives were lost. The colonial administration denounced the actions as "premeditated murder" and prepared to treat them as such. Begin refused to accept the stigma. He declared that the men whom his forces attacked were not singled out as individuals but as symbols of a government whose hands were stained with Jewish blood. His reasoning outraged the British and worried Ben Gurion, then in the midst of the delicate negotiations which, it was hoped, would bring about the long-sought goal of an independent Jewish state in a partitioned Palestine. Begin's intransigence could well scuttle whatever progress was being made.

Ironically, just as Ben Gurion was moving toward a public confrontation on policy with Begin, both had to face a small band of even more violent extremists, the Lehi (a Hebrew acronym for Fighters for the Freedom of Israel). Lehi, which broke away from Irgun in 1943, recognized no authority that deterred its war against the British, and it accepted no limitations in such a war. Its adherents were regarded as "a gang," not only by the British but also by the moderate Jewish elements. Leadership came from a young visionary, Abraham Stern, a poet and linguist close in spirit to Pádraic Pearse, the Irish Sinn Feiner who led the Easter Rebellion of 1916 and went to his death by firing squad certain that martyrdom was a necessary weapon in the achievement of independence. Lehi, at peak strength in 1944, never numbered more than 150 and drew most of its adherents from young refugees who had fled from the Arab lands of the Middle East. All had been face to face with death too often to fear it; their sole concern was never to be caught alive lest intolerable torture lead to the betrayal of comrades.

Lehi had cooperated with Irgun for a few months; but as the parleys with the British seemed to lead nowhere, and as Haganah ethical restraints increased frustration, Stern would not accept even Irgunist discipline. He remembered the history of the terror that had frozen the will of the Russian court early in the century when the revolutionaries set up the czars and their entourage as targets. He and his men followed this pattern now, waylaying British squadrons, blowing up British officials. His comrades were picked off, one by one. When Stern himself was cut down, the Lehi threw over their last remaining scruples, kidnapping British soldiers and holding them as hostages, determined to create so much havoc that the wearied British would have to surrender the Mandate.

The British reaction was to intensify reprisal. Two hundred fifty suspects were rounded up and incarcerated in the Acre and Latrun prisons. The British offered to free those who were probably uninvolved in return for the names and hiding places of the Lehi ringleaders. They could get no responsible Jewish official to cooperate. Since British intelligence reports warned that daring mass rescues were being planned for Acre and Latrun, all the prisoners were flown out to exile in Eritrea in northern Africa, there to remain until the end of the war. The Lehi responded by stepping up their sabotage. The British declared that clearly there was clandestine cooperation from the so-called moderates and struck harder against whatever dissident activity they detected. Haganah denied any relationship to the Lehi activity, but the British had broken the Haganah code and they knew that their position was accurate.

By now the critics in Parliament of British repression of Palestine began to question the policy that lost men in a "Mespot" tinpot war who were desperately needed on other fronts. Nor were the rank and file in the occupation forces, and some of the officers, entranced with an assignment that often set them against former military comrades who were seeking a new life after horrendous experiences under the Nazis. They could not believe that this was "their war."

Meantime, the tension between British and Jewish leadership in Palestine reached the point of explosion. In November 1944 it was set off when Lord Moyne, the British Minister resident in Egypt, one of Churchill's closest friends, was assassinated by two young Lehi members. His assassination did more than anger Churchill. It revolted him and curdled his long-held view of the Jewish claim to a Homeland in Palestine. He spoke sorrowfully in the House of Commons about the tragic fate of one of Britain's most beloved sons, and addressed somber words to the Jewish leaders with whom he had only the week before been negotiating for Partition after the war. "If our dreams for Zionism," he said, "should be dissolved in the smoke of the revolvers of assassins and if our efforts for its future should provoke a new wave of banditry worthy of the Nazi Germans, many persons like myself will have to reconsider the position that we have maintained so firmly for such a long time."[5]

The warning was taken to heart by Weizmann, who pleaded with the Jewish community "to cast out the members of this destructive band." He tried to placate Churchill. He issued a statement saying that the shock of Moyne's murder had been far more severe and numbing than the death of my own son."[6] He promised the Jewish Agency and the responsible authorities in Palestine that all aid would be given to the British in tracking down the extremists. Ben Gurion's reaction was also firm. Targeting the Lehi, he said: "The beast must be eliminated for it is a greater menace to us than to the authorities and to the police." The Lehi men remained unrepentant. Moderation in the face of outrage was the real treason, they stormed. They blamed the assassination on the desperation of two emotionally wrought-up boys who were driven frantic by the cold-blooded impassivity of the bureacrats. They insisted that Churchill and his government never meant to repudiate the White Paper and that the Moyne assassination was being used as a pretext for maintaining the intolerable quota system. By now the toll of Jewish dead in the extermination camps had passed five million.

Begin regretted that the Lehi boys had permitted their emotions to go to such an extreme. He could not, however, bring himself to condone Ben Gurion's cooperation with the British police by urging the Jewish community to inform on the Lehi members. As usual he turned to the Bible for his analogy, and all the Jewish world felt the fury of his scorn. "It was Cain who slew Abel, his own brother," he reminded Ben Gurion. "You have chosen your ally, Cain. . . . You are delivering men into hands which are stained with the blood of millions thrown back from the homeland's shore into the foundries of Maidanek, your own brothers. . . ."[7]

The immediate impact of the Moyne assassination was an alarming erosion of support for an independent Israel, even from former staunch friends. The intensity of Churchill's revulsion over the murder was manifested in his expressed regret that he had ever championed the Zionist cause. On May 8, 1945, all the German armies having surrendered, Weizmann sought an audience with him to explore his promise that the White Paper would be abrogated as soon as the war ended. For weeks Weizmann could get no appointment; then came a chilling note in which Churchill declined any consideration of the subject "until the victorious Allies are definitely seated at the Peace Table." On June 29, Churchill drafted another letter to Weizmann but decided not to send it; it was filed in "top secret" archives not opened until after Churchill's death. In it Churchill intimated that perhaps the United States ought to take over "the burden" of Palestine. "With its great wealth and strength and strong Jewish elements, it might be able to do more for the Zionist cause than Great Britain. . . ."

In July, another Churchill memo questioned the value of Britain's commitment to Zionist aspirations. It came close to a repudiation of thirty years of concern for a Jewish Homeland as a democratic bastion in the Near East. "I am not aware of the slightest advantage," he wrote, "that has ever accrued to Great Britain from this painful and thankless task." How much attrition had taken place in his understanding of the Jewish plight was indicated in a statement so unrealistic that one wonders whether it was meant as sarcasm: "If all those immense millions have been killed and slaughtered, there must be a certain amount of living room for the survivors, and there must be inheritance and properties to which they can lay claim." He must have been fully aware of the pogroms that had taken place when Jews returned to their native towns and villages, and were beaten to death for their effrontery. Churchill's weary *volte-face* confirmed the Irgun and Lehi in their conclusion that if the Jews were ever to live as a free people in Palestine or a partitioned state within it, they would have to fight for it themselves.

Meanwhile, the British general election, postponed during the war period, was held in July 1945. Churchill confidently expected that the responsibility for the next crucial years in

Britain would continue to be assigned to his safe and tried leadership. To his chagrin and the astonishment of the world, Labor swept into power with a gain of two hundred seats in one of the major political upsets in British history. For the Conservatives, it was not simply a defeat; it was an eviction. Conforming to the British tradition of immediate transfer of authority, Churchill resigned. His place at the Potsdam summit meeting, where decisions were being hammered out on the fate of the postwar world, was taken by Clement Attlee, who had been Deputy Prime Minister in the Coalition government. For two days Stalin was unavailable, and rumor had it that he was uproariously drunk as he celebrated Churchill's elimination.

As soon as the new ministers took their places, they were flooded with briefing memoranda from the permanent secretariat in the Foreign Office, who seized the opportunity to reinforce their traditional anti-Zionist policy. They elicited statements from their representatives in the Muslim world predicting dire consequences if there were any change in the White Paper status quo in Palestine. Ernest Bevin, who came up from a party position in the Dockworkers' Union, became the Foreign Secretary. During the Coalition period, when he served in the cabinet, he had accepted the party line of Labor that vigorously opposed the White Paper and its sharp curtailment of Jewish immigration into Palestine. But he was now Foreign Minister and imperial considerations had to be given priority.

One of the first matters Bevin had to cope with, upon assuming his new post, was the urgent request of President Truman that the White Paper be modified at least to the point of permitting 100,000 Jews, ghosts in the charnelhouse that Europe had become, to migrate to Palestine. Bevin did not confine himself to a temperate response or the plausible explanation that the adoption of such a policy, at this juncture, would weaken the British position in the Arab world. "The Jews," Bevin said, "should not want to get too much at the head of the queue." Golda Meir, later Israeli Prime Minister, suggested that Bevin had apparently forgotten that the Jews were always at the head of the queue at the gas chambers.

When Bevin met with Commonwealth journalists, he remarked that "Nothing would please him more than for all Jews to be gathered back into Abraham's bosom." He pledged resistance to any attempt on their part "to ride roughshod over Arab and Moslem rights." He advised the Jews to read the Koran as well as the Bible. Suddenly, too, he became concerned about Europe losing too many of its Jews if the doors of Palestine were opened. "It would be morally wrong," he said, "to seek a solution to the problem of the Jews by encouraging them to leave ancestral lands where they had lived for centuries and to whose welfare they had contributed." When James McDonald stopped off in London to discuss with Bevin his activities with the International Commission on Refugees, he wrote that he was stunned by the vehemence of Bevin's diatribe against the Jews.[8]

Ben Gurion did not wait long to put to test the intentions of the new Labor government. Within ten days after it had taken office in July 1945, he led a delegation to the Colonial Office to demand that 100,000 certificates be issued for entry to Palestine to relieve the alarming pressures that were building in the Displaced Persons' Camps in Europe. The Colonial Secretary, George Hall, was taken aback by the militant attitude of the delegation. He wrote that the "behaviour was different from anything which I had ever experienced." The reply to the delegation was delayed for a month. Then Hall indicated that 2,000 certificates of the unused portion of the White Paper quota would be issued, but that further concessions would come only with Arab consent. It should be noted, better to understand the Jewish reaction, that in all of 1945 only 13,000 Jews had been admitted to Palestine, 1,500 fewer than in 1944 when the war was still in progress.

All Jewish elements in Palestine now, in the autumn of 1945, submerged their differences to assume a united front in active resistance. Haganah joined its old adversaries, the Irgun and the Lehi, in repudiating restraint. Golda Meir said soberly: "We kept hearing the argument 'the Arabs can create so much trouble, therefore you have to give in.' So in the end we decided, very well, *we'll* create trouble." On October 10 the Haganah raid on the military detention camp at Athlit, south of Haifa, took place and its 210 detainees—mainly those who had been intercepted when they attempted to reach Palestine by means of illegal immigration—were set free. Athlit was followed by carefully timed attacks on two hundred points of the country's railway network, and the dynamiting of the tracks paralyzed British troop movements. Three British vessels patrolling the Mediterranean shore to prevent illegal immigrant landings were blown up. No night passed without surprise attacks on airfields, radar stations, lighthouses, and other military installations. Attacks were coordinated by joint command of the leaders of Haganah, Irgun, and Lehi.

Sir Alan Cunningham, British High Commissioner in Palestine, was obliged to request massive reinforcements, veterans of the wars in Europe, who could ill be spared since there were eruptions of colonial peoples in India, Egypt, and Malaya, and near civil war in Ireland. Cunningham ordered the detention of 14,000 Jewish civilians. The Jewish intelligence system was uncanny: the British directives were known within a few hours after they had been drafted, and they were transmitted to the underground, most of whose leaders escaped the net.

In mid-June, the Labor party had held its annual conference at Bournemouth at which Bevin announced that he pledged his political future on the reestablishment of law and order in Palestine. It was at this conference, too, that he lashed out at Truman's motives in pressing for expanded immigration of the Jews to Palestine. The American press did not take kindly to Bevin's departure from diplomatic niceties, and the editorial writers attacked him savagely. When Bevin came to New York for the sessions of the United Nations, the dockers refused to handle his baggage, and at a baseball game there were such noisy demonstrations against him that he had to be hustled out of the park.

These experiences did not divert Bevin; they simply added fuel to his rage. Upon his return to England, orders went to the military in Palestine to make an all-out effort to suppress the guerilla activity. Suspects were arrested and disarmed. Those who were identified as illegal immigrants were summarily shipped off to Cyprus or returned to the ports from which they had sailed. The Jews fought back, casualties mounting; their military kept sniping, sabotaging, and kidnapping. The populace referred to the red-bereted British paratroopers not as anemones but as anenemies—a popular song spoke of the "red anenemies with the black heart." Civilians in cities, towns, and villages, in kibbutzim and kvutzoth, oldsters, teenagers, children, blocked the search parties with their bodies. The British troops retaliated first with high-pressure water hoses, then with bayonets. A correspondent for *Time* watched as one of the colonials ordered his men to use the butts of their rifles as they routed the Jews from their homes. He heard him swear to have the troops "make such nuisances of themselves that the bloody Jews will cease protecting the Stern gang and other terrorists. And I don't care if I'm out of the Army tomorrow."[9] In the midst of the turmoil, the news was flashed that two boats from Italy, crowded with more than 1,000 survivors of the Nazi camps, had been permitted to land only after hunger strikes and threats of mass suicide. Almost simultaneously the worldwide press carried the story of new Polish pogroms.

The Jews of Palestine understood fully what Bevin was about. Every act of repression, the incarceration of hundreds of prominent citizens, the mass effort to flush out and confiscate all weapons, the deportation of survivors who had constantly challenged death to reach the Promised Land, were part of his all-out effort to end what had become a dangerous rebellion. The decision was made by the Jewish leadership to thwart the design with a dramatic retaliation. Irgun and Lehi, again with the full cooperation of Haganah, engineered the daring plan to blow up a wing of the King David Hotel, one of the nerve centers of administration, but, equally important, a symbol of British authority. Ben Gurion, then on a mission in Paris, had given his consent for Haganah participation. Later, as we have seen, a controversy arose over the responsibility for the unexpected loss of ninety-one lives—Jewish, Arab, and British—including civilians who were at their routine clerical tasks in the hotel or as part of the British apparatus.

Haganah afterward claimed that it had agreed to cooperate only on the assurance that the destruction of a wing of the hotel, or a major part of it, was to be accomplished without loss of life. It assumed that the explosion was to take place outside office hours and after ample warning to clear the hotel of guests and remaining professional personnel. The Irgunists declared that they had taken every precaution to avoid bloodshed. They had sent out signals of the intended explosion and had warned that the building be immediately evacuated. They attributed the loss of life to delay by the operators in transmitting the messages. The controversy persists over blame for the casualties, but there was no attempt to shed responsibility for the action itself.

It was in the highly emotional climate of the terrorist act that Lieutenant General Evelyn Barker made his unfortunate remark about the need for retaliation by providing "the race" where it hurt them most, "by striking at their pockets." The British ambassador to Washington, Lord Inverchapel, reported: "Implicit in much of this comment, which in some instances links General Barker's remarks to Mr. Bevin's words about Jews not being wanted in New York, is the idea that the British

Government is really anti-Semitic."[10] It was now impossible to continue negotiations for the Grady-Morrison Plan, undertaken by the American and British governments to seek some sort of compromise. Circumstances had driven the situation far beyond the problem of the admission of 100,000 Jews.

In December 1946 at the Zionist Congress in Basel came the climax when moderate leadership was repudiated. Chaim Weizmann spoke for the last time as the elected leader of world Jewry. Though he employed language more condemnatory of British policy than he had uttered in his lifetime, he could no longer serve as the symbol of revised Jewish aspirations. He said sorrowfully:

> Sometimes we were told that our exclusion from Palestine was necessary in order to do justice to a nation endowed with seven independent territories, covering a million square miles; at other times we were informed that the admission of our refugees might endanger military security through the war. . . . It was easier to doom the Jews of Europe to a certain death than to evolve a technique for overcoming such difficulties. When human need, the instinct of self-preservation, collided with the White Paper, the result was the *Struma*, the *Patria*, and Mauritius.[11]

His rebuke to the British was now not considered sufficiently condemnatory, nor did his policy of patience with the British any longer fit the times.

The unrelenting resistance to the British continued, Irgun and Lehi cooperating in the final effort to wear down the Mandatory power and to compel it to relinquish the Mandate. Nathan Yellin-Friedman, a firebrand revolutionary all his life, now head of the Lehi, whipped up the spirits of his men by reminding them that Britain, bogged down in colonial revolts, could no longer afford to sustain its Mandate in Palestine. A final spurt of resistance would inevitably drive the British out. He later explained how his tactics, adapted from those of the Irish Republican Army, had worked their attrition on the British will:

> We planted mines disguised as milestones on both sides of the road and exploded them by electricity when British vehicles came between them. Later I read that this kind of action broke the nerve of the British army. It meant that instead of their imposing

a curfew on the Jews, we imposed a curfew on them. They were afraid to leave their barracks so they had to stay there night after night, month after month. It was very bad for morale. And the casualties spread unrest among British families in England. They started demanding the evacuation of British troops. It had a political effect. That was the purpose.[12]

On January 7, 1947, Bevin made a last effort for Britain to scuttle the Balfour Declaration altogether and to ally with the Arabs so that the oil and the vital resources of the Middle East would not be jeopardized. He circulated a secret memorandum to the cabinet reminding his colleagues that "by 1950 the centre of gravity in that part of the world would shift from Persia to the Arab lands, with Saudi Arabia, Bahrain, Kuwait and Iraq being the main oil producers." The next week, in a supplementary memorandum, he wrote: "The certainty of Arabic hostility to partition is so clear and the consequences so serious, that partition must, on this ground alone, be regarded as a desperate measure." Such a decision "would contribute to the elimination of British influence from the vast Moslem area between Greece and India and would have consequences even beyond strategy. . . . It would also jeopardize the security of our interests in the increasing oil production of the Middle East."[13]

But time had run out on Bevin and his supporters. The situation in Palestine had worsened to the point that Partition had become the least of the disadvantageous options. Aneurin Bevan, the Welsh *wunderkind* of the Labor party, who had always preferred the loyalty of the Jews in Palestine to the unpredictable accords with the Arabs, wrote that, for the Jews, Partition was already a compromise solution. If it were not now put forward, leadership would pass to men who would insist upon more extreme courses. "A friendly Jewish state in Palestine," he continued, "would give us a safer military base than any we should find in an Arab state. The Jews were under the continuing influence of countries friendly to ourselves. If, however, India and other Muslim countries passed under Russian influence, for how long could we expect to retain a secure military base in an Arab Palestine?"

It was humiliating for Bevin to acknowledge defeat, especially when his adversaries had seemed to be an enfeebled people whose spirit should have been broken long before. But for a Britain so impoverished by the war, the cost of holding onto

Palestine had risen too high. With Ireland, India, Egypt, the African possessions, and other parts of the Commonwealth in disarray, even Bevin had to admit that it was time to cut losses. On April 2, 1947, he called for a special meeting of the United Nations at which he would ask for a commission to prepare recommendations for the regular session in the autumn. Perhaps he nurtured the hope that the report of such a commission would still not come to the solution of a partitioned sovereign state. In any case, it was now time, he felt, to offer to relinquish the Mandate. On May 15, the United Nations Special Committee on Palestine came into being. As detailed earlier, it reached the decision, after long sessions with representatives of Arabs and Jews, to recommend a partitioned Palestine.

The Arabs, as always, denounced the recommendations and girded for the battle in the Assembly of the United Nations to prevent them from being adopted. The British government, which had hoped for a pro-Arab decision, reacted sullenly. Bevin indicated that, if the United Nations accepted the UNSCOP recommendations, the Mandate would be relinquished as promised, but there would be no British cooperation in enforcing partition. The Jews rejoiced. The territory recommended for a sovereign state was minuscule, divided into separated segments, tenuously connected, vulnerable to attack. But it included the undeveloped Negev in the south, which could perhaps be brought to fertility by scientific resourcefulness. Partition meant recognized international authority to open the doors of the allotted areas for unrestricted immigration. Above all, it meant sovereignty, an end to the humiliation of perpetual minority status for Jews in non-democratic lands. Hence, the Jews acclaimed the recommendations and prayed that they would not end again in the sterility of empty words.

After Israel achieved statehood, there were vigorous debates about the actions that compelled the British to abandon the Mandate. More and more the people of Israel, moderates included, began to reappraise the role of the activists and their tactics of guerilla warfare. Was it conceivable, many asked, that the British would have yielded if they had not been forced to do so? A new generation had grown up in a world where most of the resolutions of the United Nations itself were cavalierly disregarded, where violence had overthrown established governments that had survived other means of resistance.

The rebuttal to this view was vigorously maintained by men

like Teddy Kollek, who knew all the Israeli leaders well. "I have always believed," he wrote with the perspective of thirty years of political activity, "that the Jewish State came about not as a result of acts of terrorism, but because of the intensive settlement throughout the country, the great numbers of illegal immigrants brought into the country by the Haganah, and the diplomatic work carried out by Weizmen and Ben Gurion.[14]

As the years passed, the mood changed. In 1975, the two boys who were hanged for Lord Moyne's assassination were proclaimed national heroes and their bodies were raised from graves of shame to be reinterred, with full military honors, on Mount Israel. In 1977, Yitzhak Shamir, one of the three Lehi leaders and admittedly part of the assassination conspiracy, was elected Speaker of the Knesset. The head of Irgun, Menachem Begin, became Prime Minister of Israel.

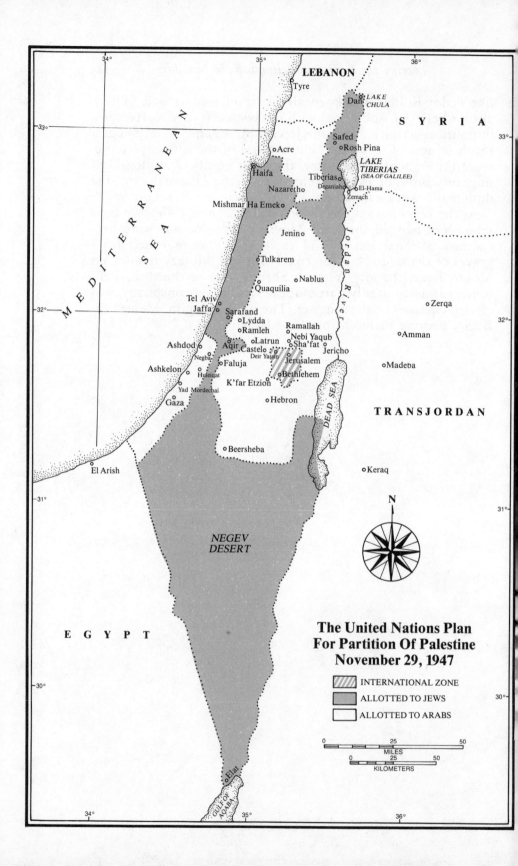

The United Nations Plan
For Partition Of Palestine
November 29, 1947

INTERNATIONAL ZONE
ALLOTTED TO JEWS
ALLOTTED TO ARABS

CHAPTER TEN

The Interregnum Vacuum:
Operation Deluge,
November 1947–May 1948

THE PARTITION VOTE came on November 27, 1947, and Britain was given a transition period of about six months to liquidate its Mandate. Britain used the period to demonstrate that Partition was unworkable. During the UN debates, a poker-faced Lord Cadogan had announced that while Britain would retain "full control" until the last moment, it "would do nothing that might be interpreted as favoring the implementation of Partition." Nor would Britain permit any UN personnel to enter Palestine to assist in carrying out the decision to create separate Arab and Jewish states. The interregnum inevitably became a deliberately contrived vacuum in which Arabs and Jews skirmished to preempt strategic areas, assigned or not, by the UN. The attacks and counterattacks often reached the level of costly pitched battles. The British paid a heavy price too, for, in what was aptly termed Operation Deluge, they continued to resist illegal immigration and the Jews fought back against all restrictions. Arthur Koestler, appropriating George Bernard Shaw's sarcastic quip in referring to insubordinate Erin as "Britain's Other Island," called Palestine "Britain's Other Ireland."[1]

The Palestine Arabs, reinforced by small bands of volunteers from neighboring Arab countries, did not wait beyond the Partition vote in the UN to demonstrate that they were in earnest when they vowed that they would never allow a Jewish state to come into being and that any line of partition would have to be drawn in blood. To be sure, they were in no position to launch any large-scale attacks. Under the Mandate they had no national army nor even a militia; there were small local units to maintain internal order under the jurisdiction of their clan heads. It would take months to achieve coordinated action. At the outset therefore, Arab opposition to the UN declaration took the form of harassment, hit-and-run raids, goaded on by the Husseini Arab religious leader, the Grand Mufti (Haj Amin el Husseini), who headed the Arab Higher Committee that he had organized in 1936.

After the Partition vote the Grand Mufti called for a three-day general strike, from December 2 to December 5; simultaneously there were attacks upon Jews in regions that abutted arterial highways and railroads, and intensified bombing in crowded commercial or residential areas. Where roads led through or near Arab towns, Jewish truck convoys had to run a gauntlet of snipers and even mines, as they tried to bring food and supplies to Jerusalem, Tel Aviv, Haifa, and to isolated settlements in Galilee and the Negev. On November 30, a Jewish bus was ambushed as it neared Lydda Airport and five passengers were killed, three of them women. A fortnight later, a patrol squad guarding a water pipeline in Upper Galilee was wiped out by villagers with most of whom their Jewish neighbors had long lived in peace. In the first twelve days after Partition, Jewish casualties mounted to eighty killed and many times that number wounded.

The Jewish Agency, now the provisional government of Jewish Palestine, did not respond with any major counteroffensive. The British had forbidden private armies, and Haganah, the unofficial Jewish militia, could count on no more than 20,000 military reserves, of whom only the 3,000 in Palmach, the shock commando forces, were regulars. The others were partially trained and most inadequately equipped for more than police duty. Ben Gurion and his staff were therefore in agreement that it was much wiser initially to maintain the traditional Haganah policy of *Havlagah*, acting only in self-defense. Until the official British withdrawal in May, they would build their striking power through accelerated illegal immigration and gather military arms and supplies from assigned agents who were acquiring them in Europe and the United States.

As the sniping and ambushing grew more serious, Ben Gurion called on the Mandatory power for military escorts for the convoys and for authority to arm the drivers for defense. The requests went unheeded. The invariable reply to expressions of outrage was that the Arab reaction had been predicted and was the reason for British opposition to Partition. On December 4, 1947, the High Commissioner wrote: "If escorts were provided by the Mandatory forces it would be interpreted as British acceptance of the UN vote." He recommended that exposed areas such as the international airport should be evacuated "for the Jews' own good." Both the leaders of the Jewish Agency and the Jewish population of Palestine were well aware that the British were determined to prove Partition could not work. Their official declarations could just as easily have read: "We told you so. We'll be back, and on our own terms."

Ben Gurion had begun, years earlier, to meet this challenge. Indeed, immediately after World War II ended, he had turned to the American Jewish community for enlistment in the impending struggle with the British and the Arabs. An old American friend, Rudolf G. Sonneborn, was asked to convene a nucleus group who would be given a candid evaluation of the crisis and be asked for help. On July 1, 1945, in Sonneborn's New York apartment, eighteen Jewish community leaders from all parts of the United States and a few from Canada met to hear Ben Gurion's appraisal of what lay ahead.

Without rhetorical embellishment, he spoke of the Holocaust and the desolation it had wrought. He predicted that Labor would win the scheduled postwar British election, but he had no faith in its promises to modify the existing policy of rigidly restricted Jewish immigration to Palestine. He believed that the Displaced Persons Camps could be emptied only by the action of the Jews themselves. They would have to resort to illegal immigration, to defy the British by every means, including force. He was convinced that after two or three years of continuous Jewish resistance, the British, encumbered by major international problems, would have to surrender their Mandate. Then the Arab states encircling Palestine would attack and, he asked, if the Israeli defenses were overwhelmed, where were the Jews to go? Would the United States, with its own rigid immigration restrictions, welcome them? Would any country receive them? Ben Gurion pledged that the Jews, prepared to fight their way past all obstacles, would give a good account of themselves. But they would need substantial military equipment to be acquired with funds that had to be readily available.

Ben Gurion explained why he had to resort to emergency appeals for the military buildup. Though the United States had placed its prestige behind the Partition plan, it was unwilling to become involved in military activity or to collaborate with Jewish Palestine to bring it about. An embargo on the shipment of arms had been imposed even though the Arab states had little difficulty in procuring them because, as Britain reminded the Jews, it had contracts of long standing with Transjordan and a number of other Arab states to sell them weaponry. Ben Gurion told his audience that whenever he asked the American Zionists for money to buy machine tools for the Haganah weapons industry, he drew a blank check.

The select audience listened in almost total shock. Sonneborn spoke for all, as years later he recalled the moment: "On that memorable day we were asked to form ourselves into an . . . American arm of the underground Haganah. We were given no clues as to what we might accomplish, when the call would come, or who would call us. We were simply asked to be prepared to mobilize like-minded Americans."[2]

The response of Sonneborn's group was unanimously positive and there were immediate contributions running into millions of dollars. Many present additionally offered to guarantee substantial bank loans to ensure a steady cash flow. Equally important, the group pledged that Ben Gurion's message would be conveyed to the business and social circles that the audience represented. Resources would thus be available to pay spot cash for planes and the cargoes they were to carry in circuitous airlifts to Palestine.

After Ben Gurion's visit, luncheons were held almost weekly in the old McAlpin Hotel in mid-New York City, new recruits constantly supplementing the core leaders and matching their generosity. It was a spectacular response because those who undertook the dubiously legal project, no questions asked, were people ordinarily involved in routine careers—bankers, manufacturers, stockbrokers, chain store magnates, men who evoked no image of adventure. Yet there was elation among them that they could participate. They felt akin to the Irish Americans of the 1920s who cooperated with their Sinn Fein compatriots by subsidizing the guerilla efforts to establish the Irish Free Republic. In the year following the end of World War II, the Sonneborn associates were providing about a million dollars a month.

The timing of Ben Gurion's appeal to prepare for the contingency he had forecast could not have been better. The American

War Assets Administration was divesting itself of billions in surplus hardware at one tenth or one twentieth of the original cost. Many of the veterans who returned from the war were restless, ready to respond to a new call to subsidized adventure. There was widely held sympathy for a people who had lost six million souls to Hitler, and admiration for the courage of the survivors who were attempting now to rebuild their lives.

In the immediate postwar period the nerve center of clandestine arms procurement activity was New York, but the operations ranged through a network that stretched to every part of the United States and Latin America. Al Schwimmer, a TWA flight engineer, had built a reputation for courageous risk in his flights "over the hump" to supply planes to China during the Pacific war. He organized the Schwimmer Aviation Corporation in Burbank, California, to acquire and renovate transports for use in Israel. With the Sonneborn-generated funds he was able to purchase ten C-46s and three Constellations. Later, as the Partition settlement neared, he located four A-20s and four B-17 bombers that had been most effective in World War II. To circumvent the American embargo, they were routed to Puerto Rico and the Azores, landing, on their way to Palestine, in a small airport, Zatec, made available by Czechoslovakia. There the planes waited again until the British Mandate was relinquished, and arrived in Palestine just as the war with the Arab states began heating up. En route, the jubilant pilots decided on a theatrical demonstration of renewed power, and their bombs fell on Gaza, El Arish, and near King Farouk's palace in Cairo.

Soon after Partition another company, Materials for Palestine, Inc., with headquarters in New York City, was organized, this time with all the accouterments of legality.[3] It was to fulfill diversified Israeli shopping lists: uniforms, overcoats, steel helmets, parachute flares, Waring blenders for shredding secret documents, camouflage paint, bales of barbed wire, brassieres for the women soldiers, anti-aircraft searchlights, generators, woolen blankets, surgical dressings, and thousands of other prosaic items. One of the routing experts wangled 350,000 burlap bags out of an importer from Calcutta. Essential items were available in bargain lots in European countries too, and the Haganah emissaries were continuously on the alert for them. Some of their bargains fell short of comfortable use, but no one troubled at this period about appearance or style. A large purchase of Polish Boy Scout coats was intended to keep Israeli soldiers warm during the winter of 1948, but the sizes proved much too small for the men. The consignment was turned over to the women in military office work, who came to their tasks in blue-gray coats that were buttoned on the wrong side.

Service Airways, Inc., headed by Irwin Schindler, also operating out of New York City, was the cover for the agency that recruited American pilots, navigators, mechanics, and other technicians for the airlifts whose final destination was Palestine. Haganah commanders and nineteen young Israeli pilots who had served during World War II in the Royal Air Force were sent over to be given refresher courses by high command American veterans. As a sideline, Service Airways sponsored an undercover school in New York to train Israelis for intelligence work. It collaborated with specially organized units that forged passports and identity cards, bills of lading, and documents that had to be produced in the continuous duel to contravene the embargo interdicts.[4]

The cooperation of American Jewish leaders was indispensable in the intensive fund-raising campaigns, the procurement of arms and equipment that stocked the Israeli arsenal, and the diplomatic influence that was exerted to prevent the emasculation of the Partition settlement. But, of course, the main reliance for achieving the combat strength to cope with the Palestine Arabs and, soon after, the assaults of the invading Arab states, had to come from the Israelis themselves.

There was Elie Schalit, a twenty-two-year-old third-generation sabra who had enlisted in Haganah while still in high school and, during the war, in the Canadian Air Force. It was his task, with the cooperation of some young American colleagues, to pack and ship bullets, explosives, blasting and primer caps for detonators, tools and dies for gun manufacture, and tons of other embargoed items and equipment. These were usually stored in scooped-out boilers or concealed beneath such cargo as onions, potatoes, screws, and other innocent items that were labeled "agricultural implements," "used industrial machinery," or "consumer goods." Small arms were hidden in drums covered with tar paper and plaster of Paris. Schalit's most ambitious undertaking was to ship tons of smokeless powder, which he obtained from a Mexican dealer, for the mortars of Israel's defenders. They were validated by invoices that identified them as refractory clay.

Haim Slavin, an agricultural engineer who had managed irrigation and hydroelectric projects in Palestine, became Haganah's expert on secret arms production. When it was learned, near the end of World War II, that the British were dumping outdated cordite into the Mediterranean, Slavin sent divers down to salvage the discarded material. He then organized a corps of young women who fashioned instruments out of razor blades to cut up the congealed chunks, dry them out, and put them to use in the manufacture of explosives.

In late 1945, Slavin was sent by Ben Gurion to the United States to become better acquainted with the latest techniques in fashioning small arms, and to apply the information in Israeli factories to reduce reliance on shipments from abroad. Once in the United States, learning his English from Conan Doyle's Sherlock Holmes stories, Slavin signed up a young Californian scientist to scour libraries and bookshops for current technical magazines and research papers that dealt with advances in military materiel. The two collated their research for guidance in the expanding Israeli arms industry. To devise a lightweight automatic machine gun for immediate use, Slavin recruited a Vermont Yankee technician, Carl Eckdahl, who had designed such a gun in World War II and was now working as a gunsmith for several New England firms. Eckdahl, although not a Jew, was soon as deeply involved in the Israeli cause as any sabra. The gun he developed was not used in the Israeli wars, but its design was adapted to create a submachine gun, the Uzi, that became Israel's standard infantry weapon. It was considered effective enough to be included in the military hardware that was later purchased by West Germany, Holland, and several other European and Asian countries.[5]

One of the knottier problems of delivering planes purchased in the United States was that, lacking the cruising range of the later jets, they could not be flown non-stop to Palestine. Diplomatic contacts, which were unusually fluid in the international scene, had to be courted and continuously reinforced to obtain refueling points in Czechoslovakia, Italy, Greece, Yugoslavia, and Bulgaria. It was through the ingenuity of Dr. Michael Felix, a Czech-born engineer who had migrated to Palestine before the war and had become a close adviser of Ben Gurion, that the government of Czechoslovakia had opened the small airfield in Zatec as a transit point. The dozen DC-4s that had been acquired in the United States were flown there. Felix simultaneously maneuvered the purchase in Europe of ten ME-109s, sophisticated fighting planes, and he put an option on another fifteen, hoping that funds would become available when the option was exercised. He must have experienced special gratification when this bargain purchase included several Messerschmitts that had been part of the Nazi air fleet.[6]

Schwimmer and Schindler's recruits and the Israeli pilots, now assembled in Zatec, were ready to fly the acquired planes to Israel. One American fighter pilot, after attending his last class at Harvard, had flown at once to Zatec. The Americans were a happily unruly, jaunty crowd who referred to themselves as "the crazy American kids," a contrast to the intense, often brooding, Israelis who were invariably duty-oriented. Nevertheless, the two groups under the skillful guidance of Yehuda Ben Chronin, a Palmach commander, complemented each other admirably, sharing risks and taking reverses in stride. A veteran ace of Canada's air force persuaded sixteen retired fellow pilots to follow him to Europe and the Near and Middle East. The mother of a former pilot from Mishawaka, Indiana, blessed her son's decision to join up in a sacred cause, hoping also it would help him to meet "a nice Jewish girl."

Expanding the original tiny air force was a crucial element in holding off the Arab attacks and, later, in fighting the War of Independence. But there had to be even greater reliance upon ships that could carry immensely heavier military cargo and manpower. Ben Gurion and Haganah sent their best men to Europe and the United States to arrange for their purchase, to coordinate routes and sailing schedules, and to load them expertly so that embargoed items could be hidden under conventional cargo to circumvent the vigilance of port authorities. Shaul Avigur, who headed Haganah operations, undertook overall direction. He counted heavily on Theodore (Teddy) Kollek, who had already created a legendary record for smuggling large numbers of refugees out of the Balkans, and Munya Mardor, who came as a boy from Russia to Palestine and rose steadily to head up "Rekesch," the name given to the project that dealt with the acquisition of ships.[7]

Kollek, who after independence became the oft-elected mayor of Jerusalem, was one of Ben Gurion's most trusted protégés. He was born in Vienna in 1911, son of a Rothschild banker who was early drawn to the He-Halutz, the activist European Zionist group. He settled in Palestine in 1934 and was soon involved in directing illegal immigration from central Europe and the Balkans. Through the war period and up to the eve of the UN Partition crisis, he was attached to the Political Department of the Jewish Agency. He was plucked from there by Ben Gurion in 1947 to represent Haganah in the United States.

It was a felicitous choice. Kollek had the capacity to kindle a sense of urgency in soliciting emergency help and he secured millions of dollars for ships and military supplies. Typical of Kollek's forthright approach was an interview with William Levitt, who had developed mass production methods to construct homes and communal buildings, whole communities, one of which, Levittown, in Long Island, became the pattern for a new industry. Said Kollek: "We need the money, but cannot tell you what it is for." Levitt was a cautious businessman but, as he later recalled, a wordy exposition would have broken the spell of "pith and moment." He answered simply, " 'OK,' and I gave him the million dollars."[8]

Kollek worked closely with Schalit. Together they managed the purchase of a U.S. Navy submarine chaser in New Orleans; with a Filipino cook, a Guatemalan radio operator, and an Annapolis graduate as third mate, the *Yucatan* arrived in Israel to become the *Nogah*, a Jewish man-of-war. Kollek also persuaded a Los Angeles hardware merchant to buy surplus landing craft that were refitted in a San Diego shipyard, and they reached Israel in December 1948 to protect the victory of the Israeli troops after the war had been won. Years later, summarizing his procurement experiences, Kollek said: "In all this, I was the traffic cop, I directed all the moving of these people to and fro."

Involved also in this frenetic activity was, once again, the chameleon Arazi. As long as the British were still in control of Palestine, most of the planes and heavy armament that would be needed to fight the Arabs had to be stored in other countries, until the way was cleared for them to reach Israel. Years later, Ben Gurion would recall in his memoirs: "You cannot hide a plane in a basement, nor a tank in an attic closet. What we had to do therefore was to try to buy them overseas, which was also nto an easy task, and hold them until the British troops would leave."[9] Ben Gurion called upon "the old man," Arazi, for special procurement missions and the fund raising to underwrite them. Arazi was now almost forty.

Daredevil he might be, yet he did not underestimate the obstacles. Partition had just been voted but, within a week, the United States had embargoed all sales of arms to the countries of the Middle East. Arazi knew that to be effective he would have to capitalize on the friendships he had garnered earlier. He moved confidently into his new assignments, combining them along the way with easy conquests of attractive women who were drawn to the broad-shouldered Lothario with the cobalt eyes. A colleague who came upon him with two women fussing over him was fearful that his amorous adventures might interfere with his crucial mission. "The least you could do," he scolded, "is to have one come on Mondays, Wednesdays and Fridays, and the other on Tuesdays, Thursdays and Saturdays." One of the Israelis who had been assigned to cooperate with him in the fulfillment of shipping needs expected that he would breeze into the rendezvous office, "accompanied by a fleet of Cadillacs, trailed by bodyguards, riding the length of Broadway through all the red lights."[10]

Arazi soon had several projects under way. He cooperated with Schwimmer to prepare the Constellations for the flight, with several stops, to Israel. But the FBI was on the alert. Schwimmer decided that it was wise to hold up the planes in the hope that a change in American policy would release them. One Constellation managed to elude the rigorous surveillance and it landed in Panama; there it was ensnarled in bureaucratic red tape. A second was stalled in Burbank for repairs. The third, which had reached Millville, New Jersey, was held up for clearance because it could not guarantee a European airport to receive it. The Constellations did not arrive in time for the buildup period, but they were of enormous help in the summer, after the Arab states launched their invasions.

Arazi would not limit himself to one project at a time any more than he would court women consecutively instead of simultaneously. He knew that he could count upon Sonneborn for purchase funds. Through one of the arms dealers, a former Marine major with whom Arazi was already in negotiation, he learned of available weaponry in Mexico—machine guns, rifles, ammunition, and 75-mm artillery. It was lend lease equipment that the United States had furnished to Mexico in return for its declaration of war against the Axis powers. Arazi made a down payment of $70,000 and closed the deal within hours. There were many other opportunities for acquisitions in Mexico and none was considered too bizarre. Only a fraction of Arazi's acquisitions reached their destination, an airstrip bulldozed out of an orange grove in Herzliah, a suburb of Tel Aviv, but he and his chiefs insisted that with the parlous situation in Israel any military victory vindicated major financial outlay.

As the time for Israeli independence approached, Arazi moved into a multitude of new projects like a juggler with half a dozen balls simultaneously in the air. He commuted between the United States and European countries, endlessly on the trail of arms dealers. Often they insisted that he had to provide the cover of some "neutral" country as "the buyer of record." Such conditions presented only a minor challenge. He met with the Nicaraguan dictator, Anastazio Somoza, who, for a price, had granted him a diplomatic passport in 1939. Now in return for several hundred thousand dollars transferred to his New York bank account, Somoza gave Arazi all the "receipts" he needed to indicate that shipments of arms from the U.S. and European countries were to be routed to Nicaragua.[11]

One such shipment, on the SS *Resurrection*, arrived in Haifa from Nicaragua on April 23, 1948, just as Jewish troops were struggling to keep the road open to besieged Jerusalem. The guns were the first to reach Haganah. They not only served well in action but sustained the confidence that major support would not taper off. Arazi waited for no congratulations. As the guns went into action, he was already in Marseilles, supervising a major shipment of French arms aboard the SS *Santa Ciara*. Another ship, the *Borea*, reached Tel Aviv with heavy artillery hidden under 450 tons of potatoes and canned tomato juice. The armies of the Arab states had begun their invasion and the artillery was used immediately against the Syrians, who were at the gates of Deganiah.

While Israeli emissaries concentrated on the procurement of planes, ships, and arms, it was crucial also that they prevent weaponry, wherever possible, from reaching the enemy. The neighboring Arab states could acquire such weaponry from Britain because of contracts completed in earlier years. They now pressed harder to keep pace with the Israelis. Ben Gurion was aware of the accelerated buildup and he authorized Shaul Avigur to create a special unit, under the command of Munya Mardor, to ferret out where Arab orders were being placed and to prevent them from reaching the Arab armory. How far Haganah intelligence was ready to go was demonstrated in the case of the *Lino*. [12]

Early in April 1948, in the last weeks before Britain relinquished its Mandate for Palestine, secret agents of Israel learned that a Syrian delegation, headed by Major Fuad Mardam, a nephew of a former President of Syria, on a military shopping mission in Czechoslovakia, had purchased some 6,000 rifles, eight million rounds of ammunition, and a quantity of hand grenades and other high explosives, all for $11 million. The arms reached the Yugoslav port of Bratislava and were loaded onto a small 450-ton Italian ship, the *Lino*. After frustrating delays, it docked in the military quay at Bari, also in Yugoslavia, on the way to augment the Arab military stores in Syria.

Munya Mardor was waiting with his comrades in Bari for the ship's arrival. Since Italian general elections were only a few days away, and there was fear of a Communist coup, Mardor intimated to the port officials that the arms were intended for the Italian Communists and he bribed some of them to delay the onward journey while the *Lino* lay in port. An Israeli frogman, familiarly known as Yossele, whom Mardor called his saboteur-in-chief, and two expert sappers managed, under cover of darkness, to row out in a dinghy to the *Lino* and attach to its side a motorcycle inner tube resistant to water, crammed with TNT. When they detonated the charge, the ship and its cargo quickly sank. Since it lay in shallow water and the arms were in sealed containers, most of the cases were recovered by Fuad; but precious time was lost as Fuad attempted to obtain another ship to transport the salvaged cargo. Frustrated by the long delay, he welcomed the alert by his innkeeper that a small freighter, the *Algiro*, had become available and hurried to complete its purchase. The innkeeper, in the confidence of Mardor, simply forgot to tell him that the ship now had in its crew some Haganah men, veterans from other illegal immigration exploits.

The *Algiro* set sail on August 19, several months after the wars in Israel were under way, and, in mid-Mediterranean, in Operation Pirate, the Haganah men seized control. Joined by two Israeli corvettes that had been tailing the ship, they steered it with its cargo to Haifa. Men and arms were rushed to the war-front to help the Israelis turn the tide of battle against the Egyptians.

To round out the story, it should be added that, after the war,

Fuad was arrested and tried for treason in Syria. He was charged with having fallen in love with "a devil in the shape of an extremely beautiful Yugoslav woman named Palmas, who had induced him to deeds of treachery." She turned out to be a Zionist spy. True or not, the court-martial reached a verdict of guilty and Fuad was sentenced to death. The Syrian government, however, was overthrown just before the execution and Fuad was freed.

Meanwhile, during the winter of 1948, military supplies and equipment were moving expeditiously to Israel through the conduits that had been established in many parts of the United States, Canada, and the Latin American countries. There were machine guns and Norden bombsights from Montreal, trucks, jeeps, and halftracks from Panama, bazookas from Manhattan's Lower East Side, aircraft engines from Texas, radar equipment from Yonkers, spare parts for planes and uniforms for the servicemen and women from factories in many of the larger American cities. Personnel to fly the planes or to help in training and defense came from diverse geographical areas: youngsters out of college, professional pilots, engineers, scientists, Jew and non-Jew, idealist and adventurer. Haganah and its special shock units—Palmach and Palyam—confident that the areas allocated for the Jewish State could now be adequately defended, were ready to go on the offensive.

Near the end of February 1948, the Jewish Agency had sent a memorandum to the UN Palestine Commission. It noted that, though the British had not relinquished responsibility for public order, they had refused to exercise it. "In this situation," the memorandum read, "the Jewish people in Palestine have come to recognize that only their own forces stand between them and annihilation. Faced with the Government's 'neutrality' in the issue of their survival or extermination . . . the Jews of Palestine have assumed a responsibility which formally rests on the Mandatory Power."

During the next few months the Jews set themselves to carry the battles to the Arabs. Where ambushes occurred, mobile Haganah forces retaliated with severity, storming villages and dynamiting known hideouts. Haganah attacked near Mount Castel, to clear the Jerusalem–Tel Aviv road. They lost a few men, but the Arabs lost forty. Haganah then proceeded to discourage Arab ambushes at the junction of the Jordan and Jezreel valleys by striking at the key town of Beisan, leaving it in ruins.[13] In March, raids were carried out in Galilee, where Syrian and Iraqi troops had infiltrated to bring aid to the Palestinian Arabs. A full-fledged battle erupted at Mishmar Ha-Emek, a Jewish settlement near the border of the Arab hills of Samaria. Here the Jews faced the British-equipped and financed Transjordan Legion, with its tanks and heavy armory. The Battle of Mishmar Ha-Emek raged for more than a week. The Haganah succeeded in routing the Legion forces, and the Arab villages were razed after their inhabitants had fled.

By the spring of 1948 the ferocity of conflict had steadily intensified. Both sides contained extremists in their midst to whom terrorism was a legitimate option. Already in January K'far Etzion, a Jewish setlement near Bethlehem, after a long siege, had surrendered to overwhelming numbers, when all but fifteen had died fighting. The survivors who emerged under a white flag were shot down. Retaliation was delayed not because Haganah forbade it, but because the Sternists, far to the right of Irgun, wanted their action to trigger such widespread panic among the Arabs that large numbers would abandon their settlements. On April 9, the Sternists were ready.

They stormed into the Arab village of Deir Yassin and wiped out its two hundred men, women, and children in a massacre that appalled the civilized world and stained Jewish honor for years ahead. The Jewish Agency went so far as to cable King Abdullah of Transjordan, an integer in the enemy coalition, deploring the excesses of the Deir Yassin tragedy. The attack gave anti-Semites a field day. It was interpreted by the British historian Arnold Toynbee as typical of Jewish ruthlessness. "The Jews were worse than the Nazis," he fumed. He was silent three days later, on April 12, when Arab terrorists ambushed and murdered the convoy of seventy-seven doctors, nurses, faculty, and students as they were making their way up Mount Scopus to the Hadassah Hospital and the Hebrew University.

The identification of the entire Jewish community and its military personnel with the irresponsibility of a fringe group had the effect that the Sternists had planned. The common Arab folk were terrified that such massacres would be their fate if they fell into Jewish hands. They abandoned villages, towns, whole regions, often without resistance, as soon as even small Jewish military contingents approached or were said to be on the way.

Of all the confrontations between the Arabs and the Jews that preceded the mid-May expiration of the British Mandate, none was as crucial as the one over control of Jerusalem, at this point governed by the British, with considerable local autonomy for the Arabs, Jews, and Christians. The city had little military significance in comparison to many other locations: in fact it was a military liability. Its defense called for major efforts to protect the roads to its eminence in the highest hills of Judea. Most of these access points were in the firm control of the Arabs. Had Jerusalem been like other revered, but little remembered, shrines—Lebanon's Heliopolis, Iran's Persepolis, the British island of Iona—which represented lost civilizations, there would have been fewer divided counsels among the Jewish military leaders about the priority of its defense. But the Old City of Jerusalem, like Athens, Rome, London, Paris, Istanbul, had a special identity and had been central in the prayers of hundreds of generations of Jews. "Next year in Jerusalem" had been invoked in every religious service—in the sorrows of the Exile, in the darkest days of the Black Death, during Torquemada's Inquisition, in the Ukrainian pogroms of Chmielnitzki. It was intoned in times of comparative peace, affluence, and security, in medieval Spain where Jehuda Halevi and Solomon ibn Gabirol vied with Jewish grand viziers to glorify six Spanish centuries as a Golden Age. Conversely, Jerusalem would be fanatically defended by the Arabs who lived in the city. To them, and to Muslim Arabs everywhere, it was one of the three most holy cities, the site of Mohammed's ascension into Heaven. The attempt by the Jews to control Jerusalem would unify all Muslims, as no political considerations possibly could. It might even launch a *Jihad*, a holy war.

Yigael Yadin, chief of staff, archeologist-turned-soldier, fully shared the conviction that a restored Israel without Jerusalem was unthinkable. Yadin's obligation, however, was to develop military strategy in what assuredly would be a long, exhausting struggle. Russian experience had proven, both in the Napoleonic and the Hitlerian wars, that temporary sacrifice of Moscow could be a key to final victory. Yadin contended, though with heartache, that Israel, facing the probability of attack by all the neighboring Arab states, had neither the manpower nor the equipment to risk on a symbol, however sacred. He believed that all effort must be concentrated to secure the rest of the country, and then to return to reclaim the soul city.

Ben Gurion argued just as vehemently that Jerusalem, precisely because it was an eternal symbol, was worth any sacrifice. The nations that voted Partition must know positively that an independent Israel could and would survive. Israel without Jerusalem? How could the Jews of Israel and throughout the world sustain their hope if, when the British surrendered control, the city of their historic dream passed, even temporarily, to exclusive Arab jurisdiction?

It should be added that Ben Gurion's view of the symbolic primacy of Jerusalem was shared by Abdullah, king of Transjordan. The king claimed that he was a direct descendant of the Prophet Mohammed, and the leader of the Hashemite Muslims, powerful in all Arab countries. He coveted the area allocated to the Palestinian Arabs, hoping to incorporate it into his Kingdom of Transjordan. Control over Jerusalem would then be easier to achieve. Secretly he had twice tried to negotiate an acceptable tradeoff with Golda Meir before she became Prime Minister of Israel. They met for the first time in November 1947, when Mrs. Meir was a member of Ben Gurion's Council of Thirteen in the provisional government just before the Partition vote. Abdullah promised then that if Arab and Jewish states came into being, he would extend a welcome to the Jewish State and would also offer strong economic cooperation. The first secret meeting did not change the course of events and war with the Arabs erupted anyway.

Now, in May 1948, only days before the British were to relinquish the Mandate, Abdullah met again with Mrs. Meir, this time in Amman. She made the dangerous journey disguised as an Arab peasant woman. She found him as amiably friendly as before, but the political situation had radically changed. Abdullah had hoped there would be no war involving the Arab neighboring states, but had become resigned to its inevitability, and he noted that when it came, his forces would have to join the other Arab armies. Mrs. Meir, knowing well the rivalries and feuds among the Arab potentates, urged the king not to enter the war against the Jews, "who were really your only friends in the Near East." Abdullah admitted the deadly enmity between his own people and the Husseini Muslims, and the hatred borne him by the Grand Mufti, who expected to become head of an Arab Palestine. As Mrs. Meir turned to leave, the king said sadly that their peoples would soon unfortunately be at war, but intimated that he, for one, had no intention of going beyond the fulfillment of an Arab state. He hoped he and Mrs. Meir might meet again as friends; that, somehow, the future Jewish and Arab states, with so much to offer one another, would find ways to cooperate.*

Abdullah was not an altogether disinterested lover of peace. He was politically acute enough to know that should he inherit from the Mandatory power East Jerusalem and the sacred site of Mohammed's ascension, he would be in a strong position to annex all of Arab Palestine and make it part of his kingdom. Once again the strange and often ironic confluences of history flowed together as the king and his court, and Ben Gurion and his war cabinet, for reasons far transcending military considerations, launched campaigns to take and hold Jerusalem before the Mandate had been relinquished.†

As the time approached for the British departure, the inhabitants of the Old City of Jerusalem found it increasingly difficult to lead normal lives. Hardly a day passed without the bombing of marketplaces, buses, business quarters, and residential districts. Arabs held the main highways leading to and from Jerusalem in all directions, over which all supplies had to be brought up the winding roads from the plains. Every mile of wooded hill was pitted with ambush spots. The Mandatory power police were rarely on guard. Only two Jewish convoys got through in February; by the end of March the Arabs had closed off all roads, placing the Old City and the New under an iron siege.

Once more General Yadin and most of his staff urged temporary retreat by the small forces that had been assigned to protect the Jewish claim. Once more Ben Gurion overruled them. His command never deviated: "Hang on to Jerusalem by your

---

*Mrs. Meir's warnings were prophetic. On the Muslim Sabbath, Friday, July 29, 1952, Abdullah was assassinated by an agent of the Mufti as he emerged from prayers in the mosque in Jerusalem. That his grandson, King Hussein, survived numerous assassination attempts in the ensuing thirty years, offered appropriateness to the title of his autobiography, *Uneasy Lies the Head.*

†Abdullah's ambition was achieved in 1952 when, with the cooperation of the British and the blessing of Bevin, Arab Palestine was formally annexed and became part of the Kingdom of Transjordan, now called Jordan. Israel captured and occupied it in the 1967 war, when it became the much-disputed West Bank. In all the fifteen years of control of the West Bank by Jordan, no Arab government urged the establishment of an independent Arab state for the Palestinians.

teeth." On March 29, he convened his Haganah commanders to take counsel on breaking the siege of the city. The code name, Operation Nachshon, was linked to the legendary biblical hero who was the first to accept the challenge of the unknown by pressing forward into the parting waters of the Red Sea. The high command, fully aware of the risk, asked for the reassignment of small contingents from each Haganah unit guarding other crucial areas of the country. Fifteen hundred men, some well-trained Palmach veterans among them, but mostly raw recruits and recent arrivals from the shambles of Europe, were assembled. This force would attempt to break the Arab grip on the access points to Old Jerusalem.

A few days before his decision Ben Gurion had directed Ehud Avriel, his agent in Prague, to send immediately, by whatever planes he could obtain, as many rifles and machine guns as had already been stockpiled in secret storage depots. On the night of April 1, a bare forty-eight hours before the first Haganah assault on the roads to Jerusalem was scheduled, a transport plane arrived from Prague, the weapons smeared with protective oil, still in packing cases. These were rushed by truck, in the darkness, to a camp near Tel Aviv where the first assault groups had been marshaled. There was time for only one firing practice session, to give the troops the feel of their weapons before going into battle. Soon after, a small freighter, the SS *Nora*, arrived. In its hold were several thousand additional Czech rifles and machine guns and 50,000 rounds of ammunition, all hidden under layers of onions. Immigrants from Salonika who were working as stevedores unloaded the guns, also encased in thick coats of grease, which were now wiped clean with hastily assembled underwear of older civilians who wished to make some kind of contribution to the war effort. The thousands of rounds of ammunition were jammed into the men's socks and fastened to their belts.

Castel, on a strategic height a few miles west of Jerusalem, and commanding one of its chief entry points, was the first objective. Some 150 members of Palmach had been selected for the surprise attack. They took Castel swiftly, and pursuing their advantage, mopped up some adjacent Arab settlements that were weakly defended, and repulsed what might have been an Arab counterattack.

This initial victory cleared enough of the road into Jerusalem to risk sending up convoys to relieve the starving Jewish population of the Old City. The first convoy was a gallimaufry of vehicles—trailers, delivery vans, hay wagons, dump trucks, almost everything but a circus pantechnicon—resembling the motley array of hundreds of taxicabs that rattled to the Marne in the opening weeks of World War I when the Germans struck at France. The often ramshackle vehicles sported posters on their sides advertising the products of their owners: soap and baby food, kosher meats, shoes, cement products. In the dark before the April dawn, the oddly unpatterned convoy, like an immense caterpillar, crawled slowly up the hills outside Jerusalem, the bulbs removed from headlights to avoid an accidental flicker. Heading the procession was Harry Jaffe, convoy commander, in his new little blue Ford with the bumper sticker, "If I forget thee, O Jerusalem."

As dawn touched the heights of Jerusalem, the convoy crossed into the Old City. When it was sighted by the first few famished inhabitants, they rushed out of their dwellings to greet the deliverers, the pious with their phylacteries and prayer shawls still in place for morning prayer. Old ladies in bathrobes and slippers forgot their infirmities and scrambled out of the Home for the Aged. One embraced a young veteran of many skirmishes, who sighed, "If only it could have been her granddaughter."[14]

The immobilization of Castel and its environs was by no means enough to secure Old Jerusalem. Indeed, within weeks Castel was retaken by heavily reinforced Arab groups. Only when the Mandate was relinquished and unimpeded immigration, supported by adequate armaments, provided reinforcements could a continuous Jewish presence in Jerusalem be undertaken. Until then, the agony had to be endured of on-and-off sieges, here a relief expedition, there a temporary gain, followed by shattering losses, a mounting toll of Jewish casualties. But Ben Gurion's faith was vindicated. The Old City did not surrender. Enough obdurate souls remained, although constricted into ever smaller areas, to deny completion of the Arab conquest.

The Jews fared better in other parts of Palestine. The UN Special Committee on Partition had assigned to them small but valuable sections of Upper Galilee, including the coastal strip from below Tel Aviv, north to beyond Haifa and Acre and the fertile Jezreel Plain. None doubted, least of all Yigael Yadin, that the stiffest Arab resistance would be mounted to prevent such precious land from coming under Jewish control. Both sides girded to preempt what they could before the British withdrew.

Haifa, Palestine's major seaport and the terminus of the oil pipeline from the oil fields of Iraq, was the key, with its 150,000 inhabitants, the Arabs slightly outnumbering the Jews. Yet, in April 1948, the armed forces available to decide such important stakes comprised an absurd minimum, not more than five hundred on each side. The decision as to who was to gain military control of Haifa lay in doubt for about a week. Unwisely, the Arab commander, General Fawzi-el-Kaukji, left his troops, ostensibly to appeal in person to the other Arab states for reinforcements. The Arab population of Haifa had already dwindled; 15,000 people, mainly the well-to-do, had left in March, when it had become clear that the city would soon be a battleground. Another 20,000 had departed in April, when the Arabs had failed to take Mishmar Ha-Emek, a crucial defense point on the Haifa–Jaffa road. While Kaukji was absent, most of the remaining Arab population of Haifa, perhaps 35,000 people, completed the Arab flight, boarding any vessel that was available, to find refuge in Beirut.

The argument to explain the exodus was to go on for years, with accusations and rebuttals, the Arabs alleging that they were threatened with terrifying reprisals and that they had fled the city to avoid massacre. The tragedy of Deir Yassin, perpetrated a fortnight earlier, was fresh in the Arab remembrance. The Jews claimed that the Arab leaders had urged their people to move out to avoid becoming casualties in the massive air attacks that had been promised to complete the Arab triumph. The Arab population had further been assured that, soon after the evacuation, they would return to have their choice of confiscated Jewish possessions. Shebetai Levy, who had won the confidence of enough Arabs in the city to be elected mayor, insisted that he deplored the flight of the Arabs who had lived successfully with their Jewish neighbors for more than forty years. They were indispensable to Haifa's economy, he said, since so many were dockworkers and the prosperity of the port city depended heavily upon their labor. The arguments continue to this day as advocates present alleged evidence to support their case. What matters, however, is that when the British withdrew and almost all of the Arabs had fled, for whatever reason, Haifa became virtually a Jewish city.

The investment of Safed, in East Galilee near the Syrian

border, was even more spectacular. Here lived about 12,000 Arabs, and 3,000 Jews, the latter under constant harassment. Responsibility for taking the city, valuable for its strategic location, was given to a twenty-eight-year-old sabra, Yigal Allon. His father, in the 1880s, had founded the Galilean settlement where Yigal was born. He had been involved in underground activity as early as the Arab riots of 1936–38. In World War II, Allon served with British intelligence in Syria and Lebanon, and in 1941 he was one of the organizers of Palmach. During his British service Allon found ways to direct projects for illegal immigration, guiding the refugees into sparsely settled Palestine areas where he supervised their military training for future contingencies.

The Jewish quarter of Safed was, like much of the Old City of Jerusalem, inhabited mainly by elderly, other-worldly Jews who spent their lives in prayer and Cabalist study. Responsibility for their protection and the ultimate control of the city itself was assigned to a unit of thirty-five Palmach men. Their tiny enclave was besieged by a force of 8,000 Arabs, drawn both from the local population and from irregulars who had come from other areas of Galilee, eager to be in on the kill. The Arabs also had working for them the hostile neutrality of the British who, when preparing to withdraw from Safed on April 19, turned over to the Arab officials the three fortress police stations that had been British headquarters, providing them with significant military advantage.

Allon, as usual, boldly improvised. He insisted that for an all-out assault on Safed, it was essential for neighboring Jewish settlements to give up whatever military resources they had amassed. The inhabitants of the smaller settlements were naturally reluctant to strip their flimsy reserves for a major gamble. They had expected from Allon more rather than less protection during this critical period. Allon insisted on his long-range objectives, and they yielded. Allon then threw everything he had in Palmach manpower and arms into simultaneous assaults on all of Safed's military strongpoints, creating the illusion, through skillfully circulated rumor and well-planted intelligence reports, that huge reserves were on the way.

Allon's objective was not only to conquer the city but, by means of such psychological warfare, to encourage the flight of the Arab population. Arab morale had never been conspicuously high. Thousands had already abandoned the city before the conflict had begun in earnest. As the fighting became more intense, the remaining defenders, though reinforced by 3,000 troops of the Arab Liberation armies, began to waver. By the fifth day of battle, when some Arab generals slipped away, most of Safed's Arab population forsook their homes to flee with the retreating troops. The majority intended to return. Few did. The fall of Safed and the flight of its Arab population had repercussions in all the Arab settlements of Upper Galilee. Their population joined the stream of refugees into Lebanon and Syria.

Since Tiberias, favorite watering spot of the Roman emperors, had already fallen without even token resistance, Operation Yiftah—the code name for Allon's coordinated assault— brought another strategically important area of Palestine, now divested of its Arab population, into the projected Jewish state.

To the conventional military mind, even to consider an attempt to capture Jaffa, the largest Arab city in Palestine and a major Mediterranean port, must have seemed wishful thinking. In 1914, some enterprising Jewish pioneers had drawn lots for plots of land on Jaffa's sandy southern suburbs. The area was transformed, in a remarkably short time, into Palestine's most unusual boom town: Tel Aviv. By 1948, the suburb had far outstripped Jaffa itself in glamour and international reputation. In the UN Partition Plan the abutting cities, Jaffa and Tel Aviv, were to be allocated, one to the Arabs and one to the Jews, each a threat to the other.

Harassment had begun on both sides, the Arabs sniping into Tel Aviv, the Jews taking reprisals against Arab shops and houses in Jaffa. There were muggings and occasional murders by Partisans of both sides, and growing numbers of casualties. It was not only the safety of the cities that was of concern. Jaffa-Tel Aviv controlled the roads south to Jerusalem and north to Haifa, and to other central points on the way to the Jordan, as well as to the international airport at Lydda. Also controlled from Jaffa-Tel Aviv were the roads to makeshift but fully operational airstrips, hastily constructed by the Jews in outlying areas to receive small planes that were guided to their landing by the headlights of parked trucks.

Like many attempts to achieve fairness in the abstract, the Tel Aviv–Jaffa solution by the UN drew the Arabs and the Jews into intense combat. Ben Gurion and his colleagues concluded that, for current and future security, the allocation of Jaffa to the Arabs had to be thwarted; snipers from Jaffa were taking a serious toll of Tel Aviv lives. The Arab leaders were equally determined that the interests of their peoples did not permit the separation of entities that belonged together. They coveted Tel Aviv with its modern facilities, which had made it a tourist center for millions from every part of the world. There was little time for long negotiation. Arab troops were already waiting for the signal to secure Jaffa and to take over Tel Aviv as well.

Yigael Yadin and his staff planned their strategy to take over, in steady progression, the villages surrounding Jaffa. Then, at the moment of British withdrawal, his forces would mount the assault on Jaffa itself. The initial forays were scheduled for the end of April, at the beginning of the Passover season. The code name for the operation was, as usual, drawn from biblical history. The campaign to occupy Jaffa and unite it with Tel Aviv was called Operation Chometz, Leavened Bread, a reference to the Passover tradition which regards as sacrilege the presence of leavened bread in the home during the celebration of the Exodus from Egypt.

The rivalry between Irgun and Haganah complicated Yadin's long-range strategy. For five months there had been skirmishes between the Arabs and the Jews in the outskirts of both Jaffa and Tel Aviv and their environs. Irgun now insisted that such nibbling tactics were counterproductive, that some dramatic sabotage attacks in scattered parts of Jaffa itself were necessary to terrify the Arabs into flight. Then, they reasoned, Jaffa could be taken without protracted struggle. On April 25, without waiting for a signal from Yadin, Irgun launched its offensive. Houses, businesses, government buildings, whole districts in Jaffa were blown up. Irgun forces penetrated to the center of the city. The government, still British, issued a stern warning that its army would employ massive military force to prevent the Jewish occupation of Jaffa. Bevin went into one of his blackest rages, vowing that his government would never permit the Jews to take over Jaffa. He ordered the British commander, Lieutenant-General Gordon Macmillan, to forbid the surrender of Jaffa to Jewish forces. Irgun ignored the warning, and Yadin, realizing that any display of divided counsels at this stage would play into British and Arab hands, authorized Haganah forces to join in the attack.

The British, following up their warning, began to shell Jewish positions, and moved some of their own units between Jewish and Arab lines. The British action succeeded in slowing down the Jewish offensive. Even the most belligerent Irgun leaders hesitated to goad the British into open warfare. In any event, Arab panic settled the problem without a showdown. For by now, of the original 100,000 there were only 4,000 Arabs left in Jaffa. The Arab Emergency Committee formally signed the surrender terms after the British withdrew from the city.

Acre, that fabled bastion of the Crusaders of the Middle Ages, provided the locus for a climactic act of Jewish effrontery. In mid-May, just as Sir Alan Cunningham, the sympathetic Scot who was Palestine's last Governor General, was going over plans formally to relinquish the Mandate, Acre, the fortress that in 1799 had defied even Napoleon Bonaparte, was attacked. Haganah's Carmeli Brigade completely surrounded the old fortress-city, and after a brief siege received its surrender. There was poetic symbolism here, for the commander, Moshe Carmel, who received the surrender, had spent many months in its prison for possession of illegal firearms. A newspaper cartoon of the time shows a Haganah soldier in rumpled uniform and rakishly tilted homemade woolen cap looking up, mockingly, at a portrait of Napoleon.[15]

The initial military danger in the creation of a Jewish Palestine had been successfully overcome. The predictions of the best informed military experts had been proven false. The Jewish settlements in Palestine had held fast, losing little of what had been assigned in the UN vote, and winning territory that would make their land more defensible and more economically viable. Large parts of Palestine that held substantial Arab inhabitants had been cleared of possible irredentists.

It was a bitter defeat for Bevin and his colleagues, who could not have foreseen that a tiny people, meagerly reinforced by survivors from the death camps of Europe, vastly outnumbered and ill armed, would be able to resist the Arab assaults upon them and the formidable obstacles of British hostility. The victory, still little more than a holding action, had been a testing point. There were times in the early months after Partition when fulfillment seemed remote and when the UN had misgivings about the practicality of its decision. Other alternatives to Partition were then several times put forward—postponements of Partition, a bi-national state, a trusteeship arrangement under the UN. But to the Israelis it was clear that any weakening of their resolve to win a sovereign state would probably end any future opportunity to retrieve international approval for such a status.

Now a new drama was enfolding. The six-month interregnum period, until the British Mandate was relinquished, had been a prologue. It ushered in the vastly greater danger from the attacks of the states ringing Jewish Palestine. The war for independence and its successful outcome was to transform the historic image of the Jew.

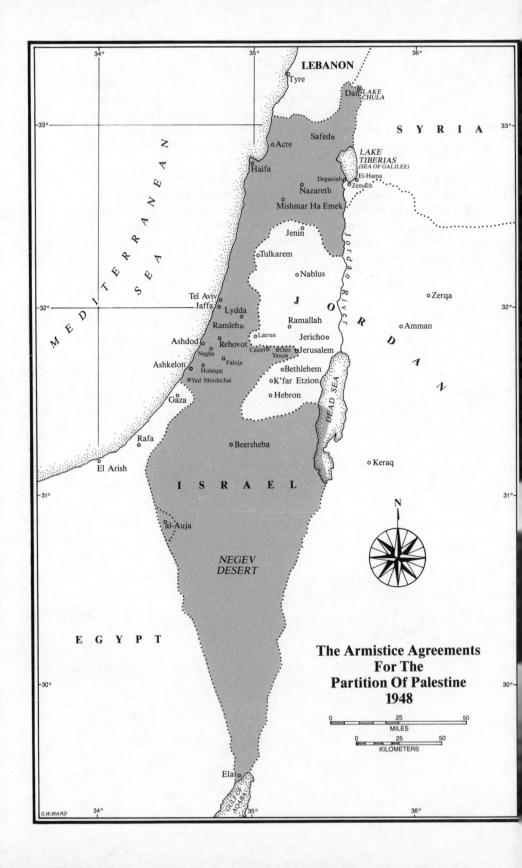

The Armistice Agreements
For The
Partition Of Palestine
1948

CHAPTER ELEVEN

The War of Independence

IT HAD BEEN HOPED by the Palestine Arabs that as soon as the Mandate was officially terminated on May 14, there would be an invasion on all frontiers by the forces of the surrounding Arab states so that the coup de grace could be given to the UN plan for a sovereign Jewish presence in Palestine. But even when the last skirls of the bagpipes by the honor guard at the British Governor General's residence had sounded "Scotland's Lament," the rivalries and the suspicions of the Arab chiefs of state had not been resolved; indecision on how to proceed still prevented coordination for a concerted attack. Abdullah of Transjordan was ready to assign his British-trained Legion for invasion, but his aim, not concealed, was to appropriate for his kingdom a considerable part of Arab Palestine, including Jerusalem, and to negotiate a separate deal with the Israelis for the areas where they were heavily settled. Syria coveted all of Galilee for its never abandoned dream of a Greater Syria. Lebanon, Iraq, Egypt, and Saudi Arabia had no enthusiasm for intervention which, even if successful, would offer them very little tangible profit.

Nevertheless, if there were conflicting objectives about the disposition of Palestine, there was united opposition, except for Abdullah, to the establishment of a Jewish enclave that impaired the homogeneity of the Arab world of the Middle East. And even Abdullah joined in the public denunciations. Arab rhetoric usually included the vow, as it had been applied to the Crusaders in the Middle Ages who had occupied Palestine for two centuries, that the Israelis would be driven into the sea. One of the

Arab League officers exulted: "How beautiful was this day, May 14, when the whole world held its breath anticipating the entry of seven Arab armies into Palestine to redeem it from the Zionists and the West. On this day Arab forces broke forth from all sides and stood as one man to demand justice and to please God, conscience and the sense of duty."[1]

Few knowledgeable military leaders and statesmen among the nations of the world disputed the Arab expectations of a quick, decisive victory. The odds, on paper, seemed overwhelmingly uneven. The Arabs drew from a population of forty-five million, who lived on three million square miles of territory, two hundred times larger than Palestine, commanding the world's richest proven oil reserves. They counted on a military force of 10,000 Egyptians, 4,500 Transjordan Legionnaires, 8,000 Iraquis, and 3,000 Lebanese. They had the undisguised support of Britain. The total Israeli population in 1948 was approximately 650,000, including the aged, the infirm, the children, and the very recently arrived. These were not concentrated in a compact territory. The Haganah had mobilized about 30,000 men and women, but they were lacking in weaponry and were especially weak in airpower. They were vulnerable to attack on three frontiers and, with no navy, the Mediterranean coast was also vulnerable.

Yet the Israelis had a special kind of strength. Their military force included a highly motivated nucleus, trained while fighting alongside the British and the Allies as comrades in arms in World War II against a common enemy. They had young, resourceful commanders. Illegal immigrants, drawn from those who had survived the war and the Holocaust within it, kept breaking through the vigilance and the opposition to the British to join the ranks of the organized Israelis. Volunteers, including committed Christian sympathizers, came from the United States, South Africa, and the western democracies. Many of these brought experience and technical sophistication to develop the air force and to cope with the complex problems of organization and supply.

Most important was the "no alternative" (ain braira) spirit with which the Israelis, and especially the immigrant reinforcements, fought. The Arabs never fully understood how powerful a weapon desperation could be. Their own men went into battle almost listlessly, not because they were cowards or shirkers, but because they could have little personal stake in the outcome. They were aware that their governments all too often regarded them as expendable. When Dr. Weizmann was asked why the Egyptians did not stand up well, he replied: "The men were too lean and the officers were too fat." The Israelis knew that the land they defended represented a last hope for them. The walls that now shut them out in most of the world were erected only partly for the protection of jobs and housing. Jewish history had prepared them not to expect to be welcomed anywhere. If Palestine were lost there would be no heart left to continue the struggle, either for them or for the survivors of the Holocaust remaining in the camps and transit points of Europe, Africa, and Asia.

The war to stave off the Arabs and protect independence was fought in a series of short, intense campaigns, punctuated by fragile truces imposed by the United Nations. The first stage of the war was concentrated into four weeks, from May 15 to June 11, and the main assaults came from the Arab forces of Syria, Transjordan, and Egypt.

It was the Syrians who, reinforcing small Palestine Arab units, attacked first; their goal was to invest the whole of the Galilee area. The Israelis—for such they had just become—were strongly entrenched in a solid belt across the south, but they were committed to the defense of many scattered settlements in the north and the east where they were almost isolated.

Leadership of the Arab Liberation campaign was assigned to the Iraqi Fawzi-el-Kaukji, who had led the Palestinians against the Israelis during the interludes before the British relinquished the Mandate. Many of the Jewish settlements were east of the Jordan, in Arab country, so that heavy fighting would not be needed to overcome resistance. Kaukji therefore struck at a front some fifty miles long in the most weakly defended north. His Syrian forces with two hundred armored vehicles, including forty-five tanks, probed the route at the lower end of the Sea of Galilee. Its ridges were already in their hands, and the valley beneath was excellent terrain for the maneuvering of armored tanks. Two brigades attacked, hitting hard about seven miles south of Lake Tiberias. At this early stage, the undermanned, ill-armed Israelis could offer little organized resistance. They had to rely on delaying actions until adequate reinforcements arrived. Only a few examples of their tactics need be cited to point up how courage and innovativeness were successfully employed.

To slow the advance of the Syrians who attacked from the east, it was necessary to destroy one of the major bridges over the Jordan. A single sapper, Emil Barak, a recent refugee from Poland, volunteered for the task. Slithering his way over sixty yards of exposed ground under heavy fire, he set a simple fuse and detonated the bomb that he carried with him. He demolished the bridge, delaying the invasion until the Syrians could put pontoons in place.

Again, in the battle for the Deganiah settlements, one of the keys to the rich valley of Jezreel, it was necessary for the Israelis to hold the town of Zemach at the lower end of the Sea of Galilee near the Syrian border. Lieutenant Colonel Netanel Lorch, who was a commander in the War of Independence and one of its respected historians, describes what was clearly ingenious dissimulation rather than military strategy:

> Feigning the arrival of reinforcements, all the settlement trucks were rounded up and instructed to ascend the mountains to the west with their lights darkened, and then to return to the valley with full lights. They were to repeat that maneuver as often as possible to create the impression of considerable forces moving into the Jordan Valley.... The tractors were assembled and their engines left running to create a noise similar to that of tanks. ... The time gained by holding out in Zemach served to organize the settlements and prepare what was later to be the Deganiah Line.[2]

All such stratagems did not of course succeed; but many did, and, as at Zemach, helped to ward off the enemy until the Israelis had approached parity in arms.

The chief aim of the Syrians, for which these probing actions were part of a softening process, was the capture of Deganiah, the first kibbutz established in Palestine in the 1880s. The main attack was launched on May 29, and the Syrians committed to it considerable manpower and heavy equipment. When they had penetrated as far as the outer perimeter of Deganiah, the commander began the composition of his victory report. The Israelis put up fierce resistance. Using improvised equipment and some old field pieces, they surprised even themselves by knocking out the first oncoming tank, then the next, hit by a Molotov cocktail thrown by a boy. The Syrians must have thought the Jews had a secret arsenal.

On the second day of heavy fighting, two ancient pieces of artillery that had just reached Israel were rushed to Deganiah to buttress the defense. The surprise opposition proved too much for the Syrians and they retreated, although they did not abandon their positions altogether. They were still on the Israeli side of the Jordan and with some Palestine Arab contingents they dug in until the first truce period in mid-June.

Azzan Pasha, the spokesman for the Arab League, had predicted that "this will be a war of extermination and a momentous massacre which will be spoken of like the Mongolian massacres and the Crusades." *The New York Times* correspondent in Damascus, apparently influenced by the premature victory announcements, wrote of a Syrian brigade "speeding toward the Galilee after a lightning feint toward the Mediterranean." But as each day passed and reinforcements kept arriving for the resistance, the Jewish forces were able, by the first week in June, to move into the offensive; and when they captured the approaches to Mount Gilboa, the Syrians muted their florid rhetoric and began to report more cautiously about "quick victories" and "an early recapture of Haifa."

Lebanon played a minor part in Arab strategy or Jewish concern. The Lebanese, divided between Christian and Muslim Arabs, had little heart for the war over Partition. They were justifiably proud of their country's reputation for amity, not only within their own Christian, Muslim, and Jewish communities, but with their neighbors. Beirut, their beautiful capital, was one of the most enterprising commercial centers in the Middle East, with extensive trade connections throughout Europe. Their well-respected American University was liberally funded by its friends in the United States and, before the Partition crisis, Beirut maintained mutually advantageous relationships with the Jews of Palestine. The Lebanese leaders may well have wondered what was so dreadful about having a Jewish entity in their midst if it did not intrude upon life in Lebanon and even opened larger opportunities for employment. In the initial campaign of 1948, however, Lebanon's Arab "big brothers" insisted that it contribute at least a symbolic share to the common effort. Its miniature army of little more than 3,000 fought briefly on the frontier of Israel and, after occupying a small border town, called a halt to invasion and turned instead to defense of Lebanese soil should an attack come. For all practical purposes the Lebanese were out of the war; the Israelis could direct their own firepower where it was more urgently needed.

The Iraqis, among the most outspoken advocates of invasion before Partition was even voted, were much tougher opponents. They had always coveted an outlet or corridor to the Mediterranean, which would guarantee control of the pipeline from their oil fields in Mosul to the refineries of Haifa. In the early stages of the war the Iraqis coordinated their efforts, first with the Syrian attacks on the Deganiah Line and then, by the side of the Transjordanians, farther south in the Jordan Valley. Though better armed and trained, they were constantly thwarted in their objectives by the Israelis, who seemed to be playing a deadly version of the children's game "Touch Last." It appeared that, even when the Israelis lost, they won. In an attack by their Carmeli Brigade on Jenin, a key point in the Galilee campaign, one of the Israeli trucks, loaded with ammunition and supplies, took a wrong turn in the road and ran straight into an Iraqi outpost guarding the approach to a strategic bridge. Driver and companion leaped out to take cover in a ditch. They had little hope of survival. The Iraqis, however, suspicious of continuous Israeli dissimulation, were convinced the action was a trap, that the truck was wired to explode and demolish the outpost. They fled and the two Israelis emerged from the ditch to take possession of the bridge without firing a shot.[3]

The cooperation of the Iraqi forces with the Syrians was similarly ineffectual. True, they thwarted Israeli efforts to dislodge them from Jenin and inflicted heavy losses upon them. But they never seemed able to achieve decisive victories in siege or attack during the Ping-Pong battles.

Perhaps the most advantageous factor for the Israelis in these opening days of the war was the widely exaggerated estimate of their military strength. They could not completely hide the flimsiness of their resources. But with an adroitness born of necessity, they gave the impression of limitless support momentarily expected from powerful friends and allies, notably in the United States and France. The leadership in Czechoslovakia was also encouraged by the Soviets to cooperate with Israel so long as such help would get the British out of the Middle East.

General Sir John Glubb, the British commander of the Trans-jordan Arab Legion, admitted in his autobiography that he had based his Legion's strategy "on the impression that the Israelis had some 65,000 armed men, among whom were about 20,000 who had served in the Russian and Polish forces in World War II."[4]

Nowhere did this illusion of potential Israeli military strength count for more than in the Egyptian calculations. Their command had ordered an attack even before the British Mandate had expired. The Prime Minister Mahmoud Nokrashy Pasha, a former professor of history, and an ardent nationalist, preferred a more favorable moment for the decisive strike. He was acutely aware that Egypt's forces, both in actual strength and in morale, were in a deplorable condition. He believed that it would be a catastrophic mistake to divert already limited forces from the much more compelling objective of wresting Egyptian control of the Suez Canal from the British. Nokrashy was also reluctant to risk his political career to indulge the personal excesses of King Farouk, a monarch who knew little about military affairs and cared less so long as he was supplied with exotic foods, pornographic comic books, and his women. The British officials despised Farouk, invariably referring to him as "the Boy."

The Prime Minister knew in what contempt the king was held by most of his key officials and his own people; no doubt he already sniffed the scent of revolution in Egyptian coffee-houses, bistros, and barracks. General Glubb warned against enlisting city Arabs, who, he believed, lacked the temperament and incentive to endure military discipline. He remembered the very much less than adequate performance of Egyptian soldiers in the desert war against General Rommel's forces.

Yet some measure of participation in the war was mandated by the internecine rivalry with the king of Transjordan. Abdullah had to be prevented from preempting the sacred Jerusalem area. The dilemma, then, for the more pragmatic Egyptian leaders, was critical: how to sustain the confidence of their troops lest they disgrace themselves and blemish the prestige of Egypt, and yet conserve resources for the long-range objective of getting the Suez Canal away from the British. The decision was made to fight hard enough to win propaganda victories, but to go no further than holding actions until the real intentions of Abdullah could be flushed out. The Minister of Defense said:

"We are not mad. We shall allow our men and officers to volunteer for service in Palestine and we shall give them weapons. But no more." Distrust invariably sat with the Arab leaders at all of their planning sessions and provided the Israelis with one of their most powerful weapons for survival.*

Several brigades under Major General Muhammed Naguib, who later became President of Egypt briefly after the 1952 revolution that expelled Farouk, moved forward into Palestine along the coastal road toward Tel Aviv. Naguib made no confident predictions that a quick triumph was to be expected. His respect for the tenacity of the Israelis was validated in the very first engagement when an Egyptian battalion attacked K'far Darom, close to Gaza, on the way up to Tel Aviv. The settlement was stoutly defended by thirty boys and girls. Elders too participated in the resistance, carrying grenades in their phylactery bags. The confusion in the Egyptian ranks was exhibited when some of the men in the rear fired on their own forward ranks, adding to the unexpectedly large number of casualties.

There was another sobering experience for the Egyptians when, on May 19, they attacked Yad Mordechai on the northern side of Gaza, a small Israeli village named for one of the fallen leaders of the Warsaw Uprising in 1943. Yad Mordechai had been founded by survivors of the uprising and of Partisan underground warfare against the Nazis. Though the Egyptians used two infantry battalions and an artillery regiment, it took five days for them to overcome the besieged. The resistance provided precious time for the Israelis to receive reinforcements for defense of the coastal road.

The lesson of these and other experiences was not lost on the Egyptian commanders, who knew that, since the defenders of Tel Aviv included many recent immigrants, the ferocity of the resistance would make further advances costly. Naguib halted his offensive at Ashdod, content to deploy some of his troops simply to remain a continuing threat to Tel Aviv. It seemed more prudent to turn south to the areas leading into the Negev to prevent the Israelis from establishing any strong positions there. It was not difficult to overrun twenty-seven small settlements, outposts in the desert established to stake out future

*Nokrashy was assassinated in Cairo on December 28, 1948, by a member of the Muslim Brotherhood.

Israeli claims to the Negev. Naguib threw nearly 8,000 men, two full battalions, against these outposts, held mainly by inexperienced, poorly equipped defenders. But he preferred not to push on and to wait for the developments at the United Nations, where clamor for a truce had now become importunate.

These first battles with the Egyptians proved to the Israeli command that their holding actions had been strategically wise. To be sure, they had lost Yad Mordechai and some indefensible Negev settlements. Some of their own attacks had failed. But they had not lost a single dunam (half acre) of land in the UN-assigned area on the coastal road. There would be time to move into the offensive when the reinforcements of arms and manpower arrived from Europe and the United States, expected during the truce period that could not much longer be postponed, as the UN orders sharpened.

It was the struggle to resist expulsion from Jerusalem that generated the fiercest fighting. The British had relinquished the Mandate without making any provision for the protection, maintenance, and disposition of even the treasures contributed to the city by pious Catholics. Indeed, in the final months before the British left, priority had been given to such matters as the assembling, accounting for, and preparing for shipment home of some thousands of tons of timber and nails. Ben Gurion thereafter, as we have seen, to save the remaining area, had thrown reserves into the fray again and again whenever Arab vigilance relaxed for even a moment. There was desperate fighting in late May 1948, around the hospice of Notre Dame and the French convent that commanded the New Gate and the Damascus Gate at the entrance of the Old City. The area was, in General Glubb's judgment, the strategic core of Jerusalem. From there the Arab Legion could break into the New City. The hospice and the convent changed hands several times in the first two weeks of the war.

The military governor of the city, Dov Joseph, described how the settlement had been defended:

For thirty-six hours from Friday morning until Saturday night, the entire city was like a single front with firing through the area, fighting being fiercer first at one point, then at another, and shells bursting throughout the day and night. Many buildings changed hands numerous times. This was no small ordeal for a civilian population but the people were not panicky. Many went into their shelters, the streets were kept clear of civilians while every able-bodied man and woman did his assigned duty resolutely and courageously. They were a people's army, if ever there was one, for all who could be, were in it, and of it. Everybody sensed that these few days would be crucial in deciding the city's fate.[5]

On May 28, what General Glubb had identified as "the vital core" had to be yielded to the Arabs. When his Legionnaires accepted the surrender from two old rabbis and realized how small were the forces against them and the scarcity of their weapons, the officer in charge remarked: "If we had known there were so few, we would have fought you with sticks instead of machine guns and mortars."

Ben Gurion did not waver in his commitment to his people in the areas of the Old City that remained. But their resistance was harder to bear if there was no way of knowing when promised help would come. Rumors were rife that it was on the way—from Russia, Czechoslovakia, France, and above all, from the United States. But each prayerful day passed in disappointment. Between May 15 and June 11 when the first UN truce was proclaimed, some 10,000 shells fell on Old Jerusalem. There were more than 1,700 military and civilian casualties. The wounded would have died in far greater numbers had not nurses and doctors given of themselves unsparingly. Temporary units were hastily created to care for the overflow from the hospitals. Many women set up first aid stations in their own homes. The Arabs inched ahead and all Israel mourned when they captured and held Mount Scopus, the site of the Hebrew University and the Hadassah Hospital, the best equipped in the Middle East, serving all faiths and creeds. The superb educational and medical facilities were to remain in Arab jurisdiction for nearly twenty years, although by a later armistice agreement responsibility for their use was assigned to an Israeli police guard.

The refugees who poured out of the Old City during the May fighting presented special problems. Place had to be found for them in outlying locations and in the already overcrowded New City, abutting the Old. In some few instances, refugees could reoccupy quarters abandoned by the Arabs. Synagogues were used for prayer by day and shelters by night. Electricity was cut off and such essentials as water had to be drastically rationed. But schools continued to function and study was not curtailed.

Rabbis and scholars conducted their Talmudic sessions, ignoring the thunder of guns around them. *Kol Jerusalem,* the Voice of Jerusalem, continued its regular radio news broadcasts in Hebrew, Arabic, and French that were heard through battery-operated loudspeakers installed at key points. The announcer was sometimes out of breath when he ran to the microphone through a hail of bullets. But it was reassuring, while shells exploded all around, to hear him calmly wind up his broadcast: "Good night and goodbye from Jerusalem."

The traditional Jewish gallows humor was often evoked to sustain morale. There was the youngster, escaping a near hit by a screaming shell, who shrugged off the episode remarking, "To the devil with life, the important thing is to keep well." A nine-year-old who served as a messenger boy during the heaviest shelling was chided affectionately for taking such risks. "But I'm still four years away from Bar Mitzvah," he explained, "and so small that as I crawl on my belly the big shells don't even see me."[6]

The forces protecting the New City continued to harass their Arab foes. Hit-and-run action often reached the level of critical confrontation. The central section of the city, set apart as a barbed-wire–enclosed compound, had been the headquarters of the British for their administrative units. It included the main post office and the telephone exchanges, a police station, the courts, several hospitals, a bank, the King David Hotel, and other installations vital to the city's government and its economic life. The Israelis had contemptuously labeled it "Bevingrad." In sporadic attacks after the British left, the Jews occupied much of the compound, relinquished it under fire, won it back, lost some parts, held others, but never gave the attacking Arabs a moment's respite. Some crack units of the Arab Legion probed for vulnerable openings in the area. They got beyond Bethlehem and to the outer suburbs of the New Jerusalem, but then the truce was imposed. The siege continued, yet the military momentum temporarily ended.

The one great objective thereafter for the Jews in Jerusalem was to survive starvation, and this depended upon getting food and water to the besieged. Relief came through the ingenious use of a narrow footpath that led into the west side of the Holy City. The footpath ran parallel to the main road, but it was just wide enough for a single traveler or a pack animal, so only minimal supplies could be brought in on it. It was wildly overgrown and there were, here and there, stretches of several hundred yards with no path at all. To clear the way and to widen the path necessitated bulldozing the terrain on both sides and chipping away at formidable rock formations. One part of the path included a precipitous incline of nearly 400 feet of mountain rock.

David (Mickey) Marcus, a West Point graduate who had flown missions over the Burma Road to China in World War II and had answered Ben Gurion's call for volunteers, was given the charge of Jerusalem's defense. He assembled all available earth-moving vehicles, including a few bulldozers, to attempt to widen the road for convoy use. Several engineers and many road construction workers were organized in the area, who were to labor at night.[7] The intention to open a supply route to be used during the truce period was not immediately fathomed by the Arabs, who apparently imagined that the movement came from trespassers or scavengers. There was desultory gunfire, but the task force labored on with less than a week to get the job done before an enforced truce would suspend all military activity. Even Marcus's colleagues spoke discouragingly. Marcus was not dissuaded—"We got across the Red Sea, didn't we?"

The road was finished on June 10, in the allotted time. The first jeep swayed its way into the city, a forerunner of the many convoys with precious cargoes that were to follow. During the truce period, 140 trucks, each with a 3-ton load, got through. The food went into storehouses, the weaponry into armories. One hundred fifty men under the supervision of a Polish-born engineer labored to lay a pipeline parallel to the road, to relieve the water shortage.

Marcus did not live to savor the triumph. On the night of June 11, when the truce was imposed, he had left his tent for a short walk, wearing a blanket that looked like an Arab gown. He was mistaken for an Arab scout. An Israeli sentinel challenged Marcus and, when he leaped over the camp barricade, the sentry fired and killed him. The distraught boy, horrified, would have committed suicide if he had not been forcibly prevented. Marcus was the last major casualty before the first UN truce was declared.

The timing of the truce had been influenced by tough diplomatic maneuvers that reflected not only the ambitions of the Arabs but also the not yet relinquished hope of the British that

Partition would be unenforceable. In the first weeks of the invasion when the Israelis lost ground, Lord Cadogan found technical reasons for continuous delay in order to give the Arabs the opportunity to broaden their advances. When the tide was reversed, it was the British who pressed for a truce. Had Cadogan or the Arab leaders realized how close to exhaustion the Israelis now were, they undoubtedly would have temporized further. When the truce went into effect there was no more than three days' supply of food left for the Jewish community. Though few believed that the truce could last very long, it was accepted all around, and a UN commission was named to supervise it.

The commission's chief responsibility turned out to be a complaint depot to receive protests about constant truce infractions. When the truce ended a month later, a report went from the Jewish government to the Security Council of the UN that the Arabs had violated its terms more than fifty times, and the Arabs had their own long list of charges. The complaints were treated with magnificent impartiality: they were uniformly disregarded.

At the outset of the truce, Cadogan called for a mediator, ostensibly to bring the warring parties together. For this thankless task he nominated Count Folke Bernadotte, president of the Swedish Red Cross, who, later in the war, as we have seen, was to help save many Jews from the concentration camps of Germany by interceding with Himmler to permit them a refuge in Sweden. The Israelis, at this stage, had some misgivings about Bernadotte's impartiality, but they went along with the recommendation. Even before the mediator had been briefed by the UN officials about his responsibilities, the British chargé d'affaires in Paris called to inform him that the British would continue to supply arms to the Arab forces. He added that if the mediator accepted any of the American proposals, particularly on expanded immigration, it would be regarded as "provocation and a flagrant breach of the UN Charter."[8] British "neutrality" was further demonstrated when Bernadotte was urged to revise the Partition Plan by turning over the southern Negev to the Egyptians. In return, the Jews would be assigned the western Galilee sections, which they had already secured in the first weeks of the war.

The truce lasted a bare month and its Latin designation, *pax in bello,* was literal. King Abdullah used the respite for a tour of the Arab capitals to negotiate for the consolidation of his alliances with the other Arab states and to persuade them that he should take over Jerusalem. Iraq assembled eleven convoys with arms and supplies to augment its resources. Egypt filled in the serious gaps in manpower that casualties had created and induced the Sudan and Saudi Arabia to encourage the enlistment of volunteers.

It was Israel that profited most from the truce. Thousands of refugees from Europe and the Arab lands poured in now without hindrance. The able-bodied were quickly absorbed and trained for military service. The acquisition of military supplies was still handicapped by embargoes and other international complications, but most of the restraints were circumvented. The planes, ships, and materiel that came through mainly by way of Czechoslovakia, vastly strengthened Israeli offensive power on land and sea and, above all, in the air. Such augmentation of military strength was in violation of the truce, which prohibited buildup of any kind. But as the Israeli leadership watched Britain "fulfill its military commitments" to the Arab states, it concluded that what was sauce for the Arabs could also be sauce for the Jews. The strengthened airforce was enabled to turn back Egyptian Dakotas that had been sent to bomb Tel Aviv and to drive off an Egyptian naval force that threatened the city and the coast line. "The truce came to us as dew from Heaven," an Israeli commander, Brigadier Moshe Carmel, acknowledged.

It was during this truce month of June and early July that the crisis of Israeli government authority weathered its most dangerous challenge. The occasional disagreements within the government were not as disruptive as the rivalries in the inner councils of the Arab states. The intransigence of Irgun, however, in the *Altalena* affair, went to the extreme of insubordination. A small ship had been purchased in France by agents of Irgun, and it sailed from Europe with nine hundred refugee-recruits. Menachem Begin insisted that the cargo, 5,000 rifles, 300 Bren guns, and some halftracks was the property of Irgun. The claim was in direct contravention of Israeli's provisional government's order that created a national military force; all armaments belonged under the jurisdiction of the government and there were to be no private caches.

Ben Gurion ordered the *Altalena,* which had arrived safely at Natanyah, to dock at K'far Vitkin and to store its cargo in government warehouses. Begin maintained that the cargo must go into Irgun warehouses, three-quarters of it to be distributed to Irgun units defending Jerusalem. Under Irgun orders, *Altalena*'s crew refused to dock at K'far Vitkin and set sail for Tel Aviv, where it deliberately ran aground on the beach. Ben Gurion considered Irgun defiance as a direct challenge to his authority as Prime Minister and he warned that Irgun was endangering "the very existence of the State." He instructed Yigal Allon and the Palmach to commandeer the ship and to use whatever force was necessary. "Your new assignment," he said, "may be the toughest one you've had so far. This time you may have to kill Jews."

Firing broke out, fifteen of the crew were killed, and the *Altalena* was set ablaze and sank. The crisis was the closest to civil war that the young state had come. Begin and Irgun never forgave Ben Gurion for the order that shed the blood of his own people. But in hindsight it seems that Ben Gurion had no alternative. His action prevented the disintegration of the government. As it worked out, the unsuccessful challenge strengthened the central administration as it girded itself for the resumption of hostilities.[9]

The truce ended abruptly on July 9, barely four weeks after it had been first imposed. Count Bernadotte had negotiated to the very end to extend this first truce into a more enduring armistice, hoping that time would cool passions and a peaceful solution emerge. He was unsuccessful because both the Arabs and the Israelis flatly rejected his recommendations. The proposal to assign Jerusalem to Transjordan not only antagonized the Israelis but was unacceptable to Egypt and the other Arab states. The proposal that the Negev go to Egypt in its entirety would slice away the largest land mass the Partition commission had set aside for Israel. As noted above, Bernadotte offered the western Galilee to the Israelis as a consolation prize; but since they had already appropriated the area, this was no "gauntlet with a gift in't." Israeli suspicions of Bernadotte as a mouthpiece for Britain hardened into certainty.

Who broke the truce several days before it was to expire precipitated a dispute where the evidence depended on which side presented it. In any case the Egyptians were soon involved in an offensive to clear out the settlements that still blocked their complete control of the Negev. Negba was a priority objective. The Egyptians, with three infantry battalions, an armored battalion, and an artillery regiment, greatly outnumbered the Israeli defenders, and at one point penetrated to within fifty yards of the perimeter fence. They were repeatedly repulsed. Each time they withdrew to reorganize, they left not only casualties but precious equipment. Since another truce was being demanded by the UN, the Egyptians decided to settle for a stalemate. An Egyptian prisoner asked his captors in astonishment how the undermanned Israelis had thrown back the Egyptians. "You had only 150 defenders and thousands of shells fell on the village." "Quantitatively," the village newspaper commented, "the balance of forces was in your favor, qualitatively it was in ours. We had a clear idea about the purpose of the battle . . . the realization that with our own bodies we barricaded the way north."

The probable imposition of an early new truce, perhaps within less than a week or ten days, impelled the Israelis to move to the offensive, to preempt whatever they could so that further negotiations would start with a more acceptable fait accompli. They rushed to eliminate the Arab pockets in the Negev that menaced the remaining Jewish settlements there. But time ran out and the Israeli drive came to a halt. The second truce was imposed on July 18; if there were to be any new decisive action, it would have to wait until, if and when, warfare was resumed.

On the northern Galilee front, during the ten days before the second truce was imposed, the battle lines rippled like a flag in a stiff breeze. The Syrian forces concentrated on keeping the Israelis on edge by sporadic attacks on targets chosen seemingly without any discernible plan. Yet the Israelis, now well reinforced, were able during the short fighting period to open the coastal road from Haifa to Tel Aviv by clearing the Arab forces out of the villages that remained as obstacles. Equally significant was the Israeli capture of the Christian city of Nazareth. It was strongly defended by Christian Arabs and it required many forays. Heavy casualties were exacted, but the Israelis felt they needed the victory to protect their Partition assignment. Sensitive to the feelings of the Christian world about the boyhood home of Jesus, the commanders issued strict orders to their troops that the greatest care be exercised to respect the sacred shrines.[10]

There were other major gains by the Israelis before the second truce went into effect. The most important was the capture of Lydda, an hour's ride from Tel Aviv, where the international airport was located. It was an audacious undertaking. The Arab leaders had built a complete system of defensive fortifications to protect Lydda, Ramleh, and the adjoining strategic territory. The core Israeli assault forces were compelled to round out their inadequate numbers with newly arrived immigrants who had been rushed to the fighting fronts with little training and were called upon for quickly executed commando assaults in which coordination and timing were indispensable. The newcomers knew little about the weapons they were to use. Few of them spoke or understood Hebrew and, coming from many lands, they often could not communicate with one another. Orders had to be transmitted through interpreters. The roads and streets were well known to the defending inhabitants but were incomprehensible dots on maps to the recruits. Yet morale was high, for now the European survivors could smite after so often being smitten.

The raid commander was a young sabra with a patch over an eye he had lost fighting the Nazis when he was part of the British forces. Moshe Dayan had already demonstrated a unique talent for improvisation in the battle to safeguard Deganiah, the kibbutz where he was born. His mechanized infantry stormed Lydda, the lead vehicle an armored car captured the day before from the Arab Legion. His shock tactics routed the defenders; within two days Lydda and Ramleh had surrendered, and the threat to the Tel Aviv area was lifted.

During this period, too, there were demonstration attacks on Arab lands by some Flying Fortresses, obtained in the United States and flown by Israeli pilots. Cairo was bombed and a small Israeli craft shelled Tyre in Lebanon. There was still time, too, for a spectacular climax if Latrun, the key to Jerusalem, could be captured. The assignment went to Yigal Allon and his experienced Palmach forces. They now had at their disposal newly arrived flamethrowers and other sophisticated weapons. But the attempt was defeated by the cream of the Arab Legion. As noted earlier, the attacks upon Latrun in the first weeks of declared independence had been repulsed, and Israel had then suffered one of its most disastrous defeats of the war. Now, facing the strongly reinforced Arab Legion, the Israelis were again thrown back and they, too, welcomed the second truce that came into effect on July 18.

It was imposed with a stern warning from the UN Security

Council. The first truce resolution had *called* upon the warring parties to desist from further military action. The second *ordered* the governments concerned to comply and added the threat of sanctions. No time limit to the truce was set; it was to continue until an agreed solution was achieved.

Count Bernadotte spent weeks during this second truce period with Arab and Jewish leaders and with delegations of the United Nations, trying to find some common ground upon which to build agreements. He again suggested that the Negev and all of Jerusalem go to the Arabs, with international supervision of the Holy Places, and that western Galilee, which the Israeli forces had won in the resumption of the war, be formally recognized as Israeli territory. Both the Arabs and the Israelis flatly rejected Bernadotte's formula. The Arabs were not ready to yield the rich Galilee area even though it was, at the moment, under Israeli control. Nor, again, would they acquiesce in any arrangement that would give Abdullah and Transjordan control over Jerusalem and Palestine's West Bank. In his rejection of Bernadotte's proposal, Ben Gurion accused him of acting like a British agent. He said bluntly that since Israel already held Galilee, the "concession" was a fraud. To yield on Jerusalem would be a betrayal of a historic right. To sign away the Negev would deprive Israel of the one undeveloped reservoir upon which depended the economic expansion of the little state and, equally important, of the possibility of absorbing large masses of immigrants.

On September 17, the world was shocked by the news that Count Bernadotte and a French assistant had been assassinated while he drove to meet with Dov Joseph in the New City of Jerusalem. The act had apparently been committed by a Jewish terrorist group even farther to the right than the Lehi that had cut down Lord Moyne in Cairo in November 1944. The Israeli government denounced the "insanity" of the gunmen who, "by their criminal irresponsibility . . . had shown themselves to be traitors to the people and enemies of its liberty." About four hundred members of the group, including their commander, Nathan Yellin-Friedman, were rounded up and jailed. If it had been the intention of the terrorists to abort the Bernadotte compromises, their action had an opposite effect. Not only the British government but moderates in the United Nations and the United States now endorsed the Bernadotte report as his "political testament." Ben Gurion and his staff realized that the Negev would be irretrievably lost unless its disposition were quickly moved from the discussion level to that of a fait accompli. It was time for new and decisive military action.

By the terms of the truce it had been agreed that on certain days convoys with food supplies would have access to the isolated Negev enclaves. On October 14, as an Israeli convoy aproached a guarded crossroad at Faluja, it purportedly was met with shellfire and bombs. A lead vehicle blew up. The Egyptians claimed that the Israelis themselves had set off the explosion, although UN observers offered no confirmation. But who did what to whom no longer mattered. Each side sensed important advantage in renewing hostilities, with fullest commitment of all military resources. As it happened, there were to be only four days before a final truce was imposed by the UN.

The strategy to be followed in the renewed Negev campaigns was reached only after another dangerous internal dispute in the Israeli high command. Yigal Allon urged that the strike in the Negev be made part of a much larger three-phase effort on the other strategic fronts, coordinated to win and consolidate a strong and secure Jewish Palestine. The chief of staff, Yigael Yadin, vigorously opposed such a massive military commitment. He feared that, despite reinforcements that had arrived during the truces, Israel still did not have enough effective power to fight simultaneously on widely dispersed fronts. Even to mount the attack upon the Egyptians in the Negev, he said, would strain Israel's resources to the limit. Ben Gurion was inclined, at first, to side with Allon; but Yadin felt so strongly about overextension that he threatened to resign if he were overruled. Reluctantly, Ben Gurion gave way.

Allon never ceased regretting Ben Gurion's decision. He had an intimate knowledge of the internecine Arab rivalries and vendettas, and he was convinced that none of the Arab states would commit their forces unless their own countries were threatened. I interviewed Allon in the fall of 1979, a few months before his death. He was now Deputy Prime Minister in the Begin coalition government, and the major problem in foreign affairs was still the unremitting Arab hostility. Our conversation centered chiefly about these "might-have-beens." Allon admitted that he spoke from hindsight, but he maintained that if he had been given the authority to proceed with the coordinated operation, central Palestine, including the Gaza Strip, even

Jerusalem, would have fallen to Israel, and the decisive Arab defeat would have avoided the wars that followed.

In any case, the control of the Negev became the prime objective of the Israelis as the third round of the war began. Allon, aiming to turn the Egyptian line, struck in mid-October at heavily fortified and defended Huleiqat, known to the Israelis as "the horror of the south." The stunning Israeli victory, announced in Allon's laconic style, "Huleiqat is ours," made it possible to encircle the key Arab position at Faluga where Naguib had billeted Egypt's prestigious Fourth Brigade with 4,000 crack troops. Naguib hoped that pressure upon the stronghold would be relieved when his Arab allies opened other fronts against the Israelis in central and northern Palestine.

Allon's prediction of Arab behavior was completely fulfilled. Instead of launching diversionary attacks immediately, the Arab leaders met on October 23 at Amman to discuss "ways to help." Many bitter words were exchanged, including insults that exposed the conflicting Arab objectives. Abdullah tore into the Egyptians for having opposed his claim to Arab Palestine and Jerusalem. He sneered at their pretensions and their loss of key strategic areas after their boasted might. The Egyptian Prime Minister replied hotly that his military were still holding their positions. "But where are the royal Jordanians and the Iraqi forces? And we all know that the Syrian forces are useless."

The conference ended in mutual recrimination. The fratricidal rivalries, the resort to braggadocio, the mistrust that contributed so largely to the humiliating Arab defeats, were not to be tempered in the years ahead. Constantine Zurayk, the rector of the Syrian University of Damascus, identified the unending discord as the primary cause of Arab vulnerability. "Declarations," he wrote, "fall like bombs from the mouths of officials at the meetings of the Arab League, but when action becomes necessary, the fire is still and quiet, and steel and iron are rusted and twisted, quick to bend and disintegrate. The bombs are hollow and empty."[11]

When the Egyptians realized there would be no relieving support, they began destroying equipment in Faluja in preparation for retreat. The Arab commander met with Allon under a white flag and indicated that, though his military situation had become hopeless, the token battle would have to continue "for the honor of the Egyptians." He reserved his anger for his Arab allies and for the British who, he raged, were responsible for the fruitless war. "What is Palestine to us? It is all a British trick to divert our attention from their occupation of Egypt."[12] It was during this period that Gamal Nasser, now a prisoner of the Israelis, later to lead the revolution that ousted Farouk, expressed his admiration for the kibbutzim. He hoped that Egypt, reorganized and rid of its governmental corruption, would some day emulate the enviable progress of the Israelis. He echoed his junior officer's harsh words about Abdullah and vowed that in time the wily king would pay for the "betrayal" motivated by his intended grab of Jerusalem and his other dynastic ambitions. Without waiting for the formal Faluja surrender, Allon sent three brigades racing down the newly opened road to Beersheba, the sleepy little "capital" of the Negev. The Egyptian garrison was caught off guard by the speed of the attack and surrendered after a brief resistance. The action isolated the eastern Egyptian forces from the Hills of Hebron and, cutting the lines of communication, made it possible to pick off the pockets of remaining Egyptian forces in the Negev.[13]

Through these tumultuous days the pressure in the United Nations for another truce, stimulated by the British, kept mounting. The Egyptians offered no protest, having come to the realization that there was no further possibility of challenging Israel's control of the west Negev. Even the evacuation of the Arabs was costly. Two of the naval vessels to which their units were assigned were sunk by Israeli demolition teams. The flagship, the *Emir Farouk*, went down off the Gaza coast with its crew and seven hundred soldiers.

Meanwhile the Egyptian Air Force, not a large one but the most professional among the Arab states, had been demolished. Israeli intelligence reports and photographic reconnaissance had operated so efficiently that it was possible to destroy most of the planes on the ground at El Arish. With almost uncontested air cover for their ground troops, sheer momentum carried Allon and the Israelis over the border into Egypt itself. Allon's forces could have moved straight into Cairo, but the UN Security Council sternly ordered a halt and Ben Gurion assented. In our 1979 conversation, Allon expressed regret that he had not found reasons to delay the acceptance of the truce of October 22 and retrieve a few extra days for the occupation of Cairo. The experience of Israeli troops entering the capital, he felt, would have chastened the Egyptians for half a century. Other Israeli columns pushed down to the southern tip of the

Negev. They took over the port of Elath with access to the Red Sea and the commercial routes to Asia and Africa.

By now Egypt was ready for an armistice. Military defeat had bred an ominous restlessness among its people. The ability and integrity of the military and the government were being openly questioned. Indeed, the events were to lead a few years later to a sweeping revolution in which the king, his counselors, and their hangers-on were overthrown. Farouk, quite philosophical so long as he could retain his harem and his secret deposits in foreign banks, went tamely and unlamentedly into exile. "Kings are on their way out," he prophesied. "Soon there will be only five left, the King of Spades, Hearts, Diamonds, Clubs, and of England."

On February 4, 1949, after weeks of patient negotiation, Dr. Ralph Bunche, the American who had taken Bernadotte's place as mediator, brought the Egyptian and Israeli representatives together on the island of Rhodes, and the armistice was signed which, for all practical purposes, took Egypt out of the war. General Walter Eytan, director of the Israeli Foreign Office, later described the festive mood of the delegates from both sides, now that the war in their sector was over:

> We did not meet socially much, but when Abdul Moneim Mustafa, the chief political adviser of the Egyptian delegation, fell ill, we sat at his bedside and comforted him and, when the armistice agreement was finally signed, Dr. Bunche had us all in to a gay party in the evening for which the Egyptians had sent in a special plane from Cairo with delicacies from Groppi's. I well remember sitting with the head of the Egyptian delegation as he showed me photographs of his family.[14]

Although negotiations for the truce with Transjordan were technically conducted under Dr. Bunche's supervision, the decisions were actually reached in personal sessions held in Amman where Abdullah met with ranking Israeli officials, including Yadin, Dayan, and Eytan. Abdullah was a gracious host through the week of intensive conferences. The Israeli chief of staff, Yigael Yadin, was in rare form. When Abdullah at the festive dinners noted that, in his leisure, he loved to listen to Arab poems, Yadin began reciting his own favorite in limpid Arabic. The king embraced him, crying out: "But that's my favorite poem too!"

Abdullah was not now too obdurate. Much of what he coveted he had achieved. He had been proclaimed king of the area of Palestine that the Partition vote had assigned to the Arabs. The New City of Jerusalem remained in Israeli jurisdiction, but he had the Old City and mollified the Jews when provision was made to keep routes open for them to have access to Mount Scopus and all the shrines on the Mount of Olives. The furious protests of the other Arab states against his unilateral appropriation of the city had left him completely unperturbed. Abdullah felt that the unity of the Arab League, headed by the Grand Mufti whose hatred was heartily reciprocated, had never been a principle worth defending strenuously. The detailed results of the negotiations were rushed to Rhodes and the official armistice was signed on April 3, 1949. It was possible at the same time to add the consent of Iraq since its government had asked Abdullah's representatives to act on its behalf as well.

Only the Syrians still held out. They, too, might have come to terms earlier, but in October 1948, in the third stage of the war, the Israelis had completely reversed the military situation in Galilee. They had been reinforced by new manpower from the floods of immigrants, and by heavy armor, including planes, that had arrived since the war began. Their drive had been felicitously named Operation Hiram for the biblical king of Lebanon who had supplied the cedars for the Temple built in Jerusalem by David and Solomon. In the operation the Israelis had recovered all but a few villages; now they refused to come to terms until the Syrians agreed to evacuate these. Negotiations dragged on for many months, the Syrians trying for last-minute concessions that would salvage something for them. The head of the delegation, who at first would not shake hands with the Israeli chief, Mordecai Makleff, demanded the return of Haifa. Makleff imperturbably countered with a mock request for Damascus. The byplay continued for several months. Then on July 20, 1949, the Syrians, along with Lebanon, joined the other Arab states in signing the armistice agreement.

By mid-August 1949 the United Nations, recognizing that in effect the war was over, recalled Dr. Bunche and terminated the office of mediator. Dr. Bunche thoroughly deserved the Nobel Peace Prize which came to him that year.

The Israeli triumph created a new power in the Near East. The Partition Plan, with numerous Jewish and Arab settlements jostling each other, reminding one observer of two snakes intertwined in deadly embrace, had now been substantially revised and most of the disputed areas were at last in Israeli hands. The Arabs had taken over fourteen sites that had been allotted to the Jewish State. Israel had won 112 villages that had been assigned to the Arabs. There was now a strong State of Israel, with a majority Jewish population, its territory small but its viability no longer jeopardized by bizarre political boundaries or grotesque economic compromises. There were still enormous problems to be faced; they could be met, not under the gun, but in a spirit of confidence and dignity.* U.S. General S. L. A. Marshall, in a foreword to Lorch's history of Israel's military achievement, noted how a free society "can build upward swiftly and surely when genius walks with courage."[15]

Meanwhile, the newly created Knesset had met in Jerusalem in February 1949, before all the armistice agreements had been completed. The choice of Jerusalem as the capital, even though only partly in Jewish control, was intended as a clear proclamation of defiance to those who still insisted that the Holy City must be internationalized. Dr. Chaim Weizmann came forward to convene the first Jewish Parliament in nearly 2,000 years. Almost thirty years before, on April 15, 1920, the representatives of the western Allies of World War I had met at San Remo, in Italy, to discuss, among other concerns, the official validation of the Balfour Declaration that had been jointly announced in 1917, by Britain and the United States, assuring the Jews a Homeland in Palestine. Weizmann, who had negotiated the original Declaration, could not participate in the San Remo validating discussions; only the emissaries of sovereign states could do so. Weiz-

---

*The largest problem that remained was, of course, the presence of hundreds of thousands of Arabs, multiplying rapidly, doomed to live as refugees under Israeli control. Israel solved the problem of more than half a million tormented Jews in the Arab lands by bringing them to Israel and integrating them into its national life. The Arab states adamantly refused to consider such a solution though they controlled millions of uninhabited and sparsely settled lands. Major General Chaim Herzog who fought in all the succeeding Arab–Israeli wars that were an unending threat to the peace of the Middle East, commented: "It is sobering to reflect that just one day's Arab oil revenues, even in 1949, would have sufficed to solve the entire Arab refugee problem. But it was not to be." Chaim Herzog, *The Arab-Israeli Wars*, N.Y., 1982, p. 106.

mann had therefore asked Balfour himself to serve as surrogate. Weizmann recalled in his memoirs how he had paced the stately halls of the San Remo palace all afternoon, waiting anxiously for the verdict upon which 2,000 years of Jewish history hung. At last the gilded doors of the conference hall opened and Balfour emerged. As Weizmann hurried toward him, he noted that the old statesman looked harried. Weizmann's heart sank. "O, Balfour," Weizmann exclaimed, "is the news so bad?" "O, no," Balfour replied, though apparently still troubled. "The news is wonderful. The decision for the Jewish Homeland was affirmative. But I am late for tennis."[16]

Weizmann had often asked himself if the moment would ever come when the destiny of his people would no longer be trivialized, dependent upon the caprice of others, even those who were friendly. Now the moment had come. Weizmann walked to the lectern, weary, infirm, in pain, scarcely able to see through the cataracts in his ailing eyes. But his voice was exultant as he linked the fate of Israel with the fate of the democratic principle in the western world. "Today is a great day in our lives," he told the audience, which included diplomatic representatives from all over the world. "Let us not be thought too arrogant if we say that it is also a great day in the history of the world. In this hour a message of hope and good cheer issues from this place, from this sacred city, to all oppressed people and to all who are struggling for freedom and equality."[17]

The venerable statesman could serve as little more than a symbol. It was a time for youth and vigor, and David Ben Gurion, a mere sixty-three, was elected Prime Minister. But the Knesset would not forget the past and what Weizmann had meant in the trying years of travail. He was elected the first President of Israel and, to the sound of the shofar, he took the oath of office.

Some months earlier, in November 1948, on the first anniversary of the Partition resolution, Israel had requested membership in the United Nations. The application was sponsored by the American and the Russian delegates. The initial application was laid over mainly because of British opposition. Sir Alexander Cadogan, still following the line that Churchill had dubbed "the sulky boycott," objected that Israel had not yet demonstrated sovereign capacity, and that it had not earned membership in the United Nations. The British government apparently required sterner guarantees from Israel than from

many of the revolution-riven African and Asian states whose
admission it had previously sponsored and supported.

The diplomatic battle was renewed in later sessions of the
Security Council and the General Assembly. On May 11, 1949,
a year after sovereignty had been achieved, when the wars to
confirm the United Nations' Partition resolution had been won
and a secure democratic government had been elected, Israel
was admitted to become the fifty-ninth member. The blue and
white of Zion joined the other flags in the UN Plaza and Moshe
Sharett, the Israeli Foreign Minister, was escorted to his seat in
the Assembly.

Equally moving was the symbolism in the return to Israel of
the body of Dr. Theodor Herzl, the father of modern Zionism.
Upon his death in July 1904, Herzl, in fulfillment of the wish
expressed in his will, was interred near his father's grave in
Vienna, "to remain there until the Jewish people carry my
remains to Palestine." On August 14, 1949, Herzl's coffin was
flown by an Israeli plane to Lydda, there to be received by Prime
Minister Ben Gurion and the entire cabinet, who accompanied
it to Tel Aviv. The bier rested on the esplanade in front of the
building used by the Knesset. Multitudes from every part of
Israel passed by to salute the man whose dream had now so
miraculously come true.

The cortège then made its way to Jerusalem, following the
route that Herzl had taken when he went to meet the visiting
German kaiser in a historic interview fifty years before. Herzl
had been begging for thirty-minute interviews from the heads
of state in countries large and small, seeking permission for Jews
to settle in their Holy Land. Only dreamers had then imagined
that the widely dispersed Jews would ever be more than wanderers. Yet Herzl had never lost faith that "if you will it, it is no
dream."

Now the dream had been realized and Herzl had come home.
His permanent grave was established on one of the highest hills
of Jerusalem, where it had been dug out of solid rock. Into the
grave with the remains of the founder of Zionism went little
bags of earth from each community, offered with reverence by
chosen delegates. The solemn ceremony ended when the guards
presented arms and the ancient mourner's Kaddish was recited.

REFERENCES

FOREWORD

1. Irving Abella and Harold Troper, *None is Too Many*. The whole volume is devoted to Canada's immigration program since World War II.
2. Jean Améry, *At the Mind's Limits*, p. 14.
3. Saturday Review Book for Newspapers, Vol. 51, Jan. 27, 1968.

CHAPTER 1

1. Leon Poliakov, *Harvest of Hate*, p. 17.
2. Dwight D. Eisenhower, *Crusade in Europe*, pp. 408–409.
3. John W. Jacobson, *"The Day Buchenwald Was Freed,"* New York Times Magazine, April 7, 1946, pp 28–29.
4. Eugene Kogon, *The Theory and Practice of Hell: The Concentration Camps and the Theory Behind Them*, pp. 52–53.
5. Paul Berben, *Dachau*, pp. 45–48.
6. Ibid., p. 183.
7. Nerin E. Gun, *The Day of the Americans*, pps. 63, 162.
8. Derrick Sington, *Belsen Uncovered*, p. 72.
9. Interview with Mrs. Josef Rosensaft (Dr. Bimko), November 9, 1981.
10. Anne Frank, *The Diary of a Young Girl*, entry for February 23, 1944.
11. Jacob Presser, *The Destruction of the Dutch Jews*, p. 518.
12. Sington, *Belsen Uncovered*, p. 73.
13. *British Medical Journal*, June 9, 1945.
14. P. Tillard, *Mauthausen*, pp. 20–21.
15. Cited in Evelyn LeChêne, *Mauthausen*, p. 452.
16. Poliakov, *Harvest of Hate*, p. 206.
17. Presser, *Destruction of the Dutch Jews*, p. 54.
18. Leonard Baker, *Leo Baeck: Days of Sorrow and Pain*, p. 299.
19. Joseph Bor, *The Terezin Requiem*, pp. 7–8.
20. Baker, *Leo Baeck: Days of Sorrow and Pain*, p. 318.

CHAPTER 2

1. Rudolf Hoess, *Commandant of Auschwitz: Autobiography of Rudolf Hoess*, pp. 16, 23.

2. Ibid., p. 190.
3. Ibid., p. 24.
4. Ibid., p. 25.
5. Testimony offered by the writer, K. Zetnik, at the Eichmann trial, cited in *Encyclopedia Judaica*. Vol. 3, p. 857.
6. Victor Frankl, *From Death Camp to Existentialism*, pp. 36–37.
7. Ibid., p. 24.
8. Reuben Ainsztein, *Jewish Resistance in Nazi Occupied Eastern Europe*, pp. 801–813.
9. Yuri Suhl, *They Fought Back*, pp. 219–223.
10. Ibid., pp. 220–222
11. Gis Weisblum, cited in Yuri Suhl, *They Fought Back*, pp. 182–188.
12. Statistics cited by Yehuda Bauer in *A History of the Holocaust*, p. 209.
13. Testimony at Nuremberg Military Tribunal Trial, cited in William M. Shirer, *The Rise and Fall of the Third Reich*, pp. 971–973.
14. Greet von Amstel, cited in Presser, *Destruction of the Dutch Jews*, p. 494.
15. Saul Friedlander, *Kurt Gerstein: The Ambiguity of Good*, pp. 110–111.
16. Ibid., p. 105.
17. Ibid., pp. 201–209.
18. Ibid. The battle for vindication is documented in the last part of Friedlander's biography of Gerstein.
19. *Commentary*, August 1965.
20. *The Black Book*, American Jewish Black Book Committee, New York, 1946. pp. 379–380.
21. Gerald Reitlinger, *The Final Solution*, pp. 296–297. The Himmler speech is preserved in transcript and in a gramophone recording.
22. Hoess, *Commandant of Auschwitz*, p. 45.
23. Suhl, *They Fought Back*. Pechersky's story, told in an autobiography in Yiddish, has been translated by Suhl, pp. 7–51.
24. Interviewed at the Hebrew University in Jerusalem, November 29, 1979.

CHAPTER 3

1. Bruno Bettelheim, "The Ignored Lesson of Anne Frank," *Surviving and Other Essays*, p. 29.
2. Hannah Arendt, *Eichmann in Jerusalem: A Report on the Banality of Evil*, p. 104.
3. Raoul Hilberg, *The Destruction of the European Jews*, p. 662.
4. Discussions during Arie Eliav's visiting professorship at Harvard University, 1979–1980.
5. Reuben Ainsztein, *Jewish Resistance in Nazi Occupied Eastern Europe*, pp. 634–635.
6. Albert Nirenstein, *A Tower from the Enemy: Jewish Resistance in Poland*, p. 105.
7. Ibid., p. 105.
8. William Zuckerman, "The Revolt in the Ghetto," *Harper's*, Vol. 352, 1943.
9. Ziphora Berman in *The Fighting Ghettos*, ed. by Meyer Barkai, p. 149.
10. Reuben Ainsztein, Spring issue of *The Jewish Quarterly*, London, 1956, cited in Yuri Suhl, *They Fought Back*, p. 143.
11. Hersh Smoliar's memoirs and interviews with Yuri Suhl are summarized in Suhl, Ibid., pp. 231–241.

12. Jacob Greenstein, *Facing the Nazis: Children-Couriers in the Ghetto of Minsk*, cited in Suhl, Ibid., pp. 241–251.
13. Isaiah Trunk, *Judenrat: The Jewish Councils in Eastern Europe Under the Nazis*, pp. 420–421.
14. Ibid., p. 470.
15. Kuznetzov (pseud.), Anatoli, A., *Babi Yar*. The whole volume is devoted to the Massacre.
16. Translated by Marie Syrkin, *Hadassah Magazine*, March, 1967, reproduced in *Encyclopedia Judaica*, Jerusalem, 1971, Vol. 4, p. 27.
17. David Schoenbrun, *Soldiers of the Night*, p. 60.
18. Yehuda Bauer, *History of the Holocaust*, p. 234.
19. Joel Colton, *Léon Blum*, p. 421
20. Schoenbrun, *Soldiers of the Night*, pp.403–405.
21. Ibid., p. 308.
22. Knout detailed the story of the Jewish Maquis in his booklet, "La Resistance Juive," Schoenbrun, Ibid., pp. 51–52.
23. Nahum Goldmann, *The Autobiography of Nahum Goldmann*, p. 160.
24. James McGregor Burns, *Roosevelt: The Lion and the Fox*, p. 421.
25. Ruth Bondy, *The Emissary: Enzo Sereny*, p. 26.
26. Masimo Adolfo Vitale, cited in Suhl, *They Fought Back*, p. 303.
27. "The Works of W. E. Henley," Vol. 1, in *Hospital XXV*, p. 40. London: David Nutt, 1908.
28. Gilles Lambert, *Operation Hazalah*, pps. 38, 200.
29. Ibid., pp. 152–154.

CHAPTER 4

1. Shammai Golan, *The Holocaust*, cited in Bauer, *A History of the Holocaust*, p. 288.
2. W. Bartoszewski and A. Lewin (eds.), *Righteous Among the Nations*, pp. 18–34.
3. Summary of unpublished manuscript made available to me by Dr. Yisroel Gutman, Scientific Secretary of Yad Vashem.
4. Philip Friedman, *Their Brothers' Keepers*, pp. 30–32.
5. Ibid., pp. 55–59.
6. Moshe Bejski in *Proceedings of the Second International Conferences, Yad Vashem*, April 1974, p. 639.
7. Ibid., pp. 645–646.
8. Ibid., p. 647.
9. Ibid., p. 644.
10. Philip Friedman, *Their Brothers' Keepers*, p. 100.
11. Yohanen Lewy, *John XXIII*, cited in *Genesis* 45:4, *Encyclopedia Judaida*, Vol. 10, p. 159.
12. Carlo Falconi, *The Silence of Pius XII*, p. 5.
13. Leni Yahil, *The Rescue of Danish Jewry*, pp. 148–151.
14. Aage Bertelsen, Address at World Jewish Congress, 1971, cited in Bejski, *Proceedings of the Second International Conferences, Yad Vashem*, pp. 640–642.
15. Yahil, *The Rescue of Danish Jewry*, pp. 223–285.
16. Hugo Valentin, *Encyclopedia Judaica*, Vol. 15, pp. 548–550.
17. Frederick B. Chary, *The Bulgarian Jews and the Final Solution*, pp. 188–189.

18. Nicholas Ivan Momtchiloff, Article on Bulgaria, *Encyclopedia Britannica*, Vol. 4, p. 393.
19. Ehud Avriel, *Open the Gates*, pp. 196 *ff*.
20. Felix Kersten, *Memoirs*, Introduction by Hugh R. Trevor-Roper.
21. Ibid., p. 307.
22. Ibid., p. 12.
23. Ibid., p. 21.
24. F.E. Werbell and T. Clarke (eds.), *The Lost Hero: The Mystery of Raoul Wallenberg*, pp. 138–140.
25. Aage Bertelsen. *October '43*, Preface, pp. vii–viii, pp. 223–282.

CHAPTER 5

1. Airey Neave, *On Trial at Nuremberg*, p. 236.
2. *Time* magazine, November 3, 1945.
3. Rebecca West, *A Train of Powder*, pp. 4–7.
4. Bradley F. Smith, *Reaching Judgment at Nuremberg*, p. 175.
5. Robert A. Jackson, *The Nuremberg Case—And Other Documents*, New York: Alfred A. Knopf, pp. 122–123.
6. Benjamin Ferencz, *Less Than Slaves*, p. 25.
7. Hugh R. Trevor-Roper, *The Last Days of Hitler*, pp. 141–142.
8. Albert Speer, *Inside the Third Reich*. Introduction by Eugene Davidson.
9. West, *Train of Powder*, p. 8.
10. War Office Papers, cited in Tom Bower, *The Pledge Betrayed*, pp. 330 *ff*.
11. Ferencz, *Less Than Slaves*, Foreword by Telford Taylor, pp. ix–x.
12. Clarence G. Lasby, *Project Paperclip*, p. 5.
13. James S. Martin, *All Honorable Men*; Josiah E. Dubois, Jr., *The Devil's Chemists*; Benjamin Ferencz, *Less Than Slaves*.
14. Martin, Ibid., pp. 204–220.
15. Ibid., pp. 12–13.
16. Ibid., pp. 73–81.
17. Ibid., p. 11.
18. Ibid., pp. 17–26.
19. Ibid., p. 264.
20. Ferencz, *Less Than Slaves*, pp. 155–158.
21. Ibid., pp. 155–158.
22. Dubois, *The Devil's Chemists*, p. 95.
23. Ibid., p. ix.
24. Tom Bower, *The Pledge Betrayed*, pp. 340–342.
25. Isser Harel, *The House on Garibaldi Street*.
26. Gideon Hausner, *Justice in Jerusalem.*, p. 247.

CHAPTER 6

1. Nelly Sachs, *O, The Chimneys, Selected Poems*.
2. Joseph Tenenbaum, *In Search of a Lost People*, Chapter 21.
3. Yehuda Bauer, *B'Richa: Flight and Rescue*, pp. 30–31.
4. Ephraim Dekel, *B'richa: Flight to the Homeland*, p. 183.
5. Bauer, *B'richa: Flight and Rescue*, pp. 154–155.
6. The PUR episode was pieced together from oral evidence gathered by Yehuda Bauer, Ibid., pp. 233–236.
7. Ibid., pp. 210–211.

8. Ibid., p. 206 *ff.*
9. Jon and David Kimche, *The Secret Roads: The "Illegal" Migration of a People, 1938–1948*, p. 119.
10. Discussion on DP camps during Dr. William Haber's visits to Brandeis University campus.
11. Discussion with Colonel Abraham Hyman, adviser on Jewish affairs to American commanders in DP camps.
12. Jorge Garcia-Granados, *The Birth of Israel*, pp. 222–225.
13. Leo Schwarz, *The Redeemers*, pp. 222–226.
14. Harry S. Truman, *Memoirs*, Vol. Two, pp. 137–139.
15. Judah Nadich, *Eisenhower and the Jews*, p. 128 *ff.*
16. George Patton, *The Patton Diaries, 1940–1945*, pp. 750–751.
17. Dwight D. Eisenhower, *Crusade in Europe*, pp. 408–409, 441.
18. Leo Srole, "Why the DP's Cannot Wait," *Commentary*, January 1947.
19. Marie Syrkin, *The State of the Jews*, p. 22.
20. Winston Churchill, *The Second World War*, pp. 188–191.
21. James F. Byrnes, *Speaking Frankly*, New York: Harper, 1947, pp. 188–191.
22. Samuel Eliot Morison, *The Oxford History of the American People*, pp. 897–898.
23. Schwarz, *The Redeemers*, pp. 46–55.

CHAPTER 7
1. Avriel, Ehud, *Open the Gates*, p. 35.
2. *Palestine Gazette Extraordinary*, April 27, 1939, cited in Koestler, *Promise and Fulfillment: Palestine 1947–1949*, pp. 59–60.
3. Avriel, *Open the Gates*, p. 112.
4. Sharett Memoir, cited in Wasserstein, *Britain and the Jews of Europe*, p. 69.
5. Memo to the British Ambassador to the United States, cited in Wasserstein, ibid., p. 77.
6. *The Diplomatic Diaries of Oliver Harvey, 1937–1940*. J. Harvey (ed.), p. 148.
7. Munya Mardor, *Haganah*, pp. 138–149.
8. The *Fede* exploit is detailed along with other daring Israeli attempts at illegal immigration in Ehud Avriel, *Open the Gates*.

CHAPTER 8
1. Niles Papers. Truman's confirming letter to author. March 10, 1959.
2. Niles Papers. Letter A, Weizmann to Niles.
3. Niles Papers. Letter B, Truman to Niles.
4. Margaret Truman, *Souvenir, Margaret Truman's Own Story*, p. 83.
5. Harry Truman, *Memoirs*, Vol. Two, p. 132.
6. Ibid., p. 133.
7. Ibid., Vol. One, p. 69.
8. Interview in Acheson's Washington Office. June 28, 1971, cited in Abram L. Sachar, *The Course of Our Times*, pp. 310–311
9. Niles Papers.
10. Truman, *Memoirs*, Vol. Two, p. 135–136.
11. Ibid., Vol. Two, 138–139.
12. Niles Papers.
13. Truman, *Memoirs*, Vol. Two, p. 142–144.
14. Richard Crossman, *Palestine Mission*, p. 57.

15. Bartley Crum, *Behind the Silken Curtain*, pp. 85, 92.
16. Niles Papers. Letters C and D, Niles to Crum and Loy Henderson.
17. Niles Papers. Letter E, Truman to Hutcheson.
18. Niles Papers.
19. Niles Papers.
20. Niles Papers.
21. Niles Papers. Letter F, Niles to Truman.
22. Niles Papers. Letter G, Truman to Taylor.
23. Niles Papers. Letter H, Truman to Niles.
24. Niles Papers. Letter I, Oscar Gass to Elath to Niles.
25. George Kirk, *The Middle East 1945–1950*, p. 225.
26. Truman, *Memoirs*, Vol. One, pp. 52–53.
27. Barnet Litvinoff, *Ben Gurion of Israel*, p. 173.
28. Niles Papers.
29. Niles Papers. Letter J, Niles to Truman.
30. David Horowitz, *State in the Making*, p. 256.
31. Niles Papers.
32. Margaret Truman, *Souvenir*, p. 482.
33. Niles Papers.
34. Niles Papers.
35. Niles Papers. Document K, Niles later service.
36. Moshe Dayan, *Story of My Life*, p.80.

CHAPTER 9

1. David Ben Gurion, *Israel: Years of Challenge*, P. 7.
2. Frank Gervasi, *Life and Times of Menahem Begin*, p. 80 *ff.*
3. Bernard Wasserstein, *Britain and the Jews of Europe*, p. 80.
4. Martin Gilbert, *Exile and Return*, pp. 267–268.
5. Nicholas Bethell, *The Palestine Triangle*, p. 183.
6. Gervasi, *Life and Times of Menahem Begin*, p. 162.
7. Bethell, *The Palestine Triangle*, p. 190.
8. James G. McDonald, *My Mission in Israel*, pp. 23–26.
9. *Time* magazine, November 4, 1940.
10. Bethell, *The Palestine Triangle*, p. 268.
11. Chaim Weizmann, *Trial and Error*, pp. 442–443.
12. Bethell, *The Palestine Triangle*, p. 268.
13. Martin Gilbert, *Exile and Return*, p. 299.

CHAPTER 10

1. Arthur Koestler, *Promise and Fulfillment*, p. 128.
2. Leonard Slater, *The Pledge*, p. 23.
3. Chaim Herzog, *The Arab-Israeli Wars*, pp. 24–25, 43.
4. Slater, *The Pledge*, pp. 104–107.
5. Ibid., pp. 38–40.
6. Ibid., pp. 260–263.
7. Teddy and Amos Kollek, *For Jerusalem*, pp. 64–80.
8. Ibid., pp. 86–87.
9. Moshe Pearlman, *Ben Gurion Looks Back*, p. 25.
10. Slater, *The Pledge*, pp. 131 *ff.*

11. Kolleck, *To Jerusalem*, pp. 70–71.
12. Munya Mardor, *Haganah*, pp. 241–258.
13. Netanel Lorch, *The Edge of the Sword*, p. 106.
14. Larry Collins and Dominique Lapierre, *O Jerusalem*, p. 235.
15. Netanel Lorch, *The Edge of the Sword*, p. 107.

CHAPTER 11

1. Netanel Lorch, *The Edge of the Sword*, p. 177.
2. Ibid., pp. 150–152.
3. Ibid., pp. 172–173.
4. Sir John B. Glubb, *A Soldier With the Arabs*, pp. 25 ff.
5. Dov Joseph, *The Faithful City: The Siege of Jerusalem*, p. 132.
6. Ibid., p. 158.
7. Teddy and Amos Kollek, *For Jerusalem*, pp. 84–85.
8. Count Folke Bernadotte, *To Jerusalem*, pp. 6–7.
9. David Ben-Gurion, *Israel: Years of Challenge*, pp. 165–177.
10. Lorch, *The Edge of the Sword*, p. 276.
11. Howard M. Sachar, *Europe Leaves the Middle East 1936–1954*, p. 578.
12. Ibid., p. 341.
13. Lorch, *The Edge of the Sword*, p. 386.
14. Walter Eytan, *The First Ten Years: A Diplomatic History of Israel*, pp. 30–31.
15. Lorch, *The Edge of the Sword*, Foreword by General Marshall, p. 7.
16. Chaim Weizmann, *Trial and Error: An Autobiography*, p. 260.
17. Ibid., p. 458–459.

SELECTED BIBLIOGRAPHY

Primarily volumes in English which are usually accessible in the libraries of colleges and fair-sized communities. The most recent authoritative studies have been given preference.

I
THE FINAL SOLUTION: WHAT THE LIBERATORS FOUND AND LEARNED

Abella, Irving and Troper, Harold, *None is Too Many.* Toronto: Lester & Orpen Dennys, 1982.

Améry, Jean, *At the Mind's Limits.* Bloomington: Indiana University Press, 1980.

Anthology of Holocaust Literature, edited by Jacob Glatstein, Israel Knox, Samuel Margoshes. Philadelphia: Jewish Publication Society, 1969.

Arad, Yitzchak (ed.), *Holocaust and Rebirth: A Symposium.* Jerusalem: Yad Vashem, 1974.

Berben, Paul, *Dachau.* London: Norfolk Press, 1975.

Bertelsen, Aåge, *October '43.* New York: Putnam, 1954.

Bor, Joseph, *The Terezin Requiem.* New York: Alfred A. Knopf, 1963.

Baker, Leonard, *Leo Baeck: Days of Sorrow and Pain.* New York: Macmillan Co., 1978.

Bauer, Yehuda, *A History of the Holocaust.* New York: Franklin Watts, 1982.

Cohen, Elie A., *Human Behavior in the Concentration Camps.* New York: W. W. Norton, 1953.

Colton, Joel G., *Léon Blum.* New York: Alfred A. Knopf, 1966.

Davidowicz, Lucy S., *The War Against the Jews, 1933–45.* New York: Holt, Rinehart and Winston, 1975.

DesPres, Terrence, *The Survivor, An Anatomy of Life in the Death Camps.* New York: Oxford University Press, 1976.

Donat, Alexander, *The Holocaust Kingdom: A Memoir.* New York: Holt, Rinehart and Winston, 1965.

———— *The Death Camp Treblinka.* New York: Schocken Books, 1979.

Epstein, Helen, *Children of the Holocaust.* New York: Inscape, Corp., 1979.

Fackenheim, Emil, *God's Presence in History.* New York: New York University Press, 1970.

Fein, Helen, *Accounting for Genocide.* New York: Macmillan Co.,/The Free Press, 1979.

Friedlander, Albert H. (ed.), *Out of the Whirlwind.* Garden City, New York: Doubleday, 1968.

Frank, Anne, *The Diary of a Young Girl.* Garden City, New York: Doubleday, 1967.

Frankl, Victor E., *From Death Camp to Existentialism.* Boston: Beacon Press, 1959.

Gutman, Yisroel, *The Jews of Warsaw 1939–43.* Bloomington: Indiana University Press, 1982.

Gun, Nerin E., *The Day of the Americans.* New York: Fleet Publishing Company, 1956.

Gurdus, Lube Krugman, *The Death Train.* New York: Holocaust Library, 1978.

Hersey, John, *The Wall.* New York: Alfred A. Knopf, 1950.

Hilberg, Raoul, *The Destruction of the European Jews.* Chicago: Quadrangle Books, 1961.

Hoess, Rudolf, *Commandant of Auschwitz: Autobiography of Rudolf Hoess.* Cleveland: World Publishing Co., 1959.

I Never Saw Another Butterfly. Compiled by Státní Zidovské for the Prague Jewish Museum. New York: McGraw Hill, 1964.

Kogon, Eugene, *The Theory and Practice of Hell: The Concentration Camps and the System Behind Them.* New York: Octagon Books, 1973.

Kieler, Wieslaw, *Anus Mundi: 1500 Days in Auschwitz.* New York: New York Times Books, 1972.

Kuznetzov (pseud.), Anatoli, A., *Babi Yar.* New York: Farrar, Straus & Giroux, 1970.

Lambert, Gilles, *Operation Hazalah.* New York: Bobbs, Merrill, 1974.

Laqueur, Walter, *The Terrible Secret.* Boston: Little Brown, 1980.

Levi, Primo, *Survival in Auschwitz.* New York: Collier, 1961.

Levin, Nora, *The Holocaust.* New York: T.Y. Crowell, 1968.

LeChêne, Evelyn, *Mauthausen.* London: Methuen, 1971.

Littell, Franklin, *The Crucifixion of the Jews.* New York: Harper & Row, 1975.

Marrus M. and Paxton, R. O., *Vichy France and the Jews.* New York: Basic Books, 1981.

Patton, George, *The Patton Diaries, 1940–1945.* Boston: Houghton, Mifflin, 1974.

Poliakov, Leon, *Harvest of Hate.* New York: Holocaust Library, 1954.

Presser, Jacob, *The Destruction of the Dutch Jews.* New York: Dutton, 1959.

Reitlinger, Gerald, *The Final Solution.* 2nd ed., rev. and enlarged. New York: A. S. Barnes, Co., 1961.

Rothchild, Sylvia, *Voices From the Holocaust.* New York: New American Library, 1981.

Sachs, Nelly, *O The Chimneys, Selected Poems.* New York: Farrar Straus & Giroux, 1967.

Schwarz-Bart, Andre, *The Last of the Just*. New York: Atheneum, 1960.

Schoenbrun, David, *Soldiers of the Night: The French Resistance*. New York: Dutton, 1980.

Sereny, Gitta, *Into That Darkness: From Mercy Killing to Mass Murder*. New York: McGraw Hill, 1974.

Shirer, William M., *The Rise and Fall of the Third Reich*. New York: Simon & Schuster, 1960.

Sington, Derrick, *Belsen Uncovered*. London: Duckworth, 1946.

Speer, Albert, *Inside the Third Reich*. New York: Macmillan Co., 1970.

Ten Boom, Corrie, *The Hiding Place*. New York: Chosen Books, 1974.

Tenenbaum, Joseph, *In Search of a Lost People*. New York: Beechhurst Press, 1948.

—— *Race and Reich*. New York: Twayne Publishers, 1956.

Tillard, P., *Mauthausen*. Paris: Editiones Sociales, 1945.

Tushnet, Leonard, *The Pavement of Hell*. New York: St. Martin's Press, 1972.

Uris, Leon, *Exodus*. New York: Doubleday, 1961.

Vrba, Rudolf and Bestie, Alan, *I Cannot Forget*. New York: Grove Press, 1964.

Wiesel, Elie, *The Gates of the Forest*. New York: Holt, Rinehart and Winston, 1966.

—— *Night*. New York: Hill and Wang, 1970.

II
JEWISH RESISTANCE AND CHRISTIAN COMPASSION

Ainsztein, Reuben, *Jewish Resistance in Nazi Occupied Eastern Europe*. London: Elak, 1974.

Bartoszewski, Wladystok and Lewin, Zofia. *Righteous Among the Nations*. London: Earlscourt Publications, 1969.

Barkai, Meyer (ed.), *The Fighting Ghettos*. Philadelphia: Jewish Publication Society, 1962.

Bauer, Yehuda, *My Brother's Keeper*. Philadelphia: Jewish Publication Society, 1974.

Bettelheim, Bruno, *Surviving and Other Essays*. New York: Alfred A. Knopf, 1979.

Bondy, Ruth, *The Emissary: Enzo Sereni*. Boston: Little Brown, 1979.

Burns, James McGregor, *Roosevelt: The Lion and the Fox*. New York: Harcourt, Brace, 1956.

Chary, Frederick B., *The Bulgarian Jews and the Final Solution*. Pittsburgh: University of Pittsburgh Press, 1970.

Falconi, Carlo, *The Silence of Pius XII*. Boston: Little Brown, 1970.

Friedlander, Saul, *Kurt Gerstein: The Ambiguity of Good*. New York: Alfred A. Knopf, 1969.

Friedman, Philip (ed.), *Martyrs and Fighters: The Epic of the Warsaw Ghetto*. New York: Praeger, 1954.

—— *Their Brothers' Keepers*. New York: Crown, 1957.

Goldmann, Nahum, *The Autobiography of Nahum Goldmann*. New York: Holt, Rinehart & Winston, 1969.

Hellman, Peter, *Avenue of the Righteous*. New York: Atheneum, 1980.

Iranek, Osmecki Kazimierz, *He Who Saves One Life.* New York: Crown, 1971.

Kersten, Felix, *Memoirs.* New York: Macmillan Co., 1957.

Kurzman, Dan, *The Bravest Battle: The Warsaw Ghetto Uprising.* New York: Putnam, 1976.

Leboucher, Fernande, *Incredible Mission: Rescue Efforts in France, Italy.* New York: Doubleday, 1969.

Leval, Jeng, *Hungarian Jewry and the Papacy: Pope Pius XII Did Not Remain Silent.* London: Sands, 1967.

Michel, Henry, *The Shadow War: European Resistance, 1939–1945.* New York: Harper & Row, 1972.

Nirenstein, Albert, *A Tower From the Enemy: Jewish Resistance in Poland* New York: Orion, 1959.

Novitch, Miriam, *Sobibor: Martyrdom and Revolt.* New York: Holocaust Library, 1980.

Proceedings of the International Conferences. edited by Yisroel Gutman and Efraim Zuroff. Jerusalem: Yad Vashem, 1971.

Ringelblum, Emmanuel, *Notes From the Warsaw Ghetto.* New York: McGraw Hill, 1958.

Rosenfeld, Harvey, *Raoul Wallenberg: Angel of Rescue.* Buffalo: Prometheus Books, 1982.

Suhl, Yuri (ed.), *They Fought Back.* New York: Crown, 1975.

Syrkin, Marie, *Blessed is the Match.* Philadelphia: Jewish Publication Society, 1947.

Trunk, Isaiah, *Judenrat: The Jewish Councils in Eastern Europe Under the Nazis.* New York: Macmillan Co., 1977.

Werbell, F. E. and Clarke, T., *The Lost Hero: The Mystery of Raoul Wallenberg.* New York: McGraw Hill, 1982.

Yahil, Leni, *The Rescue of Danish Jewry.* Philadelphia: Jewish Publication Society, 1969.

Zuckerman, Yitzchak (ed.), *The Fighting Ghettos.* New York: Lippincott, 1962.

III
THE NAZI WAR CRIMINALS: THEIR TRIALS AND "PUNISHMENT".

Arendt, Hannah, *Eichmann in Jerusalem: A Report on the Banality of Evil.* New York: Viking, 1963.

Batty, Peter, *The House of Krupp.* London: Secker & Warburg, 1966.

Blum, Howard, *Wanted: The Search for Nazis in America.* New York: New York Times Books, 1977.

Borkin, Joseph, *The Crime and Punishment of I. G. Farben.* New York: Free Press, 1979.

Bower, Tom, *The Pledge Betrayed.* New York: Doubleday, 1982.

DuBois, Josiah E., Jr., *The Devil's Chemists.* Boston: Beacon Press, 1952.

Ferencz, Benjamin, *Less Than Slaves,* Cambridge, Mass.: Harvard University Press, 1979.

Gimbel, John, *The American Occupations of Germany.* Stanford, Calif.: Stanford University Press, 1968.

Harel, Isser, *The House on Garibaldi Street*. New York: Viking, 1975.

Hausner, Gideon, *Justice in Jerusalem*. New York: Harper & Row, 1967.

Horne, Alistair, *Return to Power*. New York: Praeger, 1956.

Jackson, Robert A., *Nuremberg Case—And Other Documents*. New York: Alfred A. Knopf, 1947.

Klarsfeld, Beate, *Wherever They May Be*. New York: Vanguard Press, 1975.

Lasby, C. G., *Project Paperclip*. New York: Atheneum, 1971.

Manchester, William, *The Arms of Krupp*. Boston: Little Brown, 1970.

Martin, James S., *All Honorable Men*. Boston: Little Brown, 1950.

Maser, Werner, *Nuremberg: A Nation on Trial*. New York: Scribner, 1979.

Morse, A. D., *While Six Million Died*. New York: Random House, 1968.

Neave, Airey, *On Trial at Nuremberg*. Boston: Little Brown, 1979.

Rückerl, A., *The Investigation of Nazi War Crimes 1945–1978*. Heidelberg: C. F. Müller, 1979.

Smith, Bradley F., *Reaching Judgment at Nuremberg*. New York: Basic Books, 1981.

Trevor-Roper, Hugh R., *The Last Days of Hitler*. New York: Macmillan Co., 1947.

Wasserstein, Bernard, *Britain and the Jews of Europe*. London: Oxford University Press, 1979.

Weingertner, J. J., *Crossroads of Death*. Berkeley, Calif.: University of California Press, 1979.

West, Rebecca, *A Train of Powder*. New York: Viking Press, 1946.

Wiesenthal, Simon, *The Murderers Among Us*. New York: McGraw Hill, 1967.

IV
THE GREAT MIGRATIONS

Avriel, Ehud, *Open the Gates*. New York: Atheneum, 1975.

Bauer, Yehuda, *B'richa: Flight and Rescue*. New York: Random House, 1970.

——— *American Jewry and the Holocaust*. Detroit: Wayne University Press, 1981.

Dekel, Ephraim, *Shai: The Exploits of Haganah Intelligence*. New York: T. Yoseloff, 1959.

——— *B'richa: Flight to the Homeland*. New York: Herzl Press, 1973.

Deacon, R., *The Israeli Secret Service*. London: H. Hamilton, 1977.

Eisenhower, Dwight D., *Crusade in Europe*. New York: Doubleday, 1948.

Kollek, Teddy and Amos, *For Jerusalem*. New York: Random House, 1978.

Mardor, Munya, *Haganah*. New York: New American Library, 1964.

Nadich, Judah, *Eisenhower and the Jews*. New York: Twayne Publishers, 1953.

Schwarz, Leo W., *The Redeemers*. New York: Farrar Straus and Young, 1953.

Syrkin, Marie., *The State of the Jews*. Washington, D.C.: New Republic Books, 1980.

V
PALESTINE UNDER THE BRITISH MANDATE

Allon, Yigal, *The Shield of David: The Story of Israel's Armed Forces*. New York: Random House, 1970.

Antonius, G., *Arab Awakening*. London: H. Hamilton, 1938.

Bar Zoar, Michael, *Ben Gurion: The Armed Prophet*. Englewood Cliffs, N.J.: Prentice Hall, 1967.

Bauer, Yehuda, *From Diplomacy to Resistance*. Philadelphia: Jewish Publication Society, 1970.

——— *The Jewish Emergence From Powerlessness*. Toronto: University of Toronto Press, 1979.

Begin, Menahem. *The Revolt: The Story of Irgun*. New York: Schuman, 1951.

Ben Gurion, David, *Israel: Years of Challenge*. New York: Holt, Rinehart and Winston, 1963.

Bernadotte, Count Folke, *To Jerusalem*. London: Hodder & Stoughton, 1951.

Bethell, Nicholas, *The Palestine Triangle*. New York: Putnam, 1979.

Churchill, Winston S., *The Second World War*. Boston: Houghton Mifflin, 1953.

Crossman, Richard J. S., *Palestine Mission*. New York: Harper and Brothers, 1947.

Crum, Bartley, *Behind the Silken Curtain*. New York: Simon & Schuster, 1947.

Feingold, Henry M., *The Politics of Rescue*. New York: Holocaust Library, 1970.

Feis, Herbert, *The Birth of Israel: The Tousled Diplomatic Bed*. New York: W. W. Norton, 1969.

Frank, Gerold, *The Deed*. New York: Simon & Schuster, 1973.

Garcia-Granados, Jorge, *The Birth of Israel*. New York: Alfred A. Knopf, 1948.

Gervasi, Frank, *Life and Times of Menahem Begin*. New York: Putnam, 1979.

Gilbert, Martin, *Exile and Return*. New York: Lippincott, 1978.

——— *Auschwitz and the Allies*. New York: Holt, Rinehart & Winston, 1981.

Heckelman, A., Joseph. *American Volunteers and Israel's War of Independence*. New York: Ktav Publishing House, 1974.

Hyamson, Albert, *Palestine Under the Mandate*. Westport, Conn.: Greenwood Press, 1950.

Katz, Shmuel, *Days of Fire*. New York: Doubleday, 1968.

Kimche, Jon and David, *The Secret Roads: The "Illegal" Migration of a People, 1938–1948*. New York: Hyperion Press, 1976.

Kirk, George, *The Middle East. 1945–1950*. London: Methuen, 1954.

Laqueur, Walter, *The Israeli-Arab Reader*, New York: Citadel, 1969.

Litvinoff, Barnet, *Ben Gurion of Israel*. New York: Praeger, 1954.

Mardor, Munya, *Haganah*. New York: The New American Library, 1964.

Meir, Golda, *My Life*. New York: Putnam, 1975.

Niles, David, *The Niles Papers*, 1940–1953. Waltham, Mass.: Brandeis University, custody of Abram L. Sachar.

Patai, Raphael, *Between East and West*. Philadelphia: Jewish Publication Society, 1953.

Robinson, Jacob, *Palestine and the United Nations: Prelude to Solutions*. Westport, Conn.: Greenwood Press, 1971.

Sachar, Howard, *Europe Leaves the Middle East 1936–1954*. New York: Alfred A. Knopf, 1972.

——— *A History of Israel*. New York: Alfred A. Knopf, 1976.

Schechtman, Joseph B., *The United States and the Jewish State Movement: The Crucial Decades 1939–1949*. New York: T. Yoseloff, 1966.

Slater, Leonard, *The Pledge.* New York: Simon & Schuster, 1970.

Stone, Isidor F., *Underground to Palestine.* New York: Pantheon, 1978.

Sykes, Christopher, *Cross Roads to Israel: From Balfour to Bevin.* Cleveland: World Publishing Co., 1965.

Truman, Harry S., *Memoirs.* 2 volumes. Garden City: Doubleday, 1955.

Truman, Margaret, *Souvenir: Margaret Truman's Own Story.* New York: McGraw Hill, 1956.

Weisgal, Meyer and Carmichael, Joel, *Chaim Weizmann—A Biography.* New York: Atheneum, 1972.

Weizmann, Chaim. *Trial & Error: An Autobiography.* Philadelphia: Jewish Publication Society, 1949.

VI
THE ISRAELI WAR OF INDEPENDENCE

Burns, E.L.M., *Between Arab and Israeli.* New York: Obelensky, 1963.

Collins, Larry and Lapierre, Dominique, *O Jerusalem.* New York: Simon & Schuster, 1972.

Dayan, Moshe, *Story of My Life.* New York: William Morrow & Co. 1976.

Dunner, Joseph, *The Republic of Israel.* New York: T. Yoseloff, 1950.

Eban, Abba, *An Autobiography.* New York: Random House, 1976.

Eytan, Walter, *The First Ten Years: A Diplomatic History of Israel.* New York: Simon & Schuster, 1958.

Glubb, Sir John B., *A Soldier With the Arabs.* New York: Harper and Brothers, 1957.

Herzog, Chaim, *The Arab Israeli Wars.* New York: Random House, 1982.

Horowitz, David, *State in the Making.* New York: Alfred A. Knopf, 1953.

Hurewitz, J.C., *The Struggle for Palestine,* New York: W. W. Norton, 1976.

Joseph, Dov, *The Faithful City: The Siege of Jerusalem.* New York: Simon & Schuster, 1960.

Kirk, George, *A Short History of the Middle East 1945–1950.* London: Methuen, 1948.

Koestler, Arthur, *Promise and Fulfillment: Palestine 1947–1949.* New York: Macmillan Co., 1949.

Lorch, Netanel, *The Edge of the Sword: Israel's War of Independence, 1947–1949.* New York: Putnam, 1960.

McDonald, James G., *My Mission in Israel.* New York: Simon & Schuster, 1951.

Prittie, Terrence, *Israel: Miracle in the Desert.* New York: Praeger, 1967.

Sachar, Howard, *Egypt and Israel.* New York: Richard Marek, 1981.

Sacher, Harry, *Israel: The Establishment of a State.* London: Weidenfeld & Nicolson, 1952.

Safran, Nadav, *From War to War: The Arab-Israeli Confrontation 1948–1967.* New York: Pegasus, 1969.

Samuel, Maurice, *Harvest in the Desert.* New York: Alfred A. Knopf, 1946.

——— *Light on Israel.* New York: Alfred A. Knopf, 1968.

APPENDIX

Letters and Memoranda from the Niles Papers

A

David Niles,   20th February, 1949
White House,
Washington D.C.

Dear David,
    Meyer has been telling me of the fine cooperation we
are receiving at your hands. Need I tell you of my profound
appreciation? We are living in great days; it is perhaps too
soon to evaluate their meaning for history. For many years
now you have played no insignificant part in the making of
this history, and I feel certain that when you look back upon
these years you will have good reason to be proud and
satisfied that it had been given to you to help bring about
a proper understanding of the ideals of our cause in high
places in Washington.
    May I ask you to please convey to your great Chief my
warmest greetings and to express to him my profound gratitude for all he has done and is doing for us.
    I am looking forward to our meeting again soon,

                            Sincerely yours,
                            Ch. Weizmann

P.S. I am sending you with Meyer an autographed copy
of Trial and Error; I hope you will have a chance to read
it.

B ═══════════════════════════════════════

July 17, 1945

THE WHITE HOUSE
WASHINGTON

Dear Dave:

I am glad that at my request you are remaining on in your post as one of the Administrative Assistants to the President. I know that your long record in government will be helpful to me as it was to the late President Roosevelt.

For ten years you have taken an important part in the activities of our government in Washington. Beginning with the work of relieving the distress of unemployment, and later in the Department of Commerce, the Office of Production Management, and, for the last several years, as an Administrative Assistant you have had a hand in many of the important events of the last decade. It will be of great service to have the benefit of your ability and conscientious service, and the experience and information you have acquired during these years will be most valuable.

With kindest regards,

Very sincerely yours,
[Harry Truman]

Honorable David K. Niles
Administrative Assistant to the President
The White House
Washington 25, D. C.

C ═══════════════════════════════════════

February 20, 1946.

Mr. Bartley C. Crum,
Anglo American Commission to Palestine,
Through State Department,
Washington, D. C.

Dear Bart:

There are rumors that you are getting madder every day and that you threaten to resign with a blast. I can understand the provocation but you must be patient and calm down, if these rumors have any foundation.

The President talked to me about it this morning and he wants to assure you that he has every confidence in you and that he hopes too that you will do nothing rash. I assured him that you would not.

Yesterday we sent word to the Commission on advice that there be no interim report. Nothing is to be construed as any attempt on the part of any one over here to suggest how the Commission should conduct itself.

I know you are a good sport and will see it through as intelligently as you have always operated.

I tried to reach you by telephone but could not get through.

Cordially,
DAVID K. NILES
Administrative Assistant
to the President

D ════════════════════════════════

THE WHITE HOUSE
WASHINGTON
February 20, 1946.

MEMO FOR MR. LOY HENDERSON:

Edit this in any way you see fit. I am trying to play down my talks with the President. Confidentially, he was very much upset about this rumor.

D.K.N.

E ════════════════════════════════

April 16, 1946.

Judge Joseph C. Hutcheson, Co-Chairman,
Anglo-American Palestine Commission,
Geneva, Switzerland.

Dear Judge Hutcheson:
I have followed reports of your inquiry and delibera-

tions with great interest. The world expectantly awaits a report from the entire Commission which will be the basis of an affirmative program to relieve untold suffering and misery. In the deliberations now going on, and in the report which will evolve from them, it is my deep and sincere wish that the American delegation shall stand firm for a program that is in accord with the highest American tradition of generosity and justice.

Sincerely,
HARRY S. TRUMAN

F

May 27, 1946.

MEMORANDUM FOR THE PRESIDENT:

I have carefully examined the chart that Myron Taylor sent you, and his letter of May 15. Practically all of the comments that Mr. Taylor makes have been satisfactorily answered in the report of the Anglo American Commission. The protection of the Holy places has been taken care of in the Report in a way that ought to give additional satisfaction and confidence to Christian leaders everywhere. As a matter of fact, it is vindicating the obvious to point out that Christians, particularly Catholics, have more to fear from the Moslems than from any other competitive religious group. The Jews have always gotten along well with the Christians in the Middle East, which is something that can not be said about the Moslem group.

I am familiar with the Dr. Bowman report and particularly the report of Colonel Hoskins. As a matter of fact, I, myself, was on the State Department post-war committee with Dr. Bowman. Colonel Hoskins' report was undoubtedly colored by the fact that his father was one of the founders of the University at Beirut and the Colonel was born and brought up there as a young man.

Ambassador Kirk's report of an interview with King Ibn Saud, I think, was taken care of sufficiently by President Roosevelt's letter to Ibn Saud. You know that President Roosevelt said to some of us privately he could do anything that needed to be done with Ibn Saud with a few million dollars.

The danger of unifying the Moslem world can be discounted because a good part of the Moslem world follows Ghandi and his philosophy of non-resistance. That, too, was considered carefully by the members of the Anglo American Commission. Frank Buxton told me only a week ago that he had talked privately with many Arab Chiefs who said that outside of a few minor incidents there really would be very little opposition.

May I again respectfully point out that you are concerning yourself now only with the transference of 100,000 Jews. The other parts of the report you, yourself have publicly said that you would take under consideration for future study. Myron Taylor points out that there is an emergency need. This transference should help that emergency. Mr. Taylor's statement that Russia, Great Britain and her dominions could underwrite the migration of "pressure members," has validity but how to bring that about is not clear. I think there would be terrific resistance if we attempted at this time to bring even a small portion into our own country beyond the present quota limitations. I don't see how we could ask other countries to do what we ourselves are unable to do. I might, in this connection, point out that Brazil and Russia are opening up the gates to some refugees.

It is especially important to note that some years ago Russia set up a colony for Jews at Birobidzhan and put on a tremendous campaign in this country and other parts of the world to raise funds to support these Jews in Birobidzhan. Unquestionably this was set up by the Russian Government as a sort of buffer colony. The project seemed to die out in the past three or four years until the Anglo American Commission made its report. I have noted in the last few weeks that meetings are being staged in this country to revive interest in Birobidzhan and raise money for same. Myron Taylor suggests that Russia may use this report to encourage the Arabs to "meet the Western world, with aggressive strength in days to come". Members of the Anglo American Commission were told privately that the Russians would not look with disfavor on the transference of 100,000 Jews to Palestine. If the transference of 100,000 Jews were responsible for a future war the world is certainly in bad shape. I am inclined to think that if, God forbid, there was a future war it would not be because of the transference of these poor refugees. I am also inclined to think that 100,000 Jews would be of great assistance to us in that area as the Jews of Palestine were during the second World War, which is generally admitted by everybody who is familiar with the situation. The Allies got no help from the Arabs at all but considerable help from the Jews in Palestine.

Respectfully,
DAVID K. NILES

G

May 27, 1946.

Dear Mr. Taylor:

I want to express my great appreciation of your thoughtfulness in sending me the letter and chart in connection with entry of 100,000 Jews into Palestine.

When I proposed the immediate entry of 100,000 Jews into Palestine I had in mind, of course, the desperate situation faced by the remnant of European Jewry. I note that you also are sensitive to that emergency.

The long-range proposals of the Anglo American Commission of Inquiry, I set aside for further study, having in mind the difficulties of reconciling the aspirations of Jewish and Arab nationalism.

I fully agree with you that every country should absorb as many Jewish emigrants who wish to enter as is humanly possible. I feel, however, that the emergency need in Europe is so great that we dare not wait on this kind of consideration by a large number of individual countries.

Thank you again for writing. I am always interested in your views.

Sincerely yours,
[Harry S. Truman]
Honorable Myron C. Taylor,
The Personal Representative
   Of The President of The United States
To The Holiness The Pope,
Rome, Italy.

H

THE WHITE HOUSE
WASHINGTON
July 8, 1946.

Dr. Goldman left the following message:
Mr. Ben Gurion, Chairman of the Executive Committee of the Jewish Agency, whom I saw yesterday, just came
from Paris. He went to see Mr. Ben Cohen to ask him to
arrange for an appointment for him to see Secretary Byrnes.
Mr. Ben Cohen promised to do so the following day. He
called Mr. Ben Gurion, and left the following message:

> "Secretary Byrnes could not see him but
> wanted Mr. Ben Gurion to know that Palestine
> is in the hands of the President, and not the
> State Department. Mr. Byrnes resents Zionists
> and other criticism of the State Department
> concerning the Palestine Policy, and because of
> this—the policy is not being determined upon
> by the State Department."

Truman's handwritten response
[Dave:—I don't blame him much. Imagine Goldman, Wise
& Co each running in after a round with a bandit like
Molotov on Trieste & the Tyrol!—reparations, displaced
persons, and hell all around. Think probably I'd tell him to
jump in the Jordan.]

I

OSCAR GASS
Consulting Economist
No. 3 Thomas Circle
Washington 5, D.C.
National 8632

London
Dear Eliahu: July 28, 1946.
You cannot imagine my consternation when I got in
touch with our friends here last Monday. The Agency knew
nothing of what was going on. The Americans were going

about quietly to accept everything the British suggested. There were a few minor skirmishes going on in the financial sub-committee, but nothing serious. *To say that Grady was acting as a British "stooge" is a gross understatement. He was actually publicly reprimanding his staff for venturing to differ with the British even over secondary matters.* In private, he explained to them that there were things more important in Anglo-American relations than the question whether 100,000 Jews were admitted to Palestine.

Gaston folded up like an accordion. Dove has merely made a public fool of himself. The staff has been somewhat better. Hanna, some days ago, recommended that the Americans formally break off negotiations over the 100,000 and go home. Mikesell has taken the same line and has tried —against Grady's and Gaston's sabotage—to fight out some financial issues. Villard has also filed a memorandum of protest against the July 24 submissions to the two Governments. Even Reed says, "The [To] fight the skirmishes but cede all the battles."

It is impossible for you to go too far in emphasizing to our friends and to the press the complete abandonment of the President's declared program by Grady. I assure you that I write with measured words and in full knowledge. For instance, when the British were veering toward suggesting a starting rate of 10,000 per month, Grady broke in to indicate that 6,000 would be quite enough. There are a score of such incidents. The British simply have *not* been pressed to go ahead with the 100,000, to grant the area of Jewish settlement adequate frontiers, to give the proposed provinces any real power, or anything of the kind. Grady merely says that there is a strong Jewish lobby in Washington but that Truman exaggerates its voting strength. He, Grady, is going to ignore it.

                                 Cordially,
                                 [Oscar]

J

                                                July 29, 1947.

MEMORANDUM FOR THE PRESIDENT:

As you may recall, there was much unfavorable comment last April from certain sources about the alleged failure of the United States Delegation to the Special Session of the United Nations to carry out your policy on Palestine. Perhaps by taking some steps, we can anticipate and thus avoid more such criticism before, during, and after the Fall Session. It might become very damaging in those areas that gave us trouble last November.

The trouble lies not with your announced policy nor with the nature of the official United States Delegation. It lies, I think, with the advisers to the delegation.

I understand that the key advisers on Palestine to the United States Delegation at the Fall Session will be Loy Henderson and George Wadsworth. Because both are widely regarded as unsympathetic to the Jewish viewpoint, much resentment will be engendered when their appointment is announced and later. Moreover, on the basis of their past behaviour and attitudes, I frankly doubt that they will vigorously carry out your policy. But your administration, not they, will be held responsible.

It may not be feasible to oppose Henderson and Wadsworth as advisers to the Delegation. In any event, I believe it is most important that at least one of the advisers be a vigorous and well-informed individual in whom you, the members of the United States Delegation, and American Jewry have complete confidence. There is only one person I know who would fill the bill completely—GENERAL HILL- DRING. As you know, he is scheduled to leave his position as Assistant Secretary of State on the first of September. I respectfully recommend that you ask him as a matter of urgency to serve as an adviser to the United States Delegation to insure that your viewpoint is effectively expressed.

The following persons are the Representatives to the Second Session of the General Assembly of the United Nations:

Warren R. Austin, of Vermont
Herschel V. Johnson, of North Carolina
Mrs. Anna Eleanor Roosevelt, of New York
John Foster Dulles, of New York

and the following are the Alternate Representatives:

Charles Fahy, of New Mexico
Willard L. Thorp, of Connecticut
Francis B. Sayre, of the District of Columbia
Adlai E. Stevenson, of Illinois
Virginia C. Gildersleeve, of New York

But as you so well know, our temperamental friends, headed up by such people as Bart Crum and Silver, continue to spread the stories that Loy Henderson is the works, and that he continues to misinterpret your policy. Henderson has not yet, in my judgment, satisfactorily answered the charges made against him by Bart Crum. I think that Bart Crum was wrong in making these charges, but I do not think the State Department handled any reply in a way that has removed suspicion from Henderson himself.

DAVID A. NILES

K

ON NILES' LATER SERVICE TO PRESIDENT TRUMAN

After the UN vote that authorized the establishment of the state of Israel in a partitioned Palestine, there was still much work for David Niles. When Truman upset the predictions of all the pollsters and editors and was re-elected in 1948, Niles was asked by his chief to stay on as his confidential administrative assistant. He accepted, though with much hesitation, for his health was beginning to fail. He rejoiced to be back in harness, fulfilling many of the president's objectives in civil rights, immigration problems, and, above all, service to Israel in its infant years as a sovereign state. Niles helped to formulate the diplomatic strategy that brought Israel into the United Nations. He worked with the leadership of both parties as they shepherded through Congress the first one-hundred-million-dollar loan to Israel. He was present in the Rose Garden of the White House when an ailing but ebullient Dr. Weizmann came to express gratitude to the president who had played such a crucial part in bringing a sovereign Israel into being. Weizmann presented the president with a small Torah as a measure of his people's deep reverence for him. Niles chuckled, though with tears in his eyes, when the flustered president, lost for words, blurted out, "Oh, I have always wanted one."

But Niles found it impossible to serve out Truman's full term. He was increasingly fatigued as cancer ate into his vitals and in May 1951, he asked to be relieved. He died soon after, at sixty. He cherished the letter that Truman wrote when he accepted the resignation.

L

THE WHITE HOUSE
WASHINGTON
May 17, 1951

Dear Dave: After my conversation with you last night I am going to accept your resignation, effective May thirty-first, as you want it done, but I want it distinctly understood that when you have had your rest and vacation you will report to me and we will have a further conversation on what to do in the future.

You have been a tower of strength to me during the past six years and I can't tell you how very much I appreciate it.

I regret very much that conditions are such that you feel you must have a free lay off—that is the only reason in the world that I am accepting your resignation.

Sincerely yours,
[HARRY TRUMAN]

Honorable David K. Niles
Administrative Assistant to the President
Washington, D. C.

INDEX